The Concept of Military Objectives in International Law and Targeting Practice

The concept that certain objects and persons may be legitimately attacked during armed conflicts has been well recognised and developed through the history of warfare. This book explores the relationship between international law and targeting practice in determining whether an object is a lawful military target.

By examining both the interpretation and its post-ratification application, this book provides a comprehensive analysis of the definition of military objective adopted in 1977 Additional Protocol I to the four 1949 Geneva Conventions and its use in practice. Tackling topical issues such as the targeting of TV and radio stations or cyber targets, Agnieszka Jachec-Neale analyses the concept of military objective within the context of both modern military doctrine and the major coalition operations that have been undertaken since it was formally defined.

This monograph will be of great interest to students and scholars of international law and the law of armed conflict, as well as security studies and international relations.

Agnieszka Jachec-Neale is a visiting Research Fellow for the British Institute of International and Comparative Law, UK. Her research explores legal and doctrinal aspects of targeting and military operational practice, and examines the application of technological advancements in modern warfare. She has over 5 years' experience working with international organisations in south eastern Europe, where she specialised in monitoring domestic war crimes trials and in the enforcement of human rights standards in emerging democracies.

This is a very important work for three reasons. First, surprisingly, it is the first monograph on the subject since the adoption of the definition of military objective in 1977. Second, the quality of the research means that both the law and the practice are thoroughly covered. Third, and most important, it takes an original approach to the relevance and use of military doctrine that has implications for the study of other areas of the law of armed conflict.

Professor Françoise Hampson, University of Essex.

The law of targeting lies at the heart of international humanitarian law and no aspect of targeting is more central than the concept of military objective. Dr. Jachec-Neale has produced a masterful study of the subject that comprehensively surveys and analyzes the problematic issues it raises while placing them in a real-world contexts. It is a work that will not only be of great value to scholars and jurists, but also prove of inestimable practical use to military legal advisers and operators responsible for planning, approving, and executing attacks consistent with international humanitarian law on the battlefield.

Professor Michael N. Schmitt, Director of The Stockton Center,
US Naval War College Professor of Public International Law,
Exeter University Senior Fellow,
NATO Cooperative Cyber Defence Centre of Excellence

Routledge Research in the Law of Armed Conflict

Available titles in this series include:

Islamic Law and the Law of Armed Conflict
The Armed Conflict in Pakistan
Niaz Shah

Cluster Munitions and International Law
Disarmament with a Human Face?
Alexander Breitegger

Forthcoming titles in this series include:

Accountability for Violations of International Humanitarian Law
Essays in Honour of Tim McCormack
Jadranka Petrovic

International Law and Drone Strikes in Pakistan
The Legal and Socio-Political Aspects
Sikander Ahmed Shah

Islam and Warfare
Context and Compatibility with International Law
Onder Bakircioglu

The Concept of Military Objectives in International Law and Targeting Practice
Agnieszka Jachec-Neale

The Concept of Military Objectives in International Law and Targeting Practice

Agnieszka Jachec-Neale

LONDON AND NEW YORK

First published 2015
by Routledge
2 Park Square, Milton Park, Abingdon, Oxfordshire OX14 4RN

and by Routledge
711 Third Avenue, New York, NY 10017

First issued in paperback 2016

Routledge is an imprint of the Taylor & Francis Group, an informa business

© 2015 Agnieszka Jachec-Neale

The right of Agnieszka Jachec-Neale to be identified as author of this
work has been asserted by her in accordance with sections 77 and
78 of the Copyright, Designs and Patents Act 1988.

All rights reserved. No part of this book may be reprinted or
reproduced or utilised in any form or by any electronic, mechanical,
or other means, now known or hereafter invented, including
photocopying and recording, or in any information storage or
retrieval system, without permission in writing from the publishers.

Trademark notice: Product or corporate names may be trademarks or
registered trademarks, and are used only for identification and
explanation without intent to infringe.

British Library Cataloguing in Publication Data
A catalogue record for this book is available from the British Library

Library of Congress Cataloging-in-Publication Data
Jachec-Neale, Agnieszka, author.
    The concept of military objectives in international law and
    practice/Agnieszka Jachec-Neale.
    p. cm. – (Routledge research in the law of armed conflict)
    Includes bibliographical references and index.
    ISBN 978-1-138-81840-8 (hbk: alk. paper) – ISBN 978-1-315-
    74528-2 (ebk: alk. paper) 1. War (International law) 2. Targeted
    killing (International law) 3. Military weapons – Law and
    legislation. 4. Combatants and noncombatants (International law)
    5. War – Protection of civilians. I. Title.
    KZ5624.J33 2014
    341.6'3 – dc23
    2014019759

ISBN 13: 978-1-138-24270-8 (pbk)
ISBN 13: 978-1-138-81840-8 (hbk)

Typeset in Baskerville by
Florence Production Ltd, Stoodleigh, Devon, UK

Contents

Acknowledgements xi
List of abbreviations xiii

1 Introduction 1
  1.1 The problem 1
  1.2 The scope 2
    1.2.1 The concept and the definition 2
    1.2.2 The practice 3
  1.3 Issues beyond the scope of this study 7
  1.4 Structure 8
  1.5 Definitions and clarifications 10
  1.6 Conclusion 12

PART I
The concept and definition of military objective 13

2 The concept of military objective 15
  Part A: historical origins 16
  2.1 Pre-1923 treaty law (1863–1922) 16
  2.2 The approach to military objectives of the 1923 Hague
    Rules of Air Warfare 19
  2.3 The pre-Second World War influence of the 1923
    Hague Rules and Second World War practice 23
  2.4 Developments after the Second World War 29
  Part B: the 1977 definition of military objective 32
  2.5 Definition of the concept in API 32
    2.5.1 Shaping the concept before the conference 32
    2.5.2 Applicability of the definition 34
    2.5.3 The elements and general characteristics of
      the definition 36

viii   *Contents*

2.5.4 Customary status of the definition 37
2.5.5 Latitude and flexibility 40
2.6 Conclusion 42

3   Nature, location, use and purpose   45
3.1 Nature 46
   3.1.1 The scope of objects 49
   3.1.2 Contemporary debates 51
   3.1.3 State and political leadership infrastructure 58
3.2 Location 61
3.3 Use 65
3.4 Purpose 75
3.5 Conclusion 81

4   Effective contribution to military action   83
4.1 Effective contribution 83
4.2 Contribution to military action 84
4.3 Problematic effective contribution to military action 92
   4.3.1 Targets in economic warfare 92
   4.3.2 War-sustaining and war-fighting effort (capability) 95
4.4 Conclusion 109

5   Definite military advantage   111
5.1 The relationship between the two main parts of the
definition 111
5.2 Pursuit of a definite military advantage 116
   5.2.1 Military advantage 116
   5.2.2 The assessment of military advantage in the context
of an attack 'as a whole' 120
5.3 Definite military advantage 124
5.4 Conclusion 127

6   Methods of achieving military advantage   129
6.1 Methods of achieving military advantage 129
   6.1.1 Destruction 130
   6.1.2 Capture 131
   6.1.3 Neutralization 133
6.2 Circumstances ruling at the time 136
   6.2.1 Knowledge and information available at the time
of attack 137

Contents ix

6.2.2 Changing or evolving circumstances 142
6.2.3 The targets of opportunity 143
6.3 Conclusion 144

7 Problematic cases 147
7.1 State and political leadership infrastructure 147
7.2 Civilian morale 153
7.3 TV and radio broadcasting facilities 155
7.4 Objects involved in the commission of international crimes 162
7.5 Conclusion 166

PART II
Operationalisation of the definition of military objective 169

8 Military doctrine and international law 173
Part A: military doctrine 175
8.1 Fathers of modern targeting theories 175
8.2 The role of doctrine in military operations 180
8.2.1 Structure of the sources of doctrine 182
8.2.2 Doctrinal interoperability 183
8.3 Doctrinal perspectives on levels of warfare 184
8.3.1 Strategy and strategic military doctrine 185
8.3.2 Operational level framework 190
8.3.3 Tactical level of warfare 192
Part B: the relationship between military doctrine and the law 194
8.4 The recognition of law in doctrine 194
8.4.1 Law and the conduct of operations 197
8.4.2 Operational law and LOAC manuals 198
8.5 Legal considerations in the selection of targets 199
8.5.1 Targeting process 200
8.5.2 The application of law 204
8.6 The concept of military objective and targets 206
8.6.1 Targets 206
8.6.2 Military objectives and targets 210
8.7 Conclusion 214

x *Contents*

9 Problems of legal interoperability in relation to the identification of lawful targets   215

9.1 Targeting in Coalition operations 218

    9.1.1 1990–1 Gulf War 218

    9.1.2 1999 NATO intervention in Kosovo 225

    9.1.3 2001–2 conflict in Afghanistan 233

    9.1.4 2003 war in Iraq 239

9.2 Methods of resolving the legal interoperability problems 244

9.3 Conclusion 247

10 Conclusion   251

10.1 The definition 251

10.2 The interpretation of the definition 253

10.3 The subsequent practice in the application of the treaty 257

10.4 Problems of information 260

    10.4.1 Absence of information-sharing 260

    10.4.2 Standard of information on the basis of which a decision is made 261

10.5 Final thought 262

Bibliography   263

Index   286

Acknowledgements

This book is a result of Ph.D. thesis written under the supervision of Professor Françoise J. Hampson. I am forever in debt for her guidance and support.

For Chris, my dear husband, whose patience, encouragement and support have been beyond measure. *Dziekuje moim rodzicom za wszystko.*

List of abbreviations

ACTS	Air Corps Tactical School
AF	Air Force
AMW Manual	Air and Missile Warfare Manual
APC	armoured personnel carrier
API	Additional Protocol I to the 1949 Geneva Conventions
APII	Additional Protocol II to the 1949 Geneva Conventions
BBC	British Broadcasting Corporation
C2	command and control
C3	command, control, communications
C4	command, control, communications and computers
CENTCOM	US Central Command
CiC	commander-in-chief
CIHL	Customary International Humanitarian Law Study
CLAMO	Centre for Law and Military Operations
COG	centre of gravity
CTL	candidate target list
DOD	Department of Defense
EECC	Eritrea-Ethiopia Claims Commission
ESCR	Economic and Social Research Council
FDCPS	Swiss Federal Department of Defence, Civil Protection and Sports
FRY	Former Republic of Yugoslavia
GC	Geneva Convention(s)
GPS	Global Positioning System
GWAPS	Gulf War Air Power Survey
HoC	House of Commons
HRC	Human Rights Council
HRW	Human Rights Watch
IACs	international armed conflicts
ICC	International Criminal Court
ICJ	International Court of Justice
ICRC	International Committee of the Red Cross
ICTR	International Criminal Tribunal for Rwanda

xiv *List of abbreviations*

ICTY	International Criminal Tribunal for the former Yugoslavia
IDF	Israel Defence Forces
IHL	International Humanitarian Law
IMFA	Israel Ministry of Foreign Affairs
IP	Internet protocol
ISAF	International Security Assistance Force
JPTL	Joint Prioritised Target List
JTL	Joint Target List
KLA	Kosovo Liberation Army
KTO	Kuwaiti Theatre of Operations
LAN	local area network
LBCI	Lebanese Broadcasting Corporation
LOC	lines of communication
LOAC	law of armed conflict
LST	Libyan State Television
MOD	Ministry of Defence
NAC	North Atlantic Council
NATO	North Atlantic Treaty Organization
NCB	nuclear, chemical, biological
NGO	Non-Governmental Organisation
NIACs	non-international armed conflicts
OEF	Operation Enduring Freedom
OIF	Operation Iraqi Freedom
POL	Petroleum, oil and lubricants
RAAF	Royal Australian Air Force
RAF	Royal Air Force
ROE	Rules of Engagement
RPG	rocket-propelled grenade
RTS	Radio Televisija Srbije (Serbian Radio TV)
SAM	Surface to Air Missiles
UK	United Kingdom
UN	United Nations
US	United States of America
VPN	virtual private network
WMD	weapons of mass destruction

1 Introduction

1.1 The problem

Every armed conflict in history has been marked by some controversy about the choice of targets. In the 1999 intervention in Kosovo, the attack on the Serbian TV and radio broadcasting station caused most debate, though attacks against certain bridges were also questioned.[1] The targeting choices during the early hostilities in Afghanistan in 2001, and Iraq in 2003, were focused on objects associated with the undemocratic regimes in these countries – those of the Taliban and of Saddam Hussein respectively.[2] Increasingly, attacks on fleeting 'targets of opportunity' have started dominating the war effort in more recent conflicts. Much of the debate around specific incidents has been generated by the reporting of the mass media and non-governmental organisations. In the case of coalition or alliance operations certain targets have provoked a significant discussion between the relevant parties.[3] Although it was clear at the time that some States were not comfortable with prosecuting attacks against these objects, it was not always apparent why that was.[4]

Do these disagreements reflect a problem with the definition of military objective? Have some States been interpreting the definition differently? Even if States agree on the words of the definition, practical outcomes may differ if they do not interpret the words in the same way. Is it that the reasons behind any differences of opinion have not, in fact, been legal ones at all? If so, what has been their impact on State practice, which is supposed to assist in the clarification of the law?

The controversies around certain targets have shown the need for a clarification of the concept of military objective in law and practice. This study aims to address these issues not only through a comprehensive examination

---

1 See more detailed discussions in 3.1, 7.3 and 9.1.2.
2 See the further analysis in 3.1, 4.3.1, 7.1 and 9.1.3 and 9.1.4.
3 See the further discussion in 9.2.
4 See the further discussion in the Introduction to Part II and in Chapter 9, throughout.

2 Introduction

of all the components of the legal definition and their interpretation, but also by considering how the definition works in practice.

1.2 The scope

The two aspects of this work, namely the analysis of the concept of military objective and of State practice related to its interpretation, raise substantively different issues in relation to the scope of this work.

1.2.1 The concept and the definition

Although the notion that certain persons and objects may legitimately be attacked is long-established and uncontested, the definition of the relevant objects was formally codified only 37 years ago. The definition of military objective was first adopted in a legally binding document in 1977, as part of Additional Protocol I to the 1949 Geneva Conventions (API).[5] In Art 52.2, the definition was formulated to include two key elements. Each must be satisfied when planning an attack. The first key element is the object's *effective contribution to military action*. The second is *definite military advantage* resulting from the *destruction, capture or neutralization* of the object.[6] The focus of this study is on the content of the definition, the meaning of its elements and how the definition is put into practice. It does not address the issue of its status as a customary rule, although a brief mention of whether the rule is perceived as customary will be made where appropriate.[7]

The definition of military objective has been included in a treaty that deals entirely with one type of armed conflict: namely, an international conflict as defined by Article 1 of API in combination with Article 2, common to all four 1949 Geneva Conventions.[8] The majority of the examples in this work are from conflicts generally recognised as international in character.[9] In any

---

5 Protocol Additional to the 1949 Geneva Conventions of 12 August 1949, and Relating to the Protection of Victims of International Armed Conflicts (Protocol I), Geneva, 8 June 1977, reprinted in D. Schindler and J. Toman (eds), *The Laws of Armed Conflict*, 4th edn, Martinus Nijhoff, Leiden 2004, at 711 *et seq.* [hereinafter: API]. See the further discussion regarding pre-1977 practice and codification efforts in Chapter 2. See also n 10 below.

6 See the further general discussion in 2.5 and a more detailed analysis of the constituent elements in the chapters contained in Part I. In Chapters 2 to 7 reference is made to the term *neutralization* as used in the definition, which will be distinguished by the use of italics.

7 See part B of Chapter 2 and 4.3.2 for the relevant references in this context. See also the further discussion below, text attached to n 17 *et seq.*

8 Consequently, API is also applicable to situations of fighting 'against colonial domination and alien occupation and against racist régimes in the exercise of their right of self-determination', as per Art 1.4 API.

9 An effort was made to illustrate all the issues discussed here by examples drawn from post-1977 practice and in international armed conflicts. There may be instances where a more accurate illustration of the legal issue pertinent to the Art 52.2 definition may be found in pre-1977 practice and in the conflicts whose determination may be disputable. Unavoidably,

situations of violence referred to, the existence of an armed conflict will be assumed. The application of the relevant provisions of international law, and specifically the law of armed conflict (LOAC), to such situations will also be assumed. This will include situations involving military operations based on United Nations Security Council authorisation to use 'all necessary means' under Chapter VII of the United Nations Charter, such as the 1990–1 Gulf War.[10]

The need to assess targets flows from one of the fundamental principles of the law of armed conflict, namely the principle of distinction.[11] This principle requires that the parties to the conflict distinguish at all times between the civilian population and combatants, and between civilian objects and military objectives. In so far as objects are concerned, violent force may be directed only against military objectives.[12] Thus the concept of military objective is focused on what it is permissible to attack, and does not deal with the specific types of objects that are prohibited from being attacked. These are regulated elsewhere in the treaty, or by other, appropriate customary rules.[13] This also means that while the concept refers to both relevant human beings and physical objects, only lawful, physical objects of attack are defined in Art 52.2 API.[14] Consequently, this study will consider the concept only in relation to physical objects. More specifically, only objects located on land that can be affected by air, land or sea warfare will be considered here.[15]

1.2.2 *The practice*

To determine the meaning of the definition, it will first be necessary to explore the meaning of the terms used in it. This will take into account the records of the negotiations to agree the definition, as well as examples drawn from its practical application. In this regard, State practice, and in particular any subsequent practice in the application of the treaty, that is API, 'which establishes the agreement of the parties regarding its interpretation' in line with Art 31 of the Vienna Convention on the Law of Treaties,[16] will be considered.

---

these will be included occasionally, but for illustrative purposes only. See the further discussion in 1.3.

10 'Chapter VII' authorisation is named after the set of Articles contained in Chapter VII of the UN Charter, on which the Security Council may authorise the use of armed force to maintain or restore international peace and security. Arts 39–51 Charter of the United Nations, 26 June 1945.

11 *Advisory Opinion on the Legality of the Threat or Use of Nuclear Weapons*, International Court of Justice (ICJ), 8 July 1996, 1996 ICJ Reports, para 78.

12 Art 48 in combination with Art 49 and Art 52.2 API.

13 See Arts 53–6 API.

14 See the further discussion in 1.3 and in part B of Chapter 2.

15 The restriction to considering only objects on land results from the limited application of some API provisions, including Arts 52.2 and 49.3 API. See also 1.3.

16 Vienna Convention on the Law of Treaties, Vienna, 23 May 1969, United Nations Treaty Series, vol. 1155, at 331 *et seq.*

4 *Introduction*

However, the problem often encountered when looking at such practice is that States tend not to volunteer detailed information as to why they regarded particular targets as military objectives.[17] This is also true in respect of specifying exactly how the object effectively contributed to military action, and how its destruction, capture or neutralization offered a definite military advantage. Some limited information regarding States' views can be found in LOAC manuals and operational law handbooks, but they tend to generalise by referring to categories of targets.[18] One can find even less of an indication as to how much information – and of what kind – States need to make a decision regarding the lawfulness of a target.[19]

Subsequent practice in application of the treaty is, however, not only shaped by military manuals and the international law obligations of the State. The behaviour of the State's armed forces is also the result of military doctrine, which guides the identification of suitable targets through the targeting process. Targeting is guided by the general and specific sources of military doctrine that constitute a body of knowledge that military forces have developed in order to provide guidance on the conduct of current operations.[20]

A State's behaviour must be consistent with the law. During the targeting process, the identified targets are vetted in accordance with the relevant legal standards. If the State planning attacks is engaged in an international armed conflict, the definition of military objective must be applied in order to assess the lawfulness of the selected targets. What is being selected as a potential target, and subjected to legal scrutiny, will depend on how the military forces conceptualise the operation, which is guided by military doctrine. In other words, the starting point for any military forces, before and during an armed conflict, will be a vision and plan of their operations, including targets they would like to affect. The law is taken into account in the later stages of planning military operations. Only the targets identified by military forces as desirable would be subjected to a legal test. The practical impact of this process could be twofold.

On the one hand, this means that the objects that are eventually targeted should be regarded as a reflection of that State's view as to what is a legitimate military objective. The application of military doctrine might identify legally

---

17 The practice of all States – whether they ratified API or not – will be equally significant in the development of customary rule. Some of this practice may not be associated with legal matters, as further noted in this chapter and Chapter 8. See also text attached to n 7 above.

18 See, for instance, a discussion regarding the categories of objects in 3.1.1.

19 See also the discussion in section 1.3.

20 Targeting process is not confined to identification and selection of suitable targets; it also facilitates planning how targets are engaged. See the further discussion in 1.5 and 8.5.1.

Introduction 5

questionable targets. The risk here might be that the legal scrutiny applied would qualify the targets as lawful simply because they could not be said to be clearly unlawful. This means that pressure possibly coming from the military may affect the interpretation of the elements of the definition. If the object cannot be clearly regarded as prohibited, but can be seen as satisfying the legal requirements to some extent, then the temptation might be to go along with the military proposal and approve the target. If this turns out to be a repeated practice, then it may give the impression that this is, indeed, a preferred interpretation of the definition by that particular State. This practice would feed into the relevant practice of all States, thus comprising the subsequent treaty practice. If such a trend continues, and other States do not object or show evidence of contrary practice, the overall interpretation of the definition may appear to be modified.[21]

On the other hand, there could be other objects that, in the context of a particular armed conflict, will not even be proposed as targets by the armed forces. Does subsequent practice in application of the treaty include objects that are *not* targeted? The reason for not targeting them may be military or political, rather than legal. Does this feed into the body of subsequent practice?

The examination of military doctrine in this work has necessarily been limited in two ways. The doctrine analysed was confined to selected general or higher doctrine and more specific targeting doctrine, as well as to sources that refer to the application of the law to military activity. It is worth noting that there is a wealth of other military doctrine that may also be relevant to the discussion, but it was felt that the documents analysed were sufficient to indicate the problematic issues. In this respect, the material is thus intended to be illustrative rather than exhaustive.

The second limitation affects the choice of States whose doctrine was reviewed. The initial research goal was to acquire access to the military doctrine of a wider pool of States representing the major military powers, including the United Kingdom, the United States, Australia, New Zealand, Canada, France and Germany, as well as Russia, India, China and Arabic-speaking countries. In addition, relevant NATO doctrine was sought. The availability of the doctrinal sources varies. The UK and the US offer by far the most, and most recent, relevant doctrinal sources. Australia, New Zealand, Canada and France make some relevant documents publicly available, as does, to a limited extent, India. NATO's general doctrine is readily available, but its specific targeting document is not – even though it was not made confidential when it was adopted in 2008. However, the remaining States

---

21 If a State fails to object to the conduct of other States, particularly during operations undertaken as part of an integrated military alliance, it is unclear whether that could be viewed as a sign of the 'tacit approval' of such conduct. See the further discussion in Chapter 9 and 10.3.

6   *Introduction*

either have not developed doctrinal documents, or are not making them readily available.[22]

The military doctrine of the States discussed in this work is not necessarily the same doctrine that other States may adopt. Furthermore, even though a number of the States whose doctrine will be discussed are members of NATO, it does not necessarily mean that their relevant doctrine would be the same as NATO's. One should also bear in mind that the interpretation of NATO doctrine by other members of NATO may be different to that of the States discussed in this work.

Military doctrine is not the only factor that can shape a State's behaviour in an armed conflict. The specific context of operations may also affect how States conduct hostilities. The most obvious example is political constraints, such as those existing during the 1990–1 Gulf War.[23] Another example is the military and political constraints imposed by coalition warfare.[24] States may decide to act in certain ways because they wish to maintain the cohesion and unity of the coalition, as this is necessary to achieve the military goals. Unlike in conflicts where one State fights another, several States may need to take a position regarding a target during a conflict that involves a coalition. When they do so, some disagreements may become apparent. It may not always be overtly clear why the States disagree. The State may refrain from targeting an object not because it thinks it is unlawful or unnecessary, or because other States think it unlawful. It may decide against targeting a particular object because other States may be uncomfortable with the political implications of engaging such a target.[25] If the object is not a priority, it may never be attacked simply because one State does not want the coalition to be affected by another State's political considerations. A distinction may have to be made between *ad hoc* coalitions of 'willing' partners and multinational operations undertaken by a military alliance under the auspices of a consensus-based inter-

---

22   One source indicated that Saudi Arabian forces, for instance, started developing their own joint military doctrine from 2001 onwards (A.H. Cordesman and K.R. Al-Rodhan, *Gulf Military Forces in an Era of Asymmetric Warfare: Saudi Arabia*, Center for Strategic and International Studies, Washington, DC 2007, at 169). This, however, contrasts with other reports, such as one that states that the Saudi Arabian National Guard have outsourced military doctrine and military training to a private US company. The company allegedly teaches US Army-based military doctrine ('Saudi Arabia Outsources Training and Support to Northrop Grumman', online Defense Update Business Report, January 2010, available at defense-update.com/newscast/0110/businessnews_0110.html (last accessed on 1 May 2014).
23   See the further discussion in Chapter 9.
24   The majority of recent conflicts have not simply involved an international armed conflict between State A and State B. Instead, they have involved coalitions or alliances of States fighting, possibly with the assistance of non-State organised groups, against one State.
25   For example, the attack against the Belgrade TV and radio broadcasting station. See the further discussion in 9.1.2.

Introduction   7

governmental organisation such as the North Atlantic Treaty Organization (NATO).[26]

The problem is that targets can be regarded as unsuitable for a variety of reasons. The reasons may be related not only to the scope or interpretation of a State's legal obligations. Coalition States may require different amounts or types of information in order to make an informed assessment of a target.[27] The reasons may also include diplomatic considerations, as well as concerns resulting from national military doctrine or its interpretation, and the aims of the military mission. It should not be forgotten that both international and domestic political constraints might affect how the State acts either on its own or in coalition.

It is clear that a range of factors, other than merely legal considerations, affect the behaviour of a State's armed forces. This can make it difficult to determine what is a product of legal considerations, and what is a product of other factors. This difficulty is particularly acute in the case of coalition/alliance warfare. This makes it particularly hard to evaluate subsequent practice as a means of establishing the interpretation of a treaty.

1.3 Issues beyond the scope of this study

There are numerous issues that this book does not address. Some have been mentioned already. To recap: first, there will no discussion of whether particular situations amount to an armed conflict and/or which type of conflict is at issue. It will be assumed that LOAC is applicable.[28] Nor will specific regulations for protected objects be analysed. Second, there will be no consideration of the application of the definition to people.[29] Third, an analysis of multinational peace enforcement operations will also be beyond the scope of this study.

API's specific focus on attacks against objects on land means the application of the definition to targets at sea or in the air will not be addressed.[30]

---

26 See the further discussion in Chapter 9. No voting is undertaken in consensus-based organisations. It is the consultation process that leads to the adoption of a decision. This means that any member of the organisation can effectively veto any prospective decision. See further details in *What is NATO? An Introduction to the Transatlantic Alliance*, NATO Public Diplomacy Division, Brussels 2012, at 42.

27 See the further discussion in Chapter 9.

28 The majority of the examples in this work occurred during an active combat phase of conflict. A discussion of destruction in the post–combat phase, including periods of occupation, is outside the scope of this work. See also 6.1 and 9.1.

29 This limitation flows directly from the formulation used in Art 52.2 API. See also the discussion in the text attached to n 16 above.

30 Art 49.3 API. For a discussion of naval targeting see L. Doswald-Beck (ed.), *San Remo Manual on International Law Applicable to Armed Conflicts at Sea*, Cambridge University Press, Cambridge 1995; W. Heintschel von Heinegg 'The Law of Armed Conflict at Sea' in D. Fleck (ed.), *The Handbook of Humanitarian Law in Armed Conflicts*, 2nd edn, Oxford University Press, Oxford

8 *Introduction*

Consequently, attacks against aircraft in flight, whether military or civil, manned or unmanned, and warships or vessels at sea will not be considered here, even though they may constitute military objectives.[31]

Another important delineation must be highlighted. The concept of military objective focuses on *what* is being attacked, rather than *how* the attack can be undertaken. API recognises that there are two stages at which the same definition of military objective needs to be applied when determining the lawfulness of targets. The first stage is the planning phase, in which Art 52.2 is most relevant. The second is when the plan is implemented. Although the same definition is applied at this stage, there has normally already been a prima facie decision on *what* to attack, flowing from the prior application of Art 52.2 API. The implementation of the plans is regulated by Art 57 API, which is focused on *how* the attack should be undertaken. The issues relating to this phase of the conduct of hostilities, most notably dealing with issue of collateral damage, are beyond the scope of this book.[32]

Finally, any issues that relate to international criminal law are also not addressed, including questions relating to the burden of proof and standard of proof in such proceedings. LOAC is civil in character, even if it often enforced through national, international or hybrid criminal proceedings. The focus of this work is limited to States' obligations under LOAC relevant to targeting.[33] Some consideration will, therefore, be given to the questions of availability and sufficiency of evidence, but only in the context of the process that armed forces undertake to determine whether something is a military objective. The military standard of sufficient evidence should, at the very least, conform with the standard used in civil proceedings, such as before the International Court of Justice.

1.4 Structure

The organisation of the content of this work reflects the two underlying areas of study. Part I examines the definition itself, while Part II takes a closer look

---

2008, and W. Heintschel von Heinegg, 'The Law of Military Operations at Sea' in T. Gill and D. Fleck (eds), *The Handbook of International Law of Military Operations*, Oxford University Press, Oxford 2010.

31 Y. Dinstein, *The Conduct Of Hostilities Under The Law Of International Armed Conflict*, 2nd edn, Cambridge University Press, Cambridge 2010, at 111–17; Manual on International Law Applicable to Air and Missile Warfare, Program on Humanitarian Policy and Conflict Research, Harvard University, 15 May 2009, in, Commentary, at 110–16; The Manual of the Law of Armed Conflict, UK Ministry of Defence, JSP 383, Oxford University Press, Oxford 2004, at 308–75

32 In many cases, the concern with the proposed attack is a risk of collateral casualties. This relates to the second great principle of LOAC: proportionality. The principle of proportionality is articulated in Art 57 API and will not be discussed in this work.

33 Some examples taken from the case law of international criminal tribunals may be used to illustrate certain issues relevant to the discussion in this work.

at how the definition is put into operation. Part I starts with Chapter 2, which looks at the historical sources and presents a general commentary on the nature and structure of the text of the definition adopted in 1977. Then come four chapters that contain a comprehensive analysis of each component word of the definition. The definition comprises two crucial elements that are both supplemented or qualified by other components, resulting in an apparent state of equilibrium in its structure. Chapters 3 and 4 analyse the first key element of the definition, namely the conditions of *nature, location, use* or *purpose* through which an object can *effectively contribute to military action*. Chapters 5 and 6 focus on the second key element, which requires the *destruction, neutralization or capture* of the object to offer *a definite military advantage in the circumstances ruling at the time*. Chapter 5 also considers the relationship between the two key elements of the definition. The order of discussion of the components of the definition follows the order in which the terms are used in the text itself. There is one exception to this – the pivotal requirement of the second key element (i.e. a definite military advantage) is analysed prior to the other components of the same element, even though this does not follow the order of the original text. This emphasises the importance of this element in the structure of the definition. The analysis of the meaning of the terms used in the definition will take into account the record of negotiations. It will be supplemented by an illustration of the particular problems that have arisen in State practice since the adoption of the definition.[34] This part concludes with Chapter 7, which contains more detailed discussion of four objects, where satisfaction of the definition is problematic. They include objects associated with political leadership, civilian morale, TV and radio facilities, and objects whose contribution entails the commission of grave breaches of the Geneva Conventions, and of Additional Protocol I and/or other serious international crimes.

Part II of the book attempts to shed more light on some aspects of the operational use of the definition in States' military practice. It is composed of two chapters. Chapter 8 examines how military doctrine may affect military practice, together with its impact upon the application and interpretation of the definition. Chapter 9 focuses on identifying problems of interoperability, which may have had an impact on States' behaviour during four post-1977 multinational operations. These operations are the 1990–1 Gulf War, the 1999 NATO intervention in Kosovo, the 2001–2 international conflict in Afghanistan and the 2003 war in Iraq. The examination of the conflicts in Afghanistan and Iraq will analyse only the high-intensity, initial combat phases of these operations. Chapter 10 offers the conclusions of this work.

---

34 The practical examples used in Part II have a different function. They are used to emphasise the context of the coalition operations in which they arose. See also Introduction to Part II and Introduction in Chapter 9.

10 *Introduction*

1.5 Definitions and clarifications

Some terminology used in this study may confuse readers of both a legal or non-legal background. 'Military objective', for instance, is both a legal and a military term that carries a different meaning in each discipline. A clarification of the meaning of some selected terms at this point should assist any reader in following the analysis and arguments in this work.

Attack and attacker

The term *attack* in the LOAC is defined as an act of violence against the adversary, whether in offence or defence.[35] This approach to the understanding of the term differs to that found in military thinking, where it tends to be associated with offensive action only.[36] For the purposes of this work, the legal understanding has been adopted.

Throughout this book, the word *attacker* will be used. Attacker is not intended to indicate any *jus ad bellum* connotation of an aggressor, but merely means an initiator of military activity: the one who plans or executes the attack.

Military objective

The term *military objective*, as mentioned earlier, may be considered in both a legal and military sense. Military objective in a legal sense refers to a lawful, material target of an attack. *Military objective, as* commonly found in military doctrine, is indicative of the aim of one's efforts or actions – in this context, the goal or purpose of military operations.[37] The term military objective will be used in a legal sense in the majority of this work. However, in Chapter 8, which deals with military doctrine, the term will, unavoidably, also have to be used to mean the goals of military activity.[38]

---

35 Art 49.1 API.

36 See also 5.2.2 and 8.5.2; Y. Sandoz, C. Swinarski and B. Zimmermann (eds), *Commentary on the Additional Protocols of 8 June 1977 to the Geneva Conventions of 12 August 1949*, ICRC, Geneva, and Martinus Nijhoff, The Hague 1987, paras 1879–80; M. Bothe, K. Partsch, and W. Solf, *New Rules for Victims of Armed Conflicts: Commentary on the Two 1977 Protocols Additional to the Geneva Conventions of 1949*, Martinus Nijhoff, The Hague 1982, para 2.2.2 at 289; NATO Glossary of Terms and Definitions (English and French), AAP-6 (2013); *Campaign Execution* (Joint Doctrine Publication 3-00 (JDP 3-00), UK Chiefs of Staff, The Development, Concepts and Doctrine Centre, UK Ministry of Defence, 3rd edn, October 2009, at 3B-2, para 3B4(c); *Legal Support to Joint Operations*, Joint Doctrine Publication 3-46 (JDP 3-46), UK Chiefs of Staff, The Development, Concepts and Doctrine Centre, UK Ministry of Defence, 2nd edn, August 2010, at 1-13, para 129(b).

37 Such a difference is noted in the French LOAC Manual. *Manuel de Droit des Conflits Armés*, (French) Ministère de la Défense, Secrétariat Général Pour L'Administration, undated at 50; See also G.S. Prugh 'Armed Forces and Development of the Law of War', 21 *Revue de droit pénal militaire et de droit de la guerre* 1982, 281–4 at 282.

38 A further elaboration of this issue can be found in the introductory comments in Chapter 8.

Introduction 11

Target

The word *target* is not synonymous with a military objective in a legal sense. Target is a broad military term that denominates anything that military forces consider valuable for the purposes of military operations. This encompasses a wide spectrum of entities, things, places and even abstract concepts such as capability, will, function, understanding and the behaviour of persons or organisations, as well as objects.[39] Targets can be affected in many ways, some of which include the use of armed force. Targets selected for violent engagement will have to undergo the relevant legal scrutiny.

In this work, the term *target*, interchangeable with the word *object*, is used to denominate an object considered for an attack that has not yet been qualified as a military objective.

Targeting

Targeting is a military function by which targets are identified, selected and prioritised, and the best methods and means to pursue them are devised in the context of the operational needs and capabilities, and in pursuance of the military objectives (in a doctrinal sense) of an attacker.[40] Targeting is a process of which there are two types: deliberate targeting and dynamic targeting.[41] Deliberate targeting is focused on the prosecution of pre-planned targets, while dynamic targeting is for targets that have not previously been identified (unknown, unexpected or unanticipated targets), or that were identified but not detected, located or selected in time to be included in a deliberate targeting cycle (anticipated targets).[42] Very often, dynamic targeting involves time-sensitive targets, which require a response in a very short space of time. All targets subject to attack have to be vetted, whether during a deliberate or dynamic process. The test for what constitutes a military objective does not vary. In the case of both deliberate and anticipated dynamic targeting, it is possible to apply the test in 'normal' way.[43] In case of unanticipated targets, however, less information is likely to be available at short notice and there is likely to be insufficient time to gather more or corroborate existing information. This raises the question of whether the definition of military objective is applied in the same way to all types of targets or whether, in practice, it is applied more flexibly to unanticipated targets.

---

39 See the further discussion in 8.6.1.
40 See the further discussion in 8.5.1.
41 Ibid.
42 Ibid.
43 Ibid.

12 *Introduction*

1.6 Conclusion

At the heart of this study lies the concept of military objective. This work will explore how it is defined, how it is interpreted, how it is put into practice, and what may affect the practice and understanding of the concept.

The substantive analysis begins in Chapter 2. This chapter, which opens Part I of this study, will introduce the concept in more detail by looking at its historical origins, and the essential characteristics of the definition as adopted in 1977.

Part I

The concept and definition of military objective

2 The concept of military objective

This chapter offers an introduction to the concept of military objective. It presents the main historical developments leading to the adoption of the definition of the term in Additional Protocol I to the four 1949 Geneva Conventions (API)[1], followed by a general commentary on the nature and structure of the definition, as adopted in 1977.

Consequently this chapter is divided into two substantive parts. The first part traces the concept of military objective through the modern history of the law of armed conflict, and the early efforts at codification.[2] This insight into the historical origins also provides a brief reflection on the relevant State practice prior to 1977. This is contained in Part A, which consists of four sections. Section 1 includes a review of the seminal treaties and non-binding documents containing the early regulation of permissible targets. Section 2 is dedicated to the first legal document that sought to articulate the concept of military objective, namely the 1923 Hague Rules of Air Warfare (1923 Hague Rules).[3] Section 3 shows that even if the non-binding 1923 Hague Rules were referred to in official policies and statements as the applicable standard of the time, they nevertheless failed to encourage States to show restraint during the Second World War. Finally, Section 4 reviews the post-Second World War regulatory initiatives, culminating in the adoption of API.

Part B of this chapter, comprising section 5, offers a general introduction to the definition of military objective adopted in the API. The applicability of the definition, together with its structure, general characteristics and nature, is covered in subsections 2, 3 and 5, while brief comments on the rule's customary status is offered in subsection 4.

---

1 Protocol Additional to the 1949 Geneva Conventions of 12 August 1949, and Relating to the Protection of Victims of International Armed Conflicts (Protocol I), Geneva, 8 June 1977, reprinted in D. Schindler and J. Toman (eds), *The Laws of Armed Conflict*, 4th edn, Martinus Nijhoff, Leiden 2004, at 711 *et seq.* [hereinafter: API].
2 The status of the definition as a customary rule is beyond the scope of this work. See 1.2.1.
3 Hague Rules Concerning the Control of Wireless Telegraphy in Time of War and Air Warfare, 1923, reprinted in Schindler and Toman, op. cit. n 1, at 315 *et seq.* [hereinafter: 1923 Hague Rules].

16 *Military objective: concept and definition*

PART A: HISTORICAL ORIGINS

2.1 Pre-1923 treaty law (1863–1922)

The idea that certain objects and persons could legitimately be attacked during armed conflicts had been well recognised and developed throughout the history of warfare. Equally long-standing was the notion that certain objects and persons were excluded from deliberate attack, for a variety of reasons. Over time, these two principles have largely remained uncontested. However, their understanding and interpretation have evolved alongside the changing realities of conflict.[4] Problems arose, though, where lawful targets were surrounded by unlawful ones. It is unsurprising that early codifications primarily focused on addressing this issue.

By the nineteenth century it was commonly agreed among belligerents that the bombardment of fortresses or localities, and their armed 'defenders', was lawful. The artillery or naval bombardment of such targets was often inaccurate. It resulted, in many instances, in substantial damage to non-military buildings, and in large numbers of civilian casualties. Despite that, the primary intention appears to have been to avoid hitting unarmed locals and their property. It is more than likely that any unintended damage could have been attributed to the inaccurate bombardment of 'military' targets located within large concentrations of population. While this was accepted as an inevitable consequence, further clarification was required on how to mitigate such effects. In this respect, special protection was commonly granted to religious and cultural places, as well as hospitals and other buildings where the sick and wounded were collected within defended localities.

In the middle of the nineteenth century a process of codification of the laws of war began, during which the first regulations of land warfare were developed. The distinction between fortified/defended and undefended towns, villages or buildings, firmly set in the 'unwritten law' of the belligerent States, was reiterated in a number of non-binding documents prior to the adoption of binding acts at the beginning of the twentieth century.[5] The most significant regulation in this respect was contained in the final acts of the 1899 and 1907

---

4 For a detailed discussion on undefended towns and other places, see W. Hays Parks, 'Air War and the Law of War', 32 *Air Force Law Review* 1990, 1–225 at 14–15; E. Colby, 'Aerial Law and War Targets', 19(4) *American Journal of International Law* (1925), 702–15 extensively throughout; J.M. Spaight, 'Air Bombardment', 4 *British Yearbook of International Law* 1923–4, 21–33 at 22–3; F.E. Quindry, 'Aerial Bombardment of Civilian and Military Objectives', 2 *Journal of Air Law and Commerce* 1931, 474–509 at 484–5; and H.W. Elliott, 'Open Cities and (Un)defended Places', *Army Lawyer*, April 1995.

5 Project of an International Declaration Concerning the Laws and Customs of War, Brussels, 1874, as reprinted in Schindler and Toman, op. cit. n 1, at 23 *et seq.*; The Laws of War on Land, Manual of Institute of International Law, Oxford, 9 September 1880, as reprinted in Schindler and Toman, op. cit. n 1 at 29 *et seq.*

The concept of military objective   17

peace conferences, known as the Hague Regulations. Two Hague Conventions, regulating land warfare, permitted the destruction of 'property' if 'imperatively demanded by the necessities of war'.[6] They adopted the 'defended/undefended places' rule without listing any other particular targets as legitimate.[7]

The Hague Convention relating to naval warfare, however, provided an exception to the general prohibition of attacks against undefended towns. It recognised the right of a commander to attack certain objects such as 'military works, military or naval establishments, depots of arms or war "matériel", workshops or plants which could be utilised for the needs of the hostile fleet or army, and the ships of war in the harbour'.[8] This exception was significant in terms of identifying some military objects that may be lawfully targeted because of considerations based on their military value or importance, rather than their location. The listed objects included targets manufactured and used for military purposes, as well as facilities involved in their production (industrial objects). However, this list of permissible military targets, declared at that time by the US to represent customary international law, was already considered to be incomplete at the time of adoption, and inadequate for future conflicts.[9]

In retrospect, the Hague Regulations proved inadequate, particularly following the introduction of air warfare during the First World War of 1914–18. In general, the Hague Regulations addressed only those issues on which consensus could be reached. In respect of the regulation of lawful targets, the lack of a clear definition of the terms 'defended' and 'undefended' left the rules open to interpretation and potential abuse.[10] Furthermore, certain issues remained unaddressed, such as the question of whether the unfortified portion of a town would be exempted from attack. The Hague Regulations left open-ended the question of what could be regarded as lawful targets. Two different standards seemed to have been introduced, depending on whether the attack was undertaken by land forces or naval forces. The latter were permitted to attack specific targets irrespective of their location, including 'undefended' localities. The naval Convention was, in this respect, closer to an earlier document created during the US Civil War known as the Lieber Instructions

---

6 Art 23(g) of Convention No. IV Respecting the Laws and Customs of War on Land and its Annex: Regulations Concerning the Laws and Customs of War on Land, The Hague, 18 October 1907, as well as Art 25 of Convention No. II Respecting the Laws and Customs of War on Land and its Annex: Regulations Concerning the Laws and Customs of War on Land, The Hague, 29 July 1899 [hereinafter: Hague Regulations II], as reprinted in Schindler and Toman, op. cit. n 1 at 55 *et seq.*

7 Art 25 of Hague Regulations II, op. cit. n 6.

8 Arts 1 and 2 of Convention No. IX Concerning Bombardment by Naval Forces in Time of War, The Hague, 18 October 1907 as reprinted in Schindler and Toman, op. cit. n 1, at 55 *et seq.*

9 Hays Parks, op. cit. n 4, at 18.

10 Hays Parks, op. cit. n 4, at 15; B.M. Carnahan, 'The Law of Air Bombardment in its Historical Context', 17(2) *The Air Force Law Review* 1975, 39–60 at 43.

18 *Military objective: concept and definition*

of 1863, or Lieber Code, after its creator.[11] Art 15 of these instructions said it was permissible to destroy, among other things, 'property, and obstruction of the ways and channels of traffic, travel, or communication' if necessary for the purposes of 'armed contests of the war'.[12]

During the First World War, a target's military significance, in defended places, was a growing factor in the selection of targets.[13] Official British and French governmental communiqués referred to attacks as being 'points of military importance'. German statements stressed the distinction between objectives within and outside the zone of operations, and spoke of 'targets directly connected with military activities at the front'.[14] 'Military significance', though, appeared to have been interpreted broadly, and resulted in attacks, mainly towards the end of war, against locations whose rapidly developing industrial complexes contributed to the enemy's war effort. This was seemingly consistent with the view of permitted targets enshrined in the 1907 Hague Convention concerning naval bombardment.

The accuracy and military effectiveness of these early aerial campaigns were limited by technological constraints – relating to the aircraft and weapons systems of the time – as well as by adverse weather. Bombing operations generally affected whole cities or towns rather than individual targets.[15] Such locations often contained developing industrial centres for the mass production of armaments. These were usually located in densely populated areas with a ready supply of labour, power, water and other vital resources.[16] Inevitably, those same resources were also used by civilians in these areas. Accordingly, whole populations were coming to be seen as supporting the war effort. Their contribution to the economy – which helped sustain the national struggle – meant they could potentially have been perceived as a means of waging war.[17]

---

11 The Lieber Instructions consisted of the customary rules governing the conduct of warfare, compiled by Franz Lieber, then a professor of Columbia College in New York, and promulgated by President Lincoln during the American Civil War. Instructions for the Government of Armies of the United States in the Field, promulgated as General Orders no. 100, 24 April 1863, reprinted in Schindler and Toman, op. cit. n 1 at 3 *et seq.* [hereinafter: Lieber Code].

12 Art 15 of the Lieber Code, op. cit. n 11. It also permitted withholding of sustenance or means of life from the enemy and an 'appropriation of whatever an enemy's country affords necessary for the subsistence and safety of the army'. See also relevant discussion in the context of the evolution of notions of war-fighting and war-sustaining in 4.3.2 and 10.2.

13 The Germans justified their attacks on London on the grounds that it was a 'defended' city. J.M. Spaight, *Air Power and War Rights*, 3rd edn, Lonmans, Green, London 1947, at 220–43, as well as Spaight, op. cit. n 4, at 23–5; see also Carnahan, op. cit. n 10, at 53.

14 Spaight, op. cit. n 4, at 23–5.

15 M.W. Royse, *Aerial Bombardment and the International Regulation of Warfare*, Harold Vinal, New York 1928, at 193.

16 Spaight, op. cit. n 13, at 229.

17 G. Best, *War and Law since 1945*, Clarendon Press, Oxford 1994, at 50–1, 199–200.

The concept of military objective   19

This heralded the advent of what became known as 'strategic bombing' and the development of broader economic warfare, which reached its height during the Second World War.[18]

With time, two arguments were developed, seeking to justify the increasingly devastating effects resulting from inaccurate bombing. According to the first, the only way to ensure the successful destruction of the intended military targets was to destroy the presumed location of the target, together with some of the surrounding area. This argument was later utilised in area- or carpet-bombing tactics conducted by aircraft, and seems to have reappeared during the Second World War. The second justification was linked to belligerent reprisals. It was used, or abused, as a way to direct attacks against targets that were normally immune from direct attack, such as the civilian population. The lack of clarity regarding the meaning of 'defended' and 'undefended' permitted attacks that were often indiscriminate and seen as unlawful by the other side. These, in turn, prompted that side to conduct its own reprisal bombing, followed by counter-reprisals, and so on.[19] This trend continued during the Second World War. There was also an increasing tendency to give the word 'enemy' a broader meaning, especially in early twentieth-century military doctrine. The civilian population came to be seen as an inherent part of a belligerent's military effort. In this light, if the will of the population to wage war were broken, then its military would have to stop fighting. Attacking non-combatant targets to persuade the nation to surrender might have been seen as justifiable, and a useful explanation of otherwise inaccurate attacks. This belief was as relevant in the context of a naval blockade as in that of a bombardment. This line of argument, envisaging attacks on civilian morale as a war-sustaining resource, has reverberated ever since.[20]

2.2 The approach to military objectives of the 1923 Hague Rules of Air Warfare

While military technology was evolving during the First World War, the laws of armed conflict needed both to catch up and to clarify the areas left unaddressed by earlier treaties. A legal gap occurred in the area of aerial

---

18 See the further discussion on economic targets in 4.3.1, 8.1 and 8.6, 9.1 and 10.2.

19 M. Cherif Bassiouni, *Crimes Against Humanity in International Criminal Law*, Kluwer Law International, The Hague 1999, at 497.

20 Carnahan draws an analogy with siege warfare, where the besieging forces were permitted to attack non-combatant parts of the city in order to induce surrender. (Carnahan, op. cit. n 10, at 50–3; see also Hays Parks, op. cit. n 4, at 55). The issue also relates to the questions of who can be legitimately targeted, and how the attack can be undertaken. Both questions are beyond the scope of this book (see 1.2.1 and 1.3). See the further discussion on the issue of targeting civilian morale in 7.2 and 10.1. See 8.1 on the relevant doctrinal developments.

20 *Military objective: concept and definition*

warfare. This raised significant concern among the general public, and legal and military experts alike.

There was a somewhat fluid interpretation of what could be targeted during the First World War. It is unsurprising, therefore, that an underlying aim of the proposed regulation of aerial warfare was to impose restraint on the broad understanding of permissible targets.[21] Consequently, questions concerning what constituted a legitimate aerial bombardment became a principal concern for members of the Commission of Jurists, and its Military and Naval Advisors,[22] when they convened in the winter of 1922–3. The expert delegations explored the lawfulness of targets in the light of two main considerations. The first was the changing concept of the 'battlefield'. Technological advances and the industrialisation of Nation-States made possible attacks against targets deep in enemy territory. The second concern was of a humanitarian nature. First World War practice highlighted the need to alleviate the destruction of private property, and the suffering of individuals not engaged in hostilities.[23]

The two original proposals that ultimately shaped the resulting definition of military objectives in the 1923 Hague Rules Concerning the Control of Wireless Telegraphy in time of War and Air Warfare came from the British and American delegations. Both delegations sought to restrict the range of lawful targets, though their solutions were different. The British delegation suggested a formulation of the general principle of lawful attacks directed against military objectives without defining the term 'military objectives', or giving specific examples to illustrate it. The American delegation provided the Commission with an exhaustive list of specific objects that could lawfully be attacked, but did not include a reference to the term 'military objective'. The Americans considered the phrase 'military objective' too vague, while the British felt it was crucial.[24] The majority of the objects on the above-mentioned list were not controversial, and were soon accepted by other members of the Commission.

However, a real point of contention was determining the conditions for the bombardment of lawful targets within population centres.[25] During

---

21 For more on the failure to place restrictions on air warfare during a preliminary meeting of the 1921–22 Washington Conference on Limitation of Armament, see Royse, op. cit. n 15 at 206–8 and 210–11, as well as Hays Parks, op. cit. n 4, at 24–5.

22 The Commission consisted of the delegations of six States: the United Kingdom, United States, Japan, France, Italy and the Netherlands. The Dutch delegation was unrepresented at the 1921–2 Washington Conference, mentioned earlier.

23 Quindry, op. cit. n 4, at 486–7; also Hays Parks, op. cit. n 4, at 27 and Spaight, op. cit. n 4, at 31.

24 Hays Parks, op. cit. n 4, at 28.

25 See extensive discussion in H.M. Hanke, 'The 1923 Hague Rules of Air Warfare', 292 *International Review of the Red Cross*, Jan.–Feb. 1993, at 21–6 See also Hays Parks, op. cit. n 4, at 28, 32; Quindry, op. cit. n 4, at 489.

negotiations, the experts agreed that air attacks should be directed against those objectives whose destruction provided some advantage to the attacker. The British delegation modified its initial proposal to accommodate this conclusion after some rather troubled deliberations. It became the first paragraph of the final draft of Art 24 of the Regulations.[26] The Americans' exhaustive list was adopted into para 2 of the same provision, and the additional two paragraphs accommodated special rules to enhance the protection of civilian populations against indiscriminate or disproportionate attacks.

The 1923 Hague Rules constituted the first of many draft regulations with no legally binding authority in which the notion of military objective appeared, until its first binding codification in 1977. Art 24.1 of the Hague Rules indicated that 'aerial bombardment is legitimate only when directed at a military objective'. The same provision also contained the first formulation of the definition of this concept, which at the time was understood as 'an object whereof the total or partial destruction would constitute an obvious military advantage for the belligerent'. This formula was supported by an exhaustive list of legitimate targets that included military forces, military works, military establishments or depots, manufacturing plants producing arms, ammunition or military supplies, and lines of communication or transport used for military purposes.[27] The inclusion of these objects reflected the general agreement among participants to recognise the intrinsic liability of these particular objects to attack – even when they were found in civilian areas – so long as the targets could be struck discriminately. In other words, the Rules rejected the earlier arguments that entire cities, towns and buildings could be targeted without precision purely because they contained some military objectives.

The 1923 Hague Rules represented, to some extent, a departure from the rules enshrined in the 1899 and 1907 Hague Regulations. The 1923 Rules introduced a concept of 'military objective' that represented a different approach to regulation. This approach involved both a rudimentary definition of the concept and a list of lawful targets claimed to be exhaustive. The Rules retained some of the concepts and terminology used in the Hague Regulations, namely those relating to the bombardment of cities, towns villages or buildings located away from the immediate area of military operations.

The 1923 Hague Rules have been criticised because they fail to accommodate adequately issues concerning the dynamic nature of targeting, the practice of States at the time, and technological progress and military doctrine.[28] It was also claimed that these rules represented an about-turn in the 'then-existing bombardment philosophy'.[29] In particular, the definition of

---

26 See all works cited in n 25.

27 Art 24.2 of 1923 Hague Rules, op. cit. n 3.

28 E. Rosenblad, 'Area Bombing and International Law', 15(1–2) *Revue de droit pénal militaire et de droit de la guerre* 1976, at 76.

29 Hays Parks, op. cit. n 4, at 31–2; See also Colby, op. cit. n 4, at 713.

22 *Military objective: concept and definition*

military objectives was seen as incomplete because it failed to account for the value of the objects to the defenders' war effort, and their changing status depending on circumstances at the time of the attack.[30] Most importantly, the list of lawful objectives found in paragraph two received some criticism.[31] One commentator suggested that the drafting commission was fully aware that the list was potentially out of date at the time of adoption, and that the rules would have to be revised soon after – including the controversial list of permissible targets.[32] Other criticism related to the unhelpful use of vague language, for example describing objects as 'important and well-known centres' for the production of military supplies. Finally, it was questioned whether the list was even intended to be exhaustive, even though the words used in para 2 of Art 24 clearly suggest this.[33]

The 1923 Hague Rules represented the first – and only – formally negotiated document aiming to provide a legal definition of the concept of military objectives, until the adoption of Additional Protocol I in 1977.[34] The Rules were supposed to introduce certain restrictions in the light of previous State practice. The District Court of Tokyo, in its judgment on the use of atomic bombs in Hiroshima and Nagasaki, acknowledged the relevance of the Rules:

> The Draft Rules of Air Warfare cannot directly be called positive law, since they have not yet become effective as a treaty. However, international jurists regard the Draft Rules as authoritative with regard to air warfare. Some countries regard the substance of the Rules as a standard of action by armed forces, and the fundamental provisions of the Draft Rules are consistently in conformity with international laws and regulations, and customs at that time. Therefore, we can safely say that the prohibition of indiscriminate aerial bombardment on an undefended city and the principle of military objective, which are provided for by the Draft Rules, are international customary law, also from the point that they are in common with the principle in land and sea warfare.[35]

Although the 1923 Hague Rules were designed to serve as a legal treaty, they never became legally binding due to the lack of subsequent ratification, even by the States that took part in the negotiations. There seems to be some evidence of the Rules being incorporated into States' official policies, and/or

---

30 Hays Parks, op. cit. n 4, at 32–3.
31 See evidence cited in Hanke, op. cit. n 25, at 19–20, 29–30.
32 Ibid.
33 See discussion in A.V.P. Rogers, *Law on the Battlefield*, Melland Schill Studies in International Law, 3rd edn, Manchester University Press 2012, at 99.
34 Art 52.2 API, op. cit. n 1.
35 *R. Shimoda et al. v The State*, Tokyo District Court, 7 December 1963, translated in 8 *Japanese Annual of International Law* 1964, at 212, 237–8; 32 *International Law Review*, 626–42 at 631.

directly influencing military thinking in subsequent years.[36] Even if they are seen to represent customary practice at that time,[37] today they can be viewed only as 'reflecting, not customary law, but guidelines for proper conduct'.[38]

2.3 The pre-Second World War influence of the 1923 Hague Rules and Second World War practice

Although dissatisfaction with the 1923 Hague Rules resulted in non-ratification during the build-up to the Second World War, key military players seem to have drawn inspiration from their provisions. As early as the 1935–6 war in Abyssinia, the British government declared it would apply the relevant provisions.[39] In 1937 the British Air Ministry prepared 13 plans – the 'Western Air plans' – that proposed attacking: the German Air Striking Force and its maintenance organisation (plan 1); German military rail, canal and road communications (plan 4); and the German War Industry, including oil supplies and the German aircraft industry (plans 5 and 6).[40] All these proposed targets were considered legitimate 'military objectives' within the parameters of the test set out by the 1923 Hague Rules.[41] On 1 March 1938 the Committee of Imperial Defence issued a secret memorandum in which it implied that the definition of 'military objective', found in para 1 of Art 24 of the Rules, would have been fully acceptable. However, the subsequent list of specific objects within para 2 would have had to be revised.[42] In July 1938 the Sub-Committee for Limitations of Disarmament commissioned a report on certain legal aspects of bombing, which pointed to a number of legitimate objectives of an attack:

(a) at sea: warships, including transports and fleet auxiliaries
(b) on land: any objective may be bombarded from the air if it is within range of medium artillery, namely at a distance of ten miles from any forces of the belligerent, and the following objects within a radius of 50 miles from its nearest troops, including air forces and its allies, or in occupied territories:
   • enemy troops and air forces

---

36 S.A. Garrett, 'Airpower and Non-Combatant Immunity' in I. Primoraz (ed.), *Civilian Immunity in War*, Oxford University Press, Oxford 2007 at 166.
37 The Manual of the Law of Armed Conflict, UK Ministry of Defence, JSP 383, Oxford University Press, Oxford 2004, para 1.26.3.
38 US Air Force, *The Military Commander and the Law*, The Judge Advocate General's School, 11th edn, 2012, at 667.
39 Hanke, op. cit. n 25, at 33.
40 Hays Parks, op. cit. n 4, at 43–4.
41 C. Webster and N. Frankland *The Strategic Air Offence Against Germany 1939–1945*, Her Majesty's Stationery Office, London 1961, Vol. 1, at 94–5, 97 and 99; see also Hanke, op. cit. n 25, at 34.
42 Hanke, op. cit. n 25, at 33.

24 *Military objective: concept and definition*

- ammunition dumps, military supply depots, artillery parks and similar well-defined aggregations of distinctly military equipment, stores or supplies
- supply columns and other means of transport engaged in transporting supplies to or from the depots, etc., mentioned above.[43]

This list of apparently lawful targets was designed to limit the scope of objects that could be construed as legitimate targets.[44] Ultimately, however, this report's recommendations were abandoned. A similar fate was shared by the British Air Ministry's *Instructions to Be Observed By the Royal Air Force in War*, issued on 22 August 1939, just days before the German invasion of Poland. These Instructions not only incorporated the abstract definition of military objective proposed in the 1923 Hague Rules, but also provided a comprehensive list of the objectives *sensu stricto*. This list combined both the objects set out in para 2 of the Rules and those included in the 1907 Hague Regulations.[45]

On 21 June 1938 the British Prime Minister, Neville Chamberlain, reiterated the basic principles enshrined in the Rules while addressing the House of Commons. His remarks reaffirmed the rule requiring that air attacks be directed against targets only when legitimate 'military objectives' could be identified in advance.[46] This principle was further acknowledged in the non-binding 1938 Resolution of the League of Nations Assembly concerning Protection of Civilian Population Against Bombing from the Air in Case of War.[47] In addition, the non-binding 1938 Draft Convention for the Protection of Civilian Populations Against New Engines of War, while retaining the distinction in the 1907 Hague Regulations of defended/undefended places, specified that attacks could be 'directed at combatant forces or belligerent establishments or lines of communication or transportation used for military purposes', provided such attacks would not involve the indiscriminate bombardment of civilians.[48]

Furthermore, Italy's first law of war manual – issued on 8 July 1938 – also referred to the bombardment of 'enemy objectives' being lawful if their total

---

43 The reference here is to the so-called Malkin Report, conducted under the chairmanship of Sir William Malkin, then Legal Advisor to the Foreign Office.
44 Hays Parks, op. cit. n 4, at 43–4.
45 Air Ministry, *Instructions and Notes on the Rules to be Observed By the Royal Air Force in War* and a covering note of 22 August 1939, A.H. Self (Air Ministry) to Air Officer Commanding-in-Chief, Bomber Command, in AIR 14/249, National Archives of the United Kingdom. See also Hays Parks, op. cit. n 4, at 45; and Hanke, op. cit. n 25, at 34.
46 Spaight, op. cit. n 13, at 257–8.
47 Protection of Civilian Populations Against Bombing from the Air in Case of War, Resolution of League of Nations Assembly, 30 September 1938, reprinted in Schindler and Toman, op. cit. n 1, 329–30.
48 Arts. 2, 3 and 5, Draft Convention for the Protection of Civilian Populations Against New Engines of War, International Law Association, Amsterdam, 3 September 1938, reprinted in Schindler and Toman, op. cit. n 1, at 331 *et seq.*

The concept of military objective   25

or partial destruction could possibly benefit Italian military operations.[49] Following heavy criticism of its conduct during an earlier conflict with China, Japan declared on 26 August 1938 that it would continue to consider the 1923 Hague Rules as binding.[50] On the other hand, the US Army Field Manual 27-10 from 1914 and 1940 appeared to follow the 1899 and 1907 Hague Regulations without incorporating any other codifications.[51]

Germany's *Instructions Governing Aerial Warfare* were first issued on 20 July 1939, and seemed to follow the principles set out in the 1923 Hague Rules. The Instructions stipulated that Germany might attack only important military objectives, which were defined as being 'important to the adversary's war effort'.[52] Furthermore, Directive No. 1 of Germany's *Directives for the Conduct of War* instructed the Luftwaffe to attack enemy forces and their military-economic resources, in particular 'British supplies by sea, the armaments industry, and the transport of troops to France', as well as 'British naval units' including battleships and aircraft carriers.[53] Directive No. 9, *Principles for the Conduct of War Against the Enemy's Economy*, of 29 November 1939,[54] required naval and air forces to undertake mining, blockading and destroying ports, attacks on merchant shipping, destroying storage facilities for oil, food and grain, and destroying industrial plants within British territory.

Despite an official policy revision in May 1940, the Chief of the Air Staff had already indicated that the Royal Air Force (RAF) was not bound by the previous *Instructions to Be Observed by the Royal Air Force in War* when responding to the German Air Force attacks in Poland on 16 October 1939, and on 5 June 1940 issued new instructions entitled *Instructions Governing Naval and Air Bombardment*.[55] These new guidelines rendered attacks against identifiable 'military objectives' permissible but, in contrast with previous policy, 'military objectives' were interpreted in the broader sense of the word 'military'. Para 4 of the *Air Instructions* set out permissible targets: military forces, military works

---

49 Hays Parks, op. cit. n 4, at 40.
50 Hanke, op. cit. n 25, at 36.
51 Ibid.
52 Point 20, in Hanke, op. cit. n 25, at 35.
53 *Directive No. 1 for the Conduct of War*, The Supreme Commander of Armed Forces, 31 August 1939, published in *Fuehrer Directives and other Top-Level Directives of the German Armed Forces 1939–1941*, ATO Press, Washington, DC 1948, at 49–50. See also P.J. Goda, 'The Protection of Civilians from Bombardment by Aircraft: The Ineffectiveness of the International Law of War', 33 *Military Law Review*, 1966, 93–113 at 101. Hays Parks, op. cit. n 4, at 39 refers seemingly to the same document, giving 1936 as the date of the first issue, and 1940 as the year of the second edition.
54 Directive No. 9: *Principles for the Conduct of War Against the Enemy's Economy*, The Supreme Commander of Armed Forces, 29 November 1939, in *Fuehrer Directives and other Top-Level Directives of the German Armed Forces 1939–1941*, ATO Press, Washington, DC 1948, at 73–5.
55 Air Ministry, *Instructions Governing Naval and Air Bombardment*, 5 June 1940, in AIR 14/249, National Archives of the United Kingdom. See also Hays Parks, op. cit. n 4, at 45.

26 *Military objective: concept and definition*

and establishments involved in the manufacture of supplies and servicing military materials and equipment; power plants ancillary to such industrial centres; oil and fuel producing plants, refineries and storage installations; aerodromes, both military and civilian; storage installations; lines of communications and transportation, as well as means of communication serving military purposes; and any other objectives that might have been attacked 'for particular purposes' if their destruction would be 'an immediate military necessity'.[56] This meant including economic targets, and objects serving both civilian and military purposes.[57]

This latest formulation opened the door to a more liberal interpretation of the concept. In effect, what could be construed as 'military' was no longer interpreted *sensu stricto*. Generally, the primary focus was placed upon targets that encompassed a whole variety of objects regarded not only as upholding an enemy's ability to fight, but also as constituting its determination to wage war and its means of resistance.[58] Whole industries, and the resources supporting them, were considered legitimate targets, such as synthetic oil and benzol plants, refineries, shipping industry facilities – including submarine-building yards and U-boat bases – aircraft factories, steel works, marshalling yards, aluminium works, armament and accessory factories, communication centres, railways, canals, viaducts and road bridges of military importance.[59]

By 1943 the Allies had officially endorsed direct and intentional attacks on German civilian morale, in addition to ongoing, selective economic warfare in the Casablanca Directive.[60] While war industry targets remained the priority, Berlin was explicitly mentioned as a direct objective.[61] The Casablanca Directive superseded the earlier 1942 'Area bombing' Directive issued by the British government, which had ordered the RAF to refocus exclusively on Germany's industrial workforce – and the morale of the German population – through bombing cities and civilians.[62] The Casablanca Directive explicitly

---

56 Ibid.
57 See the further discussion regarding economic targets in 4.3.1, 8.1 and 8.6 and 10.2. See the further discussion regarding targets that serve dual civilian and military functions in 3.3.1.
58 The Ninth Air Ministry Directive from September 1940 permitted 'harassing attacks' on Berlin to disturb its industrial input and the life of the civilian population. W.A. Jacobs, 'The British Strategic Air Offensive Against Germany in WWII' in R.C. Hall (ed.), *Case Studies in Strategic Bombardment*, US Air Force History and Museums Program, Washington, DC 1998 at 118. See also Webster and Frankland, op. cit. n 41, Vol. 1, at 74.
59 Spaight, op. cit. n 13, at 268, 277–80, and Goda, op. cit. n 53, at 102–4.
60 Section 1 of the Directive to the Appropriate British and US Air Force Commanders to Govern the Operation of British and US Bomber Commands in the United Kingdom, approved by the Combined Chiefs of Staff at their 65th meeting on 21 January 1943.
61 This was likely seen as a justified reprisal for the earlier German raids on London, which, as mentioned in n 62 below, was not an isolated practice. S 2(2) of 1943 Directive, op. cit. n 59.
62 General Directive No. 5 (S.46368/111. D.C.A.S), 14 February 1942. The German cities of Cologne, Düsseldorf and Duisburg were explicitly mentioned as primary targets in this

The concept of military objective 27

endorsed the undermining of the Germans' morale 'to the point where their capacity for armed resistance is fatally weakened'. It legitimised, in effect, the continuance of strategic bombing and attacks intended to affect civilian morale.[63]

In terms of what the parties claimed, it should be noted that, following the outbreak of the Second World War, the results of actions of States on both sides of the conflict did not match the rhetoric expressed in official policies.[64] In defiance of previous statements, States conducted attacks that were not always confined to military objectives, thus establishing an ideal excuse for the other side to abandon its initial assurances. The concept of what was regarded as a lawful target appeared to evolve throughout the war, eventually expanding to include civilian morale. While both sides claimed their primary goal was attacking military objectives, there were also a number of practical reasons that influenced the results of States' actions. Most notable were the limitations of the technology of the time, and weather conditions. This meant that the intended targets were often missed.[65] The close proximity of industrial complexes to city centres meant that if the bombing was intense, and involved incendiary weapons, the effects were devastating. The resulting firestorms led to the obliteration of entire cities such as Dresden, Hamburg and Tokyo.[66] The Allies and the Axis States engaged in reprisals, which gave legitimacy to attacks that may not have been confined to potential military objectives.[67] Some places, such as Rotterdam, were initially bombed by the Germans, and then by the Allies during the German occupation. These factors, combined with the developing idea of strategic and economic warfare, left an overall impression of total, indiscriminate war.

Initially, the German bombing of British targets was limited to attacks against industry and the air force. That changed in 1940, after the RAF

---

document. The Directive also permitted the 'unrestricted' use of force. Jacobs, op. cit. n 57, at 120.

63 Webster and Frankland, op. cit. n 40, Vol. 4, app. 8 pt. 28. Attacks on German civilian morale were considered a way of inducing a German surrender, whereas the actual military defeat would be secured by other means. See the discussion of British military plans in Jacobs, op. cit. n 57, at 151.

64 On 2 September 1939, the governments of the UK and France pronounced their commitment to the restriction of bombardment to 'strictly military objectives in the narrowest sense of the word'. Hitler's declarations appeared to uphold the same principle. Spaight, op. cit. n 13, at 259–60.

65 One study in the accuracy of attacks conducted at that time indicated that the pilots managed to approach within a 5-mile radius only one-third of designated targets in localities beyond France, and further away in the Ruhr valley it fell to one-tenth of designated targets. Jacobs, op. cit. n 57, at 113; see also A.D. Coox, 'Strategic Bombing in the Pacific 1942–5', in Hall, op. cit. n 57, at 280, 305.

66 Jacobs, op. cit. n 57, at 121 and 152. Other Japanese cities included Nagoya, Osaka and Kobe. Coox, op. cit. n 64, at 320, 323–4, 331.

67 See text attached to n 20 above.

28 *Military objective: concept and definition*

bombed Berlin. The chain of reprisal attacks was triggered by the German attack of 25 August 1940, during which apparently errant bombs were dropped on the City of London. This was followed by British reprisal raids on Berlin and other cities. On 7 September 1940 the Germans carried out the 'blitz' of London as a counter-reprisal. Between 1940 and 1942 the Germans launched air strikes against numerous cities in the UK. They seem to have been broadly directed against industrial centres, such as Coventry and Birmingham, and lines of communication. The exception was the expressed denomination of the City of London and residential and governmental areas around Whitehall as intended targets. After the English bombing of Lübeck in 1942, the Germans changed their approach and started raids intended to cause the greatest impact on civilian life.[68]

This approach to targeting was not confined to the Western Front. German raids on Poland in 1939 represented a mixture of attacks against militarily significant targets and terror bombing.[69] The Russians on the Eastern Front were equally willing to use air power, for example in the 1939 campaign against southern Finnish cities. While some locations contained military facilities or railway connections, others were clearly devoid of any military nexus.[70]

In the Far East, US raids ranged from the extensive bombing of industrial sites to the strategic bombing of entire urban areas, for example the raids on Tokyo on 9–10 March 1945.[71] They reached their culmination with the nuclear bombing of Hiroshima and Nagasaki in August 1945.[72] In the Pacific theatre, the Japanese Air Force repeatedly bombed the Chinese town of Chongqing for more than four years, in addition to other towns such as Nanjing, Canton, Wuhan and Shanghai.[73]

This brief review shows that strategic and area bombing was not confined to one party or one area. The practice was common on all fronts, even if initially it was not admitted officially.[74] While the practice proved to be signifi-

---

68 It was believed that Lübeck was not a centre of war production, and did not contain important military targets (Jacobs, op. cit. n 57, at 120). The change in the German position can also be viewed as a response to the earlier British Directive, permitting similarly unrestrained attacks. See ns 57–9 above.

69 The shelling of Warsaw's Jewish quarter on 14 September 1939 indicated a possible terror bombing attack. Debatable to this day are the attacks on localities such as Frampol or Wielun in 1939.

70 See, for example, the raids on Helsinki on 30 November 1939 and numerous attacks on Porvoo town. More discussion in this respect is available at: www.elknet.pl/acestory/finbomb/finbomb.htm (last accessed on 1 May 2014).

71 American strategic bombing devastated 66 Japanese cities. Several industrial and urban targets such as steel manufacturing, aircraft industry, shipping and oil facilities were mentioned in Coox, op. cit. n 64, at 280, 282, 284, 288, 299, 305, 307, 312–15, 331, 342, 363 *et seq.*

72 Coox, op. cit. n 64, at 352–62.

73 T. Maeda, 'Strategic Bombing of Chongqing by Imperial Japanese Army and Naval Forces' in Y. Tanaka and M.B. Young (eds), *Bombing Civilians: Twentieth Century History*, The New Press, New York, 2009, at 135–53.

74 Best, op. cit. n 17, at 61–2.

The concept of military objective 29

cantly disruptive and damaging to war industry infrastructure, its effectiveness on civilian morale was very questionable.[75]

2.4 Developments after the Second World War

Both World Wars had a significant impact on the development of law when it came to the adoption of – or unwillingness to adopt – specific regulations. The atrocities of war undoubtedly made those who survived aware of the urgent need to provide greater protection for certain groups of individuals. This resulted in the updating of some treaties on the laws of armed conflict, and the adoption of entirely new ones. In 1949 the Four Geneva Conventions (GC) represented the most immediate result of these developments. These focused on enhancing and clarifying the protection of three previously protected groups, and introducing protection for a new category of civilians. The term 'military objective' was used, without being defined, in two of the Conventions – namely GC I (Art 19 of the Convention and Art 4 of the Annex) and GC IV (Art 18 of the Convention and Art 4 of the Annex) – both in the context of the protection of civilian hospitals or medical establishments, and hospital or safety zones.[76] The notion also appeared in Art 8 of the treaty that was subsequently adopted, namely the 1954 Convention for the Protection of Cultural Property in the Event of Armed Conflict.[77] In the context of protecting cultural property, Art 8 contained a list of what could be considered important military objectives. This encompassed 'an aerodrome, broadcasting station, establishment engaged upon work of national defence, a port or railway station of relative importance or a main line of communication'.[78]

The term 'military objective' was not used in any other post-Second World War treaty until 1977 Additional Protocol I. This could be explained by the general reluctance to update the treaty rules on the conduct of hostilities since their last regulation in 1907.[79] States continued to engage in attacks resembling

---

75 Jacobs, op. cit. n 57, at 156–7.
76 Convention (I) for the Amelioration of the Condition of the Wounded and Sick in Armed Forces in the Field, Geneva, 12 August 1949, reprinted in Schindler and Toman, op. cit. n 1, at 459 *et seq.* and Convention (IV) Relative to the Protection of Civilian Persons in Time of War, Geneva, 12 August 1949, reprinted in Schindler and Toman, op. cit. n 1, at 575 *et seq.*
77 Convention for the Protection of Cultural Property in the Event of Armed Conflict, The Hague, 14 May 1954, reprinted in Schindler and Toman, op. cit. n 1, at 1003.
78 Art 8.1 Convention for the Protection of Cultural Property, op. cit. n 76.
79 After World War I, the international community appeared reluctant to address and update any rules of a permissive or balancing nature. The same cannot be said about the prohibiting rules. Between 1918 and 1977 the treaties in force dealing with the means and methods of conducting hostilities on land included only the Protocol for the Prohibition of the Use of Asphyxiating, Poisonous or Other Gases, and of Bacteriological Methods of Warfare (Geneva, 17 June 1925 entered into force in 1928) and some provisions of the 1954 Convention for the Protection of Cultural Property, op. cit. n 76. In contrast, numerous treaties that focused on the protection of vulnerable groups during the same period were adopted and put into force, including the four Geneva Conventions.

30 *Military objective: concept and definition*

Second World War bombardments. Following the initial heavy bombing of North Korean cities, with their industrial and transportation hubs, in the summer of 1950, US commanders decided to stop striking civilian targets. This, though, was allegedly only to prevent the Koreans exploiting the results of such attacks to cause an international outcry.[80] After the Chinese military intervened on behalf of North Korea, the Americans abandoned their restrictive policy. The sustained bombing of urban areas, and of previously avoided targets such as hydroelectric power stations and dams, ensued.[81] The attacks were designed to damage the enemy's capacity, and to destroy the morale of the civilian population.[82] Similarly, in the Vietnam War the US initially showed restraint during the prolonged and inconclusive interdiction campaign. This was gradually replaced by a more aggressive targeting policy, and operations aimed at finally forcing the North Vietnamese leadership to resume negotiations.[83] The intention behind the US bombing campaign may not have been to devastate those countries, but this was the result.[84]

Despite States' clear unwillingness to address the shortcomings of earlier regulations, the International Committee of the Red Cross (ICRC) began to encourage some revision of the standards on the conduct of hostilities. To this effect, in 1956 it prepared Draft Rules for the Limitation of the Dangers incurred by the Civilian Population in Time of War.[85] It is worth noting that the Draft Rules were designed to apply equally to international and non-international armed conflicts.[86]

The ICRC took a twofold approach to the regulation of permissible targets. On the one hand, they proposed a prohibition on attacks against 'dwellings, installations or means of transport' exclusively used or occupied by civilians (Art 6), open towns (Art 16) and target-area bombing (Art 10). On

---

80 It appears that although such attacks offered an operational/tactical military advantage, they also involved undesirable strategic military disadvantage. T.C. Hone, 'Strategic Bombing: Korea and Vietnam' in Hall, op. cit. n 57, at 473–4, 490.

81 Ibid, at 478–9, 485, 490.

82 The military considerations in attacks on Pyongyang were apparently secondary, including attacks against Radio Pyongyang. Ibid, at 488.

83 Ibid, at 496, 498, 500, 514. See also W. Hays Parks, 'Linebacker and the Law of War', 34 *Air University Review*, Jan.–Feb.1983, 2–30.

84 The destructive effects of the attacks were compounded by the fact that neither North Korea nor North Vietnam could be said to have possessed extensive industrial and economic resources in the first place. Ibid, at 517.

85 Draft Rules for the Limitation of the Dangers Incurred by the Civilian Population in Time of War, International Committee of the Red Cross, 1956, reprinted in Schindler and Toman, op. cit. n 1, at 340–1. The 1956 Draft Rules did not seem intended to be negotiated as a treaty law. Instead, they were issued as guidance. They replaced the initial ICRC draft text from 1955 entitled Draft Rules for the Protection of the Civilian Population from the Dangers of Indiscriminate Warfare, which are discussed in more detail in J.L. Kunz 'The Laws of War', 50(2) *The American Journal of International Law* 1956, 313–37 at 323–5.

86 Art 2 of the Draft Rules, op. cit. n 84.

the other, the ICRC attempted to specify what it was permitted to attack (Art 7). Art 7 of these Rules stipulated that attacks might be directed only against military objectives. The ICRC followed with a non-exhaustive compilation of 'categories' of objects that were 'generally acknowledged to be of military importance' due to their essential characteristics. They were included in the Annex to the Draft Rules.[87] Further, the ICRC insisted that even if certain objectives belonged to any of the identified categories of objects, they could not be considered to constitute military objectives unless their total or partial destruction offered some military advantage in the circumstances prevailing at the time.

Although the Draft Rules appeared to have similarities with the definition of military objectives in the 1923 Hague Rules, they were innovative in two respects. The Draft Rules formula combined the list and definition approaches of the Hague Rules in a single rule. The rule started with a list of objects, whose eligibility as lawful targets depended on the prospective military advantage. This initial list of categories of objects was chosen according to their inherent characteristics, which suggested military significance. The list was far more extensive than that of 1923. It encompassed certain objects for the first time, such as airfields, War Ministries and other organs for the direction and administration of military operations, as well as broadcasting and television stations, and telephone and telegraph exchanges that were of fundamental military importance. However, the ICRC reiterated the 1923 Hague Rules approach regarding lines and means of communication, by specifying that only those of fundamental military importance could be considered in this context. The Draft Rules further stated that factories or plants not involved in the manufacture of supplies for military forces, but whose production and associated storage facilities were of fundamental importance for the conduct of war, had to be of an essentially military nature or purpose to satisfy the necessary requirements.

Unlike the 1923 Rules, the ICRC list was non-exhaustive. This meant that any objects not listed could be considered to be military objectives as long as they were known to be of military importance, and their total or partial destruction offered some military advantage in the circumstances prevailing at the time. The first criterion, military importance, required further clarification. The second criterion, military advantage, offered substantial improvement. By using the phrase 'circumstances ruling at the time', the ICRC made the determination of military objectives situation-dependent.

The 1956 Draft Rules, and their amendments, were presented to States but received hardly any attention, and no State responses. Another attempt was

---

87 The entire list of objects can be found in Y. Sandoz, C. Swinarski and B. Zimmermann (eds), *Commentary on the Additional Protocols of 8 June 1977 to the Geneva Conventions of 12 August 1949*, ICRC, Geneva, and Martinus Nijhoff, The Hague 1987, at 632 [hereinafter: ICRC Commentary].

32   Military objective: concept and definition

made to address the issue during the Vietnam conflict. An eight-paragraph resolution, issued by the Institute of International Law in 1969, aimed to reaffirm existing law related to 'military objectives'.[88] While upholding the general principle of distinction, the Resolution enshrined a more developed description of military objectives, consisting of objects:

> which, by their very nature or purpose or use, make an effective contribution to military action, or exhibit a generally recognized [*sic*] military significance, such that their total or partial destruction in the actual circumstances gives a substantial, specific and immediate military advantage to those who are in a position to destroy them.[89]

This formula offered a much-needed refinement of the first part of the definition. The second element of the definition was also further elaborated. The drafters finally departed from the 1923 Hague Rules and Draft Rules list approach. Instead, they used only a description of the necessary criteria. These criteria seemed more specific, though the definition did retain a vague phrase alluding to the military significance of the objects.

PART B: THE 1977 DEFINITION OF MILITARY OBJECTIVE

2.5 Definition of the concept in API

2.5.1 Shaping the concept before the conference

The definition of the International Law Institute appears to have inspired the work of the ICRC and governmental representatives on the concept of military objective during the preparatory meetings preceding the negotiations of API.[90] The proposed ICRC draft of the treaty contained two concurrent regulations in one provision. Para 2 of Art 47 related to the general protection of civilian objects, while Para 1 concentrated on a definition of military objectives:

> Attacks shall be strictly limited to military objectives, namely, to those objectives which are, by their nature, purpose or use, recognized to be

88 The Distinction between Military Objectives and Non-Military Objectives in General and Particularly the Problems Associated with Weapons of Mass Destruction, Institute of International Law, Edinburgh, 9 September 1969, reprinted in Schindler and Toman, op. cit. n 1, at 351–2.

89 Ibid, para 2.

90 B.M. Carnahan, 'Protecting Civilians Under the Draft Geneva Protocol: A Preliminary Inquiry', 18(4) *Air Force Law Review* 1976, 32–69 at 47.

The concept of military objective   33

of military interest and whose total or partial destruction, in the circumstances ruling at the time, offers a distinct and substantial military advantage.[91]

The draft also included two provisions clarifying the specific protection of objects indispensable to the survival of the civilian population, and works and installations containing dangerous forces.[92]

Although expert opinions seemed equally divided, the 1972–3 preparatory meetings, organised under the auspices of the ICRC, concentrated entirely on designing a textual definition of what were referred to as 'non-military objects' or 'objects of civilian character'[93] as opposed to military objectives[94]. The roots of some provisions that were subsequently adopted, relating to the special protection of certain civilian objects, can be traced back to the records of these particular negotiations.[95] The proposed definition of military objectives appeared in an ICRC draft of Art 43 of Protocol I, following an attempt to draft a definition of civilian objects within Art 42. Most experts thought that having two definitions in one treaty was superfluous and dangerous, as it could lead to the creation of a 'grey' category of objects that would not fall squarely within either definition.[96] Some experts thought there had to be at least one definition, either of military objective or of civilian objects, in order for the principle of distinction to be effectively operationalised.[97]

Some experts preferred to concentrate on the 'military objective' concept, from which they believed the notion of civilian objects could be drawn *a contrario*. These experts favoured deleting the suggested positive definition of civilian objects, so that anything that did not pass the 'military objective' test would be regarded as a civilian object, subject to protection. Alternatively, they

---

91 Art 47 Draft Additional Protocols to the Geneva Conventions of 12 August 1949, International Committee of the Red Cross, Geneva, June 1973; Official Records of the Diplomatic Conference on the Reaffirmation and Development of International Humanitarian Law Applicable in Armed Conflicts, Geneva (1974–7), Vol. I, Berne 1978.

92 Arts 48–9 draft API, op. cit. n 90.

93 Report on the Work of the Conference, Conference of Government Experts on the Reaffirmation and Development of International Humanitarian Law Applicable in Armed Conflicts (Second Session Geneva 3 May–3 June 1972), ICRC, Geneva 1972, in particular Vol. I, at 145–6 [hereinafter: ICRC Report 1972].

94 Consult the works of the Commission III on Protection of Civilian Population against Dangers of Hostilities in Report on the Work of the Conference; Conference of Government Experts on the Reaffirmation and Development of International Humanitarian Law Applicable in Armed Conflicts (Geneva 24 May–12 June 1971), ICRC, Geneva 1971, at 73–83.

95 For instance: Arts 53, 54 and 56 API.

96 ICRC Report 1972, op. cit. n 92, para 3.127, at 145.

97 Art 48 API, which is widely recognised as customary law. See also S. Oeter, 'Methods and Means of Combat' in D. Fleck (ed.), *The Handbook of Humanitarian Law in Armed Conflicts*, 2nd edn, Oxford University Press, Oxford 2008, at 175.

34 *Military objective: concept and definition*

favoured replacing a positive definition with a negative one, specifying which objectives were not civilian ones.[98] They asserted that retaining a definition of military objectives was necessary because it would offer a more effective means of protecting civilians.[99]

Other experts supported the proposed definition of 'civilian object' because they thought this was most appropriate within the context of international humanitarian law. They recommended a further expansion and clarification, particularly with respect to specifying which objects would fall within its scope.[100] In what became a permanent solution, a compromise was reached whereby the definition of military objectives was retained and further refined, as well as specific regulations relating to certain specially protected civilian objects.[101] This process allowed a general presumption of the civilian character of objects to replace the former definition of such objects.[102]

Although the 1977 definition was similar to that proposed in the 1969 Resolution, it appears to have been simplified and refined. The full definition reads:

> In so far as objects are concerned, military objectives are limited to those objects which by their nature, location, purpose or use make an effective contribution to military action and whose total or partial destruction, capture or neutralization, in the circumstances ruling at the time, offers a definite military advantage.[103]

2.5.2 *Applicability of the definition*

The definition of military objectives was enshrined in API, whose scope is limited to international armed conflicts (IACs).[104] This has two implications. First, API applied only to those States that ratified the treaty, and to those that did not reserve its application with respect to Art 52.2 in any way.[105] Subsequent definitions of 'military objective', formulated in Protocols II and

---

98 ICRC Report 1972, op. cit. n 92, para 3.128.
99 Ibid, paras 3.139–3.140.
100 Ibid, para 3.129.
101 It was agreed that attacks against certain objects would be prohibited in international armed conflicts, including cultural property and places of worship; objects indispensable to the survival of the civilian population, and works and installations containing dangerous forces and medical objects, save for the exceptions stipulated by law. See in particular Arts 53, 54 and 56 API.
102 ICRC Report 1972, op. cit. n 92, para 3. 130.
103 Art 52.2 API.
104 See Art 1 API. See also 1.2.1.
105 By May 2014, 173 out of 194 States had acceded to and ratified API, with most ratifications occurring in the mid/late 1980s and 1990s. The 22 remaining States include military powers often involved in armed conflicts, such as the US, Israel, Pakistan, Afghanistan, Iran, Sri Lanka and India.

The concept of military objective 35

III to the 1980 Certain Conventional Weapons Convention[106] and the 1999 Second Protocol to the 1954 Hague Cultural Property Convention, were subsequently taken verbatim from Art 52.2.[107] Unlike in API, where the definition is used to determine which objects may be lawfully attacked, the function of the definition in these treaties is subsidiary and assists in understanding and operationalising the core rules enshrined in the treaties. All three treaties apply both to IACs and non-international armed conflicts (NIACs).[108]

The applicability of this concept to NIACs was already being discussed during the 1974–7 negotiations. Records show that a draft provision, mirroring the API definition, was introduced in early 1974, although a number of delegations believed that any rule restricting attacks to military objectives provided an aura of legitimacy for acts of violence against military personnel, *matériel* and installations of a *de jure* government, as well as providing a psychological incentive to engage in rebellion.[109] The draft Article applicable to NIACs was adopted by Committee III in the shape of one paragraph, retaining only the first prong of the test – namely, the effective contribution to what was referred to as 'armed' rather than military action.[110] Ultimately, the proposal was deleted from Additional Protocol II (APII) but found expression in other treaties applicable to NIACs.[111]

---

106 Convention on Prohibitions or Restrictions on the Use of Certain Conventional Weapons which May Be Deemed to Be Excessively Injurious or to Have Indiscriminate Effects; Art 2(4) of Protocol II on Prohibitions or Restrictions on the Use of Mines, Booby Traps and Other Devices; Art 1(3) of Protocol III on the Prohibitions or Restrictions on the Use of Incendiary Weapons; all reprinted in Schindler and Toman, op. cit. n 1, at 210 *et seq.* The US has now formally accepted both documents through ratification (Protocol III was ratified on 21 January 2009).
107 Arts 6(a), 8, 13(1)(b) of Second Protocol to the Convention for the Protection of Cultural Property in the Event of Armed Conflict, The Hague, 14 May 1955, The Hague, 26 March 1999, reprinted in Schindler and Toman, op. cit. n 1, at 1037 *et seq.*
108 Protocol on Prohibitions or Restrictions on the Use of Mines, Booby-Traps and Other Devices as amended on 3 May 1996 (Protocol II to the 1980 Convention as amended on 3 May 1996); Convention on Prohibitions or Restrictions on the Use of Certain Conventional Weapons which May Be Deemed to Be Excessively Injurious or to Have Indiscriminate Effects, Amendment Article 1 in respect of the above-mentioned Protocol III (op. cit. n 105), 21 December 2001 and Art 1(f) of Second Protocol to the Hague Convention of 1954 for the Protection of Cultural Property in the Event of Armed Conflict, op. cit. n 106.
109 Draft Article 26bis mirroring Art 47(52) was introduced by Sweden and Finland on 14 March 1974 (CDDH/III/13 and Add.1, SR.5).
110 Adopted by Com. III on SR.37 on 4 April 1975 by 35 in favour to 8 against, with 17 abstentions.
111 Article deleted at the plenary by consensus (CDDH/SR.52 on 6 June 1977). Protocol Additional to the 1949 Geneva Conventions of 12 August 1949, and Relating to the Protection of Victims of Non-International Armed Conflicts (Protocol II), Geneva, 8 June 1977, reprinted in Schindler and Toman, op. cit. n 1, at 775 *et seq.*

2.5.3 The elements and general characteristics of the definition

Art 52.2 of API contains a definition of military objective consisting of two main elements: 1 an *effective contribution to military action*; and 2 an *offer of definite military advantage*.[112] Both elements contain qualifiers. The first element is qualified by four criteria: *nature, location, use* or *purpose*. The second element includes three ways of achieving military advantage: *destruction, capture* and *neutralization*. The two elements are joined in one formula, which establishes a relationship between them. All authentic texts of the definition, except the Spanish one, contain the conjunctive 'and', which resulted in some readers interpreting the relationship between the two parts as a cumulative one.[113] The definition is a threshold test, which means it is not based on balancing values. In other words, once the requirement is met, the object is a military objective. If the requirement is not satisfied, the object is not a lawful target.

The beginning of the text in Art 52.2 of API indicates that the definition has been designed only to apply to physical objects, and not human beings, as military objectives. The relevant passage reads: 'in so far as objects are concerned'. The second sentence of the authentic English text referred to the word 'objects', while the authentic French text contained the word 'biens'. Thus, both texts indicate a link to material and/or other, equally tangible targets.[114]

Dinstein implied that the drafters of Art 52.2 included a reference to 'in so far as objects are concerned', only 'to be on the safe side'.[115] However, this conclusion is not reflected in the records of the negotiations. Rogers observed that there were no apparent reasons for including these words. He based his assertion on a specific reference in one of the reports of Committee III, which was responsible for drafting the text during the 1974–7 conference.[116] This report simply acknowledged that troops, as military objects, could be considered military objectives as well.[117] It is undeniable that combatants can be attacked at all times, and regarded as valid military objectives, due to the operation of the principle of distinction, coupled with the categories of persons considered as combatants (Art 48 API and the relevant customary international

---

112 See Chapters 3–7 in Part I for a more in-depth discussion of the elements and their constituent components.

113 Art 102 API also states that the following are authentic texts: English, French, Spanish, Arabic, Chinese and Russian. See 5.1 for a further discussion of the nature of the relationship between the two parts of the definition.

114 In a similar vein, all the other authentic texts, namely Spanish, Russian, Chinese and Arabic, refer to objects.

115 Y. Dinstein, *The Conduct of Hostilities under the Law of International Armed Conflict*, Cambridge University Press, Cambridge 2004, at 85. There is no similar indication in the second edition of the book (2010), at 92.

116 Rogers, op. cit. n 33, at 104–5.

117 Report of Committee III, Second session, CDDH/215/Rev.1, Vol. XV at 277, para 64.

law read in conjunction with Art 50.1, also of customary status).[118] Furthermore, while acknowledging that combatants are valid military objectives, it is unlikely that the test from Art 52.2 could be applied to them in the same fashion as to non-human targets.[119] Those regarded as lawful combatants can generally be attacked under any circumstances, without specific consideration as to their *neutralization* or the value of their capture in terms of 'definite military advantage'.

During the API negotiations, the US delegation spoke about the objects to be defined in the context of this provision only with reference to inanimate objects.[120] Dinstein suggested that the definition covering only inanimate objects failed to accommodate living creatures such as cavalry horses or dogs.[121] Animals can fully contribute to an adversary's military effort and, in certain circumstances, it may be advantageous to neutralise or kill them. As such, dogs, mules, camels, horses and other animals utilised by military forces would count as *matériel* and would, therefore, likely be considered in the context of the definition.

2.5.4 Customary status of the definition

While this work does not seek to establish whether the definition of military objective has attained customary status, a few comments will be helpful in this

---

118 ICRC Commentary, op. cit. n 86, paras 2006–2007; E. Rauch, 'Attack Restraints, Target Limitations and Prohibitions or Restrictions of Use of Certain Conventional Weapons', 18 *Revue de droit pénal militaire et de droit de la guerre* 1979, 51–72 at 55; see also Final Report to the Prosecutor by the Committee Established to Review the NATO Bombing Campaign Against the Federal Republic of Yugoslavia, 13 June 2000, para 36 [hereinafter: ICTY Report]; Manual on International Law Applicable to Air and Missile Warfare, Program on Humanitarian Policy and Conflict Research, Harvard University, 15 May 2009, in Commentary, at 149 [hereinafter: AMW Manual].

119 Attacks on human morale or public will (whether civilian or military) are often referred to in the literature. See the further discussion in 7.2. C.J. Dunlap, 'Targeting Hearts and Minds: National Will and Other Legitimate Military Objectives of Modern War', at 120, and S. Haines, 'The United Kingdom and Legitimate Military Objectives: Current Practice . . . and Future Trends?', both in W. Heintschel von Heinegg and V. Epping (eds), *International Humanitarian Law Facing New Challenges*, Springer, Berlin 2007; and Rogers, op. cit. n 97 at 66. Compare also ICRC Commentary, op. cit. n 86, para 2017; W. Hays Parks, 'The Protection of Civilians from Air Warfare', 27 *Israel Yearbook on Human Rights* 1997, 65–111 at 84; F. Kalshoven, 'Reaffirmation and Development of International Humanitarian Law Applicable in Armed Conflicts: The Diplomatic Conference, Geneva, 1974–7', 9 *Netherlands Yearbook of International Law* 1978,107–71 at 110; and L. Doswald-Beck, 'The Value of the 1977 Protocols' in M.A. Meyer (ed.), *Armed Conflict and the New Law, Aspects of the 1977 Geneva Protocols and the 1981 Weapons Convention*, Vol. 1, British Institute of International and Comparative Law, 1989 at 155.

120 Statement of Mr Reed at the meeting of Committee III of 7 February 1975. CDDH/III/SR.15, Vol. XIV, para 11.

121 Dinstein, op. cit. n 114, at 92.

38 *Military objective: concept and definition*

context.[122] There are two aspects involved in the consideration of the customary status of a rule. First, the question arises whether a new provision was regarded as a customary rule at the time the treaty was adopted; second, if not, has it subsequently come to represent customary law?

Very few authors have commented on whether the definition of military objective embodied a customary rule at the time of adoption. US writers, in particular, expressed a view that the definition adopted in 1977 did not codify the customary rule.[123] Hays Parks argued that the agreed definition bore a striking resemblance to that espoused in the 1923 Hague Rules, and displayed the same restrictive intent that is implicit within the list of targets in Art 24.2.[124] He claimed the definition did not reflect State practice, in particular by failing to accommodate attacks on target systems that were a deeply rooted part of strategic bombing and/or targeting doctrine, and the realities of modern warfare.[125]

One should observe, though, that during the 1974–7 negotiations, there was significant agreement in respect of how the concept should be regulated in the new law.[126] Negotiators concurred that the new treaty should define what could be attacked, rather than merely set out what could not. In doing so, they recognised the need to address problems relating to protected objects in the separate set of provisions (Arts 53–6 API), in addition to the general underlying rule in Art 52. The negotiators wanted to define the concept through a definition whose two-element structure could not be disputed. Terms used to describe particular elements were, by and large, not new, and not in question. Any differences of opinion that may have arisen since appear to relate to the interpretation of the rule rather than to the formulation of the rule itself.[127]

---

122 See discussion in 1.2.1.

123 J.M. Meyer, 'Tearing Down of the Facade: A Critical Look at the Current Law on Targeting the Will of the Enemy and Air Force Doctrine', 51 *Air Force Law Review* 2001, 143–82; J. Dunlap Jr., 'The End of Innocence: Rethinking Non-combatancy in the Post-Kosovo Era', 28(3) *Strategic Review* 2000, 9–17; Hays Parks, op. cit. n 4, at 139–45; W. Hays Parks, 'Asymmetries and the Identification of Legitimate Military Objectives' in W. Heintschel von Heinegg and V. Epping (eds), *International Humanitarian Law Facing New Challenges*, Springer Publishers, Berlin 2007, at 91–5 (*A contrario* to a suggestion from Best, op. cit. n 17, at 273). For the US position regarding the rule see 4.3.2.

124 Hays Parks, op. cit. n 4, at 138–40.

125 Hays Parks' objection to the definition appears to be based on the fact that it does not pay due deference to the tenets of military doctrine on targeting practice, which goes beyond any concerns with law. Hays Parks, op. cit. n 4, at 139 and 141. See more detailed consideration of the issues related to military doctrine and State practice subsequent to ratification of the treaty Part II (in line with Art 31 Vienna Convention on the Law of Treaties, Vienna, 23 May 1969, United Nations Treaty Series, vol. 1155, at 331. See also n 129 below and 1.2.2, and Chapters 8 and 9 throughout.

126 Report of Committee III, CDDH/ 215/Rev.1, XV, paras 62, 276.

127 Hays Parks, op. cit. n 4, at 137, noting the US concerns at the time relating to the meaning of the terms used in the definition.

The concept of military objective   39

This overall union of minds, as far as military objectives were concerned, meant that even if this definition was not customary in 1977, it was more likely to be recognised as such far sooner than other rules where such unity was absent.[128] When considering, for example, Arts 54 or 56 API that deal with specific difficult situations, one clearly sees that numerous disagreements arose in the process, even if a text was ultimately accepted. Art 52 appeared to reflect a non-controversial formula, both commonly understood and accepted.

Many commentators have concluded that, with time, the formula has been widely accepted and has become a customary rule in its own right.[129] In practice, even those States that have not ratified API seem to use this test to determine military objectives.[130]

State practice, subsequent to the ratification of the treaty, assists in interpretation of the adopted provisions.[131] Distinguishing between the two could be very difficult, especially when analysing a treaty that applies only to international armed conflicts. As Part II of this work will show, establishing the relevant treaty practice will also be challenging because of the influence of various, non-legal factors on such practice.[132]

---

128 *North Sea Continental Shelf Cases*, International Court of Justice (ICJ), Judgment, 20 February 1969, ICJ Reports 1969, paras 71–4 and 76–7.

129 Compare: ICTY Report, op. cit. n 117; C. Greenwood, 'Customary International Law and the First Geneva Protocol of 1977 in the Gulf Conflict' in P. Rowe (ed.), *The Gulf War 1990–1991 in International and English Law*, Routledge, London 1993, at 71–2 and 86; F. J. Hampson, 'Proportionality and Necessity in the Gulf War', 86 *American Society of International Law Proceedings* 1992, 45–54 at 50; H.B. Robertson, 'The Principle of the Military Objective in the Law of Armed Conflict', 8 *US Air Force Academy Journal of Legal Studies* 1997–8, 35–69 at 46; M. Sassoli, 'Targeting: The Scope and Utility of the Concept of "Military Objectives" for the Protection of Civilians in Contemporary Armed Conflicts' in D. Wippman and M. Evangelista (eds), *New Wars, New Laws? Applying the Laws of War in 21st Century Conflicts*, Transnational, Ardsley 2005, at 187–90; Haines, op. cit. n 118, at 127–30; Rule 8, repeating word for word the treaty definition in J.M. Henckaerts and L. Doswald-Beck (eds), *Customary International Humanitarian Law*, Cambridge University Press, Cambridge 2005, Vol. I (Rules), at 29–32, with supplementary evidence in Vol. II (Practice), part I, at 181–232 [hereinafter: CIHL]; AMW Manual, op. cit. n 117, Commentary at 49.

130 According to CIHL, Israel claimed that its practice closely reflected the API definition of military objectives (CIHL, op. cit. n 128, Vol. II, para 349 at 186). The Israeli Ministry of Foreign Affairs Forces statement from 2006 seems to confirm the official adherence to the text of Article 52.2 API. Israel Ministry of Foreign Affairs, *Responding to Hizbullah attacks from Lebanon: Issues of proportionality Legal Background*, Jerusalem 25 July 2006. Reports of Practice in Iraq and Syria consider Art 52.2 to be customary (CIHL, op. cit. n 128, Vol. II, at 185 paras 348 and 355 respectively). The US position will be further discussed in 4.3.

131 See n 124 above.

132 See the further discussions in Part II of this work (Chapters 8, 9 and 10).

40 Military objective: concept and definition

2.5.5 Latitude and flexibility

While the definition is binding as treaty law for more than 170 States, and appears to be accepted as customary law by others, it has its critics. Academics consider the definition of military objective as not particularly constructive,[133] being abstract and generic[134] and 'so sweeping that it can cover practically anything'.[135] In this context, two particular challenges can be identified: one related to the scope of the newly adopted definition, and the other to its structure.

Practitioners' main concerns centred on the possible adverse effects of the practical application of the negotiated formula. Critics took particular issue with the apparently overly restrictive nature of the definition. Hays Parks recognised that the definition required a stricter nexus of objects with military operations, rather than accepting a broader contribution to the war effort.[136] It was therefore considered too restrictive in the light of past conflicts, and an impediment to the development of the modern concept of effects-based warfare.[137]

Hays Parks's view was not, and is not, widely shared. Supporters of this formulation acknowledged it was broad and general, but stressed its inherent flexibility[138] and highlighted its promise as a 'future-oriented approach'.[139] Other commentators trusted that the two-pronged test in Art 52.2 API was sufficiently broad to incorporate a wide spectrum of potential targets, including some economic and industrial ones.[140] The strength of the definition was indeed seen in the 'exactness of its inquiry about their [objects'] relation to the enemy's war effort'.[141]

The other problem raised related to how the definition was structured. Some commentators regretted the absence of a list, illustrative or exhaustive, akin

---

133 Rosenblad, op. cit. n 28, at 90.
134 Y. Dinstein, 'Legitimate Military Objectives Under the Current *Jus in Bello*', 31 *Israel Yearbook on Human Rights* 2002, 1–34 at 3; Dinstein, op. cit. n 114, at 90; J. Fuchs, 'Shot in the Dark: International Law of Targeting in Theory and State Practice', 3 *Acta Societatis Martensis*, 2007/2008, 21–38 at 25.
135 A. Cassese, *International Law*, Oxford University Press, Oxford 2001, at 339.
136 See text attached to n 122 above and Hays Parks, op. cit. n 4, at 137–41.
137 See also discussion in W.H. Boothby, *The Law of Targeting*, Oxford University Press, Oxford 2012, Chapter 23 'A Challenge to the Distinction Principle – Effect Based Warfare', at 489–511.
138 Carnahan, op. cit. n 89, at 47–8.
139 O. Bring, 'International Humanitarian Law after Kosovo: Is Lex Lata Sufficient?', 71(1) *Nordic Journal of International Law* 2002, 39–54 at 42.
140 Rogers, op. cit. n 33, at 109–10; Best, op. cit. n 17, at 274. Carnahan suggested that the definition was broad and flexible enough to cover targets such as raw cotton during the US Civil War (Carnahan, op. cit. n 89, at 47–8). See the further discussion in 4.3.
141 Best, op. cit. n 17, at 272.

to those included in previous documents, in addition to some form of abstract definition.[142]

Whether illustrative or exhaustive, lists of targets in the legal context implied a certain degree of rigidity in the analytical interpretation of the concept – particularly if seen through the prism of a simplified or liberally applied understanding of what constitutes military objectives.[143] Even in the past, attempts at formulating such lists in official legal documents failed, due either to their inadequacy or their controversial nature. Such lists can unnecessarily limit the range of targets regarded as military objectives in the eyes of the law, as much as they can dangerously widen its spectrum through the use of vague or 'catch-all' clauses.[144] Any object on the list would be regarded as a military objective, irrespective of the circumstances ruling at the time. A rigid set of targets presents a number of problems, including the following:

(a) It encourages automatism in the decision-making processes, and sanctions an assumption of the existence of a 'military objective' character.
(b) It does not permit any changes in circumstances (i.e. situational, technological, historical or legal) to be accommodated in the process of targeting and the legal validation of targets.
(c) It runs the risk of being outdated at the time of adoption, or shortly afterwards.

The idea of precise lists may have some useful purposes (e.g. for research purposes) and is certainly entertained in military practice as a part of target planning, but precise lists do not appear greatly helpful for jurisprudential purposes.[145] In practice, the identification of 'target sets (or systems) or target lists' consisting of groups of concrete targets, often grouped in accordance with their function or utility, such as 'electric power plants' or 'roads', is standard part and parcel of military campaign planning processes, in addition to the

---

142 Rosenblad, op. cit. n 28, at 90; Dinstein, op. cit. n 114, at 90; Hays Parks, n 122, at 92–4.
143 For an interesting debate between a list and a general definition approach, see L. Doswald-Beck (ed.), *San Remo Manual on International Law Applicable to Armed Conflicts at Sea*, Cambridge University Press, Cambridge 1995, at 114–16.
144 M. Bothe 'Targeting' in: A.E. Wall (ed.), *Legal and Ethical Lessons of NATO's Kosovo Campaign*, Vol. 78, US Naval War College International Law Studies, Newport, RI 2002, at 177–8; W. Heintschel von Heinegg 'Commentary' in A.E. Wall (ed.), *Legal and Ethical Lessons of NATO's Kosovo Campaign*, Vol. 78, US Naval War College International Law Studies, Newport, RI 2002, at 204.
145 See, for example, a compilation of the categorised examples of military objectives in the Practice section (Vol. II) of the Customary International Humanitarian Law study. CIHL, op. cit. n 128, Vol. I, at 29–32 with supplementary evidence in Vol. II, part I, at 195–232. Boothby, op. cit. n 136, n 104 at 100 and at 102.

42 *Military objective: concept and definition*

selection of individual targets.[146] Such a listing process plainly reflects a method of planning and executing attacks, which, in a rather simplified form, may find its way into academic writing.[147] Every object's qualification may change in light of the circumstances ruling at the time and should be assessed anew before the execution of the planned attack.[148] In other words, if military operations, for practical or operational reasons, use a system of target sets, they have to be able to narrow them down following legal scrutiny of individual targets. Suggesting otherwise may lead to decisions that may significantly weaken the protection of civilians, and may potentially be viewed as violations of treaty and customary law.

The drafters of the concept in 1977 clearly rejected the list approach in favour of a descriptive definition. The ICRC-proposed text of the definition, in the preliminary sessions in 1972, had already envisaged only a definition, which was a striking departure from the ICRC's 1956 Draft Rules. The assessment of military objectives through the API test is thus individualised and situational, rather than set in categories or lists. As one commentator put it:

> The object may be anything or anywhere *provided that*, at the time it is dealt with (and the attacker is reminded that he may have other choices than 'total destruction'), it is 'contribut[ing] effectively' to the other side's 'military action' *and* that dealing with it offers 'a definite military advantage'.[149]

2.6 Conclusion

There is no question that the concept of military objective has been long recognised and endorsed by States. The challenge in the period before 1977 was how to define the concept and whether to have a list, instead of or in addition to a definition.

By 1977 it appears there was a common understanding among States regarding the best way of regulating the concept to ensure it would stand the

---

146 See the further discussion in 8.4.1. Some of the examples include: *British Airpower Doctrine AP 3000*, 3rd edn, UK Ministry of Defence, 1999, paras 2.6.8–9; *UK Joint Air Operations, Interim Joint Warfare Publication*, IJWP 3-30, UK Ministry of Defence, 2003, para 507. Similarly in US practice, consult, for example, the US *Joint Doctrine for Targeting*, Joint Publication 3-60 of 17 January 2002, superseded by the Joint Publication JP 3-60, *Joint Targeting*, 31 January 2013; '*Targeting*', US Air Force Doctrine Document AFDD 2-1.9, 8 June 2006. See also K. Watkin 'Assessing Proportionality: Moral Complexity and Legal Rules', 8 *International Yearbook of International Humanitarian Law* 2005, 3–53 at 15.

147 M.W. Lewis, 'The Law of Aerial Bombardment in the 1991 Gulf War', 97(3) *American Journal of International Law* 2003, 481–509 at 488 *et seq*.

148 This subject will be further elaborated in 6.2.

149 Best, op. cit. n 17, at 272 (emphasis in original).

test of time. States agreed on the need for a definition, its structure and content. The list approach was considered largely unrealistic, as it was recognised that most target assessments in armed conflict are likely to depend on the particular circumstances at the time of the assessment. The definition adopted consists of two elements: the first concerns the characteristics of the object and their contribution to military action, while the second relates to the military advantage to be gained from removing the usefulness of the object. The relationship of the key elements, and all other terms used in the definition, will be subject to deeper analysis in subsequent chapters. The existence of significant agreement regarding the constituent elements of the definition does not in itself imply that there was a common understanding as to how the words used should be interpreted and applied to the facts.

3 Nature, location, use and purpose

The definition of military objective, adopted in 1977, comprises two key elements. The first requires that the *effective contribution to military action* is satisfied through one of more of four criteria – namely, *nature, location, purpose* or *use*. A detailed discussion of these criteria will follow in this chapter, while the meaning of *effective contribution to military action* will be analysed in Chapter 4.

The discussion of each component will begin by elaborating the meaning of the terms used in the definition, taking into account the record of negotiations. The analysis of the components will be supplemented by considering the practical application of the definition, illustrating the particular problems that have arisen since its adoption. One difficulty can be clearly identified. States tend to assert that a target is regarded as a military objective without stating exactly how it satisfies the two main elements of the definition. Specifically, with respect to the discussion in this chapter, they tend not to clarify whether they determined an object's effective contribution to military action due to its nature, location, purpose or use.

None of the four terms used in the first element of the definition has been comprehensively discussed in the literature, yet there are numerous debates surrounding their meaning and application. Experts discuss whether certain objects, or types of objects, satisfy any one of the criteria and, if so, which criterion is applicable to the object in question. Professor Schmitt rightly observes that these disputes are not purely academic, as they may affect real military operations.[1] The meaning of the nature criterion appears almost obvious and uncomplicated. However, as the following analysis will show, it represents some of the most complex legal issues. The remaining sections of this chapter will present the meaning of each term in the following order: nature, location, use and purpose. This order differs to that in the adopted definition, where use comes after purpose. The change is dictated by the logical

---

1 M.N. Schmitt, 'The Law of Targeting' in E. Wilmshurst and S. Breau (eds), *Perspectives on the ICRC Study on Customary International Humanitarian Law*, Cambridge University Press, Cambridge 2007, at 147.

46 *Military objective: concept and definition*

consideration of the meaning of these two terms, in which use denominates activity at that time, while purpose is linked to possible future uses.

3.1 Nature

The determination of the nature condition is the starting point in assessing objects. The satisfaction of this criterion implies there is no need to verify whether the other criteria are met. It is argued that if this criterion is satisfied, then so are the other elements – in all circumstances, and at all times. However, as will be shown, this may not always be the case, and the other key elements of the definition would be crucial in qualifying objects as military objectives. This analysis begins with an explanation of the nature criterion and its implications. It will then explore the scope of the objects covered by the nature criterion. The discussion will then focus on recent debates on selected types of objects, including lines of communication and transmission facilities. This section concludes with some observations regarding the relatively little-discussed objects associated with State and political leadership.

Two key qualities provide the essence of the nature criterion. One relates to the intrinsic feature of the object involved. The second requires this feature to be exclusively military. The nature criterion refers to the aggregate of features and traits that form a real, intrinsic design, characteristic state or inherent character of an object. An object can have only one nature. It signifies a particular combination of the fundamental qualities of an object that make that object a specific type. All objects of the same type have the same nature. Such inner character is constant, not time-sensitive or context-dependent. Logically, this character will be the same in all circumstances and at all times. Consequently, the nature of the object cannot change.

The intrinsic character of the object must be such as to make (intrinsically) effective contribution to military action. What is it about the object that makes its contribution so uniquely military in character? The object's nature can be found in its exclusively military features, which distinguish it from other objects. In practice, the object's qualities – which relate to its intended application, its functions and designation – will be relevant, as well as its connection to the conduct of military operations.[2] Military operational plans, for instance, are designed exclusively for military use. They simply cannot be used for any other purposes. Missiles and high explosive warheads are exclusively military weapons systems. Anti-tank grenades, such as the Russian

---

2 Some may be tempted to infer that if the object is identified as contributing by its nature, then it does not have or need a specific nexus to hostilities. Every object needs to have a specific nexus to military operations to satisfy the first element of the definition. In the case of weapons or ammunition supplies, the nexus to hostilities is clear, as it is their very nature through which such a nexus is established. See the further discussion in 4.2.

Nature, location, use and purpose 47

rocket-propelled grenade (RPG) 43, are distinctly military in nature. They have been conceived for an exclusively military application in combat operations. Weapons are developed for armed forces to defend themselves against an adversary.[3] By contrast, consider ball bearings, which are steel or ceramic components used in moving parts of various devices including cars, dishwashers or computer hard drives. Ball bearings, even if they constitute part of a military aircraft or vehicle, are not of military nature as such. They have many applications, both military and non-military.

Describing the essence of the nature criterion, the ICRC Commentary pointed to 'all objects directly used by the armed forces', giving the impression that this condition largely overlapped with the use criterion.[4] This is a misleading explanation, because the nature criterion is not defined by its use. If it were, the nature criterion would be redundant. The key point about objects regarded as fulfilling the nature criterion is that their normal condition is to be used intrinsically for military purposes only. In practice a significant majority of objects that satisfy the nature condition are also likely to satisfy the use or the purpose criteria. Consider a military barracks, which would be seen to satisfy the nature criterion. Depending on whether such a garrison is at that time used or occupied by armed forces, it could also satisfy the use requirement, or the purpose criterion because of its intended future function. As far as its nature is concerned, though, these assessments are unnecessary.[5]

Professor Dinstein argues that a military barracks retains its nature even if it is not used by armed forces.[6] This is undisputed. He also claims that the military nature of military barracks will 'change' or 'transform' if such barracks are used, for instance, to accommodate refugees.[7] Such an assertion seems to be at odds with the meaning of the word nature, which highlights the

---

3 Sometimes civilian uses of weapons can also develop with time, such as the use of smoke grenades in paintball, or Airsoft sports in which players eliminate each other with non-metallic pellets fired from replica firearms. Such smoke grenades are, however, different to those used on the battlefield.

4 Y. Sandoz, C. Swinarski and B. Zimmermann (eds), *Commentary on the Additional Protocols of 8 June 1977 to the Geneva Conventions of 12 August 1949*, ICRC, Geneva, and Martinus Nijhoff, The Hague 1987, para 2020, at 632 [hereinafter: ICRC Commentary].

5 Note that a 'potential' future use, as opposed to an immediate one, may not be enough to satisfy the purpose criterion, and would make the determination of other elements of definition debatable. See also 3.4.

6 The example actually refers to deserted military barracks, but if they were 'deserted', they would not be used by anybody. If 'deserted' meant 'abandoned' by the armed forces, then such barracks would still fulfil the nature criterion. Y. Dinstein, *The Conduct of Hostilities under the Law of International Armed Conflict*, Cambridge University Press, Cambridge 2004, at 88 (n 55). The same view is expressed in Rule 22(a), Manual on International Law Applicable to Air and Missile Warfare, Program on Humanitarian Policy and Conflict Research, Harvard University, 15 May 2009 [hereinafter: AMW Manual].

7 Dinstein, op. cit. n 6. Y. Dinstein, *The Conduct of Hostilities under the Law of International Armed Conflict*, 2nd edn, Cambridge University Press, Cambridge 2010, at 94.

48   *Military objective: concept and definition*

unchanging character of the contribution. Nature cannot change, but it might be that its effects may be suspended. If an object ceases to operate in the way that is required by its nature and serves an exclusively civilian purpose, then the effect or consequence of such nature might be regarded as temporarily suspended.[8] This means that while the nature of the object has not 'changed', the nature criterion cannot then be a determining factor for an assessment of the first element of the definition, and other criteria will become relevant. If so, this would apply only for the duration of such use, even if it were long-term. If, for example, the refugees were moved from the military barracks to another location, the object's nature would be relevant again.

Ultimately, Dinstein's view should be rejected because it is inconsistent with the logical consequence of the nature requirement. As the nature of the object relates to its intrinsic quality – which is unchanging, regardless of circumstances – then its civilian use, being such a 'circumstance', will not affect the application of this criterion in assessing the target as a military objective. The decision whether to attack such an object may depend on whether all other legal requirements are met, namely those relating to the remaining elements of the definition, and those regulating how the attack should be undertaken.[9]

Logically, this means that objects performing both military and civilian functions could not be considered legitimate targets due to their nature. Their normal condition is to be used intrinsically or essentially for both purposes and not just the military one. Such objects will be judged according to their use.[10] The decision whether to attack such an object would depend on all the remaining elements of the definition, and other provisions regulating how the attack should be undertaken.

An apparent implication may follow the identification of an object's military nature. Some commentators infer that the nature criterion implies the automatic satisfaction of the other elements of the definition.[11] Proponents of this position, whether States or academic experts, assert that, if the nature

---

8 A change in nature can occur only when the object is so fundamentally and radically transformed that it no longer retains the character by which it previously contributed to military action. In other words, the object would have to cease to exist in its current nature, and be resurrected as something else.

9 The object will be regarded as a military objective subject to further legal considerations guiding how the attacks should be undertaken. These considerations are beyond the scope of this study. See 1.3.

10 See the further discussion of dual-use objects in 1.3.

11 Dinstein, op. cit. n 7, at 96; W. Hays Parks 'Asymmetries and the Identification of Legitimate Military Objectives' in W. Heintschel von Heinegg and V. Epping (eds), *International Humanitarian Law Facing New Challenges*, Springer Publishers, Berlin 2007, at 87 and 93; W. Heintschel von Heinegg 'Commentary' in A.E. Wall (ed.), *Legal and Ethical Lessons of NATO's Kosovo Campaign*, Vol. 78, US Naval War College International Law Studies, Newport, RI 2002, at 205.

Nature, location, use and purpose   49

criterion is met, it is assumed that the object's contribution to military action is apparent at all times and in all circumstances, and that its destruction, neutralization or capture would always offer some military advantage.[12] Accordingly, once an object is classified as contributing by its nature, no further checks regarding its effective contribution to military action through its use or purpose would need to be made – nor, indeed, any further checks regarding definite military advantage.[13] The relevant targets are deemed military objectives because of that 'implied' satisfaction of all the other components of the definition.

The approach that 'assumes' the satisfaction of the remaining elements of the definition may reflect, to some extent, the logical implication of the nature condition, and may make practical sense during an armed conflict. It should be noted that there is no basis in law for such an approach, and that it is not commonly shared. The issue, however, relates to the scope of objects that can be considered to fulfil this criterion, which will be explored next.

3.1.1 The scope of objects

States and commentators alike tend to see nature-associated objects as 'types', and list examples in categories. This was apparent in the formulation of the US Operational Law Handbook mentioned in note 12.[14] The UK Manual links nature to the 'type' of object.[15] In the Commentary to Rule 22(a) of the Manual on International Law Applicable to Air and Missile Warfare (hereinafter: AMW Manual), a group of experts claimed that the following all qualify as military objectives by their *nature* at all times and, presumably, in all circumstances: military aircraft; military vehicles (other than for medical transport); missiles and other weapons; military equipment; military fortifications, facilities and depots; warships; ministries of defence; and armaments

---

12 One may find such a position expressed in the US Operational Law Handbook. This states that military personnel, equipment, units and bases are always military objectives, and the definition test is relevant only to objects that are not military in nature. (Operational Law Handbook, JA 422, International and Operational Law Department, The Judge Advocate General's Legal Center and School, 2013 edn, at 22 [hereinafter: Operational Law Handbook]). Interestingly, the UK Manual of the Law of Armed Conflict does not share the US position (The Manual of the Law of Armed Conflict, UK Ministry of Defence, JSP 383, Oxford University Press, Oxford 2004, paras 5.4.4 and 5.4.5 [hereinafter: The UK Manual]). This is also supported by Rogers (A.P.V. Rogers, *Law on the Battlefield*, Melland Schill Studies in International Law, 3rd edn, Manchester University Press, Manchester 2012, at 123).

13 The question then becomes whether the two key elements are substantively the same, and if the satisfaction of one side of the definition can be equated with the existence of the other. The relationship between the two parts will be further discussed in 5.1.

14 Operational Law Handbook, op. cit. n 12, at 22.

15 The UK Manual, op. cit. n 12, para 5.4.4(c).

50 *Military objective: concept and definition*

factories.[16] ICRC examples include 'weapons, military equipment, transports, headquarters, communication centres'.[17] Similar lists of categories can be found in publications by Rogers, Dinstein and Solis.[18] This approach appears to resemble the categories and lists of targets discussed in the preceding chapter, which was rejected when the definition was adopted.[19] While the definition should be applied as a test, the military may be tempted to enumerate the categories of targets that are regarded as qualifying under the nature criterion. There is a risk, however, that categories can be sweeping, which may result in an excessively broad application of this criterion.

Without doubt, there are objects that are exclusively designed for – and utilised in the course of – military operations. They may be used now or in the future only for military purposes. These objects could be described as satisfying the nature requirement in its full sense. Examples of such objects are weapons and ammunitions, which are inherently for military activity, even if they could also be used by civilians who participate in fighting. Other examples include fighter-bomber aircraft or submarines, whose inherent military character, function and destination can only be military in any circumstances. It is interesting to note that NATO targeting doctrine indicates that some military targets would 'virtually always' be military objectives.[20] The examples given in the doctrine appear to represent targets connected to military operations and include 'fighter aircraft, submarines, ammunition depots'.[21] One can only assume that this would be due to their nature, as the text lacks clarification. 'Virtually always' is important because it implies that such objects may not always be military objectives, though situations such as these are likely to be rare.

It could be that information became available to suggest that a target may not satisfy all the legal requirements, as previously thought. Such objects, for example, would have an intrinsic military character, but also an inherent capacity to be utilised for civilian purposes. They are not designed for civilian use, but have the capacity to be used in this way. This should not be confused

---

16 AMW Manual, op cit. n 6, Commentary to Rule 22(a) at 47 and 107. It is necessary to note that experts who participated in writing the Manual did not represent States in any official capacity, even if they were employed by their respective governments at the time. The Manual does not represent the views of individual States and is not legally binding. Boothby disagrees with the position taken in the AMW Manual (W.H. Boothby, *The Law of Targeting*, Oxford University Press, Oxford 2012, at 103).

17 ICRC Commentary, op. cit. n 4, subsequently referred to in Rogers, op. cit. n 12, at 122.

18 Rogers, op. cit. n 12, at 122–3; Dinstein, op. cit. n 7, at 96–7; G.D. Solis, *The Law of Armed Conflict: International Humanitarian Law in War*, Cambridge University Press, Cambridge 2010, para 14.3.1.

19 See the discussion in 2.5.5.

20 NATO Allied Joint Doctrine for Joint Targeting, AJP-3.9, May 2008, at 1–7, para 0113(e) [hereinafter NATO Targeting Doctrine]. See also the further discussion of military doctrine in Chapter 8.

21 Ibid.

with dual-use objects, where objects concurrently perform both military and civilian functions.[22] In this case, the normal military use is expected, unless other information is available in respect of an individual target. In practice, such occurrences may seem very unlikely, but not impossible. In this context, we can consider an armoured personnel carrier (APC) – an armoured fighting vehicle designed to transport infantry to the battlefield. It is possible to imagine that an APC could transport, for instance, displaced civilians to safety. Similarly, a military transport plane could engage in the evacuation of wounded civilians. This would not be possible in the case of fighter-bomber aircraft. Military buildings and facilities can also be used to house displaced persons, or to shield civilians from an attack. An example of this is the deserted military barracks used to house refugees in the scenario outlined by Professor Dinstein.[23]

During an armed conflict, it could conceivably be reasonable to assume that such objects, designed for the conduct of hostilities, were being used for military ends, unless one happened to know to the contrary. While it may be reasonable to assume that the quality of the nature criterion is continuous, there is no presumption of the existence of a military quality as such. If information were available that put in question the object's military use, the other components of the definition would need to be reviewed. This is because the object's determination as a military objective would depend on those other components being satisfied. There is a danger of undermining the letter and spirit of the definition if, based on the unwarranted assumption of the nature criterion, a broad range of objects were to be treated as military objectives.

3.1.2 Contemporary debates

The objects discussed so far in this section appear to be commonly recognised as satisfying the nature criterion. Until recently, a majority of commentators supported such a narrow view of the criterion. However, one leading author, Professor Dinstein, appears to embrace a broader view of the nature criterion. According to Dinstein, lines of communication, and power plants used for military purposes, may qualify as military objectives by virtue of their nature. Other experts agree that such objects can be military objectives but they have varying opinions as to whether this is achieved by the virtue of their nature or their use. The most evident debate concerns lines of communication, specifically bridges. Other possible disagreements – in respect of transmission or broadcasting facilities, and industrial facilities involved in the production and storage of power – were signalled in the 2009 AWM Manual. This subsection will first analyse lines of communication, and then transmission

---

22 See the further discussion regarding dual-use objects in 3.3.
23 See text attached to n 6 above *et seq*.

52 *Military objective: concept and definition*

facilities. Power-generating facilities will be assessed in the section dealing with dual-use objects in this chapter (section 2.3).

One of the significant and long-term disagreements relates to objects known as lines of communications and transportation (LOC), particularly bridges.[24] Lines of communication are routes (land, water and air) that connect a military force with a base of operations, along which supplies and troops move. These objects usually include the lines themselves together with connecting communication nodes such as railway lines, railway stations and embarkation points, roads, bridges, ports, airports and airfields, as well as waterways, docks, harbours, tunnels and canals.[25]

In the past, Art 8 of the 1954 Hague Convention on Cultural Property referred to 'an aerodrome, a port or railway station of relative importance or a main line of communication' within the context of an important military objective, constituting a vulnerable point.[26] As previously mentioned, transportation and communication systems, railroads, airfields and port facilities of fundamental importance for the conduct of armed conflict were also included in the non-binding 1956 Draft Rules.[27] While recognising that such objects could be considered military objectives, the authors of both documents pointed to selected LOC – and not all of them – because of their specific military significance. This does not imply that all LOC, as per their nature, could constitute lawful targets. The nature of the objects does not depend on the degree of their importance.

Since then, Professor Dinstein maintains that 'arteries of transportation of strategic importance, principally mainline railroads and rail marshalling yards, major motorways . . . navigable rivers and canals', as well as bridges, should always be recognised as military objectives under the nature condition.[28]

---

24 The two terms are used by various authors almost interchangeably. They essentially refer to the same objects. However, it might be noted that the term 'lines of communication' incorporates transportation.

25 See, for instance, a list of examples in the Dutch Military Manual, as cited in J.M. Henckaerts and L. Doswald-Beck (eds), *Customary International Humanitarian Law*, Cambridge University Press, Cambridge 2005, Vol. II, para. 538, at 212 [hereinafter: CIHL]; Art 5.1 of the 1938 Draft Convention for the Protection of Civilian Populations Against New Engines of War, International Law Association, Amsterdam, 3 September 1938, reprinted in D. Schindler and J. Toman (eds), *The Laws of Armed Conflict*, 4th edn, Martinus Nijhoff, Leiden 2004, at 331 *et seq.*), as well as Art 24 (2) of the 1923 Hague Rules, included lines of communication of fundamental military importance, or used for military purposes, in their list of potential lawful targets (Hague Rules Concerning the Control of Wireless Telegraphy in time of War and Air Warfare, 1923, reprinted in Schindler and Toman, op. cit. this note, at 315 *et seq.*).

26 The Hague, 14 May 1954, reprinted in Schindler and Toman, op. cit. n 25, at 1003.

27 M. Bothe, K. Partsch and W. Solf, *New Rules for Victims of Armed Conflicts: Commentary on the Two 1977 Protocols Additional to the Geneva Conventions of 1949*, Martinus Nijhoff, The Hague 1982), para 2.3.2, at 324.

28 Dinstein op. cit. n 7, at 97. See also Y. Dinstein. 'Discussion', comments in A.E. Wall (ed.), *Legal and Ethical Lessons of NATO's Campaign*, Vol. 78, US Naval War College International Law Studies, Newport, RI 2002, at 218.

Nature, location, use and purpose 53

There are some bridges that are not part of the LOC network. These, in his view, will qualify under the other three criteria.[29] If understood correctly, Professor Dinstein is of the opinion that some roads are more important than others. That means they will always satisfy the nature criterion, while strategically unimportant LOC can satisfy only the other criteria, presumably in certain circumstances. It is important to note that the reference to arteries only of 'strategic importance' implies a logical inconsistency, similar to that in the 1954 Hague Convention on Cultural Property. As indicated earlier, if not all targets of this type can qualify as military objectives, then they can not be regarded to have the nature required by definition.

Similar confusion can be found in the recent AMW Manual, where it is suggested in Rule 23 that:

> Objects which *may* qualify as military objectives through the definition in Rules 1(y) and 22(a) include, but are not limited to, factories, lines and means of communications (such as airfields, railway lines, roads, bridges and tunnels); energy producing facilities; oil storage depots; transmission facilities and equipment.[30]

The commentary to this Rule further specifies that this formula apparently represented a compromise between the opposing views of the drafters of the Manual. The commentary indicated that such a novel formulation resulted from the significant disagreements among the drafters of the text.[31] Three diverse, and seemingly irreconcilable, positions were noted. According to one approach, all objects enumerated in this rule always satisfied the nature condition and, in fact, belonged to the Manual's preceding Rule 22(a).[32] In the opposite view, whether these objects satisfy the definition is entirely dependent on the circumstances ruling at the time. The drafters decided to arrive at compromise approach, reflected in the formulation of Rule 23, where such objects would 'not necessarily [be] military objectives by nature, but if at all, by use, purpose or location'.[33]

The AMW Manual explains that, according to the ICRC, nature is understood as an inherent feature of the object. It does not permit temporary

---

29 Dinstein, op. cit. n 7, at 97.
30 Emphasis added. Rule 23 AMW Manual, op. cit. n 6, Rule 1(y) refers to a definition of military objective as such, whereas Rule 22(a) specifically comments on the nature criterion and reads: 'The "nature" of an object symbolizes its fundamental character. Examples of military objectives by nature include military aircraft (including military UAV/UCAVs); military vehicles (other than medical transport); missiles and other weapons; military equipment; military fortifications, facilities and depots; warships; ministries of defence and armaments factories.' Rule 22(a) AMW Manual, op. cit. n 6.
31 AMW Manual, op. cit. n 6, Commentary at 107.
32 See n 30 above.
33 AMW Manual, op. cit. n 6, Commentary at 107.

54 *Military objective: concept and definition*

fluctuations in what may be construed as the 'contribution of the object'.[34] In other words, the object cannot acquire its nature on a temporary basis; once its 'nature' is military, it cannot be changed. Furthermore, the ICRC considers that the non-exhaustive categories of targets contained in Rule 23 may only qualify as military objectives through three other definitional criteria in certain circumstances, and not by nature. One has to agree with this approach. Either the objects *do* qualify, by virtue of the nature criterion, or they *do not*. If they do not, then they cannot be classed as military objectives under the nature condition, but they *may* satisfy the definition by virtue of the three other criteria.[35] Nature is a non-contextual requirement that is incompatible with a determination dependent on circumstances, which excludes the third 'compromise' position. Given that LOC do not have an intrinsic military quality, they should be assessed in accordance with their contribution to military action by location, purpose or use. This means that the first position of the experts expressed in the Manual also needs to be rejected. The creation of two subsets of non-exhaustive categories of objects, allegedly satisfying the nature condition, may lead only to further confusion and has to be rejected.

It is worth noting that a number of other commentators, none of whom were among the experts drafting the Manual, also considered that lines of communication could qualify as military objectives only through the three remaining criteria in the definition.[36] Both Professors Kalshoven and Hampson maintain that bridges, for example, are not military objectives by nature, and each bridge must be examined individually in the context of the situation at that time.[37] Professor Bothe also asserts that bridges can qualify under the use or purpose criteria.[38] The US also takes the position that LOC are civilian in

---

34 Ibid., n 261.
35 This implies that not only the substance of Rule 23, but also the way in which it was formulated, is incoherent.
36 F.J. Hampson, 'Proportionality and Necessity in the Gulf War', 86 *American Society of International Law Proceedings* 1992, 45–54 at 49; M. Bothe, 'Targeting' in A.E. Wall (ed.), *Legal and Ethical Lessons of NATO's Campaign*, Vol. 78, US Naval War College International Law Studies, Newport, RI 2002, at 178–9; F. Kalshoven, 'Reaffirmation and Development of International Humanitarian Law Applicable in Armed Conflicts: The Diplomatic Conference, Geneva, 1974–7', 9 *Netherlands Yearbook of International Law*, 1978, 107–71 at 111; I. Henderson, *The Contemporary Law of Targeting*, Martinus Nijhoff, Leiden 2009, at 47–9.
37 Kalshoven, op. cit. n 36; Hampson, op. cit. n 36; F.J. Hampson, 'Means and Methods of Warfare in the Conflict in the Gulf' in P. Rowe (ed.), *The Gulf War 1990–1991 in International and English Law*, Routledge, London 1993, at 98.
38 M. Bothe, 'The Protection of the Civilian Population and NATO Bombing on Yugoslavia: Comments on a Report to the Prosecutor of the ICTY', 12(3) *European Journal of International Law* 2001, 531–55 at 534); M. Sassoli and L. Cameron, 'The Protection of Civilian Objects – Current State of the Law and Issues *de lege ferenda*' in N. Ronzitti and G. Venturini (eds), *Current Issues in the International Humanitarian Law of Air Warfare*, Eleven International Publishing, Utrecht 2005, at 59.

Nature, location, use and purpose 55

nature and can be assessed only according to their location, use or purpose, with use (dual use) being the predominant consideration.[39]

Hays Parks and Dinstein argue that railroads and motorways were financed and built especially for military needs.[40] This might have been the case in the past, when military forces had to build roads to allow the movement of troops. Even so, such roads would not have had an exclusively military character unless they were integrated into military infrastructure. In modern society, the prevailing civilian need for transportation dictates new connections and transport solutions. Most roads, railways and other communication infrastructure are built primarily to satisfy civilian needs. Their peacetime use is predominantly civilian. Some roads acquire military significance after the opening of hostilities, when they would be included in operational plans for transport and logistics. In a time of conflict, then, their use or purpose would become military, even though their peacetime function would not normally involve military traffic.[41] At that point, they would become dual-use objects, reinforcing the argument that determining lines of communication depends on the temporal and contextual setting of location, purpose or use, which is incompatible with the essence of the nature criterion.[42] Baghdad bridges over the Euphrates River were, for example, attacked during the 1990–1 Gulf War because they contained fibre-optic cables enabling Iraqi military communications.[43] This justification implies the attackers did not regard all bridges in Iraq as lawful targets and the ones they attacked were used for military purposes.

Although initially included in the illustrative list attached to Art 52.3 API, lines of communication were thought to show more potential than many other objects for significant military use or purpose during armed conflict.[44] This

---

39 *Air Force Operations and the Law: A Guide for Air, Space and Cyber Forces*, 2nd edn, US Air Force, The Judge Advocate General's School 2009, at 250 [hereinafter: AF Operations and the Law]. The Operational Law Handbook (op. cit. n 12, at 23) gives an example of airports and German motorways under the *purpose* criterion. This suggests that even within one State, different forces may have different views in this context. None of them suggests that LOC should be considered under the *nature* criterion.

40 Hays Parks, op. cit. n 11 at 89; Dinstein, op. cit. n 7, at 97.

41 AMW Manual, op. cit. n 6, Commentary, para 1 at 110.

42 The NATO Targeting Doctrine considers bridges as dual-use objects, different to those that it otherwise regards as 'virtually always' military objectives (op. cit. n 20). See the further discussion regarding dual-use objects in 3.3.1.

43 US State Department of Defense, US Department of Defense, *Conduct of the Persian Gulf War: Final Report to Congress*, 10 April 1992, Department of Defense Washington, DC, 1992, 1–418 at 178 and 182, and Appendix O, at O1–O36 [hereinafter: DOD Report].

44 Bothe *et al.*, op. cit. n 27, para 2.5.1; see also the Dutch delegation statement during the AP negotiations during the meeting of Committee III of 6 February1975, CDHH/III/SR.14 in Official Records of the Diplomatic Conference on the Reaffirmation and Development of International Humanitarian Law Applicable in Armed Conflicts, Geneva (1974–7), Berne 1978, Vol. XIV, para 17.

56 Military objective: concept and definition

would indicate that lines of communication or transportation should not be considered to be of a military 'nature' *per se*, unless they were deliberately built to serve military forces and were exclusively utilised by them, for example roads inside military bases or military airports. It is possible that, in specific and narrow instances, one could ascertain that such a road would contribute to military action by its nature. Access roads to such facilities, on the other hand, could also easily be used for civilian purposes. Railroads, bridges or motorways created for general purposes have no specific military nature, in which case the determining factor in the legal analysis would be their location, purpose or use at that time.[45] The practice of recent conflicts seems to reinforce such a conclusion, even though it needs to be inferred from the behaviour of States if no explanation is forthcoming.

The key to the 1992 Battle of Sarajevo was the Serb-controlled 'war road' connecting Ilidza, a central quarter of the city, to the main Serbian military base at Lukavica. The road was five miles to the south of the city centre. It ran through the mountains encircling Sarajevo to the south and connected Sarajevo to Belgrade, some 250 miles away.[46] Serb forces placed their mortars and cannon on the hills surrounding Sarajevo, and shelled central parts of the city. The road was adjacent to Sarajevo's Butmir Airport, which was also under Serbian control. The capture of the main road connecting the nearest airport and the logistical supply centre in Belgrade became a crucial military objective for Bosnian Muslims. Maintaining control of this road was also a critical military objective for the Serbs, in order to preserve their presence in the centre of the city itself. This means that the 'war road' was of significant military value because of its location and use, rather than because it had been built and used exclusively for military purposes. It was the particular context of the Sarajevo battle that made this road, in effect, contribute to military action.

Roads and bridges in South and West Lebanon were deemed by the Israeli government to be 'major transportation arteries, through which weaponry and ammunition, as well as missile launchers and terrorist reinforcements are transported'. The Israelis claimed that their destruction was 'intended to prevent or obstruct the terrorists in planning and perpetrating their attacks' and 'to prevent the kidnapped soldiers [from] being smuggled out of the country'.[47]

---

45 'The test to such objects – unaffected by the presumptions on either side of the equation – remains the two-pronged test established in para.2.' Ibid. See also the discussion in section 4 of this chapter regarding the purpose criterion.

46 *Study of the Battle and Siege of Sarajevo*, Annex VI, part 1, Final report of the United Nations Commission of Experts established pursuant to Security Council Resolution 780 (1992), S/1994/674/Add. 2 (Vol. II), 27 May 1994

47 Israel Ministry of Foreign Affairs, *Responding to Hizbullah Attacks from Lebanon: Issues of Proportionality*, Legal Background, 25 July 2006, available at www.mfa.gov.il/MFA/Government/Law/Legal+Issues+and+Rulings/Responding+to+Hizbullah+attacks+from+Lebanon-+Issues+of+proportionality+July+2006.htm (last accessed 1 May 2014). Statements by a senior Israeli military commander indicated that the connection of the potential targets to the area of active hostilities was not necessarily part of the planning of the attacks.

Nature, location, use and purpose 57

Amnesty International suggested that destruction of the main coastal road could prevent Syria rearming Hezbollah.[48] One would be tempted to conclude that it was the use (dual use) or purpose of these routes that Israeli military forces were trying to deny to Hezbollah.[49] However, without an explanation to this effect from Israel, such a conclusion remains speculation.

Another category mentioned in Rule 23 of the AMW Manual includes 'transmission facilities'.[50] It is unclear what the authors of the Manual mean by the term 'transmission facilities'. The term could be interpreted to include broadcasting and television stations.[51] This would imply a very different approach to the assessment of news broadcasting objects, such as radio or TV stations, whose effective contribution to military action may vary depending on their use, but not their inherent military quality.[52]

Para 1 of the proposed annex to Art 7(2) of the 1956 ICRC Draft Rules included in a list of examples of military objectives the installations of broadcasting and television stations, telephone and telegraph exchanges, these being of fundamental military importance.[53] This document recognised that only some fundamentally militarily important stations can be regarded as military objectives. This means that broadcasting stations are not of an intrinsically military nature, and their assessment needs to be undertaken in accordance with the three other criteria.

Radio and television stations tend to attract military attention because of their broadcasting capabilities, which may enhance or assist the usual command, control and communications (C3) centres, and because of their

---

Report of the Commission of Inquiry on Lebanon pursuant to Human Rights Council Resolution S-2/1, 23 November 2006, A/HRC/3/2, para 43.

48 Amnesty International, *Israel/Lebanon: Deliberate destruction or Collateral Damage?*, AI Index: MDE 18/007/2006, Aug. 2006 at 12.

49 The Israeli armed forces issued a warning to the civilian population south of the Litani river, urging them to move north as commanders intended to conduct numerous attacks in areas south of the river. Presumably this implies that roads in East Lebanon were assumed to be used by civilians, whereas the roads in West Lebanon were assumed to be used by Hizbullah fighters going south. Bearing in mind that roads in East Lebanon were not attacked, the use rather than the nature of roads would have been a relevant consideration.

50 See n 30 above *et seq.*

51 In the absence of any explanation in the Manual, one cannot exclude such a possibility.

52 AF Operations and the Law, op. cit. n 39, at 250, refers to use (dual use).

53 *Draft Rules for the Limitation of the Dangers Incurred by the Civilian Population in Time of War*, reprinted in Schindler and Toman, op. cit. n 25, at 340–1. See the relevant discussion in 2.4. Article 8 of the 1954 Hague Convention on Cultural Property mentioned broadcasting stations as potential military objective (Convention for the Protection of Cultural Property in the Event of Armed Conflict, 14 May 1954, the Hague, reprinted in Schindler and Toman, op. cit. n 25, at 999 *et seq.* The first reference to the military importance attached to such means of communication can be found in Article 53 of the 1907 Hague Convention. This indicated that all 'appliances . . . adapted for the transmission of news' may be seized during an occupation. Convention (IV) respecting the Laws and Customs of War on Land and its Annex: Regulations Concerning the Laws and Customs of War on Land, The Hague, 18 October 1907, reprinted in Schindler and Toman, op. cit. n 25, at 55 *et seq.*

58 *Military objective: concept and definition*

potential effects on civilian morale when performing their civilian functions. Radio and TV stations may be partially incorporated into the C3 network, whose elements are co-located in or pass through the station's physical infrastructure. Such an object does not acquire intrinsic military character if it used by armed forces to house their C3 infrastructure; therefore, its assessment needs to be carried out according to the use criterion.

Separately, stations may be militarily relevant because of their broadcasting function. They may be used to transmit purely military communications, or they may transmit military messages in addition to normal civilian broadcasts. For example, the British armed forces during the Second World War used the British Broadcasting Corporation's radio transmissions from London to send coded messages to French Resistance fighters.[54] The word *use* is operative here; all these contributions clearly depend on the use or abuse of such objects. Otherwise, such objects would undertake their normal journalistic functions, which may also involve propaganda.[55]

These possible functions do not convey a sense that TV and radio broadcasting stations, as a type of object, can be generally viewed as having an intrinsic military quality. This means that the criterion by which they were most likely to contribute to military action is use, and in fact dual use.[56]

3.1.3 State and political leadership infrastructure

The principal discussion of the infrastructure associated with political leadership is in Chapter 7. However, some remarks will be offered here to introduce the problems that may arise in regard to the assessment of such objects in relation to the nature criterion.[57] The discussion is relevant in this section because places could be attacked on account of the activity within them, which may be of intrinsic military quality. Such activity concerns supreme command and control functions over the armed forces. The places where people perform such functions may, arguably, be considered legitimate targets.[58] This study clearly does not deal with human beings as military

---

54 See the examples of such messages (in French) at http://doctsf.com/bbc/messages.php (last accessed 1 May 2014).

55 Such an object may also be used in the commission of war crimes and other international crimes such as incitement to violence against civilians. Such activities will be contrary to its normal functions, and their assessment in the context of contribution to military action will be discussed in 7.4.

56 See the further discussion of the TV and radio broadcasting stations in 3.3.1, 7.3 and 8.1.

57 This represents a far more general problem, which will be addressed through a more detailed analysis in the context of the two key elements of the definition. See 7.1.

58 States tend not to specify if they have targeted certain buildings or places on account of the activity within them or if they targeted the people inside them. If such buildings are targeted on account of their use by these individuals, the use criterion may be relevant. (See the further discussion regarding the use criterion in 3.2.) If people are attacked, the damage to the building would be collateral.

objectives. However, the various functions and roles that individuals may have with regard to the control of armed forces, will have to be considered because such functions may determine which objects, buildings and places could be regarded as satisfying the requirements of the definition.

Because of the hierarchical command structure of armed forces, it is possible that the infrastructure associated with the senior military command can be considered in the context of the nature criterion. The place where the most senior military leadership performs its defence functions is the Ministry of Defence (MOD).[59] Such functions consist of strategic command and control over armed forces. It is reasonable to conclude that, on account of such functions linked to the conduct of military activities, the MOD buildings and facilities could be regarded as being of intrinsically military character. The recently published Air and Missile Warfare Manual asserted in Rule 22(a) that Ministries of Defence were objects that would effectively contribute to military action by their nature, at all times and in all circumstances.[60]

If the MOD is viewed as a military objective because of its nature, then the question arises: how should the MOD be assessed if it has departments dealing exclusively with civilian functions? The AMW Manual gives the example of the Swiss Federal Department of Defence, Civil Protection and Sports (FDCPS), whose civil protection and sports sections are dedicated exclusively to civilian purposes.[61] The set-up of the Swiss FDCPS is unusual in that it combines governmental departments dealing with strictly civilian issues with other ones dealing with military functions. MODs normally act as both political and administrative organs, dealing with the administrative, financial and personnel affairs of the armed forces. They have the highest central defence command (General Staff), responsible for commanding troops.[62] This means that, unlike facilities associated exclusively with the Defence sector of this Department, the FDCPS as a whole cannot be regarded as military in nature, though such infrastructure is likely to satisfy the use criterion (dual use).[63]

If the infrastructure of an MOD is generally regarded as of a military nature, then a question arises regarding infrastructure associated with other State organs, individuals or political leaders whose work is vital to the prosecution

---

59 In 1956 the ICRC Draft Rules had already listed 'War Ministries' such as a Ministry of Navy, Army, Air Force, National Defence or Supplies, and other 'organs for the direction and administration of military operations' as possible military objectives. Para 1 s 3 of the annex to Draft Rules for the Limitation of the Dangers Incurred by the Civilian Population in Time of War, op. cit. n 53.

60 Rule 22(a) AMW Manual, op. cit. n 6.

61 AMW Manual, op. cit. n 6, Commentary to Rule 22(a), para 2.

62 Art 58(b) API may be a relevant consideration that the Swiss government may take into account in the future.

63 This also highlights a problem in assuming the satisfaction of all requirements of the definition by entire categories of objects.

60 *Military objective: concept and definition*

of armed conflict and who may in fact exercise the supreme command over armed forces. The infrastructure of other governmental departments (central and local) that are not linked to functions of military character, such as the Ministry of Interior or intelligence agencies, cannot be regarded as military objectives under the nature criterion.[64] During an armed conflict, they may be used for military purposes, even exclusively so, but their nature is not that required by the definition.[65]

To begin with, there are numerous other military competencies with which various political bodies can be vested as part of the civil control of armed forces. There is no single model of control over armed forces; the set-up will depend on the political system of individual countries, and the historical and cultural context. The degree of the control will differ in different political systems. In democratic systems, control over the armed forces comprises both direct and indirect management and supervision by the State authorities, such as the executive and legislative organs or the judiciary.[66] As far as the direct control of armed forces and their assets is concerned, various organs can be given diverse powers, from calling for national mobilisation to taking decisions regarding belligerent reprisals. Depending on the type of democracy, various top political posts will have different levels of control of the relevant functions.

Take, for instance, the position of commander- in-chief of the armed forces (CiC), which involves, in principle, heading the military forces and exercising supreme command powers. It is usual practice to associate CiC functions with the Head of State as holder of the highest executive powers, but this could be misleading. States can nominate a CiC who is not Head of State. This happens in Germany, where the Head of State is the President. In peacetime, the CiC is the Federal Minister of Defence, while in a state of war it is the Federal Chancellor.[67] In Sweden the monarch is the non-executive Head of State, while the CiC is the Cabinet, with the Prime Minister as chief executive.

A distinction also needs to be made in situations where the Head of State holds *de jure* authority, but exercises it either on the advice of some other organ (which *de facto* makes the decision) or delegates its command authority to other organs and institutions.[68] Indeed, the CiC position is often nominal and ceremonial, while the supreme command competencies are exercised by other executive bodies. Such bodies may include the prime minister and/or the

---

64 Rogers, op. cit. n 12, at 123, but *a contrario* to Dinstein, op. cit. n 7, at 97. Henderson provides an example of Australian forces attacking Iraqi Intelligence Service facilities during the 2003 operation in Iraq as a correct application of the definition. Henderson, op. cit. n 36, at 146.

65 See the further discussion regarding the use criterion in 3.3.

66 Such competencies are often viewed as attributes of stable, liberal democracy, but the civilian control of armed forces may not be confined to democratic States.

67 See Art 65a and Art 11b of the Basic Law of the Federal Republic of Germany, available at: https://www.btg-bestellservice.de/pdf/80201000.pdf (last accessed 1 May 2014).

68 For example, Queen Elizabeth II is the nominated Commander-in-Chief in the UK, Australia and Canada, but *de facto* and *de jure* Her Majesty's command powers are delegated to the relevant executive authorities.

Nature, location, use and purpose 61

cabinet led by the prime minister (in a parliamentary democracy), or the president (in a presidential system) or both (in a semi-presidential democracy), or even directly through a Chief of General Staff at the Ministry of Defence.[69] It is unclear whether the building where the CiC discharges his or her functions, or other places intrinsically associated with the CiC, can be considered lawful targets.

A number of other functions that can affect the prosecution of armed conflict, such as decisions relating to granting or withholding approval of certain targets, or deciding whether to engage in belligerent reprisals, may be undertaken by a president, prime minister, a whole cabinet or a whole parliament.[70] these functions are essentially military-related. The question is: could the buildings in which such functions are undertaken be considered as military objectives and, if so, is this under the nature criterion? Might it depend on whether the building is the official location of the relevant State organ, such as the British prime minister's residence at 10 Downing Street in London?

In non-democratic societies, such functions may be far more blurred or even non-existent. Institutions that sustain a dictator in power, such as government machinery or political party infrastructure, might be of military interest merely because of their role in sustaining such a dictatorship. During military operations against Iraq in 1990–1 and 2003, for instance, buildings associated with the Ba'ath party were attacked, but the legal basis for this remains unclear.[71] Greenwood argues that the combination of the highly military nature of the Iraqi government, and the close integration of the Ba'ath party in government structures, meant it was justifiable to see them as military objectives.[72]

Therefore, it is likely that not all targets involving governmental and political structures and facilities can be considered to be contributing to military action on account of their *nature*. Only some of these buildings could legitimately be characterised as such because of their intrinsic military function or destination, and not by their general association with an adversary's power base.

3.2 Location

The location criterion, unlike the nature and use criteria, was not initially included in the draft definition of 'military objective' in Art 52.2 API.[73] It was

---

69 It may be that at the start of war the ceremonial CiC can appoint a CiC nominated by the prime minister to discharge the actual functions during the war.

70 See the further discussion in Chapters 8 and 9.

71 See the further discussion in 7.1 and 9.1.1 and 9.1.4.

72 C. Greenwood, 'Customary International Law and the First Geneva Protocol of 1977 in the Gulf Conflict' in P. Rowe (ed.), *The Gulf War 1990–1991 in International and English Law*, Routledge, London 1993, at 63.

73 'Report on the Work of the Conference; Conference of Government Experts on the Reaffirmation and Development of International Humanitarian Law Applicable in Armed Conflicts' (Second Session Geneva 3 May–3 June 1972), ICRC, Geneva 1972, in particular Vol. I, at 146. See also 2.5.1.

62 *Military objective: concept and definition*

included only in 1975, during the second year of negotiations of the working group within Committee III.

Location is a specific criterion by which an object gains military significance through its relationship with other places or objects. Its assessment depends on the circumstances. Location includes areas, places and pieces of land, together with objects that are considered to be militarily important because of their particular features, or because their relationship to other things makes it necessary to capture or deny them to the enemy.[74]

Dinstein suggests that the location criterion should always be considered in the assessment of the object, regardless of the three other requirements.[75] This, however, is at odds with the nature criterion, where the satisfaction of the other criteria, such as location, is irrelevant. Dinstein argues this would be done out of concerns other than those resulting from the application of the definition, such as the presence of civilian objects within the military objectives.[76] This may be justified by considerations regarding how the attacks on such objects should be undertaken.

An object's military use, or its absence, is also irrelevant to its assessment under location.[77] Location can turn a purely civilian object into a military objective if such an object is regarded as obstructing a clear line of fire, or preventing the execution of certain military operations, including the retreat of troops. For instance, a house may become a military objective due to its location if its destruction would permit a clear view of a crossroads considered to be militarily advantageous.[78]

Tactically important mountain passes, routes through natural or man-made obstacles, a bridgehead, footbridges, crossroads, hills and tunnels can all be perceived as military objectives by virtue of their location.[79] Ground positions temporarily used by armed forces in the course of operations, or so-called 'combat objectives', are also included in this category.[80] A gathering point may

---

74 For instance, the UK Manual and AMW Manual refer only to selected areas and do not mention other objects. The UK Manual, op. cit. n 12, para 5.4.4 point 'd'; Operational Law Handbook, op. cit. n 12, at 23; AMW Manual, op. cit. n 6, Commentary to Rule 22(b), at 107; ICRC Commentary, op. cit. n 4, para 2021; Hays Parks, op. cit. n 11, at 88.

75 Dinstein, op. cit. n 7, at 100.

76 Considerations related to how attacks are undertaken are beyond the scope of this work. See 1.3.

77 AMW Manual, op. cit. n 6, Commentary to Rule 22(a), at 107.

78 Green refers to houses in areas of combat, in the assessment of which Rogers recommends caution. L.C. Green, *The Contemporary Law of Armed Conflict*, Melland Schill Studies in International Law, 3rd edn, Manchester University Press, Manchester 2008, at 156; Rogers, op. cit. n 12, at 107.

79 Hays Parks, op. cit. n 11, at 88; H.B. Robertson, 'The Principle of the Military Objective in the Law of Armed Conflict' 8 *US Air Force Academy Journal of Legal Studies* 1997–8, 35–69 at 49; Dinstein, op. cit. n 7 at 102; H. Olasolo, *Unlawful Attacks in Combat Situations: From the ICTY's Case Law to the Rome Statute*, Martinus Nijhoff, Leiden 2008, at 123.

80 S. Oeter, 'Methods and Means of Combat' in D. Fleck (ed.), *The Handbook of Humanitarian Law in Armed Conflicts*, 2nd edn, Oxford University Press, Oxford 2008, at 183.

Nature, location, use and purpose 63

become a military objective under the location criterion. For example, a hilltop could be considered as contributing to military action on account of its location if it overlooks a junction whose capture or *neutralization* offers a definite military advantage.[81]

A piece of land may become a military objective *per se* due to its location. It has been recommended that an assessment of the contribution of land should not involve a widespread area without clear features of 'military interest'.[82] This could involve gaining high ground for an observation post, or activities undertaken to prevent the enemy using a certain piece of land.

A number of States have made formal statements upon ratification of API addressing this particular issue. The formula used by the British Government reads:

> It is the understanding of the United Kingdom that:
>
> – a specific area of land may be a military objective if, because of its location or other reasons specified in this Article, its total or partial destruction, capture or neutralisation in the circumstances ruling at the time offers definite military advantage.[83]

Other States followed with the same, or very similar statements.[84] 'Piece of land' reservations have been criticised as they may possibly be inconsistent with the 'object and purpose' of API, particularly where such a statement clearly contrasts with the expressed prohibition of area bombing in Art 51

---

81 It is worth noting that such a hilltop is not used by the adversary, and may not otherwise contribute to their military action. This raises a question as to whose military action the object should contribute. See a further discussion of the issue in 4.2.

82 ICRC Commentary, op. cit. n 4, paras 1955 and 2026; Dinstein, op. cit. n 7, at 101; Rogers, op. cit. n 12, at 107–8.

83 The language used to express the statement suggests this is an interpretative declaration rather than a reservation. UK statement on the vote on Article 47 of draft API (CDDH/DR.41, VI, para 153) and on the ratification of API made on 28 January 1998. Protocol Additional to the Geneva Conventions of 12 August 1949, and Relating to the Protection of Victims of International Armed Conflicts (Protocol I), Geneva, 8 June 1977, reprinted in Schindler and Toman, op. cit. n 25, at 711 *et seq.* hereinafter: API].

84 Canadian statement of 20 November 1990; French declaration of 11 April 2001; German statement on vote on Article 47 of draft API (CDDH/DR.41, VI, at 188) and on ratification of API of 14 February 1991; Italian declaration of 27 February 1986, Dutch declaration on vote on Article 47 of draft API (CDDH/DR.41, VI, at 195) and on ratification of API of 26 June 1987; New Zealand statement of 8 February 1988 and the Spanish declaration of 21 April 1989. The US made the same statement on the vote on Article 47 of draft API (CDDH/DR.41, VI, at 204) and on its signature in 1977, and Pakistan made a declaration of this type on its ratification of the 1996 Amended Protocol II to the United Nations Convention on Prohibitions or Restrictions on the Use of Certain Conventional Weapons which May Be Deemed to Be Excessively Injurious or to Have Indiscriminate Effects, on 9 March 1999.

64   *Military objective: concept and definition*

API.[85] This would be particularly important in the context of specific types of weapons – landmines or cluster weapons – because the laying of mines to neutralize a piece of land, in order to deny the enemy access to it, is a fully permissible military operation.[86] In this respect, the Swedish IHL Manual specifies that although Art 52.2 API applies only to objects and property, an area of land, not being an object, can become a military objective if it is militarily advantageous to impede the advance of the enemy by means of artillery fire or mining.[87]

Henderson warns against too liberal an interpretation of this condition, permitting the extensive destruction of objects based on speculative assumptions as to their contribution on account of their location. He further argues that the destruction of large buildings, or large numbers of buildings, from an area that may be militarily useful – and where such buildings may obstruct the land's potential in future – is unacceptable, as it would yield no definite military advantage.[88] This author agrees that caution should be applied in making generalised conclusions, since any assessment of the object's status, with the general exception of those that satisfy the nature condition, should be made on a case-by-case basis.

Location is a more dominant factor in targeting analysis in some conflicts because of specific geographical features. This is particularly true where the exploitation of the natural landscape dominates operations. For example, natural crevices or ridgelines in deep valleys surrounded by mountain ranges can be used to avoid detection by even the most sophisticated surveillance systems. Extensive vegetation or foliage also can provide effective cover.[89]

Stupni Do Hill, near Grbavica village, was regarded as militarily significant because it would have enabled the army of Bosnia and Herzegovina to block Bosnian-Serb access to the Travnik–Busova road, one of the main lines of

---

85   E. Rauch 'Conduct of Combat and Risks Run by the Civilian Population', 21 *Revue de droit pénal militaire et de droit de la guerre*, 1982, 66–72 at 68. See also discussion in E. Rosenblad, 'Area Bombing and International Law', 15(1) *Revue de droit pénal militaire et de droit de la guerre* 1976, at 90; Dinstein, op. cit. n 7, at 118–19; S.A. Garrett, 'Airpower and Non-Combatant Immunity' in I. Primoraz (ed.), *Civilian Immunity in War*, Oxford University Press, Oxford 2007; T. Marauhn and S. Kirchener, 'Target Area Bombing' in N. Ronzitti and G. Venturini (eds), *Current Issues in the International Humanitarian Law of Air Warfare*, Eleven International Publishing, Utrecht, 2005, at 87–105.

86   Bothe, *et al.*, op. cit. n 27, at 325 para 2.4.5. The use of landmines and other weapons in military operations intended to neutralise the area will be further discussed in 6.1.3.

87   CIHL, op. cit. n 25, Vol. II, at 225 para 616; also in ICRC Commentary (op. cit. n 4, para 1955), though confined to the combat zone, a restriction that is challenged by Rogers, op. cit. n 12, at 108.

88   Henderson, op. cit. n 36, at 57. See also the further discussion of definite military advantage in 5.2 and 5.3.

89   Foliage and vegetation were exploited by North Vietnamese fighters. See also 2.4.

Nature, location, use and purpose 65

transportation and communication in the area.[90] Mount Srd, a prominent geographical feature of the Croatian city of Dubrovnik, contained a communications tower and a historical Napoleonic fortress. It was attacked by Serb forces because it gave Croatian troops an advantage, being the only high ground around the city, which was not under Serbian control in 1991.[91]

During a large Israel Defence Forces (IDF) offensive in the Gaza Strip in 2009, Israeli forces destroyed the el-Bader flour mill – the last functioning mill in the area. A UN-commissioned inquiry noted that the mill may have been viewed as a military objective by the IDF because, being one of the tallest structures in the area, it could possibly have served as an observation and sniping post for Palestinian forces.[92] The Israel Ministry of Foreign Affairs (IMFA) maintained that the mill was not a pre-planned target. However, given the object's location in the adversary's defensive zone, as well as evidence of its 'potential use' by Palestinians, the mill could be considered a legitimate military target in the circumstances of active combat.[93] Interestingly, though, the IMFA suggested in the same document that the mill had already been identified during the preparation of Israel's operations in Gaza because of its importance as a 'strategic high point'.[94] Two potential justifications were given by the IMFA. One related to purpose, while the other suggested a location criterion. This may be a sign of the fact that some objects may qualify through more than one criterion. Controversy still surrounds the attack on the mill, and it is impossible to conclude with certainty why it was targeted. Bearing in mind the mill's proximity to active hostilities, it is reasonable to conclude that if it was considered a military objective, its location (or purpose) may have been a determining factor.

3.3 Use[95]

The *use* criterion refers to the current function of an object, whether inside or outside its normal or habitual use; what it is made for, and what it is supposed

---

90 *The Prosecutor v Tihomir Blaskic*, IT-95-14-T, ICTY Trial Chamber Judgment of 3 March 2000, para 551.
91 *The Prosecutor v Pavle Strugar*, IT-01-42-T, ICTY Trial Chamber Judgment of 31 January 2005, paras 70 and 99.
92 The authors of the report nevertheless seem to question the necessity of the attack and how it was undertaken. UN Human Rights Council, Report of the United Nations Fact-Finding Mission on the Gaza Conflict, UN Doc. A/HRC/12/48, 25 September 2009, para 929.
93 Israel Ministry of Foreign Affairs, *Gaza Operation Investigations: An Update*, January 2010, paras 164, 166, 170–3, available at: http://mfa.gov.il/MFA/ForeignPolicy/Terrorism/Pages/Gaza_Operation_Investigations_Update_Jan_2010.aspx (last accessed 1 May 2014).
94 Ibid.
95 The *use* criterion, as mentioned earlier in this chapter, was chosen to be analysed before *purpose*. Although this clearly does not follow the order in Art 52.2, it is logically more fitting to discuss activity at the time followed by future activity, in line with the purpose requirement.

66 *Military objective: concept and definition*

to do.[96] Use can signify a practice that is either habitual or customary, as well as a singular, *ad hoc* event, perhaps even including its accidental use. Both meanings seem equally applicable to the analysis of an object. The law does not indicate whether use should have any particular qualities such as volume, duration or intensity. Use could, therefore, be continuous or singular, random and sporadic, or regular. The law does not specify if use should be of a particular kind, with the exception that it should effectively contribute to the military action of the adversary for the object to satisfy the first element of the definition.

As with the location criterion, what is crucial here is the consideration of context. The use of the object will depend on the factual circumstances in each case. As those circumstances are fluid, they could change rapidly, and so, potentially, could the status of the analysed object.[97]

A normally civilian object can become a lawful, military objective if it is used by armed forces.[98] Dinstein convincingly argues that 'virtually any object or location may become a military objective through use (or abuse) by a belligerent'.[99] In other words, the use or misuse of any object or place by an adversary will be relevant in any determination. The unlawful behaviour of the other side is not a bar to attacking such objects, though other constraints may ultimately prevent the attack.[100]

With some objects, there is a positive presumption regarding non-military use enshrined in Art 52.3 API.[101] This presumption applies to objects that are normally used exclusively by civilians.[102] This does not cover objects that are, or can be, habitually used for both military and civilian purposes (known as

---

96 ICRC Commentary, op. cit. n 4, para 2022; The UK Manual, op. cit. n 12, para 5.4.4 point 'e'; Operational Law Handbook, op. cit. n 12, at 23, AMW Manual, op. cit. n 6, Commentary to Rule 22(d), at 108–9.

97 This is further informed by reference to 'the circumstances ruling at the time', enshrined in the definition of military objective. See the further discussion in 6.2.

98 One can also argue that the object can satisfy the use criterion when it is controlled but not necessarily used by the adversary. This may occur when the object remains captured. See also 6.1.2.

99 Dinstein, op. cit. n 7, at 98.

100 See also Solis, op. cit. n 18, at 527. During the 1990–1 Gulf War, for instance, Iraqi MIG-21 fighter jets based next to the ancient temple of Ur were not targeted, despite their obviously military *nature*. The US Department of Defense report, following the war, alluded to the proportionality principle as the reason for not attacking the planes, rather than the lawfulness of the target *per se*. US Department of Defense, *Conduct of the Persian Gulf War: Final Report to Congress*, 10 April 1992, Department of Defense Washington, DC, 1992, 1–418 at 133, and Appendix O, at O14.

101 'In case of doubt whether an object which is normally dedicated to civilian purposes, such as a place of worship, a house or other dwelling or a school, is being used to make an effective contribution to military action, it shall be presumed not to be so used.' Art 52.3 API.

102 Some military targets, such as military bases or military ports, may contain civilian objects. The presence of non-combatants or civilian objects in or around military objectives does not change their status as lawful targets.

Nature, location, use and purpose 67

dual use).[103] These will be considered separately below. The implication of the presumption is that some evidence is required to show that such objects are, in fact, used for military purposes. The presumption rests entirely on the existence of doubt as to the use of such an object at that time, and not on it being used in future. The presumption had already become controversial during its adoption, and continues to be so, mainly because the 'degree of doubt' required for the presumption to be applied remains disputed.[104] The presumption is of no value when such doubt does not exist, and if one is confident that, for example, a nursery is being used for military purposes, it could be recognised as satisfying the first part of the definition.

There is a temporal dimension to the use criterion. In principle, an object will be a military objective only while it is used for military purposes.[105] Consider a scenario in which a clock tower is used as a sniper position for one day, because troops are passing by the village where the tower is located. The attackers would consider attacking the tower only on that particular day, while it was used for a military function. On any other day, it is more likely that the tower would not be used for a military purpose. If a doubt exists as to its use, the presumption of its civilian character should be applied.[106] The mere suspicion of an object's use, unsupported by evidence, would not suffice.[107] Should questions arise concerning the reliability of the evidence gathered, the presumption of the object's civilian character must be taken into account.[108] Numerous civilian buildings, including schools and nurseries, were apparently used by South Ossetian forces in and around Tskhinvali to set up firing positions. Such buildings could have been reasonably determined to be legitimate targets if they were attacked by Georgian forces with a view to neutralising the Ossetian positions.[109]

Common sense must be applied in every case. Consider a different scenario, where the village clock tower has been used as a sniper's position every day

---

103 C. Greenwood, 'The Law of War (International Humanitarian Law)', Chapter 25 in M.D. Evans (ed.), *International Law*, Oxford University Press, Oxford, 2003, at 786.

104 The ICTY seems to suggest 'a reasonable belief' standard: 'an object shall not be attacked when it is not reasonable to believe, in the circumstances of the person contemplating the attack, including the information available to the latter, that the object is being used to make an effective contribution to military action'. (*The Prosecutor v Stanislav Galic*, IT-98-29-T, Trial Chamber, Judgment of 5 December 2003, para 51). The US and Israel oppose this rule, as they believe it imposes an unfair legal burden on the attacker. For more, see Dinstein, op. cit. n 7, at 98 and A. Boivin, 'The Legal Regime Applicable to Targeting Military Objectives in the Context of Contemporary Warfare', Geneva Academy of International Humanitarian Law and Human Rights, Research Paper 02/2006, at 19–20.

105 Good examples here are the 'Taxis of the Marne', ordinary cabs used to transport French troop reserves to the front in 1914, as recalled in Dinstein, op. cit. n 7, at 97.

106 AMW Manual, op. cit. n 6, Commentary to Rule 12(b), at 88.

107 The UK Manual, op. cit. n 12, para 5.4.2 n 16.

108 AMW Manual, op. cit. n 6, Commentary to Rule 12(b), at 88.

109 Human Rights Watch, *Up in Flames*, Report of 23 January 2009, Part 2, section 2.2.

68   Military objective: concept and definition

for three months. In a 'regular use' scenario, the likelihood of the tower being used for military purposes on the day of a planned attack is certainly greater, as there is a pattern of past military use. Here, the presumption of normal civilian use would not apply because of that past use.[110] During the war in Bosnia, for example, the Hotel Vitez was used as the Croatian Defence Council Military Police headquarters and, as such, was undoubtedly a legitimate target.[111]

Is it permissible, though, to infer a present military use from regular past military use? The law does not envisage a presumption of military use. While, in practice, such use is likely to be viewed as a strong indication of the adversary's intentions, it might also be taken as a reflection of the continuation of the object's function at that time. In the second scenario, the clock tower could, nevertheless, qualify by its purpose, defined as intended future use, if the attackers were convinced that such an intention existed.[112]

A variation of the second scenario occurs when a school is regularly used by armed forces for overnight stays over a longer period of time. In other words, the building functions as a school during the day, but at night it provides accommodation for armed forces. Again, the presumption of its civilian use cannot be applied, as there is no doubt that it is used by armed forces. It is possible that the school satisfies both the use and purpose criteria, and can thus be regarded as a lawful target both during the day and night.

The third kind of situation concerns an erratic and/or sporadic use of the same object over a long period of time. Take the school, which is used every now and then to store ammunition and weapons. There is no regularity in the frequency and length of use. This sort of use cannot be indicative of military use at that time. It may also be necessary for a presumption to be applied, when there is doubt as to the object's use, on the day the attack is envisaged.

When considering use as a criterion for satisfaction of the first element of the definition, it is also worth mentioning so-called 'dual-use' objects. 'Dual-use' object is not a legal term,[113] yet it is widely and increasingly used in the

---

110 See also Bothe *et al.*, op. cit. 27, para 2.5.1 at 326.

111 *The Prosecutor v Zoran Kupreskic (et. al)*, IT-95-16-A, ICTY Appeals Chamber Judgment of 23 October 2001, para 282.

112 It is debatable if such an object can satisfy even the *purpose* criterion, if purpose relates to what the object was made for. After all, a clock tower is not made to be used as a sniper post. Solis argues that the satisfaction of the *use* (and *purpose*) criterion does not depend on the object's original intended use, but does not elaborate further on this point (Solis, op. cit. n 18, at 526). See the further discussion of the purpose criterion in 3.4. See also the further discussion regarding the importance of the reliability and credibility of information in the assessment of objects in 6.2 and 10.4.

113 Dinstein, op. cit. n 28, at 218–19; C. Greenwood 'Current Issues in the Law of Armed Conflict: Weapons, Targets and International Criminal Liability', 1 *Singapore Journal of International and Comparative Law* 1997, 441–67 at 461; Sassoli and Cameron, op. cit. n 38, at 57.

Nature, location, use and purpose   69

public domain.[114] Dual-use targets are those objects that happen to facilitate both military and civilian ends.[115] Any objects that are used or misused for military purposes, in addition to their civilian use, should be regarded as falling under the *use* criterion.[116] Any object is either a military objective or it is not; there is no separate category of dual-use objects.

Dual-use objects are understood as being used for civilian and military purposes, such as an airport that deals with military and civilian traffic. Whether the military or civilian function is primary is irrelevant in terms of assessment in the context of the definition of military objectives. Even if the military use is secondary, it would imply the satisfaction of the first element of the definition. However, the substance of the object's civilian use will be a prominent consideration when deciding *how* to attack a dual-use target.[117] It has been suggested that a 'dual-use' object can be a military objective depending on 'whether its military use is sufficient to bring it within the test laid down in Article 52(2)'.[118] It should be made clear that the issue is not that there is a requirement for a sufficient volume of military use, but whether the use is of military quality such as to take it across the threshold.[119]

When there is an 'alternating use' – namely, when the object's use fluctuates between an exclusively civilian function and an exclusively military one – then the object cannot be regarded as dual use. It could still satisfy the purpose

114 See the reports of NGOs including Human Rights Watch (HRW), *International Humanitarian Law Issues in a Potential War in Iraq*, February 2003; HRW, *Off Target: The Conduct of the War and Civilian Casualties in Iraq*, December 2003; and UN reports such as Report of the Commission of Inquiry on Lebanon pursuant to Human Rights Council Resolution S-2/1, 23 November 2006, A/HRC/3/2 and Report of the Special Rapporteur on extrajudicial, summary or arbitrary executions, Philip Alston; the Special Rapporteur on the right of everyone to the enjoyment of the highest attainable standard of physical and mental health, Paul Hunt; the Representative of the Secretary-General on human rights of internally displaced persons, Walter Kälin; and the Special Rapporteur on adequate housing as a component of the right to an adequate standard of living, Miloon Kothari, Mission to Lebanon and Israel, 2 October 2006, A/HRC/2/7.
115 The notion of dual use, in this context, should not be confused with the meaning of dual use attached to technology, which indicates a potential to be used for hostile and/or peaceful purposes. S.A. Evans, 'Defining Dual-Use: An International Assessment of the Discourses around Technology', Presentation given to the ESCR New Directions in WMD Proliferation Seminar, 27 February 2006, at 4.
116 Hays Parks, op. cit. n 11, at 106.
117 Such a discussion is outside of the scope of this work (see 1.3). Boothby, op. cit. n 16 at 105; H. Shue and D. Wippman, 'Limiting Attacks on Dual-Use Facilities Performing Indispensable Civilian Functions', 35(3) *Cornell International Law Journal* 2002, 559–79 at 563.
118 Greenwood, op. cit. n 103, at 785.
119 Greenwood, op. cit. n 113, at 461; AMW Manual, op. cit. n 6, Commentary to Rule 22(c), at 108. See discussion regarding the threshold in 2.5. Assessing the use of objects *ex post facto* attacks could be problematic, as use may be concealed – and not obvious to third parties making the assessment.

70   *Military objective: concept and definition*

criterion, though.[120] An object that is only occasionally known to be used for military ends must not be assumed to serve both uses at any given time, simply because it has been categorised as 'dual use' in the past. This is particularly important when the object is rarely utilised for military ends. An analysis of any object must factor in the context and circumstances at the time.[121] This dependence on circumstances implies that dual-use objects cannot be considered to satisfy the nature criterion, which is not situation-dependent.[122]

An interesting illustration is provided by the water reservoir near the village of Harsile, in a desert region of Eritrea. The reservoir was subject to several strikes by the Ethiopian Air Force in 1999 and 2000, but did not suffer any long-term, significant or irreparable damage. Ethiopia believed that by attacking the reservoir, it would deprive the Eritrean troops of access to drinking water, which would affect the Eritreans' military capacity on the Eastern Front of their operations.[123] Apparently, the Ethiopians possessed evidence of the reservoir's military use, but they were also aware of its civilian function. Eritrea argued before the Eritrea-Ethiopia Claims Commission that the reservoir served only civilians, and that its army in that area had its own wells and underground storage tanks.[124] The Commission agreed with Eritrea, and asserted that Ethiopia's purpose in targeting the reservoir was to deprive civilians of fresh water. It rejected Ethiopia's justification for attacking the reservoir – namely, the military use of this object.[125] It is not known whether the Commission rejected the evidence obtained from Ethiopia that it had relied on for the purpose of the attacks, or whether Ethiopia had failed to provide sufficient proof to support its claims.[126] The Commission simply focused on the alleged intent behind the attacks on what it regarded as an object indispensable to the survival of the Eritrean civilian population, and thus subject to the customary rules regulating the special protection of such civilian objects.[127] The legitimacy of attacking objects performing these types of specific

---

120 AMW Manual, op. cit. n 6, Commentary at 107.

121 See the further discussion in 6.2.

122 See the relevant discussion in 3.1.

123 Eritrea-Ethiopia Claims Commission, Partial Award: Western Front, Aerial Bombardment and Related Claims Eritrea Claims 1, 3, 5, 9–13, 14, 21, 25 and 26 between The State of Eritrea and The Federal Democratic Republic of Ethiopia, The Hague, 19 December 2005, para 98.

124 Ibid, para 99.

125 The Commission found a violation of the customary rule (arguable) codified in Art 54 API. Ibid, paras 103–105.

126 There is a problem with the supply of evidence for what the attacker knew or thought they knew about the target. See further discussion throughout this work and especially in 10.3 and 10.4.

127 Art 54(2) API and Art 14 APII. Art 54 API prohibits attacking, destroying or rendering useless objects that are indispensable to the survival of the civilian population, with the specific purpose of denying them sustenance. Examples of such objects include foodstuffs, agricultural areas for the production of foodstuffs, crops, livestock and drinking water installations, and supplies and irrigation works if the purpose of such an attack would be

Nature, location, use and purpose 71

dual functions would depend on the purpose and ultimate consequences of such action. Attacks on dual-use targets may seem advantageous to the adversary because of their intended or unintended physical and/or potential psychological effects on the civilian population. Nonetheless, this example shows the problems that may occur in future disputes arising from attacks on objects concurrently serving both military and civilian functions, and the practical problem of establishing the information on which the decision to attack is taken.[128]

In recent years, the term dual use has been associated with energy and electricity generation and distribution facilities such as electricity grids, other utility establishments, oil refining installations, and telecommunications networks and transmission facilities such as TV and radio broadcasting stations. Other examples include bridges, rail and road transportation systems, and airports, which are all part of lines of communication. The latter are discussed earlier in this chapter (section 1.2), together with transmission facilities. It was indicated there that such objects cannot be considered to satisfy the nature condition. They should, instead, be regarded as satisfying the use criterion (and viewed as dual-use targets).[129]

The modern transmission and communications network of computers is known as the Internet. It also provides a broadcasting medium. The Internet may seem an abstract notion, but its infrastructure is, in fact, physical and finite.[130] The difficulty in seeing the Internet as one physical object may be attributed to the sheer volume and scale of its constituent connections. A point where its segments can be isolated, such as a website or a connection, can

---

to deny civilians the sustenance value of the objects. In international armed conflicts, if such objects are also used as the sole source of sustenance to armed forces, or in direct support of the military action, then those objects can be attacked provided the resulting damage would not leave civilians with inadequate food or water for their survival.

128 See the further discussion of some these issues particularly in 6.2, Chapters 8 and 9 and 10.4.

129 See also Rogers, op. cit. n 12, at 111–12; AF Operations and the Law, op. cit. n 39, at 39, 250.

130 In essence, there are two types of computer network that allow computers to share data, namely local area networks (designed to cover the internal space of a single building) and wide area networks that connect several buildings Such networks tend to be based on a communication standard known as the Internet protocol (IP). An IP-based network used within an organisation is known as an intranet. In an extranet, all or some parts are made available to external organisations or the public via a link or the Internet. The Internet is, in effect, a wide area network on a very large scale. There are two types of connection between local area networks – a dedicated link, and a virtual private network (VPN). A dedicated link is a physical link in the form of a cable or fibre-optic cable, a leased line, or a satellite or radio link. A VPN is a secure connection between the local area networks (LANs) using a less secure or public network, such as the Internet. Just like telephone exchanges or switching centres in telecommunications networks, computer networks are based on numerous interlinked Points of Presence. Such points are normally at data centres, but may also be co-located alongside the telephone lines in telephone exchanges.

72 *Military objective: concept and definition*

potentially be considered in the context of the definition. Such selected segments cannot be viewed as being intrinsically military in character, so their assessment will depend on their use (or purpose). Interestingly, some military communications networks may share or rely on elements of the civilian infrastructure.

The 'Cormorant' network, for example, used by the chain of command of the British Joint Theatre Forces, is designed to interconnect with the 'Falcon' system.[131] 'Falcon' provides integrated services to UK Joint Forces Command Centres across all levels of command. It is also used externally to communicate securely with Allied and multinational military communications frameworks. Both networks support the 'Bowman' system, which provides joint tactical secure communications for land-based forces across all their services. The soldier on the ground using 'Bowman' feeds data into the 'Falcon' system. This would then be relayed to command centres in the UK using the Skynet 5 satellite system.[132] This means that even some digital telecommunication networks might be entirely military in character, and could be regarded as such under the nature criterion. In practice, however, any networks that share digital or physical infrastructure with a civilian network, such as the Internet, can only be considered objects used for both military and civilian purposes.

While energy production and distribution facilities are not inherently military in character, their use (or purpose) is likely to be for both military and civilian purposes.[133] The 1956 ICRC Draft Rules thought 'installations providing energy mainly for national defence, e.g. coal, other fuels, or atomic energy, and plants producing gas or electricity mainly for military consumption' to have been fundamentally important to the conduct of war.[134] The operative word here is 'mainly', which implies concurrent civilian and military use.

---

131 S. Butler, 'Acquisition Support to the Operational Arena', presentation for the 11th International Command and Control Research and Technology Symposium, US available at www.dodccrp.org/events/11th_ICCRTS/html/presentations/Butler_Acquisition_Support.pdf (last accessed 1 May 2014).

132 The latest Skynet 5 system of four geostationary satellites provides a secure, military satellite-based communications network for all UK forces, and complements the ground military networks system comprising Cormorant, Falcon and Bowman. While the British MOD is the main and primary guaranteed leaser of the communication traffic bandwidth, the private consortium managing the satellite systems is free to sell the excess capacity to other military entities, such as NATO and other governments, and possibly to private clients. J. Amos, 'UK Skynet: Not to Be Confused with The Terminator', 10 March 2010, BBC Spaceman Blog, available at: www.bbc.co.uk/blogs/thereporters/jonathanamos/2010/03/uk-skynet-not-to-be-confused-w.shtml (last accessed 1 May 2014); also in B. North, 'UK Space Capability Development', Presentation for Defense iQ Military Satellites, 12 July 2010, at 4.

133 *A contrario* to AMW Manual, op. cit. n 6, Rule 23 and the attached Commentary.

134 Para 1(e) of the proposed annex to Art 7(2) Draft Rules for the Limitation of the Dangers Incurred by the Civilian Population in Time of War, reprinted in Schindler and Toman, op. cit. n 25, at 340–1.

Nature, location, use and purpose 73

The production and distribution of energy involves all the energy and power supply sources for the manufacture of products sustaining military operations. This includes petrochemical industries, coal mines and petroleum, oil and lubricant (POL) production, storage, distribution and transport installations, and transport facilities used to supply their products. The installations, facilities and all infrastructure used to manufacture products destined for military purposes would be recognised as satisfying the use condition (dual use where the output serves civilian purposes, too).[135] Products used for national defence, such as fuel, are likely to satisfy the use condition. During the Korean War, targets included chemical plants and oil refineries.[136] There is a report on the Iranian practice that listed refineries, petrochemical complexes and power stations as examples of objects subject to attack during the 1980–8 Iran–Iraq war.[137] During the 1990–1 campaign to liberate Kuwait, oil refining and distribution facilities and electricity production facilities were all targeted with the aim of 'reducing Iraq's military sustainability'.[138] A list of NATO's choice of targets in the 1999 operations in Kosovo and Serbia encompassed refineries.[139] Attacks on the Pancevo petrochemical complex, which included an oil refinery and the petroleum storage areas at the Novi Sad refinery, took place on 15 and 18 April 1999 respectively.[140]

Electric power is essential for the functioning of manufacturing facilities in many industries. Armament and war *matériel* production facilities are particularly affected. Additionally, military forces rely on the constant provision of electricity for all their communication, command and control, as well as for air defence systems, which are usually all computer-networked and power-supported. The provision of basic civilian commodities, such as drinking water, is dependent on the power supply.[141] Modern, integrated, electrical grid network facilities tend to supply electricity for both civilian and military

---

135 If the subcontractors' products or services are of exclusively military character in any circumstances, then one presumably cannot exclude the determination of their contribution being based on their *nature*.

136 CIHL, op. cit. n 25, Vol. II, at 220, para 584.

137 Ibid, para 581.

138 UK Report to UN Security Council, 1991 in CIHL, op. cit. n 25, Vol. II, at 220, para 582.

139 ICTY Final Report to the Prosecutor by the Committee Established to Review the NATO Bombing Campaign Against the Federal Republic of Yugoslavia, 13 June 2000, paras 47 and 55.

140 Ibid, para 9.

141 The access to fresh water for Serb military forces, as well as some 70 per cent of the Serbian civilian population, was restricted as a result of NATO attacks on Serbian electricity sites in 1999. O. Medenica, 'Protocol I and Operation Allied Force in Kosovo: Did NATO Abide by Principle of Proportionality?', 23(3) *The Loyola of Los Angeles International* and *Comparative Law Review* 2001, 329–426 at 412.

74 *Military objective: concept and definition*

consumption.[142] This practical problem relates to the difficulty of establishing a clear-cut separation between military and civilian objects in an industrial society.[143] Ascertaining whether a given power plant is contributing to military action, by being a sole source of energy for national defence, is difficult unless it can be shown it is the only source of electricity for the whole country. An integrated electricity grid means power can be shifted countrywide, and separating the generation and/or distribution of it between the two groups of customers is clearly almost impossible.

Finally, the facilities associated with the metallurgical, chemical and engineering industries, such as steel mills or aluminium plants, tend to be viewed as dual-use targets.[144] Such manufactures are involved in production of materials such as steel, which are then used in the production of parts of military equipment and weapons, such as ball bearings.[145] Unless they have specific characteristics required only in a military application, either such materials or the ultimate products should also generally be regarded as dual use. A modern example of such parts could be computer microchips, which are used by armed forces in computers serving numerous uses, such as telecommunications infrastructure or computer systems designed for operating aircraft. Such microchips are commonly also used for civilian purposes.[146] Similarly, other elements of computers, such as disks, memory chips and central processing units, are utilised for both civilian and military computers. There is nothing distinctly military in their character or use, which suggests that their assessment should be based on their use (dual use).

In the modern age, subcontractors making various products and parts are likely to be dispersed throughout the whole of an enemy's territory, rather than being concentrated in one location.[147] While Hays Parks favours the inclusion of a subcontracting infrastructure in the consideration of objects as military objectives, the particular dangers of implementing this idea were also raised.[148]

---

142 Rogers, op. cit. n 12, at 114 referring to Hays Parks's comments, who says elsewhere that an assessment of a particular power plant's contribution would be impossible, in light of the complexity of integrated electricity systems. See W. Hays Parks, 'Air War and the Law of War', 32 *Air Force Law Review* 1990, 1–225 at 141.

143 O. Schachter, 'United Nations in the Gulf Conflict', 85(3) *American Journal of International Law* 1991, 452–73 at 466.

144 AF Operations and the Law, op. cit. n 39, at 39.

145 See also the earlier discussion in 3.1. The Operational Law Handbook considers classifies infrastructure involved in the production of ball bearings under the purpose criterion, presumably because intended future use involves military purposes. This author does not concur with such a position for reasons elaborated further in 3.4.

146 Some microchips are referred to as being 'of military grade', but that is due only to their higher quality, and not as a result of a specific military character or destination. 'Military grade' chips are used in medicine, aviation and other complex civilian infrastructures requiring higher quality parts.

147 Hays Parks, op. cit. n 142, at 140.

148 Oeter, op. cit. n 80, at 185.

3.4 Purpose

Purpose is the last of the four criteria attached to the first key element of the definition and is concerned with the future contribution of targets. Purpose can be defined in two ways. The ordinary meaning of the word 'purpose' refers to the reason behind an object's creation or design. It is a reflection of the present assessment of what the object is made for, which could have been conceived before or at the time of its creation. It includes its use but also implies several other qualities. Such purpose has to be inherently military. Purpose, in this context, is closer to the nature criterion in meaning, which may suggest potential significant overlap between the two. A school building, for example, is intended to facilitate education. This does not mean it cannot be used for storage or accommodation, though these are not its intended uses.

Professor Dinstein notes that the purpose of an object is often determined by its nature or use.[149] He claims that purpose must be distinguished from other criteria, or otherwise it would be redundant. He argues that purpose 'must be assumed not to be stamped' on the object from the beginning, as that would make it qualify by nature.[150] He then suggests the purpose of civilian objects, to distinguish this from their nature, will be inferred from the intention of the adversary as to the target's future use, as opposed to use at that time. Purpose, as such, will materialise after the object's nature is known and before its use takes place.[151]

Professor Dinstein therefore upholds the interpretation favoured by the ICRC, which has been referred to by numerous commentators.[152] The ICRC Commentary indicates that the purpose means the intended, future use of an object.[153] This is not the meaning of the word 'purpose' normally understood in the English language, which relates to the object's design.[154] The Commentary refers to an object not at that time of a military nature, location

---

149 Dinstein, op. cit. n 7, at 99.

150 Ibid.

151 This could be illustrated by an example of a bridge that a group of soldiers is preparing to cross, and that is destroyed before their eyes just minutes before they would have crossed it. It would imply that the nature of the bridge had been known since the time it was built, but the object had not yet been used by the soldiers. This example is not given by Professor Dinstein; it was inspired by an incident referred to by Lambeth in which a bridge about to be crossed by Taliban forces was destroyed before their eyes by three US missiles. S. Lambeth, *Airpower Against Terror: America's Conduct of OEF*, National Defense Research Institute, RAND, 2005, at 153.

152 It is unclear whether academic experts, as well as the States that referred to this description, actually agree with this position or whether they simply repeated the ICRC interpretation.

153 ICRC Commentary, op. cit. n 4, para 2022. Examples of other commentators include: Solis, op. cit. n 18, at 525; Rogers, op. cit. n 12, at 105; The UK Manual, op. cit. n 12, para 5.4.4 point 'e'; Operational Law Handbook, op. cit. n 12, at 23. See text attached to ns 175 *et seq.* above.

154 For example, the French word used in the French version of the authenticated text is 'destination', which relates to the purpose for which something is created.

76 *Military objective: concept and definition*

or use, which, by virtue of the attacker's knowledge about what is going to happen, converts it into a military objective.[155] In other words, the object's purpose requires a future change, which will be ascertained from the adversary's intentions.

There are at least three crucial differences between the two meanings. The first meaning is concerned with the object's quality at that time, while the second looks at a future quality. Second, the ICRC view appears to shift attention from the purpose of objects to the purpose of military operations. For example, a railway's purpose as an object is to transport anything and anybody, but the purpose of armed forces would be to use the railways to transport their equipment. Third, unlike the first description, the second also assumes a future change in circumstances, which is deduced from information possessed by the attacker.

There could be at least three different types of 'future change' of circumstances. The first involves geography. There may a change in the areas where the fighting is occurring. For example, hostilities are conducted in areas A and B, but not in C and D. In areas A and B, all schools are used as weapons storage facilities. Does that mean that all schools in C and D can be assumed to satisfy the purpose criterion because of the likelihood of them being used as weapons depots? This is a contingent kind of future use that depends on other factors, such as fighting moving into unaffected areas. The second type of change in circumstances will occur as a conflict evolves. As the conflict progresses, an object may gain more importance and become a military objective after other targets, which were initially higher priority, have been attacked. One example of this was the attack, during the 1990–1 Gulf War, on the Al Firdus/Amariyah (Ameriyya) bunker, a structure that gained significance only after numerous other command and control centres had been destroyed.[156] The third possible change involves the object itself being converted or altered in the light of future circumstances. An object that contributes to military action may be purely civilian in peacetime, but may be redirected to suit military needs during times of armed conflict. For example, a textile factory producing civilian clothes could be converted to produce uniforms.[157]

It is unclear what 'future' means in terms of length of time. It is possible that it is not linked to any specific length of time, though it should not be infinite. The purpose requirement must not be assessed outside the context of

---

155 Two situations may be relevant in this context. One is where the object is purely civilian in nature and is expected to be used for military purposes. In the second, a dual-use object is expected to be used only for military purposes in the future. On a practical level, it is possible that less evidence would be required to determine the military nexus in the second scenario.

156 See the further discussion in 6.2.2 and 9.1.1.

157 Dinstein, op. cit. n 7, at 95.

Nature, location, use and purpose 77

the entire first part of the definition, which requires that the object 'makes' a contribution to military action, which is indicative of the 'present' and not some time in the future.[158]

The most problematic issue in the context of intended future use is the understanding and/or evaluation of the enemy's intentions. The degree of knowledge about what the enemy is seeking to achieve with a particular object will be crucial in ascertaining the adversary's intent.[159] Bearing in mind that the intent of the defending party is not usually readily available to the adversary, such evaluations could be speculative, thereby leaving the attacker with some degree of doubt.[160] Are such determinations – presumably based, to some extent, on speculation – acceptable in satisfying the test of Art 52.2 API?

Two distinguished commentators, Dinstein and Rogers, suggest that a determination of the purpose criterion in practice requires a more substantive action to occur – namely, the materialisation of 'use', and not just 'potential use' – before an object can be regarded as satisfying the first element of the definition.[161] In other words, while they advocate a standard of actual knowledge of the enemy's intentions, they also appear to require evidence of an adversary's action in support of these intentions. The drafters of the AMW Manual follow Rogers and Dinstein's line of thought. For example, they propose that the adversary's intentions could be inferred from the 'specified preconditions prior to actual implementation of any existing plans'.[162] They insist that reasonable information must suggest that either:

1 the plans are in the process of implementation, and thus indicative of positive action towards the achievement of the purpose, as supported by other commentators; or
2 the plans will be implemented in the near future.

---

158 M. Sassoli, 'Targeting: The Scope and Utility of the Concept of "Military Objectives" for the Protection of Civilians in Contemporary Armed Conflicts' in D. Wippman and M. Evangelista (eds), *New Wars, New Laws? Applying the Laws of War in 21st Century Conflicts*, Transnational, Ardsley 2005 at 199; O. Bring, 'International Humanitarian Law after Kosovo: Is Lex Lata Sufficient?', 71(1) *Nordic Journal of International Law* 2002, 39–54 at 41.
159 AMW Manual, op. cit. n 6, Commentary, at 107.
160 The ICTY suggested that the 'reasonable belief' standard should be applied in the assessment of the *mens rea* of those who decide the status of an object normally dedicated to civilian purposes (*The Prosecutor v Stanislav Galic*, op. cit. n 104, para 51); also in AMW Manual, op. cit. n 6, Commentary to Rule 22(c), at 107; and *a contrario* to Boivin, op. cit. n 104, at 20.
161 Dinstein, op. cit. n 7, at 90 and Rogers cited therein. This is further implied in P. Benvenuti, 'The ICTY Prosecutor and the Review of the NATO Bombing Campaign against the Federal Republic of Yugoslavia', 12(3) *European Journal of International Law* 2001, 503–30 at 516.
162 AMW Manual, op. cit. n 6, Commentary at 108.

78 *Military objective: concept and definition*

The second suggestion implies that even reasonable evidence of the *mere possibility* of the potential implementation of the plans will suffice, thus creating quite a remote substantive link between the object and its future use.[163] One could ask how 'near' should near future be in order to be acceptable.

No doubt, the 'intended future use' of certain civilian objects inferred from overt contingency plans for time of war appears to comply with the standard. This would also be acceptable if, for example, the attacker has evidence that the adversary has compiled a list of selected private commercial airfields that its armed forces would be entitled to use in time of war.[164]

Professor Schmitt advocates a different standard of assessment. He suggests that 'reasonable reaction to reasonably reliable evidence of enemy intentions' should suffice, without the need for evidence for any positive action.[165] Consequently, suspecting the intentions of the enemy, the attackers may not need to wait until the object is actually used for military purposes before launching the attack.[166] 'Reasonably reliable evidence' could consist of publicly announced enemy plans, indicating their intention, or satellite photographs of movement around the observed targets. It may be that, in order to achieve a reasonably reliable standard of evidence, one would have to acquire evidence from various sources, and assess its quantity and quality so as to avoid, for example, a sole reliance on unconfirmed human intelligence.[167] In this situation, the supporting evidence does not need to be fully convincing. That makes it susceptible to becoming part of an operation based on doubt, in which case the presumption of Art 52.3 could be relevant.

However, Professor Schmitt seemed also to have indicated that the purpose criterion could be met even in the absence of any evidence of the enemy's

163 Sassoli and Cameron, op. cit. n 38, at 58.
164 AMW Manual, op. cit. n 6, Commentary at 108. The Manual further gives an example of an intercepted military communication with specific information as providing a good reason to believe that a civilian airfield, normally capable of being used for military purposes, is actually planned to be used as an alternative recovery node for the armed forces once the primary military airfield has been rendered inoperable. It is unclear what is meant by 'alternative recovery node', which may indicate the recovery for wounded and sick, in which situation it would be questionable that such airfield could be attacked due to the special protection afforded to the wounded and sick. If it means simply recovery node for healthy combatants, then it would be acceptable to consider this as a relevant example.
165 Schmitt, op. cit. n 1, at 147–8. Henderson supported Schmitt's suggestion without any due analysis of this issue. Henderson, op. cit. n 36, at 61.
166 AMW Manual, op. cit. n 6, Commentary at 107.
167 The AMW Manual stressed that reliance on hard evidence in the assessment of the enemy's intentions is paramount, particularly when those intentions are not clear. As intelligence may not be always reliable, the Manual suggested, the test required a reasonable determination as to whether 'the intelligence was reliable enough to conduct the attack in light of the circumstances ruling at the time'. AMW Manual, op. cit. n 6, Commentary at 108. See the further discussion in 6.2, 8.4 and 10.4.

Nature, location, use and purpose 79

intentions, as long as 'the assumed enemy course of action is that which any reasonable war fighter would take'.[168] In other words, he appears to reject any need for any evidence of action and intention, and accepts the mere likelihood of future military use based on a certain assumption.

In practice, this means that in the previously given example of schools being used as weapons storage in areas A and B, schools in C and D would be regarded as satisfying the purpose criterion according to either of Schmitt's views. Schools in C and D would not satisfy the condition, as far as Rogers and Dinstein are concerned, until the armed forces in C and D started moving some of the weapons. It is unclear whether the evidence of 'positive action' would be necessary for all the schools or just a few, on the basis of which the future use of the remaining schools will be inferred. Either way, this would indicate that the use at that time (mostly dual use) may be relevant to a determination of a future use.[169] To infer such use, only the likelihood of the fighting moving to areas C and D would need to be shown.

The danger with this approach is that it appears to invite the inclusion of whole groups of objects, in a similar manner to the nature criterion. The evidence required would have to be less general than proposed by Professor Schmitt, and in fact to be more specific to each object under consideration.[170]

Another risk is that less than rigorous adherence to even the ICRC's understanding may permit an unjustifiable latitude in the application of the terms. A recent US Operational Law Handbook indicated that future use can be: intended, suspected, possible and/or potential.[171] The practical implication is that 'intended' use conveys a substantially different standard of required evidence compared to suspected use. The mere suspicion of the use would not suffice. There is also a significant difference between intended use and a possible or potential use. The latter is too vague and invites a substantially broader interpretation of the criterion. A 'clear-cut' intention would be necessary, even if it were dependent on or conditioned by other circumstances.[172]

Surely, there is a difference between the existence of intention and the existence of evidence of such an intention. The nature, volume and scope of the evidence remain a matter of debate. Evidence of some intention is both

---

168 Schmitt, op. cit. n 1, at 147–8.
169 A separate question arises as to whether the volume of the use at the time (such as regular, but not routine or universal use) is a relevant consideration in ascertaining intended future use. See also the discussion in 3.3.
170 This shows the differences in the type and scope of the evidence necessary for such evaluations. The information necessary to show, for example, the intended conversion of car manufacture into tank production would be fundamentally different to one relating to the fighting. See the further discussion in 6.2, 8.4 and 10.4.
171 Operational Law Handbook, op. cit. n 12, at 23.
172 AMW Manual, op. cit. n 6, Commentary at 110; Henderson, op. cit. n 36, at 61, Sassoli and Cameron, op. cit. n 38, at 59.

80 *Military objective: concept and definition*

necessary and crucial. Otherwise, most, if not virtually all civilian objects would have the *potential* to be used for military purposes, consequently creating a sort of underlying presumption that they are military objectives.[173] The legal standard is not some remote, potential use that may or may not come to fruition at some point in the future. The legal standard requires that the intent to use civilian objects for military purposes is actually expected, and that such objects will most likely be used for such purposes in future. The risk with inferring potential use may be that the attackers will be inclined to make assumptions based on their own experience, doctrine and technical possibilities, which may be very different from those of the other side.

Two key indicators might assist in ascertaining the existence of the purpose criterion. These may include, but should not be limited to, the consideration of:

- previous use for military purposes of: (a) the same object and/or (b) the previous use of the same type of objects located elsewhere in the territory of the enemy, or by the enemy outside its territory;
- the capacity or capability to convert to an allegedly military function: (a) without any substantive changes; and (b) with a comprehensive conversion that presumes an examination will be made to determine if such a conversion would impact on the intrinsic character of the object and evidence of a specific intent to convert a specific object to serve a military function.[174]

With regard to the first indicator, the physical distance of an object from the location of hostilities may play an important role.[175] With respect to the second indicator, the nature of the object may predetermine its functional capacity. A civilian school or community centre can easily be turned into billets. However, it is more difficult to convert a dairy farm into a weapons manufacturing facility.[176] Thus the analysis of the object remains contextual with respect to factual circumstances and other definitional conditions.

It is, finally, necessary to consider an issue that will be more fully addressed in the next chapter. It has been argued that it is legitimate to target 'war-sustaining' objects.[177] This refers to objects that are seen as enabling or

---

173 Similarly in Sassoli, op. cit. n 158, at 197, 199 and in Henderson, op. cit. n 36, at 60.
174 The Hartha thermal power station, the fourth largest power station in Iraq, was repeatedly struck as it was regarded as the only one capable of supplying oil to the pipeline pumps that the Iraqis intended to use to fuel their fire trenches in southern Kuwait. T.A. Keaney and E.A. Cohen, *Gulf War Air Power Survey* Operations and Effects and Effectiveness, US Department of Air Force, US Government Printing Office 1993, Volume II, at 298.
175 Schmitt, op. cit. n 1, at 146–7.
176 Hays Parks refers to the relatively easy conversion of civilian airports to serve military needs. Hays Parks, op. cit. n 11, at 105.
177 See 4.3 for the relevant discussion.

Nature, location, use and purpose 81

sustaining the continuation of the war by the adversary. For example, a factory that does not contribute to military action itself produces items that are then exported. The revenues obtained through their sale are utilised to sustain the armed conflict. It is difficult to see such objects in the framework of the requirements of the definition and, in particular, how they satisfy nature, location, purpose or use. Nature does not seem to be the relevant criterion, unless it is regarded as including objects supporting war. The present tense of the phrase 'war-sustaining' suggests a form of current activity most closely linked to the use criterion. This could also be due to the current use of equipment and resources to make the objects, even if such objects provide a future contribution. If such a future intended use is the factor under consideration, then the purpose criterion could, arguably, be appropriate.[178] These assertions have yet to be confirmed or rejected by the United States, from where the war-sustaining concept originates.

3.5 Conclusion

Nature, location, purpose and use are criteria that, in practice, will be unlikely to be scrutinised individually. Although an object needs to satisfy only one of these criteria to fulfil the first part of the definition, in practice all four should be considered in the analysis as they sometimes overlap, reinforce or preclude each other. The established presence of only one criterion is sufficient to satisfy the test, though very often there is evidence of a combination of them. It is possible that this is how States view their application. So long as the object satisfies one or more of the four criteria, then it satisfies this component of the definition. This could then explain why States do not specify clearly how individual targets fit into one or more criteria.

Completing an artificial analysis of each criterion separately may result in a distorted and incoherent view that does not take into account the possible relationship or conflict between the criteria. Rule 23 of the AMW Manual, for example, and the associated debates, imply that some disagreements arise where experts do not question that the object satisfies the definition criterion – but disagree as to which criterion is relevant. This also shows some level of confusion among experts regarding the meaning of the words. While the disagreements do not really matter as far as the practical application of the definition is concerned, the lack of clarity as to what the individual criteria entail may lead to an unwarranted broadening in practice of the interpretation of the definition when applied by States.

Significantly, this analysis has shown that certain potential targets have not yet received sufficient attention. These objects are associated with political

---

178 Parallels could be drawn with the ball bearing production facilities for the assembly of aircraft, which are regarded in some sources as satisfying the *purpose* criterion. Operational Law Handbook, op. cit. n 12, at 23.

82 *Military objective: concept and definition*

leadership infrastructure. Their analysis involves complex considerations that are, to some extent, beyond the scope of this book.[179] The consideration of other objects highlights a key problem involving the quality and quantity of the information on which decisions regarding military objective status is made.

Regardless of their configuration, any of the criteria must entail an effective contribution to the military action of the enemy. The following chapter will focus on an examination of the meaning of this central component of the first element of the definition.

179 This refers, for example, to the question of the assessment of people's status as military objectives.

4 Effective contribution to military action

The nature, location, purpose and use criteria are firmly set in the context of the main component of the first element of the definition, namely *effective contribution to military action*. As the definition states, the contribution must be both *effective* and connected to *military action*. A discussion of both conditions follows in the first and second sections of this chapter.

The third section presents certain types of objects whose 'contribution', in the context of effective contribution to military action, has been disputed. They are often objects whose nexus to military action has been challenged because of an apparent lack of such a connection, or its remoteness. This section deals with economic targets, and analyses in more detail the claim that some objects can be regarded as satisfying the first element of the definition because they have a 'war-fighting' or 'war-sustaining' effort (capability).

4.1 Effective contribution

Contribution relates to the object's role in connection to military action. While this role is inevitably shaped by the four qualifying criteria, that is nature, location, use and purpose, discussed in the preceding chapter, the substance of this role must display a nexus to military action. It can be described as an input by which the object adds to one's military action. This contribution must be *effective*.

The use of the adjective *effective* implies that a contribution to military action must be real and discernible, rather than theoretical, speculative or hypothetical.[1] The effective contribution generates a certain outcome, or should be capable of delivering such an outcome. In this sense, the contribution should produce an identifiable, intended or expected result, which should

---

1 The view of the Air and Missile Warfare Manual is that a connection between the target and military actions, which is, in effect, the contribution, must have such qualities. Manual on International Law Applicable to Air and Missile Warfare, Program on Humanitarian Policy and Conflict Research, Harvard University, 15 May 2009, Commentary to Rule 24, para 3 at 110 [hereinafter: AMW Manual].

84 *Military objective: concept and definition*

display an actual connection with the military action. The scale or volume of the contribution is irrelevant unless it is of such quality or quantity that it disables the effectiveness of the contribution.

The assessment of effective contribution to military action involves a determination that an object that was earlier identified to be military significant on account of, for instance, its use is actually used in a way that makes the required contribution. Ascertaining the effective contribution of an object that satisfies the purpose criterion may be seen problematic, because it relates to the contribution expected to actually occur in the future. In this case, the assessment has to be made as though the future contribution were taking place in the present.

4.2 Contribution to military action

The definition requires that the contribution must be connected to military action. The nature and scope of this nexus require a more comprehensive analysis.

First, though, a brief note is necessary regarding the contribution's connection to an adversary. There may be a temptation to assert that the first element of the definition should be interpreted as being linked to the opposing side's actions. In other words, the object will either belong to, or otherwise be associated with, the adversary's military action. This is sometimes referred to as an 'objective' assessment.[2] An early ICRC draft of the definition suggested a link between the contribution to the adversary's activities.[3] There is, however, nothing specific in the current text of the definition to support that assertion. It could be argued that the contribution could potentially be related to one's own side – for example, an area of land that one intends to capture will be effectively contributing, because of its location, to one's own side's military action. Furthermore, what is regarded as contributing to the opposing side's military action may, in effect, also contribute to one's own, displaying certain 'mirror' effects of the definition.[4]

The definition requires that an object's contribution be connected to military action. The term *action* suggests an emphasis on positive activity or conduct of some kind. Such action has to be *military* in substance. Logically, the term denotes some kind of conduct undertaken by military forces. Bearing in mind the wide range of activities conducted by armed forces, one wonders which specific acts the term is meant to encompass.

---

2 S. Oeter, 'Methods and Means of Combat' in D. Fleck (ed.), *The Handbook of Humanitarian Law in Armed Conflicts*, 2nd edn, Oxford University Press, Oxford 2008, at 180.

3 See text attached to ns 4 and 13.

4 This may also be true in respect of the second element of the definition, which clearly requires an assessment of definite advantage benefiting one's own military operations, and presumably those of one's coalition partners, where the third parties may be gaining the advantage. (See also 5.2 and 9.1.2.)

Effective contribution to military action   85

Although the term *military action* was not specifically addressed in the context of the definition of military objectives, there is some evidence suggesting that other terms were considered in place of it. A very early draft of the definition of military objectives, proposed by the ICRC, contained a reference to the 'military effort of the adversary'. These drafts included the qualifying adjective 'directly', in addition to 'effectively', in the first part of the proposed article, which was subsequently deleted during negotiations. The draft Art 43 read:

> Only those objects which, by their nature or use, contribute effectively and directly to the military effort of the adversary, or which are of a generally recognised military interest, are considered as military objectives.[5]

During the meetings preparatory to the conference, some experts felt that a link to 'military effort' was too restrictive for military commanders, while others viewed the term 'military interest' as lacking precision. Both groups agreed that neither description was fitting, and that retaining two terms in one text was superfluous.[6] The underlying concern was that the effective protection of civilian objects could have been put at risk by relaxing the boundaries of the military force constraints. At the outset of the conference in 1974, the ICRC nevertheless chose to retain the term 'recognised to be of military interest' for further negotiation.[7]

During the 1974–7 meetings, governmental, military and academic members of the delegations regarded the formula suggested in the ICRC draft as vague and subjective.[8] Consequently, they attempted to find a clearer wording. Several propositions were put forward. The Vietnamese delegation pointed to objects 'serving military ends',[9] while Poland favoured objects that were 'of military character or nature'.[10] France suggested that the target should contribute 'directly or indirectly to the maintenance or development

---

5 Report on the Work of the Conference; Conference of Government Experts on the Reaffirmation and Development of International Humanitarian Law Applicable in Armed Conflicts (Second Session Geneva 3 May–3 June 1972), ICRC, Geneva 1972, in particular Vol. I, at 145–6 [hereinafter: ICRC Report 1972].

6 Ibid, paras 3.141–3 at 147.

7 Draft Article 47 para 1, CDDH/1; I, Part III, at 16. See also the relevant discussion in 2.5.1.

8 Statements of the Australian, French and Dutch delegations at the meeting of Committee III on 9 February 1974, CDDH/III/SR.14, XIV, paras 16–17, 21 at 109, as well as the UK statement on the meeting of Committee III of 7 February 1975, CDDH/III/SR.15, XIV, 117.

9 Statement at Meeting of Committee III of 10 February 1975, CDDH/III/SR.16; XIV, 127, para 16.

10 Statement at Meeting of Committee III of 10 February 1975, CDDH/III/SR.16; XIV, 127, para 15.

86 *Military objective: concept and definition*

of the military potential of the adverse party'.[11] The notion of 'military effort' was invoked again, this time by the Dutch delegation, and seemed to gain support during negotiations concerning the definition of military objectives.[12]

Ultimately, the Working Group devised a formula of *effective contribution to military action*, which was included in both the definition of military objectives and in the text of the presumption of the civilian character of certain objects.[13] These provisions were first adopted by Committee III in February 1975,[14] and later at the plenary session, to form part of the final text of API.[15] Although this issue was clearly discussed at length, the reasoning behind the wording that was ultimately adopted was not fully explained. Inspiration may have come from the 1969 Institute of International Law Resolution referring to military objectives. The Resolution also referred to the 'effective contribution to military action', which seemingly covered objects of a civilian nature, contributing by their use (or misuse), purpose or location.[16]

In order to clarify the meaning of the term *military action* that was ultimately adopted in the definition, it may be useful to examine it in light of other terms discarded by the experts involved in negotiating the API provisions. During the early negotiations of the Additional Protocols to the Geneva Conventions, the ICRC attempted to define some of the above-mentioned terms, albeit in the context of the protected status of civilians, and the particular circumstances in which their active involvement in a conflict may deprive them of such protection. Three concepts were considered: 'military operations', 'war effort' and 'military effort'. A 'military operation' was regarded as a 'movement of attack or defence by armed forces'. 'War effort' denoted 'all national activities which by their nature or purpose would contribute to the military defeat of the adversary'.[17] The term clearly encompassed military activities at all three levels of warfare – tactical, operational and strategic – as well as potentially civilian activities.[18] The third term coined by the ICRC was

11 CDDH/III/41 of 15 March 1974, III, 209.
12 The Dutch delegation's proposal of 19 March 1974 (CDDH/III/56, III, 209) and proposed amendment by Australia of 18 March 1974 (CDDH/III/49, III, 209).
13 CDDH/III/229 of 25 February 1975, in Report of Committee III, CDDH/215/Rev.1, XV, 306.
14 CDDH/III/SR.24, XIV, 217.
15 CDDH/SR.41 of 26 May 1977, VI, 141.
16 The Distinction between Military Objectives and Non-Military Objectives in General and Particularly the Problems Associated with Weapons of Mass Destruction, Institute of International Law, Edinburgh, 9 September 1969, reprinted in D. Schindler and J. Toman (eds), *The Laws of Armed Conflict*, 4th edn, Martinus Nijhoff, Leiden 2004, at 351–2. See the relevant discussion in 2.4.
17 CDDH/III/SR.2 of 12 March 1974, XIV, para 8,14. M. Bothe, K. Partsch and W. Solf, *New Rules for Victims of Armed Conflicts: Commentary on the Two 1977 Protocols Additional to the Geneva Conventions of 1949*, Martinus Nijhoff, The Hague 1982, n 6 attached to para 2.2.2, at 294.
18 Military doctrine distinguishes between three main levels of warfare – tactical, operational and strategic, the latter sometimes divided into grand and lower planes. Compare this with the notion of attack and the three levels of warfare, as discussed in 5.2 and in part A, in particular 8.3.

Effective contribution to military action   87

'military effort', which seemed to be positioned between the wider perspective of war effort and the narrowly focused military operation. 'Military effort' was defined as 'all the activities . . . [that] are objectively useful in defence or attack in the military sense, without being the direct cause of damage inflicted, on the military level'.[19]

Eventually, references to 'military effort' were dropped from the adopted text of API with respect to people to avoid ambiguity in ascertaining their legal status. However, a few of these proposed or considered terms reappeared in the final text in relation to specially protected objects.[20]

The difficulty in interpreting the nuances in the meaning of these formulations had long been recognised. A year after they were adopted, Professor Kalshoven observed that there might be difficulty in differentiating between the specific terms:

> It is to be feared that those called upon to apply this provision may in practice experience some difficulty in appreciating, first, the subtle difference between 'sustenance solely for enemy combatants' and 'direct support of military actions'; once accepting that the latter concept evidently must be the wider of the two, they will search in vain for an indication *how much* wider it is; what is 'military action', when support is 'direct'?[21]

Although inherent complexities exist, drawing some summary observations in this context may prove useful. The broadest of the terms − 'war effort' − appears to encompass both military and non-military activities conducted by members of the adversary's population, with the overall aim of supporting the war. It denominates the general direction in which a nation directs its activities. It may involve activities that have no connection to the actual prosecution of hostilities. 'Military effort' appears to be less broad, and covers all the activities undertaken by military forces as part of the overall war effort.[22] It comprises both direct and indirect connections to military operations. In other words, it

---

19 Bothe *et al.*, op. cit. n 17.

20 In addition to the adoption of the notion of 'military effort' in a provision regulating the protection of a cultural property (Art 53 API), the 'regular, significant and direct support of military operations' was used in a provision regulating the protection of works and installations containing dangerous forces (Art 56 para 2 API). The phrase 'direct support of military action' was included in the article about objects indispensable to the survival of civilians (Art 54 para 3 API) Protocol Additional to the Geneva Conventions of 12 August 1949, and Relating to the Protection of Victims of International Armed Conflicts (Protocol I), Geneva, 8 June 1977 reprinted in Schindler and Toman, op. cit. n 16, at 711 *et seq.* [hereinafter: API].

21 F. Kalshoven, 'Reaffirmation and Development of International Humanitarian Law Applicable in Armed Conflicts: The Diplomatic Conference, Geneva, 1974–7', 9 *Netherlands Yearbook of International Law* 1978, 107–71 at 127 (emphasis in original).

22 Bothe *et al.*, op. cit. n 17, n 15 attached to para 2.4.3, at 324. See also discussion in 4.3.6.

88 *Military objective: concept and definition*

includes all the activities of military forces, some of which may not be specific to the conduct of military operations in an armed conflict: for example, recruitment or the training of armed forces. It seems reasonable to conclude that *military action* could be interpreted as a more specific term that refers to military operations conducted towards achieving a military goal.[23]

The drafters of API considered and rejected the notion of 'military effort', as well as other phrases, which meant they were looking for a more precise and refined standard. They found this in *military action*. Clearly, the term *military action* is focused on the actions of the armed forces rather than of the whole nation. This signifies a clear departure from the practice during the Second World War, in which the whole State was considered to have been put on a war footing.[24] It also indicates a shift from an 'effort' encompassing both physical and mental struggle, to an 'action' clearly denominating activity. The term *military action* appears to cover the conduct of one or more military operations by armed forces in the prosecution of hostilities in a specific armed conflict. It may involve several military operations[25] and, where necessary, missions outside battlefield-specific activities undertaken for a specific military goal. Military action may not be confined to tactical operations, but will involve operational-level conduct. Consequently, viewing military action simply as the 'military phase of the Party's overall war effort', or the 'prosecution of the war', may be overly broad, and may overlap with the concept of 'military effort'.[26] Hays Parks observes that military action may include activities of 'fundamental importance for the enemy's conduct of the armed conflict, including his will to resist'.[27] First, this view appears to assume that the object will contribute to an adversary's activities that comprise the entirety of its prosecution of war, and not just its conduct of military operations. Second, Hays Parks may merely be observing that contribution to military action may include conduct that is fundamentally important to the other side, though his comments may also indicate that he takes a broader view on military action, similar to war effort. If so, such an explanation of the term would appear broader.

---

23 This description would also be consistent with a military understanding of the term. See Part A of Chapter 8.
24 See the relevant discussion in 2.3.
25 The Manual of the Law of Armed Conflict, UK Ministry of Defence, JSP 383, Oxford University Press, Oxford 2004, para 5.4.4 point 'g' [hereinafter: The UK Manual]; The US Operational Law Handbook indicates that military action should be interpreted in the ordinary sense of the words, and is not intended to encompass a limited or specific military operation. Operational Law Handbook, JA 422, International and Operational Law Department, The Judge Advocate General's Legal Center and School, 2013 edn, at 23 [hereinafter: Operational Law Handbook].
26 A.P.V. Rogers, *Law on the Battlefield*, Melland Schill Studies in International Law, 3rd edn, Manchester University Press, 2012, at 109; Bothe *et al.*, op. cit. n 17, at 324 para 2.4.3.
27 W. Hays Parks 'Asymmetries and the Identification of Legitimate Military Objectives' in W. Heintschel von Heinegg and V. Epping (eds), *International Humanitarian Law Facing New Challenges*, Springer, Berlin 2007, at 97.

Effective contribution to military action 89

An interesting example in the context of the assessment of effective contribution to military action is the Eritrea-Ethiopia Claims Commission's assessment of the May 2000 attack by the Ethiopian Air Force on the Hirgigo Power Station in Eritrea.[28] The Commission grappled with the facts of the case.

Ethiopia argued that, on that day, the original object of the attack was to have been the nearby port of Massawa, the main port serving Eritrea. Two planes en route to the port detected anti-aircraft missile launchers within the Hirgigo power plant site. The pilots immediately requested permission to strike, received approval and engaged the launchers. Eritrea contested this explanation, claiming that the attack was deliberate and against the plant itself. Eritrea alleged the Ethiopians must have encountered difficulties in maintaining radio contact as their planes were low-flying, which would have disrupted their communications and receipt of approval for the new targets. Furthermore, they noted that the anti-aircraft missile launchers were located near the plant site, and not at the site itself, as indicated by Ethiopia.[29] This, combined with the fact that the power plant itself received a load of seven bombs, called into question the Ethiopians' claim.[30]

The Commission ruled that the Hirgigo power plant was the intended target. In its analysis of the object's contribution to military action, the Commission observed:

> electric power stations are generally recognized to be of sufficient importance to a State's capacity to meet its wartime needs of communication, transport and industry so as usually to qualify as military objectives during armed conflicts. The Commission also recognizes that not all such power stations would qualify as military objectives, for example, power stations that are known, or should be known, to be segregated from a general power grid and are limited to supplying power for humanitarian purposes, such as medical facilities, or other uses that could have no effect on the State's ability to wage war.[31]

---

28 As in the case of the Harsile water reservoir, the Commission found that the customary definition of a military objective was applicable to the conflict between the parties and that the text of Art 52.2 API represented customary law. (For discussion about the Harsile water reservoir see 3.3.) Eritrea-Ethiopia Claims Commission, Partial Award: Western Front, Aerial Bombardment and Related Claims Eritrea Claims 1, 3, 5, 9–13, 14, 21, 25 and 26 between The State of Eritrea and The Federal Democratic Republic of Ethiopia, The Hague, 19 December 2005, para 113 [hereinafter: EECC Award].

29 Ibid, para 116.

30 The Eritreans argued that when the pilots spotted the launchers, they should have been able to identify their location, especially when flying slowly at low altitude. The Award did not contain any further elaboration on whether the launchers were left undamaged by the attack.

31 EECC Award, op. cit. n 28, para 117.

90 *Military objective: concept and definition*

It appears that the Commission upheld a standard in which a power plant can be regarded as satisfying the first element of the test, unless it is clearly detached from the integrated power grid and serves no military function or otherwise contributes to the State's ability to wage war.

A question has arisen as to whether the power plant was, in fact, generating electricity at the time of attack. Eritrea asserted that, as of May 2000, the Hirgigo power plant was in the final stages of construction and was not producing power. The plant was not intended to support any military action. One Eritrean witness statement implied, though, that construction was advanced enough for the plant to be capable of being operational. Furthermore, the witness indicated it was designed to replace power supplies coming from an old station in Grar, which sustained the functioning of the port and, most likely, the naval base there.[32] It was also supposed to supply electricity reliably to most parts of the country through the integrated grid system. The Commission concluded that the Hirgigo plant effectively contributed to military action on purpose as it was going to be used to generate power directly for the needs of military objectives, such as the port of Massawa.[33]

It is interesting to note that the Commission also observed that by placing anti-aircraft missile launchers in the vicinity of the power plant, the Eritreans themselves considered it to be of military value. This, however, did not seem to be consistent with the general Eritrean line of argument, which, as already mentioned, indicated that the plant had no intended military function. The Commission's finding as to the plant's purpose seems to contradict the Eritrean position. This raises an interesting question as to the Commission's role in reconciling the claims put before it by the two sides. Eritrea claimed the plant did not have a military use or purpose, while Ethiopia maintained it did not intend to attack the plant. So, presumably, the Ethiopians did not make an assessment of the target in line with legal requirements. Assuming that the Commission was correct in its view of the power plant as the actual target, it would have been a target of opportunity for the Ethiopians. It is unclear how much Ethiopia knew about the plant's functioning, bearing in mind this issue was not entirely clear even to the Eritrean side. The Commission did not reflect or acknowledge any practical difficulties involved in the dynamic targeting of targets of opportunity, some of which concern the availability of relevant information. It may be that the Commission took all these issues into account, but this is simply not included in the text of Award.[34]

While agreeing with the Commission's overall conclusion regarding an object's actual contribution to military action, a word of caution is necessary.

---

32 The port contained the (former) Ethiopian navy headquarters and, as such, was, in the opinion of the Commission, a legitimate target. Ibid, para 120.
33 Ibid, para 119–20.
34 See the further discussion in 6.2, 8.4 and 10.4.

Effective contribution to military action   91

The Commission envisaged the possibility that an object that can affect the State's ability to wage war will also satisfy the requirement. If the Commission made its assessment based on this standard, it would have to be questioned. The API test clearly does not extend beyond contribution to military action.

In order to meet the standard of effective contribution to military action, the object must display a connection to the conduct of military operations as part of the ongoing prosecution of hostilities in a specific armed conflict. This connection will be primarily related to tactical or operational activities undertaken for the purposes of military operations. A strategic-level warfare contribution could be accepted on condition that it was connected to military action and not to the broader military or war effort.[35]

Finally, a question was raised in relation to the nature of the relationship between contribution to military action and the object itself. Does the law require such a relationship to be direct? The very first ICRC draft of the definition included the words 'direct' and 'effective' as qualitative conditions of the contribution, but the text of the definition adopted retained only the latter requirement.[36] This prompted some commentators to concede that such a relationship does not have to be direct.[37] This approach is also adopted in US documents pertaining to the law applicable to military operations. In this context, the US claims that economic targets, which indirectly but effectively sustain the adversary's overall war effort, may qualify as military objectives. In such cases, the connection between the object and the military action becomes indirect, and sometimes possibly too remote.[38] It would appear that a direct contribution is generally required, but it remains unclear if indirect contributions to military action could be acceptable. Whether direct or indirect, the contribution must be effective, and thus real, discernible and capable of producing results. This approach, in relation to economic objects as well as other objects whose nexus to military action is debatable, will be discussed in the following section.

35 Some contributions, for example some targeting decisions taken because of a target's sensitivity, will be taken at a high political or military level, but that does not make them strategic. Contributions that are relevant to the overall prosecution of an armed conflict, such as what strategy will be applied, are strategic. Some targets can be considered strategic because of their significance. See further discussion in 8.1 and 8.6 and in 9.2.

36 See 2.5.1.

37 It has been observed in, among others, AMW Manual, op. cit. n 1, Vol. I Rule 24 at 13, and the attached Commentary in Vol. II, at 110. See also discussion in 8.6.2.

38 This approach, in relation to economic objects as well as other objects whose nexus to military action is debatable, will be discussed in the Chapter 7. See 4.3 and 7.1–4.

92 *Military objective: concept and definition*

4.3 Problematic effective contribution to military action

In most cases, an object's satisfaction of this element of the definition would not be problematic. In relation to some specific types of objects, there will be no apparent effective contribution to military action; or there may be a connection to military action, albeit an indirect one. Examples of such problematic targets include objects associated with political leadership, civilian morale, TV and radio facilities, and objects whose contribution entails the commission of grave breaches of the Geneva Conventions, and of Additional Protocol I and/or other serious international crimes. These objects will be discussed in more detail in Chapter 7.

The analysis in the subsections below, however, will endeavour to highlight the problems in determining effective contribution to military action in respect of one specific category of target – economic targets. This section begins with an introduction to economic targets, which is followed by a more comprehensive analysis of the claim that economic objects can be regarded as satisfying the first element of the definition, because they indirectly but effectively sustain a 'war-fighting' or 'war-sustaining' capability. This claim appears to be unique to the US view of the concept of military objective. It seems to rests on the premise that objects also providing non-military means of waging war, such as monies from exports, may enable the required contribution.

4.3.1 Targets in economic warfare

The notion of economic targets derives from a concept of economic warfare.[39] Economic warfare indicates all measures that are aimed at impairing the economic capacity of the adversary, particularly in relation to its capacity to sustain the war effort.[40] Economic warfare embraces all sorts of measures designed to impact either directly or indirectly upon the execution of military operations. They include, for instance, arms embargoes, blockading enemy harbours, attacks on merchant shipping and striking at the oil refineries producing fuel for armed forces.[41] In practice, much of the discussion of economic warfare has arisen in the context of naval warfare, and referred to the disruption of, or damage to, the adversary's maritime trade by the use or threat of force.[42]

---

39 The term 'economic warfare' does not have a precise definition. V. Lowe and A. Tzanakopoulos, 'Economic Warfare' in R. Wolfrum (ed.), *Max Planck Encyclopaedia of Public International Law*, Oxford University Press, Oxford 2012.

40 F. Kalshoven, *Reflections on the Law of War: Collected Essays*, International Humanitarian Law Series 17, Brill, Leiden 2008, at 21.

41 Ibid.

42 As specified in 1.3, this work does not deal specifically with maritime or air warfare, but may include a discussion of such in the context of land targets, including economic targets. In regard to naval warfare, see also Aquila, 'Air Power in Economic Warfare, A Comparison with Naval Blockade', 94(576) *Royal United Services Institute Journal*, 1949, 572–5, as well as

Kalshoven views economic warfare as all measures aimed at impairing the economic capacity of the adversary, which includes capacity to sustain the war effort. According to him, this includes anything from cutting off supplies to measures taken against raw materials and other goods necessary for the war industry.[43] This would be consistent with how such targets in land warfare have been seen in the past. Historically, while economic targets on land were associated with the overall commercial activities of States, they were also closely linked to the war effort. During the Second World War, this was reflected in the attacks against industrial sites involved in production connected to war.[44] The so-called 'oil plan' was a strategy designed to impair German oil production, in the knowledge that the German Air Force used fuel generated by refining crude oil to operate their planes.[45] Steel plants and manufacturers of ball bearings generated parts that were necessary for the production of aircraft.[46] All these objects were undeniably linked not just to the war or military effort; they also enabled the further prosecution of military operations.

Lawful interference with the economic interests of the enemy is very limited. In maritime warfare, an adversary's exports can be interfered with through a blockade, and their imports through the law of prize.[47] 'Economic targets' is not a legal term. Any objects that are significant to the economy must satisfy the test to be seen as lawful targets.[48] There is no doubt that some of the objects may well satisfy the legal requirements. Some of these objects will also be dual

---

D.A. Melson, 'Targeting War-Sustaining Capability at Sea: Compatibility with Additional Protocol I', *The Army Lawyer*, US Department of Army Pamphlet 27–50–434, July 2009, at 44.

43 Kalshoven, op. cit. n 40, at 21; see also G.D. Solis, *The Law of Armed Conflict: International Humanitarian Law in War*, Cambridge University Press, Cambridge 2010, at 522.

44 W.A. Jacobs, 'The British Strategic Air Offensive Against Germany in World War II', in R.C. Hall (ed.), *Case Studies in Strategic Bombardment*, US Air Force History and Museums Program, Washington, DC 1998, at 137, 149–50, 155–6; S.L. McFarland and W.P. Newton, 'The American Strategic Air Offensive Against Germany in World War II', in R.C. Hall (ed.), *Case Studies in Strategic Bombardment*, US Air Force History and Museums Program, Washington, DC 1998, at 189–90; A.D. Coox, 'Strategic Bombing in the Pacific 1942–1945' in R.C. Hall (ed.), *Case Studies in Strategic Bombardment*, US Air Force History and Museums Program, Washington, DC 1998, at 278, 306, 315.

45 Jacobs, op. cit. n 44, at 149,157; McFarlandand Newton, op. cit. n 44, at 223, 226. Attacks on railways were designed not only to cut off supply routes, but also to deny the transportation of coal on which the German war industry heavily relied. (Jacobs, op. cit. n 44, at 157, 159; McFarland and Newton, op. cit. n 44, at 238).

46 McFarland and Newton, op. cit. n 44, at 192–3, 197–8, 207.

47 Aquila, op. cit. n 42; see also throughout W. Heintschel von Heinegg, 'The Law of Military Operations at Sea' in T. Gill and D. Fleck (eds), *The Handbook of International Law of Military Operations*, Oxford University Press, Oxford 2010.

48 See also discussion in 3.3. It is likely that considerations in regard to how an attack is conducted could be relevant in the context of economic targets, but this discussion is beyond the scope of this book. See 1.3.

94   *Military objective: concept and definition*

use.[49] A question arises, though, about whether objects can be targeted solely on account of their contribution to the economic health of the State attacked.[50]

Although it is not clear why the following objects were attacked, these examples raise a question about the targets' contribution to military action, as opposed to the economic strength of the adversary.

Concerns were raised by the destruction of some objects during Israeli operations in 2008–9 in Gaza. These included the Sawafeary chicken farm and other egg factories, food processing plants of the al-Wadiyah Group and many greenhouses. These attacks were all deemed by the UN to be unjustified, and were considered part of a wider, systematic and wanton activity constituting a grave breach of the Geneva Conventions.[51] Bearing in mind the UN Inquiry's problems with securing access to the relevant evidence, particularly from the Israeli side, such conclusions must be viewed with caution. While it is striking that all these targets appear to have been economically important to the civilian population, it is impossible to draw firm conclusions regarding their military nexus without more detailed information.

During the 34 days of the 2006 conflict in Lebanon, Israel caused extensive damage to the commercial, industrial and agricultural sectors of the Lebanese economy. It has been reported that more than one hundred factories[52] and hundreds of industrial enterprises were damaged or destroyed.[53] These included Liban Lait, the largest dairy farm in the country, and the Maliban glass works in Tanayel.[54] The former produced more than 90 per cent of Lebanese long-life pasteurised milk, as well as other dairy products for the national market. The Israel Defence Forces (IDF) never provided a clear or detailed justification for these attacks; one's analysis must therefore be based on publicly available factual reports and speculative inferences.

On the one hand, it is possible that the Liban Lait Company's production farm in Baalbeck could have been used – or was intended to be used – to directly support military action through the storage of weapons and military

---

49   See the discussion regarding dual-use objects in 3.3.

50   The objects in question would not be military objectives on any other basis, in contrast to industrial facilities, which serve both military and civilian purposes. See also discussion of the Hirgigo power plant in 4.2.

51   UN Human Rights Council, Report of the United Nations Fact-Finding Mission on the Gaza Conflict, UN Doc. A/HRC/12/48, 25 September 2009, paras 961, 1018–21.

52   UN reports like Human Rights Council, Report of the Commission of Inquiry on Lebanon pursuant to Human Rights Council Resolution S-2/1, 23 November 2006, A/HRC/3/2, para 144.

53   HRC, op. cit. n 52, para 144; Amnesty International, *Israel/Lebanon: Out of All Proportion – Civilians Bear the Brunt of the War*, AI Index: MDE 02/033/2006, November 2006 at 50.

54   Dairy factory and agricultural facilities were also attacked in the first Gulf War; see Chapter 4 of Middle East Watch (Human Rights Watch), *Needless Deaths in the Gulf War: Civilian Casualties During the Air Campaign and Violations of the Laws of War*, New York 1991, available at: www.hrw.org/legacy/reports/1991/gulfwar/index.htm#TopOfPage (last accessed 1 May 2014).

equipment, or as a shelter for the adversary – Hezbollah fighters. As such, the farm would have satisfied the effective contribution to military action test. At the other extreme, the farm could have been attacked purely because of its significance to the Lebanese economy. Unlikely as this may be, the possibility should not be excluded as the company apparently catered for more than 90 per cent of milk consumption in Lebanon. Should this be the case, there would have been a problem in determining the object's contribution. An economic contribution alone could not meet the definition. As Israel claimed Hezbollah operated from Lebanese territory, a third possibility arises.[55] The IDF may have regarded the farm as associated with Hezbollah fighters, and therefore that the profits from the site were used to arm Hezbollah forces. In other words, members of Hezbollah could have benefited financially from the company's production, and used the profits to fund military action.

The attack on the glass bottle and jar factory in Tanayel also raises doubts regarding its contribution to Hezbollah's military action. The target cannot be considered to have met the first part of the military objective test, based purely on the production of these goods, which could potentially be used to supply food to soldiers.[56] Similar to the previous example, the problem is that there is insufficient factual information to be able to address the issues resulting from the application of law. Admittedly, there is no legal obligation for the State that conducted the attack to disclose such information. The objects may well be used for military purposes, yet such use may be concealed and not clearly visible to others. If third parties cannot 'see' the use being made, they may question the actions of the attacker, which may have implications for the enforcement of the rules.[57]

The definition of military objective clearly does not permit the object solely contributing to the economy to be seen as a lawful target. There has been a claim that objects that are economic in character but that, in some sense, are linked to the war, can be attacked. This will be discussed in more detail in the subsequent subsection.

4.3.2 War-sustaining and war-fighting effort (capability)

While it is undeniable that targeting objects simply because of their contribution to the general economic health of the State is not regarded as

---

55 It is worth noting that Hezbollah is a non-State organisation. This, combined with the fact that Israel is not a party to API, implies that the customary definition of military objectives would be more relevant to the legal analysis (see 1.2). For the Israeli position, see *The Second Lebanon War – One Year Later*, Israel Ministry of Foreign Affairs, 12 July 2007, available at www.mfa.gov.il/mfa/foreignpolicy/issues/pages/the%20second%20lebanon%20war%20-%20one%20year%20later%20-%20july%202007.aspx (last accessed 24 July 2014).

56 Another example could be the paper mill in Kafr Jara. Amnesty International, op. cit. n 53.

57 See also 10.3.

96 *Military objective: concept and definition*

lawful, there is a claim that attacks against some targets could be justified on account of their economic contribution to the prosecution of war.[58] There are two types of economic contribution that could be made to a military or war effort. One is an economic contribution to war-fighting, and the other is an economic contribution to the ability to wage a war or war-sustaining effort (capability). For about thirty years there has been a constant but not uniform reference to both of these contributions in the literature of the United States to which other States do not appear to make a reference.

The meaning of both terms is not entirely clear. Different sources may give different explanations. Conceivably, the term 'war-fighting', being associated with objects enabling the fighting, could include targets, such as oil, that may directly power military vehicles and machines, or may be used less directly to enable industrial plants to produce military aircraft.[59] The term may include power-generating plants and war-supporting industry. Their contribution to military action, whether direct or indirect, will be undisputed. The term 'war-sustaining', however, seems to be substantively different. It may include objects, such as oil, that are sold as commodities. The profits from these sales will assist in funding the war effort. In such a context, the term refers to trade goods and exports or imports. It is very questionable whether such a contribution could be considered to satisfy the test.[60]

The question arises as to whether there is any evidence that, even though the phrases 'war-fighting' and 'war-sustaining' effort (capability) are not used in the definition in Art 52.2 API, the meaning of this provision includes them. If, however, these concepts convey a different meaning of contribution to military action, or the US applies them differently, would they still be covered by the definition? In an attempt to clarify issues around the US position, the origins and meaning of these terms will be discussed at greater length in the following subsection.

4.3.2.1 *The US position*

The United States regards the effective contribution to military action as encompassing economic objects that sustain both war and fighting. There could be a historical reason as to why the US takes this position.

During the US Civil War (1861–5), there were two striking features of the conduct of Union forces, which they claimed were legally justified.[61] The first related to General William Sherman's march through Georgia in 1864, involving what could be described as a 'scorched earth' policy. Sherman's

---

58 See also 8.1 and 8.6.
59 Kalshoven, op. cit. n 40; Melson, op. cit. n 42, at 46.
60 These terms will be further discussed in 4.3.2.2.
61 The legal justification appears to have been confirmed in a number of cases; see reference in ns 69 and 70 below.

Effective contribution to military action 97

campaign was remembered for its widespread damage to property, and in particular the damage to industry, infrastructure and civilian property.[62] Sherman's armies lived off the land and, as they proceeded, all surplus food stocks were destroyed. The soldiers seized food from local farms and brought widespread devastation to railroads and to the local manufacturing and agricultural infrastructure.[63] Sherman justified this policy with a twofold argument. On the one hand, Sherman wanted to deny the Confederate troops any food supplies. On the other hand, he thought this would demoralise the civilian population. Sherman subscribed to the idea that the war could be won only if the Confederacy's economic, strategic and psychological support for the conflict had been severely diminished, and that this could be achieved through the devastation that affected civilians.[64] Sherman believed that:

> [we are] . . . not only fighting armies, but a hostile people, and must make old and young, rich and poor, feel the hard hand of war, as well as their organized armies. I know that this recent movement of mine through Georgia has had a wonderful effect in this respect.[65]

It is worth noting that the 1863 Lieber Code[66] suggested that military necessity permitted the 'withholding of sustenance or means of life from the enemy; [and] of the appropriation of whatever an enemy's country affords necessary for the subsistence and safety of the army'.[67] The issue of the denial of food

---

62 Military historians mention damage to a large percentage of the railroads, numerous bridges and miles of telegraph lines. Sherman's Army was reported to have confiscated millions of pounds worth of 'corn and fodder, and destroyed uncounted cotton-gins and mills'. L. Kennett, *Marching through Georgia: The Story of Soldiers and Civilians During Sherman's Campaign*, HarperCollins, New York 1995 at 309; H. Hattaway and A. Jones, *How the North Won: A Military History of the Civil War*, University of Illinois Press, Urbana 1983, at 655; also G. Best, *Humanity in Warfare*, J.W. Arrowsmith (Bristol), 1983, at 207–11.

63 Military Division of the Mississippi, Special Field Orders No. 120, 9 November 1864 in point IV contained the following orders: 'The army will forage liberally on the country during the march. To this end, each brigade commander will organize a good and sufficient foraging party, under the command of one or more discreet officers, who will gather, near the route travelled, corn or forage of any kind, meat of any kind, vegetables, corn-meal, or whatever is needed by the command, aiming at all times to keep in the wagons at least ten day's provisions for the command and three days' forage.'

64 Best, *Humanity in Warfare*, op. cit. n 62, at 208–10; B. Catton, *The Civil War*, First Mariner Books, Houghton Mifflin, Boston 2004 at 243 and B. Catton, *This Hallowed Ground: The Story of the Union Side of the Civil War*, Wordsworth Editions, Ware 1998, at 359–60.

65 Letter from Sherman to Henry W. Halleck, 24 December 1864, cited in US War Department, *The War of the Rebellion: a Compilation of the Official Records of the Union and Confederate Armies*, US Government Printing Office, 1880–1901, Series I, Vol. XLIV, Part 1, at 798.

66 Instructions for the Government of Armies of the United States in the Field (Lieber Code), 24 April 1863.

67 Ibid, Art 15.

98 *Military objective: concept and definition*

supplies to the Confederate troops seems to relate to the concept of the contribution that enables the continuation of fighting.[68]

The other striking feature of the Civil War relates to the destruction of raw cotton. The Union side seems to have recognised the value of the revenues obtained from the sale of cotton, which they believed had financed the Confederate war effort. Union forces therefore mounted a naval blockade to prevent the export of cotton,[69] and also separately destroyed bales of cotton.[70] Undoubtedly, the cotton in Confederate territories was recognised as being such a highly valuable economic commodity that it was worthy of expropriation or even destruction because it was war-sustaining. In 1871 the American–British Claims Commission, otherwise known as the Alabama Commission or the Claims Tribunal of Arbitration, was set up to hear and resolve the maritime grievances of the United States against Great Britain that had accumulated during the American Civil War. These grievances included Britain breaking its neutrality when it provided weapons and fighting manpower, and constructed, equipped and/or refitted warships belonging to the Confederate States of America.[71] The Confederacy paid the British with raw cotton and grain shipments for armaments, hoping that British dependency on this trade would eventually result in Britain recognising Confederate independence. The Alabama Commission concluded that General Sherman's order to destroy civilian property during his march through Georgia,[72] and the related destruction within Confederate territory, constituted justified acts of warfare.

The practice followed during the Civil War resulted in two strands of economic contributions that were subsequently legitimised by domestic courts. Official US sources do not then appear to contain any substantive references to the two concepts for more than a century. It is possible that no relevant references are to be found even during the Second World War because the

---

68 Scorched earth policy is nowadays regulated in Art 54 API, a consideration of which is beyond the scope of this work. See a related discussion on civilian morale in 4.3.2 and 5.4.

69 In 1870 an international Arbitral Tribunal recognised that the destruction of raw cotton was justified as the sale of cotton provided funds for the acquisition of almost all Confederate arms and ammunition. See also relevant case law: *Mrs. Alexander's Cotton*, US Supreme Court, 69 U.S.2 Wall. (1864) at 407, 420–3 and *Lamar v Browne*, US Supreme Court, 92 U. S. (1875) at 194.

70 *Young v United States*, 97 U.S. 39 (1877) at 605–6. Destruction of cotton, albeit on the Confederates' orders to prevent the seizure of cotton by Union forces, was also discussed in *Ford v Surget*, US Supreme Court, 97 U.S. (1878), at 594, 596.

71 Art IV of the Treaty between Great Britain and The United States for the Amicable Settling of All Causes of Difference between the Two Countries, 8 May 1871, Washington (so-called Treaty of Washington) in C. Perry (ed.), *The Consolidated Treaty Series*, Oceana Publications, Dobbs Ferry 1977, Vol. 143 at 145.

72 Point V of Military Division of the Mississippi, Special Field Orders No. 120, 9 November 1864.

Effective contribution to military action 99

Second World War concept of economic warfare was all-encompassing and subsumed the US position in relation to economic targets.

From the end of the Second World War until the late 1980s, there is very limited reference to the US position with respect to economic targets that are linked to military effort. Some academic commentators refer in this context to the US 1953 dam-busting attacks. Towards the end of the Korean War, the US undertook attacks against hydroelectric irrigation dams such as the Toksan dam on the Yalu river.[73] The North Koreans relied heavily on the water supply for farming rice, and this supply depended on the functioning of the dams. The flooding resulting from the attacks achieved two outcomes. It not only damaged lines of communication and transportation, as well as numerous underground bunkers in the area, but also threatened the rice crops.[74] The latter were thought to sustain military effort because the rice was apparently sold to finance the fighting.[75]

There is no obvious reference to war-sustaining or war-fighting capabilities until the late 1980s. The experience of the US Navy in the 1987–8 stage of the Iran–Iraq war made the war-sustaining and war-fighting concepts of economic targets emerge again, this time in military sources. Although ships had been struck throughout the entire conflict, it was not until the 1984 Iraqi attack against Iranian tankers carrying oil and the oil production terminal at Kharg Island that such attacks became common. Iran responded by attacking tankers carrying Iraqi oil from Kuwait, and declaring its readiness to attack tankers of any of the Persian Gulf States supporting Iraq. At the same time, Iraq declared that all ships going to or from Iranian ports in the northern zone of the Gulf were subject to attack. Both nations subsequently engaged in attacks against oil tankers and merchant ships ('the tanker war'), including those of neutral nations. It was not until spring 1987 that the US, following a Kuwaiti request for assistance, engaged its Navy in maritime escorts and in reflagging Kuwaiti vessels.[76] In response to Iranian attacks on US-flagged Kuwaiti tankers in May and October 1987, the US launched attacks against two Iraqi oil platforms, one in the Rostam field and another nearby.[77]

---

73 Sui-ho Dam, at the time the world's fourth largest hydroelectric station, was not attacked, but only because of the nearby presence of an air force base. T.C. Hone, 'Strategic Bombing Constrained: Korea and Vietnam' in R.C. Hall (ed.), *Case Studies in Strategic Bombardment*, US Air Force History and Museums Program, Washington, DC, 1998, at 485, 488.

74 Hone noted there was a serious disagreement in the US command prior to the attacks, due to the possible consequences for the civilian population. Ibid, at 488 and 490.

75 W. Hays Parks, 'Air War and the Law of War', 32 *Air Force Law Review* 1990, 1–225 at 208 citing R. Futrell, *The United States Air Force in Korea, 1950–1953*, 1953, at 481–9; W.G. Hermes, *United States Army in the Korean War: Truce Tent and Fighting War*, Center of Military History, US Army, Washington, DC 1992, at 461.

76 The operation was codenamed Operation Earnest Will and lasted from 24 July 1987 to 26 September 1988.

77 Another attack on oil platforms followed in May 1988.

100 *Military objective: concept and definition*

It is striking, but not entirely surprising, that in 1987 the US Navy decided to include a reference to economic targets that can contribute to the war-sustaining or war-fighting capability of the enemy, when it issued its *Commander's Handbook on the Law of Naval Operations*.[78] The Handbook contained a definition of military objectives akin to the one in API, except that it replaced the words 'military action' in the first element of the definition with the terms: 'war-fighting or war-sustaining capability'. The definition read:

> military objectives are combatants (see Chapter 5), military equipment and facilities (except medical and religious equipment and facilities), and those objects which, by their nature, location, purpose, or use, effectively contribute to the enemy's *war-fighting* or *war-sustaining capability* and whose total or partial destruction, capture, or neutralization would constitute a definite military advantage to the attacker under the circumstances at the time of the attack.[79]

The *Commanders' Handbook* indicated that economic objects that 'indirectly but effectively support and sustain the enemy's *war-fighting capability* may also be attacked'.[80] Issued in 1997, the *Annotated Supplement to the Commander's Handbook*, an unofficial commentary on the Handbook, added that the cotton-destruction ruling of 1872 was an example of a legitimate economic target that was sustaining a war effort.[81]

This appears to be the first reference in US military literature to both terms. While the US Navy's approach in this matter remains consistent and uniform, there is less clarity in the military doctrine and operational law sources between and within the three services.[82] Subsequently, the US Department of Defense issued documents that referred to the definition in the text where the words

78 The Handbook represents the operational law source. See n 82 below. US Navy, Marine Corps and Coast Guard, *Commander's Handbook on the Law of Naval Operations*, Department of Navy, Office of the Chief of Naval Operations, Headquarters, US Marine Corps, Department of Transportation, US Coastal Guard, NWP 1-14M, MCWP 5-2.1, COMDTPUB P5800.7 (formerly known as Naval Warfare Pub. No. NWP 9 (Rev. A)/FMFM 1-10, 1989) 1987; 2nd edn 1995, superseded by the third and current version of July 2007 [hereinafter: *Commander's Handbook*].

79 *Commander's Handbook*, op. cit. n 78, para 8.2, in 2007 version, at 8–3, para 8.2.5 (emphasis added).

80 Ibid, (emphasis added).

81 The Supplement lists the following targets as 'proper economic targets' for naval attack: enemy lines of communication, rail yards, bridges, rolling stock, barges, lighters, industrial installations producing war-fighting products, and power generation plants. It further states that economic targets that indirectly but effectively support and sustain the enemy's war-fighting capability may also be attacked. *Annotated Supplement to the Commander's Handbook on the Law of Naval Operations*, Oceans Law and Policy, US Naval War College, Newport, RI 1997, at 8–3.

82 The sources that relate to this section include both documents issued as part of the military doctrine of the US armed forces and legal sources outlining the law applicable to military operations. Operational law is generally considered to comprise the domestic and international rules relevant to military operations. It includes many legal issues, including the laws of war. See the relevant discussion in 8.5.3.

Effective contribution to military action 101

'war fighting or war-sustaining capability' were used in place of 'military action'. In 2003 such a reference also appeared in 'Instructions for the U.S. Military Commission at Guantanamo Bay'.[83] More recently, the 'war fighting or war-sustaining capability' formulae also found their way into the 2006 Military Commission Act.[84]

As far as doctrinal sources are concerned, three documents must be mentioned. The US Air Force first used both terms in a 1998 doctrinal pamphlet entitled *Intelligence Targeting Guide*.[85] Subsequently, the 2006 Air Force targeting doctrine drew from the description in Additional Protocol I to the Geneva Conventions and described military objectives as 'those objects [that] by their nature, location, purpose or use make an effective contribution to military action'.[86] The targeting doctrine further specified that economic objects 'ma[de] an effective (though not necessarily direct) contribution to an adversary's military capability'.[87] The document stressed that, as in the case of dual objects, economic targets would require 'a higher level of approval because of the particular facts and circumstances regarding the nature, location, use, and purpose of the target'. This approach was repeated in the newest version of the Air Force document, except for an initial description akin to the definition in API. This was replaced by entirely novel definition of civilian objects, which contained *a contrario* a description of military objectives as 'those used to support or sustain the adversary's war fighting capability'.[88]

Published in 2007, and applicable to the Army, Navy and Air Force, the Joint Targeting Doctrine contained a definition of military objective without a reference to effective contribution to military action. The text read:

> Military attacks will be directed only at military targets. Only a military target is a lawful object of direct attack. By their nature, location, purpose, or use, military targets are those objects whose total or partial destruction, capture, or neutralization offer a military advantage.[89]

---

83 Department of Defense Instructions for the US Military Commission at Guantanamo Bay Military Commission Instructions No. 2, Crimes and Elements for Trials by Military Commission, 30 April 2003, para 5D.

84 Military Commissions Act, 2006, 10 U.S.C §§948a–950w, 30 September 2006, s 3930–26, para 950 v. 'Crimes triable by military commissions'.

85 US Air Force, *Intelligence Targeting Guide*, Air Force Pamphlet (AFP) 14-210, Secretary of the US Air Force, 1 February 1998, para 1.7.1 at 12 and para A4.2.2 at 147. This document superseded AFP 200–17, 23 June 1989 and AFP 200–18 Volumes I and II, 1 October 1990.

86 *Targeting*, US Air Force Doctrine, Document AFDD 2-1.9 of 8 June 2006, at 89 [hereinafter: Air Force Doctrine (2006)]; the same definition can be found in other Air Force publications, namely US Air Force, *The Military Commander and the Law*, The Judge Advocate General's School, 11th edn, 2012, at 667.

87 Air Force Doctrine (2006), op. cit. n 86, at 91.

88 *Annex 3-60, Targeting*, US Air Force Doctrine, 10 January 2014, at 91.

89 The language used in this paragraph refers only to military targets, as opposed to 'military objectives'. It is difficult to tell whether this text was worded in this way to highlight the difference between the two terms, or whether that was merely accidental. *Joint Targeting*, US Joint Publication JP 3–60, US Joint Chiefs of Staff, 13 April 2007, Appendix E at E-3 [hereinafter: JP 3–60 (2007)].

102 *Military objective: concept and definition*

On the other hand, the 2013 version of the Joint Targeting Doctrine referred to the treaty definition of military objectives, citing the entire treaty text. In contrast to the 2007 version of the doctrine, this recent version dispensed with the indication that legitimate 'military targets' included economic objects, such as plants and factories, that 'make an effective contribution to the adversary's military capability'. Furthermore, an earlier suggestion that some objects that 'indirectly, but effectively, support and sustain the adversary's war fighting capability' could be dual-use targets was also omitted from the 2013 version of the Joint Targeting Doctrine.[90] Just like the Air Force targeting doctrine, the 2007 joint doctrine document contained a reference only to 'war-fighting capability', and did not refer to a 'war-sustaining' contribution. However, the commentary to the purpose and use terms of the definition in the 2013 Joint Targeting Doctrine alluded to 'war-fighting' as well as to 'war-sustaining' effort in the following explanation:

> [T]he connection of some objects to an enemy's war fighting or war-sustaining effort may be direct, indirect or even discrete. A decision as to classification of an object as a military objective and allocation of resources for its attack depends upon its value to an enemy nation's war fighting or war sustaining effort (including its ability to be converted to a more direct connection), and not solely to its overt or present connection or use.[91]

As far as operational law and LOAC publications are concerned, the earliest documents – even predating API – embraced the definition as formulated in Art 52.2 of API. These include the 1976 US Air Force Operational Manual (Pamphlet)[92] and the *Law of Land Warfare* manual, which was also amended a year before the adoption of API.[93] The changes included the negotiated text of the definition of military objectives *in toto*.[94] The *Law of War Handbook*, the guide for Judge Advocates practising the laws of war, also relied on the text

---

90 JP 3–60 (2007), op. cit. n 89, at E-3, ss 4(a)(2) and 4(b). Elsewhere in that text, the document stressed that civilians and civilian objects, 'other than those used to support or sustain the adversary's war-fighting capability', must not be attacked. Ibid, at E-2, s 4(a). See also the discussion of dual-use objects in 3.3.

91 *Joint Targeting*, US Joint Publication JP 3–60, US Joint Chiefs of Staff, 31 Jan. 2013, Appendix A at A2–3 [hereinafter: JP 3–60 (2013)].

92 H.B. Robertson 'The Principle of the Military Objective in the Law of Armed Conflict', 8 *US Air Force Academy Journal of Legal Studies* 1997–8, 35–69 at 45, referring to the Department of Air Force, *International Law – The Conduct of Armed Conflict and Air Operations* (AFP 110–31, 19 November 1976, at 5–8 and 5–9, para 5–3b(1). See also a discussion on the relevant source in 8.4.

93 *Law of Land Warfare*, Field Manual 27-10, US Department of Army, 18 July 1956 with subsequent amendments of 15 July 1976.

94 Ibid, Appendix A, para 40(c), at iv. Older versions of this document, namely the Basic Field Manual Rules of Land Warfare of 1914, 1934 or 1940, do not mention a definition of military objectives in any form.

Effective contribution to military action 103

of the API definition for many years, and each edition of the Handbook repeatedly contained the API definition.[95]

The most recent version of the annually published *Operational Law Handbook*, designed for Judge Advocates practising operational law, similarly argues that the US followed the treaty definition, which was regarded as an expression of customary rule, as incorporated into the 1956 US Army Field Manual 27-10 in 1976.[96] However, it later included the formula that appeared in earlier versions of this Handbook, as well as in the very recent Joint Targeting Doctrine.[97] Although the text used is exactly the same as in the doctrinal document, it is located in a separate part of the commentary.

It would appear that both the US doctrinal and legal documents released in 2013 seem to have been made generally consistent with each other by the usage of the same formula in the commentary. It is uncertain whether the different location of the same statement in the commentary bears any significance for a differential analysis. What is certainly important, though, are the expressions used. Both documents departed from the earlier terminology of 'capability', substituting instead the notion of 'effort', which has a substantively different meaning. It is also difficult to ascertain exactly what was meant by a 'discrete connection' to war-fighting or war-sustaining effort. The publications did not offer any further commentary. It remains unclear if the specific connection referred to relates to economic targets or any objects.[98]

The most recent Air Force publications, such as *Air Force Operations and the Law*[99] and *The Military Commander and the Law*,[100] reproduced the API formula.[101] The former stated the concept is an 'accurate restatement of customary international law'. The *Air Force Operations and the Law* publication noted that economic objects made an *effective* but not necessarily *direct* contribution to the

---

95 *Law of War Handbook*, JA 423, International and Operational Law Department, The Judge Advocate General's Legal Center and School, 2004 and 2005 edns, at 165–6 and 168–9.

96 Operational Law Handbook, op. cit. n 25, at 22.

97 The formula read: '[T]he connection of some objects to an enemy's war fighting or war-sustaining effort may be direct, indirect or even discrete. A decision as to classification of an object as a military objective and allocation of resources for its attack depends upon its value to an enemy nation's war fighting or war sustaining effort (including its ability to be converted to a more direct connection), and not solely to its overt or present connection or use.' Operational Law Handbook, op. cit. n 25, at 23; see also text attached to n 90 above.

98 The 2009 version of the Operational Law Handbook contained a list of categories of military objectives, which included economic targets such as 'power', 'industry (war supporting manufacturing/export/import', 'transportation (equipment/LOC/POL)'. Operational Law Handbook, op. cit. n 25, 2009 edn, at 19.

99 *Air Force Operations and the Law: A Guide for Air, Space and Cyber Forces*, US Air Force, The Judge Advocate General's School, 2nd edn, 2009.

100 *The Military Commander and the Law*, op. cit. n 86, at 667.

101 Respectively *Air Force Operations and the Law*, op. cit. n 99, at 248 and *The Military Commander and the Law*, op. cit. n 86, at 615.

104 *Military objective: concept and definition*

adversary's 'military capability'.[102] The document further stressed that such economic objects would require a higher level of approval.[103]

It is striking that all the documents mentioned above, with the exception of the *Commander's Handbook of Law of Naval Operations* and documents pertaining to military law, recognise and uphold API's version of the definition as their primary reference.[104] Some of them then supplement the API definition with a reference to economic targets. The contribution of economic targets is said to be: 'war-fighting' or 'military capability'.[105] The 2013 Joint Targeting Doctrine, *Commander's Handbook on the Law of Naval Operations* and the *Operational Law Handbook* also mention, respectively, 'war-sustaining capability' and 'war-sustaining effort' as relevant considerations. This implies that the fundamental difference in the US position, albeit initially inconsistent, exists in the interpretation rather than the replacement of an otherwise accepted customary definition. This interpretation, however, could be expanding the scope of the definition.

The inclusion of the term 'war-fighting or war-sustaining effort (capability)' in official documents has increased with time. In 1990 only the *Commander's Handbook on the Law of Naval Operations* contained these phrases. By 2010 the number of documents mentioning economic targets' contributions to war-fighting or military capability had risen to seven, and they were no longer limited to regulation of naval operations. The 2013 versions of the leading doctrinal and legal publications invoked also include 'effort' in place of the earlier references to 'capability'. They both lacked any mention of the context

102 *Air Force Operations and the Law*, op. cit. n 99, at 248.
103 The contemporary example that the publication supplied related to the pursuit of Taliban-controlled heroin, as well as drug-related assets and facilities thought effectively to contribute to the Taliban's military capability, with the profits from the drug trade being used to sustain the insurgency. *Air Force Operations and the Law*, op. cit. n 99, at 250.
104 The US *State Practice Report* had already confirmed by 1997 that, although the *opinio juris* of the US recognised the customary nature of Art 52.2 of the API definition, the US in practice interpreted the definition broadly, with 'war-supporting economic facilities' fitting into the military objective test (J.M. Henckaerts and L. Doswald-Beck (eds), *Customary International Humanitarian Law*, Cambridge University Press, 2005, Vol. I (Rules), with the supplementary evidence in Vol. II (Practice), in Vol. II, at 221,para 589 [hereinafter: CIHL]. See also Remarks of M.J. Matheson cited in 'The United States Position on the Relation of Customary International Law to the 1977 Protocols Additional to the 1949 Geneva Conventions', 2 *American University Journal of International Law and Policy* 1987, 419–31 at 436, also reprinted in US Army Field Manual FM 27-10, op. cit. n 93; Air Force Doctrine (2006), op. cit. n 86, at 89, stating: 'Though the US is not a signatory to the Additional Protocol it views this definition as an accurate restatement of customary international law that we recognize and with which we comply'; A. Roberts 'Air Power, Accuracy and the Law of Targeting: Why No Brave New World?' in R.B. Jaques (ed.), *Issues in International Law and Military Operations*, Vol. 80, Naval War College, International Law Studies, Newport, RI 2006, at 140.
105 Barring the general nature of the commentary in the Operational Law Handbook (op. cit. n 25), which does not clarify whether it also covers economic targets or other objects.

Effective contribution to military action 105

of economic targets, and both included the 'war-sustaining' term alongside 'war-fighting'. Interestingly, the terms in question are no longer confined to military matters, but also appear in domestic criminal legislation.

Only a few States officially endorse the possibility that the first element of the test might be satisfied by specific economic objects that indirectly contribute to military action.[106] It is worth noting that Ecuador's military manual replicates, word for word, the US 'war-fighting or war-sustaining' formula in the definition of military objectives.[107] Australia's military manual indicates that economic targets that indirectly but effectively support military operations are also military objectives, provided that the attack would also satisfy the second prong of the definition.[108] The same position is taken in documents from Sweden[109] and New Zealand.[110] None of these documents refers to a 'war-sustaining' contribution. This indicates that there is a substantive difference between the two terms, and that other States are willing to accept only one of the claims the US is promoting. The following section will examine the meaning of the key concepts used by the US, and their consistency with the test of effective contribution to military action.

It is not clear how US uses the 'war-sustaining' and 'war-fighting' terms. It may be that different sources could define them differently. This may give an impression of that the US position is inconstant and possibly inconsistent. The discussion in the next subsection will be focused on trying to ascertain how these terms may be used, the relationship between them and how they may relate to the requirement of effective contribution to military action.

4.3.2.2 War-sustaining and war-fighting effort (capability)

US sources refer to various related concepts in both military doctrine and legal documents. It would seem that the two terms denominating capabilities, that is 'war- sustaining' and 'war-fighting', are not synonymous, and are in fact so substantively different that States other than the US may accept one but not

---

106　AMW Manual, op. cit. n 1, Commentary, point 2, at 110.

107　CIHL, op. cit. n 104, Vol. II, at 183, para 331. It has been suggested to the author that a number of other countries, particularly in Latin America, adopted the US position in the process of translation of the *Commander's Handbook* (op. cit. n 78) into their national languages for use by their forces. This author was unable to confirm this suggestion. Even if this was the case, it remains unclear whether such 'adoption by translation' reflects a considered position of such States.

108　CIHL, op. cit. n 104, Vol. II, at 217, para 565. Note that the Royal Australian Air Force (RAAF) Operations Law Guide for the RAAF Commanders, on the other hand, argued that 'mere contribution to a country's economic output is unlikely to be sufficient to meet the criteria required for a military objective'. (*Operations Law for RAAF Commanders*, Royal Australian Air Force, Air Power Publication AAP 1003, 2nd edn, 2004, at 64–5, para 8.6).

109　CIHL, op. cit. n 104, Vol. II, at 219, para 575.

110　CIHL, op. cit. n 104, Vol. II, at 218–19, para 573.

106 *Military objective: concept and definition*

the other. Both the 2013 Joint Targeting Doctrine and the *Operational Law Handbook* refer to war-sustaining and war-fighting 'effort', and not 'capability'. Some recent US documents also use the term 'military capability', particularly in the context of economic targets. How, then, can all these terms be defined?

'Military capability' is defined by the US armed forces as the 'ability to achieve a specified wartime objective – namely, winning a war or battle, or destroying a target set – and includes four elements: the structure of the force, modernisation, readiness and sustainability'.[111] They are all clearly linked to military forces, but the main difference to 'military action' is that 'capability' is a broader term that covers 'action', but is not confined to it. For instance, one of the four elements, 'sustainability', is defined as the provision and maintenance of the requisite level of operational activity for the forces, material and consumables to support the 'military effort'.[112] The ability to fight during wartime will require training and recruitment activities prior to, and/or during the conflict. They are not, as such, directly linked to military operations. An object's capability also refers to its potential, or the quality that permits its intended use. In this sense, the term may be associated with targets that are considered in the context of the purpose criterion.[113] This means the term encompasses a wider range of military activities, some of which would be connected to the conduct of military operations indirectly. If this is indeed the meaning of this term, resembling that of 'military effort', then it may not be entirely compatible with the requirement of the definition of military objectives.

'Effort' is different to 'capability' because it entails concerted activity directed towards the achievement of an objective. The term 'military effort' denominates the activities of armed forces with a common purpose. This phrase is substantively closer to the meaning of 'military action', although it is still broader, as per the discussion earlier in this chapter.[114] In short, the word 'effort' appears to encompass both physical and mental activities, and may involve activities of entities other than armed forces. In this context, 'war-fighting effort' is likely to denominate both physical and non-physical endeavours towards the goal of fighting. This way, the term seems to be more specific, as it appears linked to concrete military activity – the conduct of hostilities.[115] While it seems narrower, there could be contributions that, arguably, fall outside the definition. If, for instance, diamonds were said to be

---

111 *Joint Doctrine for Multinational Operations*, JP 3-16, US Joint Chiefs of Staff, 7 March 2007 at GL-9; omitted from the recent version of the document (16 July 2013).

112 Ibid.

113 This position would be compatible with the position expressed in the 2013 Joint Targeting Doctrine. See text attached to n 91 above. See 3.4 for a discussion regarding the *purpose* criterion.

114 See discussion in 4.2.

115 In this sense, a willingness to attack objects that increase the enemy's ability to fight resembles the American Civil War practice of 'scorched earth', which was aimed, among other things, at denying food to the Confederate troops.

Effective contribution to military action 107

used as payment for the supply of missiles or other weapons used in an armed conflict, some commentators may be compelled to accept that the contribution made by such exports might correspond with the test. This, again, would be acceptable only if it could be shown that no alternative way of financing such a contribution existed, and that without these weapons the adversary would have been much less effective in the conduct of hostilities.[116] The use of the word 'effort', just as in the context of 'military effort', may imply that contributions that are not linked to the conduct of hostilities in a specific armed conflict would be unlikely to satisfy the test.

The meaning of the term 'war-sustaining' effort (capability) appears to be the broadest and least precise.[117] This term is qualitatively different to the 'war-fighting' phrase. It relates to 'war'-supporting 'capability', which could conceivably encompass all the activities and potential of all members of society who assist the war effort, and not just 'military effort', let alone military action.[118] The term 'war-sustaining' does not appear to be used in US sources in a specific connection to economic targets. This may suggest that it represents a broader group of objects than economic targets. It is unclear if it is separate to what are considered 'military targets', and should be viewed as an additional category. Its relation to objects contributing to 'war-fighting' effort (capability) is also uncertain.

It is not entirely clear whether economic targets and other targets, which could satisfy the definition, are two stand-alone categories of objects, or whether one is included in the other. One US source suggests that economic targets are part of 'military' targets. This may suggest that economic targets are not a separate category of targets. In US sources, economic targets appear to be associated with concepts related to the prosecution of hostilities, such as lines of communication, industrial installations, workshops and power plants. This means that some defined targets would in any case be considered to satisfy the definition by virtue of the use criterion (dual use), even where their contribution may not do so. The most recent doctrinal and legal documents appear to dispense with references to economic targets altogether, thereby implying the irrelevance of the term in the context of the current US position.

---

116 Such a position appears to be found in 'Explanation' to the San Remo Manual on International Law Applicable to Armed Conflicts at Sea. L. Doswald-Beck (ed.), *San Remo Manual on International Law Applicable to Armed Conflicts at Sea*, Cambridge University Press, Cambridge 1995, para 40.12; I. Henderson, *The Contemporary Law of Targeting*, Martinus Nijhoff, Leiden 2009, at 62 and 144.

117 The Operational Law Handbook (op. cit. n 25) and 2013 Joint Targeting Doctrine (op. cit. n 89) use the term 'war-sustaining effort'.

118 As mentioned earlier, the practice of destroying cotton during the American Civil war was associated with attacks against objects contributing to the 'war-sustaining effort' of the adversary. The notion is associated with the economic dimension of maritime operations, in particular attacks against enemy or neutral merchant vessels and their cargo. Robertson, op. cit. n 92, at 50; W.J. Fenrick 'Legal Aspects of Targeting in the Law of Naval Warfare', 29 *Canadian Yearbook of International Law* 1991, 238–82.

108 *Military objective: concept and definition*

'War-sustaining' effort (capability) is a notion that could potentially subsume many objects of psychological (including civilian morale or will to wage war), commercial or financial (exports, stock markets, taxation or revenue collections) value to the enemy.[119] Although its meaning is not established with certainty, the term may cover an excessively broad scope of potential objects. Their contribution to the conduct of hostilities seems not just ineffective but also non-military. It may permit a consideration of the contribution to the adversary's will and capability to wage war. As was indicated, the satisfaction of such objects of the effective contribution to military action requirement is debatable.

A reliance on the broader interpretation of the first element of the definition triggered a number of critical responses. It was thought to 'justify unleashing the type of indiscriminate attack that annihilated entire cities during that war'; a reference alluding to the Second World War practice of strategic bombing.[120] It was suggested that such an approach removed civilian protection, through a reliance on a potentially distant link to influencing war-related activities.[121] The 'war-sustaining' term was perceived as entailing a connection between the object and military action that was 'too remote' to be acceptable.[122] It was denounced as a significant substantive departure from the letter and spirit of the definition in Art 52.2.[123]

It should be noted that there is no need for such expansive interpretation, as the existing formulation of military action is broad enough to accommodate a wide scope of economic objects without risking the infringement of the principle of distinction. One commentator not only links the term with 'economic targets', but also suggests that, to satisfy the law, the object contributing to war-sustaining capability would need some nexus to

---

119 Compare this with a discussion of the attack on the Hirgigo power plant: see 4.2 and 5.2.1.

120 L. Doswald-Beck, 'San Remo Manual on International Law Applicable to Armed Conflicts at Sea', *American Journal of International Law* 1995, 192–208 at 199.

121 M. Sassoli, 'Targeting: The Scope and Utility of the Concept of "Military Objectives" for the Protection of Civilians in Contemporary Armed Conflicts' in D. Wippman and M. Evangelista (eds), *New Wars, New Laws? Applying the Laws of War in 21st Century Conflicts*, Transnational, Ardsley 2005, at 196.

122 Ibid; Doswald-Beck, op. cit. n 120, para 67.27; K.W. Watkin, 'Coalition Operations: A Canadian Perspective' in M.D. Carsten (ed.), *International Law and Military Operations*, Vol. 84, Naval War College, International Law Studies, Newport, RI 2008, at 255; S. Oeter, 'Comment: Is the Principle of Distinction Outdated?' in W. Heintschel von Heinegg and V. Epping (eds), *International Humanitarian Law Facing New Challenges*, Springer, Berlin 2007, 56; AMW Manual, Commentary, op. cit. n 1, point 2, at 110, Oeter, op. cit. n 2, at 185; W.H. Boothby, *The Law of Targeting*, Oxford University Press, Oxford 2012 at 106.

123 Y. Dinstein, *The Conduct of Hostilities under the Law of International Armed Conflict*, 2nd edn, Cambridge University Press, Cambridge 2010, at 95–6; Rogers, op. cit. n 26, at 109–10; A. Boivin, 'The Legal Regime Applicable to Targeting Military Objectives in the Context of Contemporary Warfare', Research Paper Series no. 2/2006, Geneva Academy of International Humanitarian Law and Human Rights, at 29–30.

military capability.[124] He observes that there is confusion and a lack of clarity as to what the terms mean.[125]

This is indeed a problem. The US position is not constant or well explained, and only very recently began to be more uniform. This means firm conclusions cannot be reached as to whether the use by the US of terms different to those in Art 52.2 represents a substantively different view on this element of the definition. It may be a combination of these aspects. It is likely that objects contributing to 'war-fighting' effort (capability) will satisfy the definition. In this case, there is no difference between the US position and that of other States, except that the US uses a different term to describe this contribution. At the same time, the US use of the 'war-sustaining' term, assumed to include a substantially broader scope of objects, may imply a broader interpretation of the Art 52.2 requirement. It is worth noting that perception of mere 'remoteness' between the object and military action could sometimes be insufficient and misleading. 'War-sustaining' objects are likely to comprise substantively different targets than those contributing to military action or even to 'war-fighting' effort.

4.4 Conclusion

The first key element of the definition of military objective contains a requirement of the existence of the object's contribution, based on certain of its characteristics, to military action. The nature, location, purpose and use criteria of the contribution are not considered in the abstract, but in close relationship to military action. The required contribution not only has to be linked to the conduct of military operations, but also has to be effective and therefore capable of achieving a result.

There are certain objects whose contribution was questioned because no information about them was provided by the State that initiated the attack. It is possible that they might genuinely have lacked the required connection. Uncertainty has been introduced by the US interpretation of the definition, which is not necessarily shared by other States, and which assumes that the contribution to the 'war-fighting' and 'war-sustaining' effort (capability) of the adversary is covered by the term *effective contribution to military action*. The US no longer appears to link economic targets to the interpretation of the definition of military objectives. While it is possible that objects that contribute to war-fighting effort (capability) may well be covered by the definition, there is a concern that the US interpretation of the first element of the definition may also include objects that do not contribute to military action. It is unclear if

---

124 It would seem that Melson claims that natural resources can be war-sustaining objects. This would be consistent with the concept of economic targets in the context of naval warfare. Melson, op. cit. n 42, at 50–1.

125 Ibid, at 54.

110 *Military objective: concept and definition*

that is the case, as it remains uncertain what meaning the US attaches to either of these terms.

This chapter concludes the discussion of the first key element of the definition. Chapters 5 and 6 will analyse the meaning of the terms used in the second key element. Chapter 5 will specifically address the nature of the relationship between the two elements, in addition to considering the requirement of a *definite military advantage*.

5 Definite military advantage

There is an apparent state of equilibrium in the structure of the definition of military objective. The definition comprises two crucial elements, which are both supplemented or qualified by other conditions. Chapters 3 and 4 addressed the meaning of the terms used in the first key element of the definition. As the discussion moves towards the second key element, one must first consider the nature of the relationship between the two. This relationship is discussed in the first section of this chapter.

The chapter then examines the second part of the definition. Like the first element, the second consists of one pivotal requirement, namely *definite military advantage*. The meaning of this standard will be addressed first. This clearly does not follow the order of the actual structure of the definition. This change is justified by the importance of this crucial component.

The requirement of definite military advantage will be discussed in two sections, starting with a discussion of the concept of *military advantage* and followed by an analysis of the term *definite*. The discussion of the meaning of the terms in the definition will take into account the record of negotiations. This will be supplemented by an illustration of the particular problems that have arisen since its adoption, drawn from relevant examples of State practice since 1977.[1]

5.1 The relationship between the two main parts of the definition

Pivotal to the practical operation of the definition is the relationship between the two key elements. It may be that the first element, *effective contribution to military action*, is, in effect, identical in substance with the second element, namely *definite military advantage*. The two elements may be seen as referring to the same things, viewed from two different perspectives (defender and

---

1 An exceptional reference might be made to a pre-1977 example if it is thought to illustrate the problem.

112 *Military objective: concept and definition*

attacker).[2] They may then be seen as a single requirement, articulated in two different ways. In this situation, the issue of any relationship would be irrelevant, as a relationship can only be between two distinct parts. If the two elements are perceived as two ways of expressing the same content, it would not matter which element was used. There may be a temptation to infer that the two elements represent the same thing simply because in most, if not all, cases, the second element will be satisfied upon the fulfilment of the first. This, however, cannot be taken as an indication of their meaning.

If the substantive content of the two elements is not identical, then the question arises whether it is necessary to satisfy both elements or just one of them. The requirement to satisfy both elements would suggest a cumulative relationship. If they are considered as cumulative requirements, what will matter is the simultaneous satisfaction of both requirements. The need to satisfy only one would imply an alternative type of relationship, where the scope and precise meaning of each element will be particularly important as an object can be regarded as a military objective if only one element of the test is met.

The definition of military objective contains the conjunctive 'and' in five out of the six authentic texts.[3] The Spanish authentic text is the only version of Additional Protocol I to the four 1949 Geneva Conventions (API) that uses the word 'or' to connect the two elements of the definition. It is unclear why such an inconsistency appeared in the authentic texts. Should the terms used differ in meaning between two or more authentic texts of a treaty, the Vienna Convention on the Law of Treaties recommends that one should consult the subsequent practice in the application of the treaty, and use supplementary means of interpretation, such as the preparatory materials of the treaty and the circumstances of its adoption.[4] Without such a resolution, the meaning that best reconciles the texts, having regard to the object and purpose of the treaty, should be adopted.[5]

Interestingly, the choice of connecting word was discussed at the time of the negotiations.[6] Records show that the use of the disjunctive 'or' was also

---

2 See also the discussion regarding the first element of definition in this context in 4.2 and the discussion regarding the notions of attacker and defender in 1.5.

3 Art 102 of Additional Protocol I (API) specifies that the Arabic, Chinese, English, French, Russian and Spanish texts of the original are equally authentic. Art 102 of Protocol Additional to the Geneva Conventions of 12 August 1949, and Relating to the Protection of Victims of International Armed Conflicts (Protocol I), Geneva, 8 June 1977, reprinted in D. Schindler and J. Toman (eds), *The Laws of Armed Conflict*, 4th edn, Martinus Nijhoff, Leiden 2004, at 711 *et seq.* [hereinafter: API].

4 Arts 31–3, Vienna Convention on the Law of Treaties, 23 May 1969, United Nations Treaty Series, vol. 1155, at 331.

5 Ibid.

6 The disjunctive 'or' was used previously in the 1969 Edinburgh Resolution. The Distinction between Military Objectives and Non-Military Objectives in General and Particularly the Problems Associated with Weapons of Mass Destruction, Institute of International Law, Edinburgh, 9 September 1969 and in Schindler and Toman, op. cit. n 3, at 351–2.

Definite military advantage 113

considered. The Dutch delegation proposed a change to the original ICRC draft, which used 'and', to that end.[7] This idea was subsequently supported by Canada,[8] France[9] and the US,[10] but opposed by other States.[11] The Netherlands experts implied that there was a difference in the substantive content of the two elements, one being more general then the other.[12] Qualification through only one of the parts of the definition was, therefore, regarded as less restrictive.[13]

Eventually, the conjunctive 'and' was used to connect the two elements in the definition, except for the Spanish version. These elements, as was suggested during the negotiations, were considered not to be substantively identical.[14] The Spanish version, containing the disjunctive 'or', appears to have been transcribed into the 1996 Spanish and 1989 Argentinian Law of War military manuals, as well as into Spanish criminal law.[15] The second edition of the Spanish LOAC Manual refers to the definition containing 'and', which indicates a substantive change.[16] The second version of the Argentinian LOAC Manual follows the previous text, including 'or', without any change.[17]

7 CDDH/III/56, 19 March 1974.
8 CDDH/III/79, 25 March 1974, withdrawn in support of the Dutch proposal. See also statement on the meeting of Committee III, CDDH/III/SR.14, 6 February 1975, para 19.
9 Meeting of Committee III, CDDH/III/SR.14, 6 February 1975, para 21.
10 Meeting of Committee III, CDDH/III/SR.15, 7 February 1975, para 9.
11 While Sweden felt that such rules could give too much latitude to the belligerents, Honduras argued that it would substantively weaken the protection of civilian objects. Meeting of Committee III, CDDH/III/SR.15, 7 February 1975, paras 3 and 38.
12 The Dutch delegation thought that the first element was apparently aimed at those who had a general view of the military situation, such as high-ranking officers in a 'static' military situation. It was suggested that the second element was directed at soldiers in the battlefield, or other military personnel in a more 'dynamic' environment, who normally had a limited view of the situation (Meeting of Committee III, CDDH/III/SR.14, 6 February 1975, para 17; Meeting of Committee III, CDDH/III/SR.16, 10 February 1975, paras 9 and 24.) It is striking that these comments also appear to reflect, perhaps inadvertently, the different circumstances in which the definition is applied under Art 52.2 and Art 57 API. The latter is outside the scope of this work. See 1.3.
13 Meeting of Committee III, CDDH/III/SR.16, 10 February 1975, paras 24, 28.
14 There is no evidence that, during the voting, some States still objected to the final version. In particular, there is no indication of Spanish-speaking countries objecting. Art 52 was adopted by 79 votes in favour with no objections. Seven States abstained, including Australia and France, but not for reasons related to the structure of the definition. See Plenary Session, CDDH/SR.14, 26 May 1977, at 168, 176–7, 186.
15 For instance, Art 613(1)(b) Spanish 1995 Penal Code prescribes punishment for those who, during an armed conflict, attack civilian objects of the adversary that do not offer a definite military advantage or make an effective contribution to military action. J.M. Henckaerts and L. Doswald-Beck (eds), *Customary International Humanitarian Law, Vol. II (Practice)*, Cambridge University Press, Cambridge 2005, part I, para 342 [hereinafter: CIHL].
16 *Orientaciones. El Derecho de los Conflictos Armados*, OR7–004, Ministry of Defence of Spain, 2nd edn, 2007, Vol. I, para 1.3.b(1) at 1–16.
17 *Manual De Derecho Internacional De Los Conflictos Armados*, Ministry of Defence of Argentina, 2010, para 3.52 at 76.

114 *Military objective: concept and definition*

Colombia's Operational Law Manual includes the definition with 'and', instead of 'or'.[18] There is some evidence that other Spanish-speaking delegations, such as Honduras, objected to the use of the word 'or', and preferred 'and'.[19] There is no record of the Spanish or Argentinian view during negotiations, or even upon ratification of API.[20]

Spain is also a member of NATO and participated in drafting its joint targeting doctrine.[21] NATO defines military objectives in an identical way to Art 52.2 API by using the conjunctive 'and' between the two key elements.[22] There would appear to be no record of Spanish objections in respect of the adoption of such a formula in the NATO document. Spain participated in combat operations during the NATO 1999 intervention in Kosovo. There are no available documents suggesting that the Spanish version of the definition caused interoperability problems, or that Spanish military planners suggested a broader scope of targets on that basis.[23]

A Spanish academic expert has recently suggested that the Spanish version of the authentic text of Art 52.2 could simply have been a mistake in translation, which was then transferred into national legislation.[24] This seems reasonable. Bearing in mind that the Spanish authentic text is the only one to contain the disjunctive 'or', and that the negotiating records showed a conscious rejection of the option to include it instead of 'and', one could reasonably infer that the preferred nature of the relationship between the two elements of the definition was based on the conjunctive 'and'. This could be reinforced by the fact that, although both Argentina and Spain clearly adopted verbatim the Spanish authentic text, neither has made any subsequent reference to their potentially divergent version of the definition – not even in the declarations upon ratification of API. The possibility may not be excluded, however unlikely, that should one of the Spanish-speaking States engage in an armed conflict, they may invoke a different standard.

When considering the two texts of the definition, one should not forget that API was adopted with a view 'to reaffirm[ing] and to develop[ing] the provisions protecting the victims of armed conflicts'.[25] As mentioned above,

---

18 *Manual de Derecho Operacional*, FF. MM 3-41, El Comando General de las Fuerzas Militares, Republic of Colombia, 2009, at 56.
19 Consult the position of Honduras, n 11 above.
20 Spain ratified API on 21 April 1989. Its interpretative statement does not contain any relevant reference. Argentina ratified API on 26 November 1986 and its interpretative declaration does not refer to the definition of military objective.
21 The evidence of such participation can be seen from the national reservations note at the beginning of the NATO Allied Joint Doctrine for Joint Targeting, AJP-3.9, May 2008, at x [hereinafter: AJP-3.9]. See also further discussion of the document in 7.4 and 7.5.
22 AJP-3.9, op. cit. n 21, para E at 1–7.
23 See discussion regarding interoperability in Chapter 9.
24 H. Olasolo, *Unlawful Attacks in Combat Situations: From the ICTY's Case Law to the Rome Statute*, Martinus Nijhoff, Leiden 2008, at 123.
25 Preamble to API, op. cit. n 3.

the proposed version of the definition containing the disjunctive 'or' was seen as providing a lesser standard of protection of civilian objects, by broadening the scope of objects that could be considered lawful targets. Compared to the version of the definition containing 'and', this would have been less consistent with such an object of API. It appears, therefore, more likely that the connection between the two elements was intended to be based on the conjunctive 'and', as this construction provides a higher standard of protection of civilian objects.[26] The elements do not have to be substantively related to each other.[27]

The two key elements of the definition must be satisfied simultaneously when determining the lawfulness of the target.[28] In other words, they both need to exist in respect of the same object at the same time. Both elements are most likely to exist at all times simultaneously in regard to objects contributing to military action under the nature criterion.[29] In the case of other criteria, however, there would be situations when changing circumstances will affect whether the requirement of the anticipated definite military advantage is met.[30] This does not necessarily mean that the circumstances that determine the second element would be relevant in an assessment of the first element of the test.[31]

It is very likely that if the object is militarily significant to one side, it is also going to be valuable to the other side, even if not in the same way. The first element is quite specific in its description, but encompasses a wider range of potential targets. The second element seems quite broad, but its application is limited by the requirement of *circumstances ruling at the time*. The cumulative

---

26 This is a position that is going to be taken in the following discussion regarding the second element of the definition. This position is also supported, for example, by Hampson and Boothby. See F.J. Hampson, 'Proportionality and Necessity in the Gulf War', 86 *American Society of International Law Proceedings* 1992, 45–54 at 49; W.H. Boothby, *The Law of Targeting*, Oxford University Press, Oxford 2012, at 100, n 106.

27 M. Bothe, K. Partsch and W. Solf, *New Rules for Victims of Armed Conflicts: Commentary on the Two 1977 Protocols Additional to the Geneva Conventions of 1949*, Martinus Nijhoff, The Hague, 1982, para 2.4.4 at 325; A.V.P. Rogers, *Law on the Battlefield*, Melland Schill Studies in International Law, 3rd edn, Manchester University Press, Manchester 2012, at 106.

28 Y. Sandoz, C. Swinarski and B. Zimmermann (eds), *Commentary on the Additional Protocols of 8 June 1977 to the Geneva Conventions of 12 August 1949*, ICRC, Geneva, and Martinus Nijhoff, The Hague 1987, para 2018 [hereinafter: ICRC Commentary].

29 See the discussion regarding the nature criterion in 3.1.

30 P. Rowe, 'Kosovo 1999: The Air Campaign – Have the Provisions of Additional Protocol I Withstood the Test?', 82(837) *International Review of the Red Cross* 2000, 147–65 at 150; see further discussion in 6.2.

31 M. Sassoli, 'Targeting: The Scope and Utility of the Concept of "Military Objectives" for the Protection of Civilians in Contemporary Armed Conflicts' in D. Wippman and M. Evangelista (eds), *New Wars, New Laws? Applying the Laws of War in 21st Century Conflicts*, Transnational, Ardsley 2005, at 186; Rogers, op. cit. n 27, at 106; The Manual of the Law of Armed Conflict, UK Ministry of Defence, JSP 383, Oxford University Press, Oxford 2004, para 5.4.4(f) [hereinafter: The UK Manual].

116 *Military objective: concept and definition*

application of both elements thus appears to have a limiting effect on the scope of lawful targets. In other words, a much wider pool of objects would be effectively contributing to the defender's military action, but only some of them might offer a real military advantage in concrete circumstances.

5.2 Pursuit of a definite military advantage

Experts suggested that the second element of the definition is different in meaning to the first. The definition of military objective requires that total or partial destruction, capture or *neutralization* of the object offers a definite military advantage in the circumstances ruling at the time. A notion of *definite military advantage* will therefore be central to this analysis.

5.2.1 Military advantage

The term 'military advantage', in the context of military objective, was first mentioned in the 1923 Hague Rules.[32] Art 24 specified that an objective whose 'total or partial destruction would constitute an obvious military advantage for the belligerent' was considered a military objective.[33] The original ICRC draft of Art 52.2 (then Art 47) also contained the phrase. It was ultimately retained in the adopted text, despite one proposal to do away with this element of the definition.[34]

Gaining a military advantage will result in benefits that help attain one's military goals. In other words, military advantage is an expected contribution to the success of military operations, and is often thought of as necessarily being beneficial to the attacker's side.[35] This approach is described as a 'subjective' determination relating to the 'military purposes' of the attacker.[36] The 'subjectivity' of this element of the definition relates not only to the perspective from which it is assessed, but also to how it is defined by the other side, or what it means to that side. It is worth noting that military advantage is not always beneficial to the attacker. It was thought, for example, that NATO's attacks on Serbian security forces and equipment in Kosovo were advantageous

---

32 Hague Rules Concerning the Control of Wireless Telegraphy in time of War and Air Warfare, drafted by the Commission of Jurists of the United States, France, Great Britain, Italy, Japan and the Netherlands at the Hague, 11 December 1922–17 February 1923, reprinted in Schindler and Toman, op. cit. n 3, at 315–25.

33 Ibid.

34 The French proposal of 15 March 1974, CDDH/III/41. In contrast, the Australian proposal favoured retention only of the second element of the definition (CDDH/III/49 of 18 March 1974).

35 See the discussion regarding the notion of 'attacker' in 1.5.

36 S. Oeter, 'Methods and Means of Combat' in D. Fleck (ed.), *The Handbook of Humanitarian Law in Armed Conflicts*, 2nd edn, Oxford University Press, Oxford 2008, at 180; Boothby, op. cit. n 26, at 100, n 108.

Definite military advantage 117

to Kosovo Liberation Army (KLA) units, and not to NATO forces.[37] Bearing in mind that NATO did not appear officially to regard the KLA as friendly forces, the actual advantage seemed to benefit a third party. It is possible that an attack on a specific target may result in a definite military disadvantage to the adversary. It is unclear whether such disadvantage could be deemed sufficient to fulfil the requirement of advantage.

The advantage has to be of a military nature. The articulation of military advantage thus necessarily involves a clear belligerent nexus or other connection to ongoing or planned military operations in a specific armed conflict. In this context, the ICRC Commentary suggested that '[a] military advantage can only consist in ground gained and in annihilating or weakening the enemy armed forces'.[38] There is more to consider in this context than what the Commentary suggests. The weakening of armed forces does not comprise only killing the adversary's combatants. The choice of potential military objectives will go beyond the armed forces, *matériel* (resources) and tactical positions and will include depriving them of the means of fighting. Striking at a fuel dump will benefit one side by depriving its adversary of fuel and thus weakening the adversary's ability to fight in a different way to, say, capturing a unit of soldiers. Damaging a steel plant that produces parts for military planes can also weaken the enemy, and it is certainly militarily advantageous. Interruption of military communications may also bring significant military benefits.[39]

The requirement of military advantage means non-military advantages, such as political or economic ones, will not satisfy the test. Even if the destruction or capture of a target could result only in a significant negative impact on the adversary's economy or political system, it would not be enough to fulfil the requirement of military advantage. The question arises as to whether the economic or political dislocation caused to an adversary, measured against the ultimate goal of 'ending the war', is permissible. The Eritrea-Ethiopia Claims Commission's assessment of the attack by the Ethiopian Air Force on the Hirgigo Power Station in Eritrea appears to suggest it would be justified.[40] On 28 May 2000 the Ethiopian Air Force set out to launch an attack on the port of Massawa. On the way, the pilots spotted missile launchers in the vicinity

---

37 See further discussion in 9.1.2. See also discussion in 4.2.
38 ICRC Commentary, op. cit. n 28, para 2218.
39 Boothby, op. cit. n 26, at 506.
40 See also the discussion regarding the first element of the definition in 4.2. As in the case of the Harsile water reservoir (see discussion in 3.3.1), the Commission found API was not applicable *de jure* to the conflict, but applied Art 52.2 API as customary law. Eritrea-Ethiopia Claims Commission, Partial Award: Western Front, Aerial Bombardment and Related Claims Eritrea Claims 1, 3, 5, 9–13, 14, 21, 25 and 26 between The State of Eritrea and The Federal Democratic Republic of Ethiopia, The Hague, 19 December 2005, para 113 [hereinafter: EECC Award].

118 *Military objective: concept and definition*

of a power plant and requested permission to attack them. Eritrea disputed that claim. Eritrea accepted that the launchers were located not far from the power plant, but maintained that the plant itself had been targeted. Eritrea based its conclusion on the fact that all seven bombs released by the Ethiopian pilots landed within the boundaries of the power plant. The Commission determined that the actual target was the power plant and retrospectively applied the definition. The Commission concluded that the power plant satisfied the first part of the test, though it is not clear whether the plant was generating electricity at the time of the attack, or whether it was going to do so imminently.[41] The Commission then needed to consider whether the destruction of the plant offered Ethiopia a definite military advantage. In regard to its assessment of the second key element of definition, the Commission argued:

> In general, a large power plant being constructed to provide power for an area including a major port and naval facility certainly would seem to be an object the destruction of which would offer a distinct military advantage. Moreover, the fact that the power station was of economic importance to Eritrea is evidence that damage to it, in the circumstances prevailing in late May 2000 when Ethiopia was trying to force Eritrea to agree to end the war, offered a definite advantage. 'The purpose of any military action must always be to influence the political will of the adversary.' The evidence does not – and need not – establish whether the damage to the power station was a factor in Eritrea's decision to accept the Cease-Fire Agreement of June 18, 2000. The infliction of economic losses from attacks against military objectives is a lawful means of achieving a definite military advantage, and there can be few military advantages more evident than effective pressure to end an armed conflict that, each day, added to the number of both civilian and military casualties on both sides of the war.[42]

The Commission concluded that the second half of the test was satisfied through the operational benefit in depriving Eritrea of electricity. Given the Commission's finding that the power generated by the plant was likely to be used in the future military operations of the port and the naval base therein, it was clear that the destruction of the Hirgigo plant would offer a definite military advantage to Ethiopia by depriving Eritrea of that power. On this account, the Commission's finding that the destruction of the Hirgigo power station thus offered the Ethiopians military gain is uncontroversial. The Commission's remarks that followed this assessment are far more disconcerting.

41 See also discussion regarding the first element of the definition in 4.2.
42 EECC Award, op. cit. n 40, para 121 (footnotes omitted).

Definite military advantage 119

The Commission also appeared to suggest that action designed to bring closer an end to the war, and prevent further loss of life on both sides, gives rise to definite military advantage. They appeared to link it to the goal of influencing the political will of the adversary. They further implied that the expectation of bringing the war to an end constitutes military advantage, even if this is caused by a significant economic impact alone.

The Commission's remarks suggests that definite military advantage may be anticipated from the application of pressure to end the conflict and prevent further loss of life. It is possible that some strategic military benefits, such as the early cessation of hostilities, will be closely linked to political goals. It may be that some benefits towards strategic military goals may be considered in the context of military advantage, though caution here is advisable.[43] The expectation of only political advantage does not meet the test. Therefore, expecting to influence the will of an adversary would not suffice.[44] The expectation that an attack against one object will end the entire conflict is too uncertain and remote for it to meet the requirement of *definite military advantage*, even if the existence of *military* advantage was argued.[45] The danger of the Commission's approach is that it could potentially justify the Second World War attacks on Nagasaki and Hiroshima, and give rise to a far broader interpretation of the definition than that anticipated at its adoption.[46]

The Commission was also of the opinion that the requirement could have been fulfilled by a strategic advantage resulting from causing economic losses.[47] The formulation of military advantage, in the context of both gains, resulted from an attack that appeared to be a relatively restricted act of violence. The issue of whether the anticipated advantage may, in principle, entail operational as well as strategic benefits relates to the discussion of military advantage in the context of an attack 'as a whole', which is presented in the next subsection.

---

43 K. Watkin, 'Canada/United States Military Interoperability and Humanitarian Law Issues: Land Mines, Terrorism, Military Objectives and Targeted Killing', 15(2) *Duke Journal of International and Comparative Law* 2005, 281–314 at 307.

44 Y. Dinstein, *The Conduct of Hostilities under the Law of International Armed Conflict*, Cambridge University Press, Cambridge 2010, at 93.

45 The important limitation lies also in a requirement of *effective contribution to military action*. See 4.2 and 4.3 and 5.4. See also G.D. Solis, *The Law of Armed Conflict: International Humanitarian Law in War*, Cambridge University Press, Cambridge 2010, at 522. See the further discussion in 5.3.

46 See 2.3.

47 It is interesting to note that the Commission was making its evaluations with hindsight. This raises the question of how much evidence was presented to them to enable their conclusions, which should have taken into account Ethiopia's information about the target, and its military goals. The evaluations in the Award suggest that, even on the Eritrean side, there could have been a question about whether the plant was in operation. See the discussion in 4.2, 4.3.5 and 4.3.6.

120   *Military objective: concept and definition*

5.2.2 The assessment of military advantage in the context of an attack 'as a whole'

Upon ratifying API, Canada and Spain issued statements in the context of Art 52.2 indicating that *military advantage* was intended to refer to the advantage anticipated from an attack 'as a whole', and not from isolated or particular parts of it.[48] The UK Manual also contains a reference indicating the same understanding.[49] It is unclear if other States, which did not make similar statements, take the same position.

Such statements suggest that the military advantage anticipated from an attack will be expected from the attack in its entirety, and not from selected actions. It is unclear whether this implies that military advantage is required to result from a single action of a single military unit, a number of actions constituting a specific attack of such a unit (or both), or a number of attacks that are part of a broader military operation, executed not by one formation but by a number of them.[50]

The key to defining anticipated military advantage thus seems to be the understanding of the concept of 'attack'. There is a difference between the legal definition of attack and the general military understanding of the term. The legal definition covers acts of violence, whether in offence or defence.[51] The military normally uses the term to mean offensive operations.[52]

---

48 See the Canadian statement of 20 November 1990 and the Spanish declaration of 21 April 1989. States that are not party to API, such as Israel and the US, also appear to support the same interpretation of the assessment of definite military advantage. For the US: CIHL (op. cit. n 15), Vol. II, Chapter 2, para 361 and *Operational Law Handbook*, JA 422, International and Operational Law Department, The Judge Advocate General's Legal Center and School, 2009 edn, chapter 2 s X, point A(5), but the 2013 edition of the Handbook contains only a reference to the UK position on this issue as applied to the principle of proportionality (p 13). For Israel: e.g. Israel Ministry of Foreign Affairs [IMFA], *The Operation in Gaza – Factual and Legal Aspects: 27 December 2008–18 January 2009*, 29 July 2009, para 105, available at: www.jewishvirtuallibrary.org/jsource/Peace/GazaOp Report0709.pdf (last accessed 1 May 2014).

49 It is worth noting that numerous States, most of which are NATO members, including the UK, Australia, Belgium, Canada, Germany, Italy, Netherlands, New Zealand, Spain and France, made the relevant statements in respect of Art 51 and/or Art 57 API (e.g., the British statement at CDDH/SR.41, VI, para 120). Since the phrase these States are seeking to clarify is also used in Art 52.2, it would be reasonable for them to take the same approach to the term military advantage in the definition of military objective. Bothe *et al.*, op. cit. n 27, at 325; UK Manual, op. cit. n 31, para 5.4.4 point 'j'.

50 Oeter, op. cit. n 36, at 186.

51 Art 49 paras 1 and 2 API.

52 ICRC Commentary, op. cit. n 28, paras 1879–1880; Bothe *et al.*, op. cit. n 27, at 289 para 2.2.2; W. Hays Parks, 'Air War and the Law of War', 32 *Air Force Law Review* 1990, 1–225 at 114–15; E. Rauch 'Conduct of Combat and Risks Run by the Civilian Population', 21 *Revue de droit pénal militaire et de droit de la guerre* 1982, 66–72 at 66; A.P.V. Rogers, 'Armed Forces and Development of the Law of War', *21 Revue de droit pénal militaire et de droit de la guerre* 1982, 293–317 at 207; and G.S. Prugh 'Armed Forces and Development of the Law of War', 21 *Revue de droit pénal militaire et de droit de la guerre* 1982, 281–4 at 281.

Definite military advantage 121

The term 'attack' was interpreted as representing a substantially narrower notion than that of 'military operation'.[53] Some sources described the term 'attack' as 'acts of violence committed against the adversary by means of arms, in the course of hostilities, whether for purposes of offence or of defence',[54] and others as a 'combat action',[55] a violent military operation of a specific unit against an adversary's unit.[56] Attacks were thought to involve coordinated acts of violence 'by a specific military formation engaged in a specific military operation',[57] or acts 'involving the use of armed forces including means of warfare', namely weapons.[58] Depending on the circumstances, an attack could encompass only the particular acts of individual combatants contributing to such operations.[59] Commentators associate attack with acts such as the capture of a piece of land, deceiving an enemy, preventing countermeasures, or diverting attention from friendly forces engaged in combat.[60]

International criminal courts use the term 'attack' to define military actions specific in time and place.[61] Such actions include, for example, a set of strikes against targets in one location, like a village or town, or on one particular day, or a combination thereof.[62] Specific 'incidents' of sniping, artillery fire and mortar attacks against urban and rural areas of Sarajevo were all representative of the attacks that formed a general, coordinated and prolonged campaign by the Bosnian Serb Army.[63] The comprehensive and sustained shelling of

---

53 Committee III, Summary Record of the Sixth Meeting, Second session, CDDH/III/SR.6, Vol. XIV, at 44, para 4; Proposal by Working Group, Committee III, Second session, CDDH/III/54 of 19 March 1974; Statement from Swedish representative, Committee III, Second session, Fourth Meeting, CDDH/III/SR.4 of 13 March 1974, at para 37; Bothe *et al.*, op. cit. n 27, at 289 paras 2.2.2 and 2.3 and 366 para 2.8.1.2; and Oeter, op. cit. n 36, at 175.

54 Committee III, Summary Record of the Sixth Meeting, Second session, CDDH/III/SR.6, Vol. XV, at 44 para 4.

55 ICRC Commentary, op. cit. n 28, para 1880.

56 See Oeter, op. cit. n 36, at 176, 186; C.-I. Skarsted, 'Armed Forces and Development of the Law of War', 21 *Revue de droit pénal militaire et de droit de la guerre* 1982, 230–31 at 230.

57 Bothe *et al.*, op. cit. n 27, at 288 para 2.2.

58 The UK Manual, op. cit. n 31, para 5.20.2.

59 Bothe *et al.*, op. cit. n 27, at 288 para 2.2; The UK Manual, op. cit. n 31, para 5.20.4; Oeter, op. cit. n 36, at 186; A.P.V. Rogers, 'Conduct of Combat and Risks Run by the Civilian Population', General Report, 21 *Revue de droit pénal militaire et de droit de la guerre* 1982, 293–317 at 302–3.

60 The UK Manual, op. cit. n 31, para 5.20.2; Rauch, op. cit. n 52, at 66.

61 *The Prosecutor v S. Galic,* Judgment and Opinion of 5 December 2003, Trial Chamber, ICTY No. IT-98-29-T, para 52.

62 Note that the Trial Chamber of the Special Court for Sierra Leone adopted 'attack' as denominating a 'campaign, operations or course of conduct', but applied it to a particular event, again specific in time and place. *The Prosecutor v Fonfana and Kondewa*, The Judgement of 2nd August 2007, Trial Chamber, Special Court for Sierra Leone, Case no. SCSL-04-14-J, para 111 *et seq.* and in *The Prosecutor v Fonfana and Kondewa,* Judgement of 28 May 2008, Appeals Chamber, Special Court for Sierra Leone, Case no. SCSL-04-14-A, paras 303–4 *et seq.*

63 *The Prosecutor v S. Galic*, op. cit. n 61, paras 27 *et seq.*

122   *Military objective: concept and definition*

Dubrovnik on 6 December 1991 was regarded as an attack, and as part of more protracted 'combat operations' in the Dubrovnik municipality.[64] The 1993 attack on Vitez was not only geographically and temporally specific, but was also divided into separate phases (artillery and infantry attacks) constituting one assault.[65]

The majority of commentators seem to view 'attack' as a more complex action than an isolated incident, even though some indicate that the latter should not be excluded from the analysis.[66] An assessment, therefore, of military advantage from an attack 'as a whole' is more likely to require a consideration of a series of incidents or engagements, rather than of each in its own right.[67] This would mean the assessment could encompass several individual incidents against specific targets, together constituting a single, coherent, military operation. This would correspond to the scope of the notion of 'attack' at the operational level of warfare.[68]

Experts caution against an expansive interpretation of military advantage.[69] Dinstein advises that 'attack as a whole' should not be confused with 'entire war'; it must be seen as a 'finite event'.[70] This position has been supported by other commentators.[71] A more recent source, the commentary to the Manual

---

64 *The Prosecutor v P. Strugar*, Judgment of 31 January 2005, Trial Chamber, ICTY No. IT-01-42-T.

65 *The Prosecutor v Kordic and Cerkez*, Judgment of 3 March 2000, Trial Chamber, ICTY No. IT-95-14-T, paras 497–510. The Appeals Chamber in the same case further recognised a number of actions in various villages and towns in central Bosnia and Herzegovina as attacks. *The Prosecutor v Kordic and Cerkez*, Judgment of 17 December 2004, Appeals Chamber, ICTY No. IT-95-14/2A.

66 Final Report to the Prosecutor by the Committee Established to Review the NATO Bombing Campaign Against the Federal Republic of Yugoslavia, 13 June 2000, 39(5) *International Legal Materials* 1257–83 at 1257, para 78 [hereinafter: ICTY Report].

67 The UK Manual, op. cit. n 31, para 5.20.4.

68 Military doctrine organises military activity into three levels: strategic, operational and tactical. The strategic level of warfare is the level at which national resources are applied to achieve the government's (national) policy goals, which usually requires a combination of military force (military component of strategy), diplomacy and economic measures. The operational level of warfare is the level at which campaigns or major operations are planned, conducted and sustained to accomplish strategic objectives. The tactical level of warfare is the level at which formations, units and individuals ultimately confront an opponent or situation on the ground at the level of the battlefield. *Campaigning*, UK Ministry of Defence, Joint Doctrine Publication JDP 01, 2nd edn, December 2008, at 2–1 and 2–2, and in *British Airpower Doctrine AP 3000*, 3rd edn, UK Ministry of Defence, 1999, at 1.1.2. See also the discussion of military doctrine in 8.2 and 8.3.

69 At the strategic level, such a consideration would have to take into account an entire military campaign encompassing diverse military operations and tactical attacks conducted in the pursuance of strategic military goals, or even armed conflict *in toto*.

70 Dinstein, op. cit. n 44, at 95. This would also question the view expressed in EECC Award, see op. cit. ns 40 *et seq.*

71 F.J. Hampson, 'Means and Methods of Warfare in the Conflict in the Gulf' in P. Rowe (ed.), *The Gulf War 1990–1991 in International and English Law*, Routledge, London 1993, at 94. In respect of proportionality, see Olasolo, op. cit. n 24, at 155–88; Solis, op. cit. n 45, at 522.

on International Law Applicable to Air and Missile Warfare, also cautions against an overly broad interpretation of the term. It suggests that only the impact on the operational and tactical military capacity of the enemy should be considered.[72]

On the other hand, in the commentary to the handbook for German military forces, Oeter objects to advantage being considered in the context of one specific military operation, let alone attack.[73] He views 'attack' as a separate action within an operation. He advocates that definite military advantage has to be understood in the context of modern military operations, which means that advantage has to be evaluated in the context of the overall goal of military operations – a whole campaign.[74] It is not possible to conclude whether Oeter intended to say that the strategic advantage related to a whole conflict would be relevant in this context.[75] He undoubtedly stressed that restricting the interpretation to tactical gains flowing from single engagements would be misleading, as one should also contemplate the operational advantage.[76]

Problems in interpretation may arise when the advantage is viewed 'as whole', and not in the context of the 'attack as a whole'. In other words, the requirement will be met when an expectation exists that the 'attack as whole' will make a definite contribution to the success of the operation. The term 'attack' involves 'acts' of violence, and may encompass several engagements. Sometimes, an attack on several targets may offer the same military advantage considered in the context of the attack as a whole.[77] Executing a number of actions against targets in one area, in order to deceive the adversary into believing that the main thrust of the attack would follow in the same location, is lawful.[78] Consider a diversionary attack, undertaken to permit an intended

---

72 Manual on International Law Applicable to Air and Missile Warfare, Program on Humanitarian Policy and Conflict Research, Harvard University, 15 May 2009, Commentary, at 93 [hereinafter: AMW Manual].

73 Oeter, op. cit. n 36, at 186 and 205.

74 Oeter said: '[t]he separate action within an operation, that could be described as a specific 'attack' is hardly ever an end in itself', and elsewhere in the same paragraph '"military advantage" . . . must result from a specific military operation which constitutes "the attack"'. Oeter, op. cit. n 36, at 186.

75 As alleged by Olasolo, op. cit. n 24, at 173, and it also has been a position taken by the Eritrea-Ethiopia Claims Commission, op. cit. ns 40 *et seq*. See also n 69 above and the accompanying text.

76 Oeter, op. cit. n 36, at 205, last sentence in para 456.2.

77 'If there are, for instance, two bridges across a strategically significant river, the destruction of one only may give no military advantage; only the destruction of both would achieve this objective.' In Rowe, op. cit. n 30, at 152; also in AMW Manual, op. cit. n 72, Commentary, at 45 and 93.

78 Bothe *et al.*, op. cit. n 27, at 325, para 2.4.4; Dinstein, op. cit. n 44, at 95; M.N. Schmitt, 'The Law of Targeting' in E. Wilmshurst and S. Breau (eds), *Perspectives on the ICRC Study on Customary International Humanitarian Law*, Cambridge University Press, Cambridge 2007, at 146.

124   *Military objective: concept and definition*

action to take place elsewhere. Viewing the attack as a whole, these two actions would be considered to be parts of the same attack. In such a case, it is possible to claim a military advantage results from the diversionary action.[79] During the 1990–1 Gulf War, US Marines engaged in decoy actions from the sea. These were aimed at making the Iraqi defence units believe the Coalition was going to launch an amphibious assault in the direction of central Kuwait.[80] The definite military advantage offered by the attacks on Iraqi defences, forming part of these operations, would have been regarded in the context of the whole ground operation aimed at liberating Kuwait.

5.3 Definite military advantage

The adjective 'definite' relates to the quality of military advantage. It specifies that military advantage must be clearly defined, not vague or general.

The insertion of this, or a similar, modifying adjective, was extensively debated during the 1974–7 negotiations on the Additional Protocols. Numerous other adjectives were proposed, such as 'substantial' and 'direct', which were used in the original ICRC proposal,[81] and 'clear', 'immediate', 'obvious' or 'specific'. Most of these essentially attempted to set a requirement to prevent situations where the attack against the object would bring no military advantage, or an unspecified one. All these adjectives, with the exception of 'substantial', refer to the quality of the advantage. Substantial refers to its quantity. 'Distinct' was thought to hold substantively the same meaning as the current adjective, 'definite'.[82] One should appreciate a subtle difference between the two words. 'Definite' implies something capable of being clearly determined and precise, rather than something certain or guaranteed, while 'distinct' denotes something distinguishable and not identical. In this sense, the term is closer to 'concrete', which is used in relation to military advantage elsewhere in API. Even though the reasons behind the final choice of wording remain unclear, it is worth noting that the precise wording was discussed

---

79 An old example of such a situation, to which current law cannot be applied, is the Allied attack on the bridges, airfields, fuel dumps and railroads in the Pas de Calais during the Second World War to divert German attention from the beaches of Normandy, where the actual offensive was planned (Bothe *et al.*, op. cit. n 27, at 325, para 2.4.4). Meyer stressed that these attacks brought little immediate military advantage at the tactical level, yet strategically they were crucial for the success of the Normandy operation (J.M. Meyer, 'Tearing Down the Facade: A Critical Look at the Current Law on Targeting the Will of the Enemy and Air Force Doctrine' 51 *Air Force Law Review* 2001, 143–82 at 169–70).

80 J. R. Pope, 'U.S. Marines in Operation Desert Storm' in C.D. Melson, E.A. Englander and D.A. Dawson, *U.S. Marines in the Persian Gulf, 1990–91: Anthology and Annotated Bibliography*, US Marines Corps Headquarters, Washington, DC 1992, at 79–80.

81 Art 47, Draft Additional Protocol, CDDH/1.

82 F. Kalshoven, 'Reaffirmation and Development of International Humanitarian Law Applicable in Armed Conflicts: The Diplomatic Conference, Geneva, 1974–7', 9 *Netherlands Yearbook of International Law* 1978, 107–71 at 111.

Definite military advantage 125

intensively during the treaty negotiations.[83] Ultimately, whichever words were to be used, they all conveyed the underlying idea that 'a concrete and perceptible military advantage rather than a hypothetical and speculative one' was required.[84] There is no question, though, that an essentially indeterminate or generalised military advantage that is not identifiable would not comply with the test.[85]

A similar 'military advantage' phrase is found in API, but with the addition of two words. In the definition of proportionality in Arts 51 and 57, the harm to civilians and civilian objects must not be excessive in relation to the 'concrete and direct' military advantage anticipated.[86] Clearly, having used the phrase in Arts 51 and 57, the drafters in the same working group could have used it in Art 52.2.[87] The fact they did not use it in the definition is, presumably, significant, in that there is something added by the word 'direct' that was not included in 'definite'. Some commentators have indicated that, for reasons of expediency during hostilities, the phrases applied in the context of military objective and in proportionality could be considered quite similar in practice. There is no legal reason to support that assertion.[88]

A definite military advantage can be challenged on four main grounds. First, the advantage can be viewed as hypothetical and too abstract. The requirement of definite military advantage implies that it cannot be simply 'wishful thinking' on the part of the attacker. Similarly, the advantage may be seen as speculative. In both cases, the test will not be met. Speculation regarding the advantage may be connected to the issue of the credibility, volume and relevancy of the information on which the decision is made.[89]

Second, the advantage itself may be seen as not 'sufficient'. There is no minimum quantity of advantage required to satisfy the requirement. As the test is not related to the volume of the advantage, but to its quality, even a limited advantage could, arguably, suffice. However, the question can be asked, at what point can the quantity of the military advantage affect its quality. A separate question is raised when there is a range of types of advantage expected

---

83 The Rapporteur of Committee III noted that one was 'unable to draw any clear significance from this choice'. Report to Committee III on the work of the working group', CDDH/III/224, 24 February 1975, at 6.

84 Bothe *et al.*, op. cit. n 27, at 326, reproduced verbatim in The UK Manual, op. cit. n 31, para 5.4.4 point 'i'.

85 The UK Manual, op. cit. n 31, para 5.4.4 point 'j' and para 5.33.3. Boothby, op. cit. n 26, at 101.

86 This work does not deal with issues of proportionality. See 1.3.

87 It is worth noting that the original ICRC drafts of both regulations contained the same qualifying adjectives, which were changed during the negotiations.

88 Bothe *et al.*, op. cit. n 27, at 365, para 2.7.2; The UK Manual, op. cit. n 31, para 5.33.3; K. Watkin, 'Assessing Proportionality: Moral Complexity and Legal Rules', 8 *International Yearbook of International Humanitarian Law* 2005, 3–53 at 18.

89 See the further discussion in 6.2 and 10.4.

126 *Military objective: concept and definition*

from an attack on the target. Consequently, while anticipating some presumably definite military advantage from an attack, the attacker may also expect that political, psychological, economic and other advantages, while not military in character, may offer a substantial improvement to its chances of winning the war.[90] Does:

> the requirement of article 52(2) regarding a definite military advantage prohibit an attack where the principal purpose of the attack is psychological or political rather than military?[91]

Undoubtedly, if the sole purpose behind the attack on a specific object is to gain an advantage other than a military one, then the attack's lawfulness has to be questioned.[92] Even if the primary purpose behind the attack is, in reality, not purely military, the fact that definite military advantage can be clearly identified and expected is sufficient to pass the test of Art 52.2 API. Provided that a definite military advantage exists, the underlying motives of the attacks are irrelevant to the legal assessment of a possible military objective.[93]

A third challenge arises when the anticipated military advantage is so distant that it may not be determinable. This might be the case with objects perceived to satisfy the purpose criterion, defined as intended future use.[94]

Finally, the advantage may be viewed as so remote that it cannot plausibly be associated with definite military advantage. Indirect advantage might also depend on other conditions, which would introduce further uncertainty. An example relevant to both challenges may be found in the case of the Hirgigo power plant, discussed earlier. The 'end of war' induced by economic losses resulting from an attack on the plant would simply be so remote and uncertain that it could not be considered definite.

---

90 See also the discussion on the Hirgigo power plant, text attached to ns 40 *et seq.* above.

91 Hays Parks, op. cit. n 52, at 143.

92 Hays Parks argued that psychological advantage could be regarded as a military tool and used the pre-1977 example of the Doolittle raid on Tokyo in April 1942 as an illustration. The material damage caused was allegedly insignificant, but the attack brought about a significant boost to the morale of the American people. The attack's anticipated advantage was that if it were successful, it was supposed to remind the Japanese people of their vulnerability, and that the pride and short-sightedness of their leaders could cost them their lives. Hays Parks, op. cit. n 52, at 141–3. Best disagreed with this assessment, indicating that such an advantage alone would not suffice to comply with the current requirement. G. Best, *War and Law Since 1945*, Clarendon Press, Oxford 1994, at 275.

93 The prohibition that addresses the purpose of the attack is dealt with in another provision, namely Art 51.2 API, which stipulates that acts (or threats) of violence, i.e. attacks 'the primary purpose of which is to spread terror among the civilian population', are prohibited (Art 51.2 API). Acts of violence against the adversary, whether in offence or in defence, define the notion of 'attacks' (Art 49 API).

94 See the discussion regarding the purpose criterion in 3.4.

The definite military advantage considered in the context of an attack as a whole may sometimes not be obvious or realised immediately following the attack. There is no evidence that immediate military advantage is required for an object to qualify.[95] However, there is a requirement for it to be unambiguous.[96] The UK Manual of the Law of Armed Conflict stresses that a 'pious hope that it [military advantage] might improve the military situation in the long term' or remote future is clearly unacceptable.[97]

Finally, the second half of the definition requires that definite military advantage is 'anticipated'. It is possible that military advantage may not be clearly visible to others. In general, this does not matter, as API is directed at the armed forces. Provided the armed forces are satisfied that the requirement is fulfilled, the fact that the advantage is not visible to the world at large is irrelevant. It will, however, make it more difficult for potential victims to know what military advantage had been anticipated, and also for third parties trying to ensure that the parties to the conflict respect the rules. Potentially, this could be an enforcement problem, because parties outside the conflict may not see what the definite military advantage is, and therefore call into question its existence. Destroying a certain bridge may not readily show a military advantage, though that advantage may reveal itself afterwards. For instance, if the expected advantage is prevention of the retreat of the enemy, this may become apparent once the offensive has taken place.

5.4 Conclusion

The relationship between the elements in the definition is important to its effective application. There might have been a concern that if the two elements of the definition had been alternative requirements, the alleged vagueness of definite military advantage might have caused problems. However, given that the two halves of the definition are cumulative, this appears not to be a matter of concern.

95 The UK Manual, op. cit. n 31, para 5.4.4 point 'j'; W. Hays Parks, 'Asymmetries and the Identification of Legitimate Military Objectives' in W. Heintschel von Heinegg and V. Epping (eds), *International Humanitarian Law Facing New Challenges*, Springer, Berlin 2007, at 90.
96 The 1969 Edinburgh Institute of International Law definition contained the requirement of 'substantial, specific and immediate military advantage' and is discussed in 2.4. See also a discussion regarding the 'circumstances ruling at the time' part of the second element of the definition in 6.2. See 1969 Edinburgh Resolution: The Distinction between Military Objectives and Non-Military Objectives in General and Particularly the Problems Associated with Weapons of Mass Destruction, Institute of International Law, Edinburgh, 9 September 1969, in Schindler and Toman, op. cit. n 3, at 351–2.
97 The UK Manual, op. cit. n 31, para 5.4.4 point 'i'.

128 *Military objective: concept and definition*

As the determination of lawful targets turns on the existence of definite military advantage, the lack of it will mean that the object cannot be subjected to attack.[98] In a number of cases the problem will not result from legal considerations, but from a determination of the facts. This is clearly relevant to identifying the military nexus of objects such as TV and radio stations. This may also be a factor in establishing whether war crimes are being committed and, if so, of which type, as this is the basis on which States may take action against the places where unlawful activity is taking place. The basis on which States decide whether a target meets the test is not always clear. Even if some information is given, it is very difficult to evaluate an attacker's claim that the object does, in fact, satisfy the test.[99] As with the Hirgigo power plant, it was unclear not only why the target was attacked, but what was the intended target in the first place.

There is a claim that military advantage should be anticipated from the attack as a whole, and not from isolated or specific parts of it. This, however, does not suggest that an attack can be interpreted broadly. Specifically, it is questionable if an attack on one object can affect the entire war and, if so, whether it could be accepted as satisfying the definition. Even if shortening the war could be seen as a valid military advantage, the object that is being attacked to achieve that goal needs to fulfil the requirement of effective contribution to military action in order to become a military objective. In most cases this will exclude the objects relevant in this context, such as those associated with civilian morale, from satisfying the test. It is unclear, prior to the discussion in the next chapter, whether the second key element of the definition would ever prevent an attack on a target that satisfies the first element of the test.

A *definite military advantage* achieved through the *destruction, capture or neutralization* of objects must also exist in the *circumstances ruling at the time*. The understanding of these components of the second element of the definition will be analysed in the next chapter, which will conclude with a discussion of all the elements of the definition.

---

98 Meyer, op. cit. n 79, at 181; M.N. Schmitt, 'Targeting and International Humanitarian Law in Afghanistan' in M.N. Schmitt (ed.), *The War in Afghanistan: A Legal Analysis*, Vol. 85, US Naval War College International Law Studies, Newport, RI 2009, at 323; W.J. Fenrick 'Targeting and Proportionality during the NATO Bombing Campaign against Yugoslavia' 12(3) *European Journal of International Law* 2001, 489–502 at 498.

99 See 10.3 and 10.4.

6 Methods of achieving military advantage

The definition of military objectives indicates that the definite military advantage may be achieved through three methods: *destruction*, *capture* or *neutralization*. The meaning of each of these technical terms will be discussed in a separate subsection in the first section of this chapter.

The second section will analyse the final component attached to the second element of the definition, namely *circumstances ruling at the time*. This requirement is very important, as it ensures that the second element of the definition has to be satisfied at the particular point of time.[1]

6.1 Methods of achieving military advantage

Definite military advantage may be achieved through *destruction*, *capture* or *neutralization*. These three methods are aimed at preventing the object being used by the other party to contribute effectively to military action. Stopping such a contribution through *destruction* means nobody can use such an object following the attack. By *capture* and *neutralization*, the objects are simply denied to the adversary – but not necessarily used by the party gaining the advantage. It remains unclear whether the methods mentioned in the definition are the only ones through which definite military advantage might be achieved.

The definition serves as a reminder to the attacker that destruction is not the only option in attack. Does the definition indicate any preference with regard to the choice of method? In other words, if you could capture or neutralise as oppose to destroy, are you required to do so? The definition does not appear to contain a specific implication that one should try a 'less' destructive method first.[2] It is possible that even the partial destruction of a military objective, rather than its capture, might appear more advantageous to the decision-maker, who will exercise discretion in choosing the appropriate

---

1 This will not be relevant to objects which effectively contribute to military action based on the nature criterion. See the discussion about such objects in 3.1.
2 The issue of how the attack should be undertaken is beyond the scope of this work. See 1.3.

130 *Military objective: concept and definition*

way of achieving the anticipated military advantage. The choice of method will depend on the characteristics of the object, the goals of military operations and the circumstances.

6.1.1 Destruction[3]

Destruction means, in essence, the carrying out of an act that renders an object no longer usable, or unable to perform its function. The important effect of destruction is that the destroyed object is rendered unusable to both sides – the side to which the object belongs, and the side that initiates the attack.[4] Acts of destruction do not involve seizing control of the object.

Destruction means the total and permanent annihilation of the target, through which the object is demolished or damaged to such an extent that neither can it function as intended, nor can its previous functionality be restored by repairs. This will mean different effects for different objects, from physical annihilation to the impairment of critical functionality. Consequently, if one is entitled to 'destroy', one is not required to justify 'damage'. Both are equally acceptable in the context of the definition.

The question of destruction is sometimes raised in the context of the principle of military necessity. It arises from Art 23(g) of the Hague Regulations, which stipulates that the destruction or seizure of enemy property is prohibited unless 'imperatively demanded by the necessities of war'.[5] This was reiterated in one of the post-Second World War war crimes trials in the context of belligerent occupation. The international court asserted that:

> [d]estruction as an end in itself is a violation of international law. There must be some reasonable connection between the destruction of property and the overcoming of the enemy forces.[6]

---

3 A distinction has to be made between the nature of destruction resulting from combat actions on the one hand, and destruction imposed in the period after active hostilities on the other. The discussion in this chapter does not address the latter. See 1.3.

4 It is possible that the party initiating the attack and the party to whom the object belongs are the same. See the relevant discussion in 4.2 and 5.2.

5 Art 23(g) of Convention No. II respecting the Laws and Customs of War on Land and its Annex: Regulations Concerning the Laws and Customs of War on Land, The Hague, 29 July 1899 [hereinafter: Hague Regulations II], and in Convention (IV) Respecting the Laws and Customs of War on Land and its Annex: Regulations Concerning the Laws and Customs of War on Land, The Hague, 18 October 1907 [hereinafter: Hague Regulations IV]; both in D. Schindler and J. Toman (eds), *The Laws of Armed Conflict*, 4th edn, Martinus Nijhoff, Leiden 2004, at 55 *et seq.*

6 The international war crimes court explained that 'military necessity permits a belligerent, subject to the laws of war, to apply any amount and kind of force to compel the complete submission of the enemy with the least possible expenditure of time, life, and money'. *United States v W. List et al.* (Case no. 7), American Military Tribunal, *Trials of War Criminals before the Nuremberg Military Tribunals*, Vol. 11, Nuremberg 1950, at 1253–4, also mentioned in essence at 757, 1230 [hereinafter: The Hostage Case].

Methods of achieving military advantage 131

Some commentators infer that this means that destruction that is not needed to secure definite military advantage is unlawful.[7] In other words, they require that the destruction not only assists in the attainment of military goals, it has to be necessary to the attainment of such goals.

In The Hostage case, cited above, the international war crimes court explained that a 'reasonable connection' was necessary between destruction and the military aims of defeating the enemy. Objects such as railways, lines of communication, or any other property that might be utilised by the enemy, could be lawfully destroyed; even 'private homes and churches' (normally civilian objects) may be damaged if it is necessary for military operations.[8] The tribunal stressed that wanton destruction was not permitted.[9]

'Modern laws of war take full account of military necessity',[10] and so does the definition.[11] The requirement of definite military advantage expected from an attack, in the circumstances ruling at the time, establishes the implicit 'reasonable connection' between destruction and what the armed forces are trying to achieve.[12] Only the destruction of an object that offers definite military advantage will be lawful; destruction that offers no such advantage will not be legally justified and, as such, will be wanton.[13]

6.1.2 Capture

The term *capture* was not originally included in the draft provision of the definition. It was proposed, together with the term *neutralization*, by the

---

7 A.P.V. Rogers, *Law on the Battlefield*, Melland Schill Studies in International Law, 3rd edn, Manchester University Press, Manchester 2012, at 10; M.N. Schmitt, 'War and the Environment: Fault Lines in the Prescriptive Landscape' in J.E. Austin and C.E. Bruch, *The Environmental Consequences of War*, Cambridge University Press, Cambridge 2000, at 101; see also *Prosecutor v Rajic*, Judgment of 8 May 2006, Trial Chamber, ICTY No. IT-95-12-T, para 159; G.D. Solis, *The Law of Armed Conflict: International Humanitarian Law in War*, Cambridge University Press, Cambridge 2010, at 265.

8 The Hostage Case, op. cit. n 6, at 1254.

9 Post-trial legislation explicitly prohibits wanton destruction. Art 147 of the Fourth Geneva Convention considers 'extensive destruction and appropriation of property not justified by military necessity and carried out unlawfully and wantonly' to be a grave breach.

10 The Manual of the Law of Armed Conflict, UK Ministry of Defence, JSP 383, Oxford University Press, Oxford 2004, at 23 para 2.3; see also at 21–2 para 2.2 after Amendment of September 2010. [hereinafter: The UK Manual].

11 This consideration does not refer to any other legal considerations, such as proportionality, that may be relevant in the context of military necessity (see 1.3).

12 Y. Dinstein, *The Conduct of Hostilities under the Law of International Armed Conflict*, 2nd edn, Cambridge University Press, Cambridge 2010, at 252; B.J. Bill, 'The Rendulic "Rule": Military Necessity, Commander's Knowledge, and Methods of Warfare', 12 *Yearbook of International Humanitarian Law* 2009, 119–55 at 132.

13 Dinstein, op. cit. n 12, at 6 and 252. Numerous ICTY cases contain the same conclusion. See for instance: *The Prosecutor v Kordic and Cerkez*, Judgment of 17 December 2004, Appeals Chamber, ICTY No. IT-95-14/2A; *The Prosecutor v S. Galic*, Judgment and Opinion of

132   *Military objective: concept and definition*

Netherlands delegation on 19 March 1974, and subsequently adopted.[14] This was presumably done in recognition that there are other ways of denying objects to the adversary without destroying them, and gaining the resulting definite military advantage.

Definite military advantage from capture is gained from acts of seizing and maintaining control or possession of objects, by which a threat associated with such objects is removed. Capture is aimed at denying the object's effective contribution to military action to the other side. It is up to the party that captured the object whether it can be made to contribute to that party's own action. Capture does not necessarily involve causing damage to seized structures, buildings or places. Its role appears to be most often referred to in the context of areas of land and buildings contributing to military action by virtue of their location, but it may equally apply to any other objects.[15] For instance, if a weapons dump were seized, the capturing party might decide to use it, or merely keep it in its control, in order to deny its use to the other side. In other words, it does not necessarily mean that the party controlling the object uses it, or is going to use it. Having control of it prevents the adversary using it.

The regulation of what may happen to captured objects – including military equipment and property acquired during hostilities, war booty and other property – will depend on whether such objects belong to the State or are privately owned.[16] All these issues are regulated by separate rules.[17]

---

5 December 2003, Trial Chamber, ICTY No. IT-98-29-T and *Prosecutor v P. Strugar*, Judgment of 31 January 2005, Trial Chamber, ICTY No. IT-01-42-T.

14 Dutch proposal, CDDHIIII/56 of 19 March 1974.

15 The analysis in this work is confined to objects on land. See also 1.3 and the discussion in 3.2.

16 All military equipment, buildings and assets found or captured on the 'battlefield', except for personal belongings and protective gear, can be seized and used without limitation by the adversary, but never for personal gain. This includes military medical transport, vehicles and supplies under the condition of guarantee of care of the wounded and sick (Arts 33, 35 First Geneva Convention). Only selected private military property can be captured in the same manner, namely weapons, ammunition, military equipment and documents; the rest is protected. 'Battlefield' here should be considered broadly, i.e. in the context of the theatre of operations, rather than a specific battle. Dinstein, op. cit. n 12, at 247; The UK Manual, op. cit. n 10, at 299–305; J.M. Henckaerts and L. Doswald-Beck (eds), *Customary International Humanitarian Law*, Cambridge University Press, 2005, Rules 49–51, Vol. I, at 73–182 with the accompanying evidence in Vol. II [hereinafter: CIHL].

17 Arts 53 and 56 Hague Regulations IV, op. cit. n 5, at 55 *et seq.*; Art 7 of Convention (IX) Concerning Bombardment by Naval Forces in Time of War, The Hague, 18 October 1907 and Art 4(3) of Convention for the Protection of Cultural Property in the Event of Armed Conflict, The Hague, 14 May 1954, both in Schindler and Toman, op. cit. n 3, respectively at 1079 *et seq.* and at 999 *et seq.*; Rule 52, CIHL, op. cit. n 16, Vol. I, at 182–5 with the accompanying evidence in Vol. II; The UK Manual, op. cit. n 10, at 88.

6.1.3 Neutralization

Neutralization, like *capture*, was introduced into the text of the definition only during the negotiations of API, and was eventually adopted.[18] *Neutralization* is broadly perceived as disabling objects so that they are incapable of functioning as intended – either by their removal or destruction. This is achieved by removing the threat of the object being used by the other side to contribute effectively to its military action. It does not necessarily involve seizing control of the object. Objects may be rendered ineffective or unusable either in the short term or long term.[19] Depending on the characteristics of the damaged object, and the technical and financial capabilities of those in charge of repairs, the object's original function may be restored relatively quickly. This may influence the decision about how the attack is undertaken, and which elements of the intended targets are affected.[20] For example, if the aim of an attack on electricity supply facilities is to deprive the enemy of such power in the area of operations, the attacker may decide to damage the power lines rather than the generating station, because widespread damage to numerous power lines would take more time to repair.[21]

A good example of denying things without destroying them is laying mines. This involves covering a piece of land within the area of active hostilities with land mines, in order to prevent enemy forces entering. Although it has been noted that the precise benefits resulting from mining may be difficult to formulate at the time the attack is planned, the neutralisation of a militarily significant area of land, in order to deny its use or access to it by the adversary, is viewed as a permissible method of achieving military advantage.[22] The key in an analysis of such attacks is the assessment of the expected definite military advantage, and not the benefits that eventually transpire.[23]

Outside the specific context of neutralising areas of land by mining them, *neutralization* applies equally to other objects. In the 2006 conflict in Lebanon, for example, the Israeli government justified its extensive attacks as they were aimed at rendering the runways of Beirut International Airport unusable.

---

18 M. Bothe, K. Partsch and W. Solf, *New Rules for Victims of Armed Conflicts: Commentary on the Two 1977 Protocols Additional to the Geneva Conventions of 1949*, Martinus Nijhoff, The Hague 1982, at 325 para 2.4.5.

19 D. Mandsager (ed.), *Rules of Engagement Handbook*, International Institute of Humanitarian Law, Sanremo November 2009, at 84.

20 The issues related to how the attack is undertaken are beyond the scope of this work. See 1.3.

21 F.J. Hampson, 'Means and Methods of Warfare in the Conflict in the Gulf' in P. Rowe (ed.), *The Gulf War 1990–1991 in International and English Law*, Routledge, London, 1993, at 97.

22 G. Würkner-Theis cited in Rogers, op. cit. n 7, at 107–8; Bothe *et al.*, op. cit. n 8, at 325; Y. Dinstein, 'Discussion', comments in A.E. Wall (ed.), *Legal and Ethical Lessons of NATO's Kosovo Campaign*, US Naval War College International Law Studies, Vol. 78, Newport, RI 2002, at 218.

23 See the further discussion in 6.2.

134 *Military objective: concept and definition*

Ministers claimed the destruction 'constituted the most appropriate method of preventing reinforcements and supplies of weaponry and military *matériel* reaching the terrorist organisations', as well as 'a response to reports that it is the intention of the terrorists to fly the kidnapped Israelis out of Lebanon'.[24]

Modern examples of the neutralisation of military objectives include affecting power lines and transformers with a special kind of dispersible munitions filled with graphite filament material. This was pioneered in the 1990–1 Gulf War, and used more systematically in Kosovo in 1999 and in Iraq in 2003.[25] The so-called 'soft bombs', or 'blackout bombs', showered the electricity infrastructure with a very fine dust layer of chemically treated carbon fibre filament. This caused short-circuits, which resulted in an initial disruption of electricity supplies to vast areas. The operational aim was to disable the distribution of power in order to deny it to the enemy for a limited period, without causing long-term damage to the power-generating capability, and therefore generally reducing the risk of extensive collateral damage.

There are two operational downsides to neutralisation by graphite bombs. First, they are effective only on power lines that are not insulated. Second, the effects are easily removable, so the recovery time could be shorter than in the case of damage to other parts of the electrical infrastructure. Also, the actual result may not always be as expected. In Iraq, the instant short-circuiting of the *matériel* ignited the affected lines and structures, resulting in long-term – and often permanent – damage.[26] The initial effect was the same: frequent power outages. Recovery times ranged from a few days to a few weeks. Even where the damage was long-term, it was not as devastating as total destruction, where entire plants would have to be rebuilt.

It has been suggested that the *neutralization* of electrical infrastructure in such a way could be regarded as not meeting the requirement of definite military advantage from Art 52.2 of Additional Protocol I to the four 1949 Geneva Conventions (API), because the military advantage yielded appeared to be only temporary.[27] The temporary disruption of power supplies may seem insignificant, especially to the end-users who regain electricity in a short period of time. However, the effect might be very important to commanders in a conflict conducted entirely through air strikes, and in particular high-altitude

---

24 Israel Ministry of Foreign Affairs, *Responding to Hizbullah Attacks from Lebanon: Issues of Proportionality*, Legal Background, Jerusalem 25 July 2006, available at www.mfa.gov.il/mfa/aboutisrael/state/law/pages/responding%20to%20hizbullah%20attacks%20from%20lebanon-%20issues%20of%20proportionality%20july%202006.aspx (last accessed 1 May 2014) [hereinafter: IMFA Statement].

25 Human Rights Watch, *Off Target: The Conduct of the War and Civilian Casualties in Iraq*, December 2003, at 42–5.

26 Ibid, at 44.

27 J.M. Meyer, 'Tearing Down the Facade: A Critical Look at the Current Law on Targeting the Will of the Enemy and Air Force Doctrine' 51 *Air Force Law Review* 2001, 143–82 at 178–9. Protocol Additional to the Geneva Conventions of 12 August 1949, and Relating to the Protection of Victims of International Armed Conflicts (Protocol I), Geneva, 8 June 1977, reprinted in D. Schindler and J. Toman (eds), *The Laws of Armed Conflict*, 4th edn, Martinus Nijhoff, Leiden 2004, at 711 *et seq.* [hereinafter: API].

Methods of achieving military advantage 135

air attacks aimed at reducing risks to their own soldiers. Gaining even a few hours of safer air corridors might open windows of opportunity for conducting attacks, which might otherwise involve a high risk of casualties on one's own side.[28] It may also be useful for ground forces passing through an area.

Neutralization as a method of achieving definite military advantage is becoming increasingly relevant in the context of cyber warfare.[29] Modern society has seen a massive change in the way our lives depend on computers and computer networks, including the Internet.[30] It is feasible that attacks using computer networks could be undertaken to neutralise the functioning of the objects whose operations they manage. System resources, including computer hardware, operating systems and applications software, may be subject to physical or cyber attack, the effects of which range from minor disruption on individual computers, through disabling entire computer networks and preventing the affected organisation working, to disrupting major segments of the Internet.[31] There are no examples of cyber attacks conducted during international armed conflicts that can be attributed to a particular State, though attacks against governmental or military cyber targets have taken place in the past.[32]

28 A similar observation is noted by the author without further elaboration, even though, in the context of the nature of military operations in Kosovo, it should be seen as a valid argument. Meyer, op. cit. n 27, at 179 n 204.

29 M.N. Schmitt (ed.), *Tallinn Manual on The International Law Applicable to Cyber Warfare*, Cambridge University Press, Cambridge 2013, at 112.

30 Each and every computer, as well as the links between them, needs electricity in order to operate. Command, communications and control centres, as well as the data centres that contain computers used for military needs, could potentially be paralysed simply by denying them electricity. It is likely, though, that armed forces will have alternative power sources.

31 H.T. Tavani, *Ethics and Technology: Controversies, Questions, and Strategies for Ethical Computing*, 3rd edn, John Wiley & Sons, Hoboken 2009, at 178.

32 During the Israeli–Palestinian conflict some protracted cyber operations were initiated, which affected the Israeli government, the banking and finances sector and commercial targets on one hand, and Hamas and the Palestinian National Authority on the other hand (M. Zanini and S.J.A. Edwards, 'The Networking of Terror in the Information Age' in J. Arquilla and D. Ronfeldt (eds), *Networks and Netwars: The Future of Terror, Crime, and Militancy*, RAND, Santa Monica 2001, at 48–9; D.E. Denning, 'A View of Cyberterrorism Five Years Later' in K.E. Himma (ed.), *Internet Security: Hacking, Counterhacking and Society*, Jones and Barlett, Sudbury, MA 2007, at 129–30). During the 1999 Kosovo conflict activists sent email bombs against both the Yugoslav government and NATO sites, as well as allegedly deleting data on US Navy computers. Moreover, virus-spreading emails were unleashed against numerous Western economic and educational institutions causing damage to the affected computers (D.E. Denning, 'Activism, Hacktivism, and Cyberterrorism: The Internet as a Tool for Influencing Foreign Policy' in J. Arquilla and D. Ronfeldt (eds), *Networks and Netwars The Future of Terror, Crime, and Militancy*, RAND, Santa Monica 2001, at 269, 273–4, 280). Before and during the 2008 conflict in Georgia, sustained and repeated cyber operations ensued that caused significant economic damage to the Georgian financial sector as well as disruption to the functioning of Georgia's government, including early stages of coordination of defence against the 2008 Russian intervention. (Overview by The US Cyber Consequences Unit of the Cyber Campaign Against Georgia in August 2008, US-CCU Special Report, August 2009, at 5–6; Independent International Fact-Finding Mission on the Conflict in Georgia, Report of September 2009, at 217–18).

136 *Military objective: concept and definition*

6.2 Circumstances ruling at the time

The element of the definition of military objective that places it at the very centre of combat in time and space is the phrase *circumstances ruling at the time*. The definite military advantage resulting from destruction, capture or *neutralization* must exist in the circumstances ruling at the time. The phrase relates to the time and situation-specific factors that must be taken into account when ascertaining the lawfulness of the intended targets.[33] By including this condition in the text, the negotiators recognised the dynamic nature of military operations.[34] Each will be discussed in turn.

It has been observed that definite military advantage is 'intricately tied' to the effective contribution to military action of the enemy.[35] Other commentators have added that both elements of the definition must be fulfilled in the circumstances ruling at the time.[36] The contextual setting of the definite military advantage in circumstances ruling at the time, combined with the connective 'and' between the two elements of the definition, in effect compels States also to apply the first element the definition.[37] As both parts of the definition must be satisfied simultaneously, it is reasonable to conclude that, although primarily set in relation to the second element of the test, this requirement is likely to have an impact on the assessment of the existence of its first element.

The determination of military advantage in the circumstances ruling at the time is not only relevant to objects that are considered to contribute effectively to military action through military use, but also by location or purpose.[38] The assessment of objects that contribute to military action by nature results in

---

33 Dinstein, op. cit. n 12, at 93–4; S. Oeter, 'Methods and Means of Combat' in D. Fleck (ed.), *The Handbook of Humanitarian Law in Armed Conflicts*, 2nd edn, Oxford University Press, Oxford 2008, at 180.

34 Meeting of Committee III, CDDH/III/SR.14, 6 Feb1975, Vol. XIV, paras 8 and 17.

35 Manual on International Law Applicable to Air and Missile Warfare, Program on Humanitarian Policy and Conflict Research, Harvard University, 15 May 2009, Commentary, at 45 [hereinafter: AMW Manual].

36 M. Sassoli, 'Targeting: The Scope and Utility of the Concept of "Military Objectives" for the Protection of Civilians in Contemporary Armed Conflicts' in D. Wippman and M. Evangelista (eds), *New Wars, New Laws? Applying the Laws of War in 21st Century Conflicts*, Transnational, Ardsley 2005, at *186*.

37 While there could be numerous objects that can satisfy only the second element of the definition, it would be very hard to find an example of an object that satisfies the first element but not the second. This means that application of the first element is unavoidable in any situation.

38 It is worth noting that in the case of objects satisfying the nature criterion, such satisfaction will not depend on the context. The requirements will always be satisfied in all circumstances, except when the nature of the object is suspended. See the discussion in 3.1. W. Hays Parks, 'Asymmetries and the Identification of Legitimate Military Objectives' in W. Heintschel von Heinegg and V. Epping (eds), *International Humanitarian Law Facing New Challenges*, Springer, Berlin 2007, at 90; H. DeSaussure, Commentator, The American Red Cross-Washington College of Law Conference: International Humanitarian Law, 11–12 March, 1982 proceedings, 31 *American University Law Review* 1981–2, at 885.

Methods of achieving military advantage 137

definite military advantage, irrespective of the situation.[39] Some experts claim that attacking objectives of a military nature – when the purpose of the attack is to affect civilian morale rather than to damage the military capability of the adversary – would be unlawful, because it would not be militarily advantageous in the circumstances ruling at the time.[40] One example given in this context involves the MiG fighter jets parked near the temple of Ur in Iraq, which, because of their location and inoperability, presented no military advantage.[41] In such circumstances, where the mere location of the object and a lack of access to it by the Iraqis or the Coalition made the object effectively unusable, the expected military advantage resulting from its destruction might not have been definite.[42] This is also supported in military thinking:

> In theory, even if the object is clearly military in nature, such as a tank, . . . [i]t cannot be a valid military objective. In reality, such a target would be extremely low on the target list anyway as it would not be considered an effective use of limited resources.[43]

6.2.1 Knowledge and information available at the time of attack

The contextual setting of the anticipated military advantage entails a consideration of a variety of information about the military situation. Such information has two features. First, the assessment must be carried out on the information available at the time to the side initiating the attack, and not afterwards. Second, the information must be timely and reliable. Both features will be discussed in more detail.

Even though the wording of the definition is clear, a number of States emphasised that any considerations relating to the planning of attacks – which include an assessment of the status of objects as potential military objectives – should be based on information from all sources available at the time of the attack.[44] This reflects the so-called *Rendulic* rule. According to this rule, the

---

39 See the discussion in 3.1.
40 DeSaussure, op. cit. n 38; Sassoli, op. cit. n 36, at 186; M.W. Lewis, 'The Law of Aerial Bombardment in the 1991 Gulf War', 97(3) *American Journal of International Law* 2003, 481–509 at 487–8.
41 Lewis, op. cit. n 40, at 487–8.
42 See 3.1.
43 US *Law of War Handbook*, JA 423, International and Operational Law Department, The Judge Advocate General's Legal Center and School, 2004 and 2005 edns, at 169.
44 Declarations upon ratification to this effect were made by Austria, Canada, Belgium, Germany, Ireland, Italy, the United Kingdom (also in The UK Manual, op. cit. n 10, at 55, para 5.4.3; CCDH SR.41 para 121), Spain, Netherlands and New Zealand, in Schindler and Toman, op. cit. n 3, at 792 *et seq*. Israel upholds the same understanding in public statements, e.g. IMFA Statement, op. cit. n 24, para 102; the US statement to this effect can be found in *Operational Law Handbook*, JA 422, International and Operational Law Department, The Judge Advocate General's Legal Center and School, 2013 edn, at 12 [hereinafter: Operational Law Handbook].

138   *Military objective: concept and definition*

court must judge commanders' decisions only in the light of the knowledge and information available to them at the time.[45] The determination of definite military advantage cannot be made with hindsight, *ex post facto* and inferred from the result. The actual results of an attack are irrelevant to the prior assessment of the expected definite military advantage at the time when the attack is planned.[46]

The results of an action may not always match expectations. During the 1990–1 Gulf War, for example, the Iraqis' skill, determination and creativity in overcoming the destruction of their major bridges took the US military leaders by surprise. Witnessing the Iraqis' successful rerouting of traffic to bypass the disrupted lines of transportation, General Horner observed:

> Anybody that does a campaign against a transportation system had better beware! It looks deceivingly easy. It is a tough nut to crack. The Iraqis were very ingenious and industrious in repairing them or bypassing them . . . I have not seen so many pontoon bridges. When the canals near Basra were bombed, they just filled them in with dirt and drove across the dirt.[47]

As a result of these effective Iraqi measures, and the limited mobility of the 'essentially inert' Iraqi army, the attacks during the Coalition air campaign achieved only a reduction in supplies to the Kuwait theatre of operations (localised supply shortages), instead of a complete disruption of transportation lines.[48] It was the subsequent Coalition ground operation that put the Iraqi forces under increased pressure because of a lack of supplies.[49]

---

45 Lothar Rendulic was tried as a military commander at Nuremberg and found guilty of attacks on civilians in Yugoslavia. He was cleared of charges concerning the 'scorched earth' policy in Lapland because he believed his actions were a militarily necessary in the face of the advancing Russians, based on the information available to him at the time. The Hostage Case, op. cit. n 6, at 1253–4, also mentioned in essence at 757, 1230. See also the text accompanying n 6 above and in Bill, op. cit. n 12.

46 AMW Manual, op. cit. n 35, Commentary, at 44. Distinction should be made between the Art 52.2 API obligation to determine lawful targets and the obligation to verify that such targets are indeed military objectives enshrined in Art 57 API. The assessment in the context of Art 52.2 will normally be part of the planning process (see also 6.2.2), whereas Art 57 is more relevant to verification immediately prior to or during the attack. K. Watkin, 'Assessing Proportionality: Moral Complexity and Legal Rules', 8 *International Yearbook of International Humanitarian Law* 2005, 3–53 at 38; F. De Mulinen, Report on the Question 'What Is Military and What Is Civilian?', Meeting of the Committee for the Protection of Human Life in Armed Conflict, 39 *Revue de droit pénal militaire et de droit de la guerre* 2000, 401–5 at 402; W.H. Boothby, *The Law of Targeting*, Oxford University Press, Oxford 2012, at 418.

47 Cited in T.A. Keaney and E.A. Cohen, *Gulf War Air Power Survey Summary Report*, US Department of Air Force, US Government Printing Office 1993, Vol. I, at 95.

48 Lewis, op. cit. n 40, at 494.

49 Keaney and Cohen, op. cit. n 47, at 99.

Methods of achieving military advantage 139

In order to have a full picture of the military situation, one needs timely, credible and reliable information.[50] The ICRC Commentary specifies that '[t]hose ordering or executing the attack must have sufficient information available' in order to determine correctly the expected military gains.[51]

What, in practice, would this entail? What type of information is required? Would that be information gathered to confirm something specific, or any information? How much is enough? Certain practical impediments, for instance the availability of technology facilitating greater access to better quality intelligence, will invariably influence the substance, volume or reliability of the collected data. Does the satisfaction of the requirement depend on the means available? If so, is the test relative or absolute? In other words, is the requirement different for States with more sophisticated technology?

The better informed one is, the more prepared one is to make an informed decision. This means that gathering as much relevant and reliable information as reasonably possible would be preferable. This may involve questions of what the decision-makers knew, what they thought they knew and what they ought to have known.[52] Upon ratification of API, the UK made a general statement to API that asserted that:

> military commanders and others responsible for planning, deciding upon, or executing attacks necessarily have to reach decisions on the basis of their assessment of the information from all sources which is reasonably available to them at the relevant time.[53]

The information gathered before and during operations will consist of the general context of the planned operations, and specific information relevant to particular targets. So far as the general context of battle is concerned, this will include such considerations as the environment in which operations occur, the opponent, the political and economic state of affairs, and social, cultural and religious traditions.[54] It will also require an appraisal of the compatibility of the chosen targets with the overall aims of the military operations, which

---

50 Bothe *et al.*, op. cit. n 18, at 326 para 2.4.6; S. Haines, 'The United Kingdom and Legitimate Military Objectives: Current Practice . . . and Future Trends?' in W. Heintschel von Heinegg and V. Epping (eds), *International Humanitarian Law Facing New Challenges*, Springer, Berlin 2007, at 130.

51 Y. Sandoz, C. Swinarski and B. Zimmermann (eds), *Commentary on the Additional Protocols of 8 June 1977 to the Geneva Conventions of 12 August 1949*, ICRC, Geneva, and Martinus Nijhoff, The Hague 1987, para 2024 [hereinafter: ICRC Commentary].

52 See also 10.4.2.

53 UK statement of 28 January 1998 upon ratification of API.

54 For example, fire originating from a building may be perceived as fire against one's own forces, or may be a traditional sign of wedding celebrations. *British Defence Doctrine*, JDP 0-01, British Ministry of Defence, 2011, at 4-01 to 4-03, 5-06 and 5-09. See the discussion about military doctrine in Chapter 8.

140　*Military objective: concept and definition*

should be much more specific than the political or moral aims of the war.[55] This would then comprise the subjective intent, the declared purpose of the operation and the objective character of the entire mission, as mentioned above.[56] It should be noted that policy decisions may also affect the choice of objects, and their legal qualification, in a particular campaign.[57] The quality of the information collected is important, and not just its volume or relevancy.[58] Having updated maps or GPS information may reduce the risk of simple mistakes regarding location coordinates.

Specific information in respect of individual targets will be assessed during the targeting process.[59] It is important that information is credible and the sources are verified as much as possible. Timely and accurate information will further help avoid mistakes.

Different types of information will be required in respect of different objects. Information on the basis of which elements of definition are determined may differ in cases where change of use occurs in respect of objects used for civilian purposes, or where the objects serve both civilian and military purposes.[60] When the object is normally used for civilian purposes, the military use needs only to be established. When object is used for both purposes, it is unclear whether only military use needs to be established or only the end of civilian use. The air attack on the Al Firdus/Amariyah (Ameriyya) bunker in Baghdad on 13 February 1991 illustrates this issue. The object was originally built as a civilian and civil defence shelter. It was used as such during the Iran–Iraq conflict in the early 1980s. Subsequently, it was supposedly hardened and adjusted so it met military needs.[61] By the time the 1990–1 Gulf War had begun, it was considered a secondary command and control facility, which,

---

55　Fenrick limits such consideration to 'dual-use' objects, without giving any further explanation (W.J. Fenrick, 'Targeting and Proportionality during the NATO Bombing Campaign against Yugoslavia' 12(3) *European Journal of International Law* 2001, 489–502 at 494); Oeter, op. cit. n 33, at 180; M. Bothe, comment in 'Discussion' in A.E. Wall (ed.), *Legal and Ethical Lessons of NATO's Campaign*, US Naval War College International Law Studies, Vol. 78, Newport, RI 2002, at 217; a thought also promoted by Professor Hampson in Hampson, op. cit. n 21, at 100 and found in Final Report to the Prosecutor by the Committee Established to Review the NATO Bombing Campaign Against the Federal Republic of Yugoslavia, 13 June 2000, 39(5) *International Legal Materials* 1257–83 at 1257, para 37 [hereinafter: ICTY Report].

56　Bothe, op. cit. n 55.

57　Hays Parks, op. cit. n 38, at 99. See the discussion in especially part B of Chapter 8 and throughout Chapter 9.

58　G. Best, *War and Law since 1945*, Clarendon Press, Oxford 1994, at 273; Oeter, op. cit. n 33, at 180–1; ICRC Commentary, op. cit. n 51, para 1952.

59　See 8.5.1.

60　Solis, op. cit. n 7, at 257. See the discussion in the context of the use criterion in 3.3.

61　A.L. DeSaussure, 'The Role of Law of Armed Conflict During the Persian Gulf War: An Overview', 37 *The Air Force Law Review* 1994, 41–68 at 65.

Methods of achieving military advantage 141

according to intelligence, remained inactive during the initial phase of the war, and was kept off the targeting list altogether.[62]

In other words, it seems the bunker was considered to have the capacity to be used in the future. However, as the air campaign progressed, information regarding the structure indicated an increased military use of the facility.[63] The structure became camouflaged, cordoned off with barbed wire and secured by armed guards.[64] Reportedly, there was movement of military vehicles delivering communication equipment to the site.[65] The week before the attack, US intelligence intercepted the first communications originating from the shelter.[66] In such circumstances, the neutralization or destruction of the shelter began to offer a more significant military advantage, while the object was effectively contributing to the military action of the adversary. All the intelligence pointed towards the military status of the object, and the Coalition was correct in considering it to be a military objective. If other intelligence had also been sought or had come to light, it would have indicated that, apart from the shelter's military use, it still served its civilian role.[67] This would have been a key consideration for other obligations related to the attack, for example how and when to attack it.[68]

It is unclear how much information is required to make an informed determination, as well as whether the information sought can be selective. Put another way, is the party initiating the attacks required to look for any and all information about the object, or would it suffice to seek the information that would confirm or invalidate a particular piece of intelligence? The answer may depend on the characteristics of the object, the nature of the conflict and the time available to the attacker before the target is no longer within its reach.[69]

---

62 C.B. Shotwell, 'Economy and Humanity in the Use of Force: A Look at the Aerial Rules of Engagement in the 1991 Gulf War', 4 *United States Air Force Academy Journal of Legal Studies* 1993, 15–58 at 33; Lewis, op. cit. n 40, at 503. See also 9.1.1.

63 If, at the beginning of the conflict, the bunker had not had the capacity to be used as a command and control centre, then it might not even have been recognised as a military objective. For a discussion of the *purpose* criterion, see 3.4.

64 DeSaussure, op. cit. n 61; Shotwell, op. cit. n 62.

65 DeSaussure, op. cit. n 61.

66 Lewis, op. cit. n 40, at 503; DeSaussure, op. cit. n 61.

67 The US claimed it had no knowledge of civilian use. See 9.1.1. See also Middle East Watch (Human Rights Watch), *Needless Deaths in the Gulf War: Civilian Casualties During the Air Campaign and Violations of the Laws of War*, Human Rights Watch, New York 1991, Chapter 4, available at www.hrw.org/legacy/reports/1991/gulfwar/index.htm#TopOfPage (last accessed 1 May 2014) [hereinafter: Needless Deaths].

68 Hampson, op. cit. n 21, at 96; Needless Deaths, op. cit. n 67, Chapter 3.

69 See the further discussion regarding such targets in the subsequent subsection of this chapter, as well as in 8.5.1.

142 *Military objective: concept and definition*

The requirement has to be relative to one's means.[70] It would be hard to expect less technologically sophisticated States to attain the same standard as those that possess more advanced means. If means are available to permit the acquisition of information of better quality, or in less time, then not deploying them may seem negligent.

6.2.2 Changing or evolving circumstances

Circumstances can change rapidly on the battlefield during an armed conflict, and the definition of military objective permits an adjustment of the commander's reaction to a developing situation. The test highlights the inherent 'plasticity' of the definition, as it permits a competent decision-maker to adapt military operations, if necessary, and respond to unanticipated events.[71] It assists the verification of the continued validity of pre-planned targets. It also encourages the ongoing prioritising of military objectives, according to how hostilities are progressing. This is consistent with the military way of thinking and conducting military operations.[72]

Two types of situation may affect the application of the definition. When circumstances rapidly change, some objects may become military objectives, while others cease to be so. As circumstances evolve, the relative importance of objects may gradually increase or decrease.

Evolving circumstances entail situations in which objects originally identified as potential military objectives of low priority become more significant targets as the conflict progresses. What this means is that such objects appear to satisfy both the key elements of the definition. However, their effective contribution to military action, and/or the definite military advantage offered by their destruction, capture or neutralization, is not significant enough for the target to be engaged. As the military situation develops, such objects start to contribute more substantially to military action, and thus the potential military gains might also increase. The military objective becomes the targeting priority, even if it was not so at the start of the conflict.[73]

---

70 Schmitt, op. cit. n 29, at 117 para 9; *a contrario* to Oeter, op. cit. n 33, at 181, who appears to suggest an absolute requirement.

71 The UK Manual, op. cit. n 10, at 56 para 5.4.4(h) and almost verbatim in Operational Law Handbook, op. cit. n 44, at 23. In respect of the verification of targets, see The UK Manual, op. cit. n 10, paras 5.32.2–5.

72 See, for instance, Army Doctrine Primer, UK Army Publication, AC 71954, May 2011, at 5–4. See the further discussion regarding the military doctrine in Chapter 8.

73 The example of the Al Firdus/Amariyah (Ameriyya) bunker, mentioned earlier, is also a good illustration of an object's military advantage becoming more significant during the latter stages of a conflict. In the light of the circumstances ruling at the start of the war, if the bunker had been included in target lists *ab initio*, it would have been destroyed with limited, or no apparent, definite military advantage. A limited military advantage would have resulted only if, as alleged by the US, the target had, at the start of the conflict, been considered a military objective of low priority.

Methods of achieving military advantage 143

The second type of evolving circumstances involves the evolution of a conflict, which may influence whether a civilian object becomes a military objective. Consider a hypothetical example of bridges in a city.[74] Individual bridges may be military objectives depending on their location, the use that is made of them or their purpose.[75] In our hypothetical example, there are nine bridges in the city. The military forces of the adversary inform local residents that they are going to be using bridges 1, 2 and 3, but not the other six. Bridges 1, 2 and 3 can thus be considered military objectives, unlike bridges 4 to 9. Following the destruction of bridges 1, 2 and 3, the adversary announces he is going to need to use bridges 4 to 6, while bridges 7 to 9 remain exclusively for civilian use. Clearly, as circumstances evolve, bridges 1–6 become used for military purposes, as a result of which they are likely to become military objectives.

The anticipated military advantage resulting from the destruction, capture or neutralization of certain bridges may diminish or increase during the course of the conflict.[76] If the adversary stops using bridge 6, this bridge will not only offer no military advantage, but will also no longer contribute to the military action. In Professor Kalshoven's words, the circumstances ruling at the time requirement of the definition:

> effectively precludes military commanders from relying exclusively on abstract categorisations in determination of whether specific objects constitute military objectives ('a bridge is a military objective'; 'an object located in the zone of combat is a military objective', etc.). Instead, they will have to determine whether, say, the destruction of the particular bridge, which would have been militarily important yesterday, does, in the circumstances ruling today, still offer a 'definite military advantage': if not, the bridge no longer constitutes a military objective and, thus, may not be destroyed.[77]

6.2.3 The targets of opportunity

The definition of military objectives is applicable to two types of military processes, whose context appears dramatically different. Most of the thinking

---

74 There is no such category of 'bridges' *per se*, as there are no categories of any objects that can be military objectives. See the discussion in 2.5.5 and 3.1.

75 For example, during the 1990–1 Gulf War the bridges in northern Iraq, away from the main theatre of operations, were not attacked. This was because they were not used by the Iraqi military forces during this conflict.

76 Hampson, op. cit. n 21, at 94.

77 F. Kalshoven, 'Reaffirmation and Development of International Humanitarian Law Applicable in Armed Conflicts: The Diplomatic Conference, Geneva, 1974–7', 9 *Netherlands Yearbook of International Law* 1978, 107–71 at 111.

144 *Military objective: concept and definition*

about the definition occurred in the context of pre-planned operations, during which target lists are drawn up and validated with the luxury of time and a variety of potential means of verification.[78]

The other situation in which the test also has to be applied concerns particular fleeting targets, also known as targets of opportunity.[79] Targets of opportunity encompass, broadly speaking, two types of targets – unanticipated and unplanned ones. Unanticipated targets represent targets of opportunity *sensu stricto* as they comprise objects not known, or not expected to be present in the operational environment. Unplanned targets, although seen as targets of opportunity, include known objects from a list of targets, but which are not selected for engagement in the given time. In such cases, targeting decisions have to be made in a matter of seconds. There will be substantially less time, and much reduced opportunity, to gauge the context before deciding whether to engage such a target. The decision in these circumstances may be based entirely on what the attacking side thinks it has seen, or what it has been told that other people think they have seen. Would this be sufficient to be considered as the context in which one anticipates definite military advantage? Would the side initiating the attack be required to attempt to check any other information about such a target of opportunity, or perhaps just to confirm the information originally obtained?

The definition of military objectives does not contain answers to these specific questions; it requires only a consideration of definite military advantage in the circumstances ruling at the time, without specifying the substance of the standard. If the information is not checked at all, there is a risk of making more mistakes, and there is nothing in the definition of military objectives to mitigate that. It may well be that, in practice, such steps are undertaken as part of a subsequent targeting analysis that would include a consideration of the precautions to be taken in the attack. This would indicate that law may address the issue, but it does not address it in the definition of military objective.

6.3 Conclusion

This chapter concludes the discussion of all the elements and components of the definition of military objective. The definition adopted in 1977 comprises two pivotal elements connected by the conjunctive *and*, implying the simultaneous application of both elements. These two elements do not appear to have the same meaning.

---

78 See the relevant discussion in 1.5 and 8.5.1.
79 Ibid. See also *Joint Targeting*, Joint Publication JP 3-60, US Joint Chiefs of Staff, 31 January 2013, at x–xi.

Methods of achieving military advantage 145

The first element relates to the characteristics of the object that describe its contribution to military action. Three out of four of the criteria, namely *location*, *use* and *purpose*, are contextual, which means their satisfaction will depend on the circumstances. The fourth criterion, *nature*, refers to an inherent characteristic of the object that will always be the same. The *purpose* requirement's meaning relates both to its inherent design for future purposes, and to its 'intended future use'. This latter point gives it a substantively broader interpretation in comparison with its other meaning. All four criteria are firmly anchored in the requirement of *effective contribution to military action*. This element clearly requires the contribution to be connected to the conduct of military operations in a specific armed conflict.

The first element of the definition is connected to the second, *definite military advantage* offered by *destruction, capture or neutralization*, in a way that not only appears to require both elements at the same time, but also, and more importantly, guarantees that the first element will always have to be fulfilled. This is an important feature of this relationship, with far-reaching practical consequences. While there are objects that can easily satisfy the second element of the definition without satisfying the first, one would struggle to find an object that satisfies the first element but fails to fulfil the second. *Definite military advantage*, broadly interpreted, may also be seen as accruing from psychological or economic advantage if it leads to the achievement of a strategic military or political goal, including the ultimate aim of the 'end of war'. The potentially broad interpretation of the second element is guarded by the terms *circumstances ruling at the time*, which is a key factor in the contextual assessment of targets. It allows the continued adaptation of the legal analysis to the actual situation. The conjunctive *and* in the definition linking both halves matters not only because it requires simultaneous application of both requirements, but also because it ensures that the application of the first element is unavoidable.

One of the difficulties in ascertaining the practice of States after they have ratified the treaty is the fact that, when it comes to targeting an object, States rarely, if ever, disclose how they believe it satisfies the two main elements of the definition. They tend not to specify whether they determine an object's effective contribution to military action due to its *nature, location, purpose* or *use*, or what they anticipate to gain from its *destruction, capture* or *neutralization*. States also tend not to reveal the specific reasons or evidence on the basis of which they thought the objects satisfied the definition. By withholding more specific information, States open themselves up to questioning by third parties in relation to the lawfulness of targets. The crux of the problem rests on the fact that such objects cannot be considered in the abstract. The satisfaction of the test must be based on specific information regarding the object's function or use, and the expectations of the party initiating the attack. More detailed information is often unavailable in the public domain, even after the events have taken place.

146 *Military objective: concept and definition*

Finally, there are certain targets whose determination in accordance with the requirements of the definition is problematic. It is unclear whether the definition is at all applicable to some targets. If the law of armed conflict is to be applied, then there are inherent problems with the application of the test to such objects, even if the factual situation is fairly clear. These problematic targets will be subject to more detailed discussion in the following chapter.

7 Problematic cases

This chapter presents certain types of objects whose 'contribution', in the context of effective contribution to military action, or 'advantage' in the second element of the definition have been disputed. They are often objects whose nexus to military action has been challenged because of an apparent lack or remoteness of such a connection. This section deals with objects associated with political leadership, civilian morale, TV and radio broadcasting facilities and with commission of serious international crimes.

There are objects whose satisfaction of the test is arguable. It would seem that there could be instances in which objects related to the political leadership, or TV and radio broadcasting, could satisfy the second element of the definition. This does not imply that such objects become military objectives. For this to occur, as explained earlier in this study, both elements of the definition must be satisfied simultaneously. This will be illustrated first, by an analysis of the requirement in the context of objects related to political leadership and civilian morale, and then by a discussion of TV and radio broadcasting stations. Finally, some observations relating to objects involved in the commission of international crimes will be offered.

7.1 State and political leadership infrastructure

The assessment of objects associated with the direction and control by the political leadership of the conduct of war raises questions not just about the way they satisfy the criteria attached to the first element of the definition, but also whether the definite military advantage resulting from an attack on them may be determined.[1] The analysis in this section will begin with an examination of the potential effective contribution of these objects to military action. It will then continue with a discussion of the second key element of the definition.

First and foremost, it is unclear if, and to what extent, buildings, facilities or other physical objects linked to the political leadership are in fact targeted

---

1 See the relevant discussion in 3.1.3.

148 *Military objective: concept and definition*

for their own contribution. It is not always clear whether the building, or the person in it, was targeted.[2] Considerations relating to people as military objectives are, in principle, outside the scope of this work, but must be addressed where they relate to the determination of objects used or associated with the people being attacked.[3] In situations where people are the actual targets, the damage to the building will be collateral.[4]

Second, buildings, places and locations may be targeted on account of their association with the activity of the people in them. Such targets could be targeted because they are used for the exercise of functions that relate to the prosecution of armed conflict. Determination of the effective contribution of military action of such objects will not be possible without the identification of two key factors:

1 which functions of the people are relevant in this context, and
2 whether there is any time limitation that may affect when such objects can be considered military objectives.

The analysis in this section will focus primarily on the issue of the functions of people, which is relevant to both situations mentioned earlier. The time factor will depend on the nature of the situation, and will be specifically addressed when each situation is discussed.

Where infrastructure is targeted because of its use, this will normally be because of use by combatants, for example when combatants stay overnight at a hotel. Its contribution will be undisputed, as it is used for purposes closely related to military action. Whether it can be considered to satisfy the contribution will depend on the type of 'use'. This issue was addressed in Chapter 3.[5] The question arises whether the same assessment will also be relevant to people who do not wear uniforms and are not members of armed forces, but who are involved in taking decisions relating to the prosecution of armed conflict – such as a Minister of Defence. Can a hotel where the Minister of Defence stays be regarded as contributing to military action? The answer to this may depend on whether, and to what extent, the Minister's functions

---

2 In 2003 Coalition forces started their operations in Iraq with an attack on a farm where Saddam Hussein was believed to have been staying. It appears that, in this case, the Iraqi leader was the actual intended target. See further discussion in 8.1.4.
3 See also 1.3.
4 Issues related to how attacks are executed are beyond the scope of this work. Ibid.
5 Rogers considers all central and local government buildings, except for those that are 'military related', as civilian objects. (A.P.V. Rogers, *Law on the Battlefield*, Melland Schill Studies in International Law, 3rd edn, Manchester University Press, Manchester 2012, at 123). Dinstein asserts that civilian political leaders other than those 'associated with the armed forces' cannot be considered lawful targets (Y. Dinstein, *The Conduct of Hostilities under the Law of International Armed Conflict*, 2nd edn, Cambridge University Press, Cambridge 2010, at 108). See also 3.1.3.

Problematic cases 149

relating to military action are undertaken during his or her stay in the hotel. A Ministry of Defence, for example, is considered a lawful target on account of the command and control functions of the Ministry as an institution.[6] It could be targeted at any time as its contribution does not depend on whether individuals use the facility or are present at a given time.

The necessary connection of people's activity to military action means that only selected functions will be relevant in this context. These functions will be limited to the management, control or supervision of military operations undertaken as part of a specific military action. Any contribution also has to be effective, which means that the requirement will not be met in regard to buildings associated with people who may be nominated *de jure* to hold certain powers, but who *de facto* do not exercise their authority. In some cases their authority could be officially delegated, and in such cases that may become a relevant consideration in respect of the person to whom the functions have been delegated.[7]

The specific nexus to the prosecution of hostilities required by the first element of the definition means that not all objects connected to the political leadership would be able to satisfy the test. Some objects associated with the political leadership may be considered lawful targets in relation to the role that some individuals play in the decision-making process during war, in combination with their being used in connection with the conduct of a specific armed conflict. The functions here would include decisions relating to the deployment or redeployment of armed forces, or decisions regarding the granting or withholding of approval of attacks against specific targets. These may be viewed as effectively and directly linked to the prosecution of hostilities in an armed conflict.[8] It would not be too unreasonable to consider denying the adversary the use of venues that house military activity, thereby significantly disrupting the adversary's conduct of military operations. It is likely that this will encompass *de facto* executive control over the armed forces.[9] One of the positions often associated with this function is that of commander-in-chief, who is regarded as the supreme commander of a State's armed forces. This was discussed in more depth in Chapter 3 in the context of the nature criterion.[10]

---

6 This will very often be connected to the use of the buildings. See Dinstein, op. cit. n 5, at 108.
7 This could, possibly, also exclude people vested with the relevant functions only for ceremonial purposes where, in practice, someone else executes such functions. See the discussion regarding the commander-in-chief position in 3.1.3.
8 For a further discussion in relation to high-level decisions in targeting, see Chapters 8 and 9.
9 It is worth noting that control can be direct and indirect, such as the role of parliament in approving laws that affect the conduct of hostilities. It is not clear, but rather unlikely, that the latter may also be considered. During the Second World War, the Helsinki Parliament was attacked, but it remains unclear on what basis. See n 69 in Chapter 2.
10 See 3.1.3.

150 *Military objective: concept and definition*

When considering the infrastructure associated with the people in charge of these functions, any analysis becomes complicated in at least three aspects. First, the question may be asked as to whether such buildings can, in principle, be targeted at any time, or only when the people vested with the relevant functions are exercising them in such facilities. Second, if any such functions are exercised collectively, does that mean the only place that can be targeted is where all the people involved are engaged in such functions, such as places where the Cabinet meets, or meetings that involve control functions? Third, is the association between the people and objects involved limited to the places where the functions are discharged, or does it extend to places where they work, where they travel on official business, or even where they live during their tenure in office (official residences)?

It is not clear whether such people's private property can be targeted because of their functions. Dinstein argues that the White House would constitute a lawful target on account of the status of the US commander-in-chief.[11] If the functions of the commander-in-chief give rise to an assessment of objects linked to the person who holds this post, would it similarly have been justified to attack Slobodan Milosevic's private villa on account of his capacity as supreme commander? If that would be legitimate, would it be also legitimate to attack the villa in his absence? The Belgrade residence that he occupied *ex officio*, as well as his private villa in Dobanovci, were attacked during the 1999 NATO intervention in Kosovo, but the justification given was not related to him or his functions.[12] Similarly, during the 2011 NATO action in Libya, President Gaddafi's palace in Tripoli was struck. NATO argued that Gaddafi was not a target himself, and that the compound contained military communications infrastructure.[13] It is therefore unclear if, in the absence of any military use, such objects could be considered as contributing to military action merely because of their association with such leaders, whether in their capacity as commanders-in-chief, or otherwise.

Sometimes other governmental and legislative objects may become targets. It is unclear whether they may be regarded as effectively contributing to military action, and if so, on which basis. During the 2008–9 Israeli offensive in Gaza, the Palestinian Legislative Council building was attacked. The reasoning behind the strike was given as the strong association of the Palestinian governing authorities with the Hamas party. The authors of a

---

11 Dinstein also claims that the commander-in-chief, as such, will be targetable. This, however, makes it very difficult to distinguish whether the object or the person was the actual target of attack. Dinstein, op. cit. n 5, at 107.

12 In both cases NATO argued the buildings contained command and control infrastructure. B.S. Lambeth, *NATO's Air War for Kosovo: A Strategic and Operational Assessment*, RAND, Santa Monica 2001, at 36.

13 T. Shanker and D. Sanger, 'NATO Says It Is Stepping Up Attacks on Libya Targets', *The New York Times*, 26 April 2011.

Problematic cases   151

UN Report analysing this attack concluded that Gaza's 'governmental' infrastructure, barring 'war ministries' if they existed, could not be regarded as effectively contributing to military action.[14] One commentator implied that the Palestinian Ministry of Interior oversaw the Hamas-controlled governmental forces in Gaza, and that this relationship was relevant in considering attacks on Palestinian governmental buildings.[15] It is unclear on what basis such objects were considered to satisfy the test, unless there was evidence of military use.

A distinction needs to be made between State and executive functions, such as being in charge of the conduct of operations, and political functions related to being in charge of a political party that are not related to the conduct of operations. The building at 10 Downing Street in London is an official workplace of the British prime minister, the leader of the Cabinet who exercises control powers over the armed forces. It could be targeted on account of these specific functions of the prime minister. It would not be acceptable, though, to target the party headquarters on account of the prime minister being the leader of the ruling party. In other words, only the infrastructure related to the prime minister, in his or her capacity as executive in charge of the conduct of operations, can be relevant in this context.

A problem with the connection to political parties may arise in single-party political systems, or indeed in what is regarded as a dictatorship. In such cases, distinguishing between State and party-political functions might be difficult or even impossible. An example of such a close relationship may be seen in Iraq during Saddam Hussein's rule. The Ba'ath party was seen as a tool for exercising power over the civilian population, which in itself would not give rise to a connection to military action. Greenwood suggests that the party was integrated into governmental structures whose nature was military.[16] Even if he were correct, this would be relevant only to particular party members, and not to the party as a whole. It would still be problematic to see how an attack on the party headquarters, as opposed to government offices, would have been justified.

The assessment of objects associated with the political leadership depends on several factors that determine their contribution to military action, as well

---

14   UN Human Rights Council, Report of the United Nations Fact-Finding Mission on the Gaza Conflict, UN Doc. A/HRC/12/48, 25 September 2009, para 387.

15   L.R. Blank, 'The Application of IHL in the Goldstone Report: Critical Commentary', 12 *Yearbook of International Humanitarian Law* 2009, 347–402 at 359. This position, however, has been challenged for an absence of supporting evidence. Z. Yihdego, 'Gaza Mission: Implications for International Humanitarian Law and UN Fact-Finding', 13(1) *Melbourne Journal of International Law* 2012, 158–215 at 24.

16   C. Greenwood, 'Customary International Law and the First Geneva Protocol of 1977 in the Gulf Conflict' in P. Rowe (ed.), *The Gulf War 1990–1991 in International and English Law*, Routledge, London 1993, at 63; see also the discussion in 3.1.3.

152   *Military objective: concept and definition*

as the advantage resulting from their destruction, capture or neutralization.[17] In this context, it is first necessary to establish the target of an attack, that is whether the attack is directed at the people using the buildings, or at the buildings themselves.[18] If the latter is the case, one would have to distinguish between the places utilised by the national governmental authority involved in the direction and control of military operations, and other political institutions, for example those related to political parties.[19] It is conceivable that the destruction, capture or *neutralization* of facilities that house the organs that take decisions regarding the prosecution of military operations would offer a definite military advantage. There is little doubt that objects such as a Ministry of Defence would offer such an advantage. There is less certainty that this would also be the case in targeting a building occupied by the commander-in-chief who, in reality, has delegated supreme command authority to other State organs.[20] The destruction of the buildings where a *de jure* and *de facto* commander-in-chief is taking decisions may bring substantial political and military benefits. There may also be other civilians in the State political structure who exercise other functions that may impact on the conduct of military operations. It is unclear whether such people – and the buildings and places associated with the exercise of their functions – can be regarded as satisfying the definition.

The same cannot be said for buildings or places that appear to be linked to other political structures of the State, but that do not seem to exercise any functions relating to the conduct of hostilities. This could be a political party's facilities or local government buildings. Destroying the place where party members normally meet, or work, does not appear to involve any military advantage, though it may be viewed as attractive for political reasons. Unless there could be shown to be some other military nexus, then attacks on such facilities, on account of their association with the State political system, cannot offer military advantage. A distinction could be made in States in which the political system, especially a dictatorship, is based on a single party closely incorporated into governmental structures. Where such an association exists,

---

17 Note that such objects, like any other buildings, can also be used for military purposes, which would be subject to consideration in the context of the *use* criterion. See 3.3.

18 This is not altogether clear, as States tend not to share publicly any detailed explanations when they engage such targets. Recent indications that attacks could have been directed against people rather than facilities can most commonly be found in the context of counter-insurgency attacks in Afghanistan. In 2003 Coalition forces started their operations in Iraq with an attack aimed at Saddam Hussein, who was believed to have been visiting the al-Dora farm on the outskirts of Baghdad. This clearly indicated that the object of the attack was a human one. This is not to say that the facilities in the farm might have separately been of military significance. See the further discussion in 9.1.4.

19 See the discussion regarding the political leadership infrastructure in 3.1.3.

20 See the related discussion in 3.1.3.

Problematic cases 153

the distinction between the State and party functions will be hard to separate. It is not entirely clear, though it may have been possible, that definite military advantage could have been expected from the attack against the Ba'ath party headquarters in Iraq in 2003. To consider an attack against the Socialist Party headquarters in Belgrade in 1999 in the same way would be more difficult.

7.2 Civilian morale

Civilian morale is undoubtedly an important factor to consider in wartime.[21] Legitimate attacks against adversaries, with the aim of leaving a lasting psychological effect, have been conducted from the very outset of warfare.[22] They were deemed largely counter-productive, failing to achieve results other than causing extensive civilian casualties and the widespread destruction of centres of civilian population.[23] Direct attacks with the sole aim of affecting civilian morale are, however, uncommon. Even during the Second World War, attacks viewed as being directed against civilian morale generally also included military targets.[24] Hays Parks observes that, even from the military efficiency point of view, it would be hard to see morale as a primary objective of military actions.[25]

21 For example, in US Air Force Basic Doctrine: 'While physical factors are crucial in war, national will and leadership are also critical components of war.' US Air Force Basic Doctrine, Document 1, 17 November 2003, at 15; see also W.J. Fenrick, 'Targeting and Proportionality during the NATO Bombing Campaign against Yugoslavia' 12(3) *European Journal of International Law* 2001, 489–502 at 497.

22 One such example could be the Romans' siege of the rebellious town of Masada. The town was crushed by a whole Legion of Roman soldiers to demonstrate Rome's strength and ferocity, not only to the inhabitants of Masada, but also to any other tribes thinking of revolt in even the most remote locations of Empire. E.N. Luttwak, *The Grand Strategy of the Roman Empire from the First Century AD to the Third*, The Johns Hopkins University Press, Baltimore 1976, at 4.

23 For an extensive discussion of the origins, theory and practice of strategic bombardment until the 1990–1 Gulf War, see R.C. Hall (ed.), *Case Studies in Strategic Bombardment*, US Air Force History and Museums Program, Special Studies, Washington, DC 1998. See also W. Hays Parks, 'Asymmetries and the Identification of Legitimate Military Objectives' in W. Heintschel von Heinegg and V. Epping (eds), *International Humanitarian Law Facing New Challenges*, Springer, Berlin 2007, at 111; Dinstein op. cit. n 5, at 116.

24 It was often the way in which the attack was conducted that resulted in destruction and casualties that could have affected the civilian morale, with the possible exception of German Baedeker raids directed at British five cultural cities and some attacks against selected German cities such as Lübeck. British Broadcasting Corporation Online Archive, available at www.bbc.co.uk/history/ww2peopleswar/timeline/factfiles/nonflash/a1132921.shtml (last accessed 1 May 2014). See also 2.3 and 2.4.

25 W. Hays Parks, 'Air War and the Law of War', 32 *Air Force Law Review*, 1990, 1–225 at 22; similarly in Hays Parks, op. cit. n 23, at 99, 107 and 116; also reiterated in military doctrine: *British Defence Doctrine*, UK Ministry of Defence, Joint Warfare Publication JWP0-01, 3rd edn, August 2008, Annex 6 at B-06. See the further discussion of military doctrine in Chapter 8.

154   *Military objective: concept and definition*

Targeting civilian morale needs to be distinguished from planning and engaging in attacks against it. While civilian morale can be and often is a target during armed conflict, attacking civilian morale directly means using lethal force against civilians and civilian objects. This approach is contrary to the legal obligation to distinguish between military objectives and civilian objects enshrined in API.[26] Further concerns relate to an understanding of the first element of the definition of military objectives. The morale of civilians, and political leaders, cannot be considered as contributing to 'military action'.[27] If objects are planned for engagement merely because of the impact they have on civilian morale, then in the absence of any more concrete nexus to military operations, they would not satisfy the test. This, however, does not preclude attacks on objects that satisfy the test, but where the impact on civilian morale is a secondary result.[28]

Separate issues arise where the contribution to military action is not clear-cut. Is the consideration of the impact on civilian morale a factor that may influence whether the decision to attack an object is taken? In other words, may an effect on civilian morale be taken into account in the context of the first element of the definition for an object that could not otherwise satisfy the test? In principle, this may be a relevant factor, as long as it is not the sole factor. Even if it were argued that it was a relevant factor, it could not be accepted as satisfying the requirement of *effective* contribution to military action. One also cannot ignore the fact that the impact on civilian morale has not been proven in practice.[29] It is, therefore, questionable whether reliance on a factor that has never produced the anticipated results in practice can be acceptable in a legal consideration.

Attacks on civilian morale are aimed at inflicting hardship on the civilian population in order to reduce support for a political leadership determined to continue the war. Can attacks against such objects be reasonably expected

26 In principle, the use of force directed at civilians who are not actively participating in hostilities is strictly prohibited both in treaty and customary law. The prohibition covers any direct attacks on civilians and/or civilian objects, unless they lose their protection because of particular circumstances. The law forbids intentional attacks and threats of such attacks aimed at causing psychological harassment or terror among the civilian population. See, for example, Arts 48, 51–2 and 57 of API, most of which are regarded as customary rules; see J.M. Henckaerts and L. Doswald-Beck (eds), *Customary International Humanitarian Law*, Cambridge University Press, Cambridge 2005, Vol. I (Rules) with the supplementary evidence in Vol. II (Practice) [hereinafter: CIHL].

27 M. Bothe, 'Targeting' in A.E. Wall (ed.), *Legal and Ethical Lessons of NATO's Kosovo Campaign*, Vol. 78, US Naval War College International Law Studies, Newport, RI 2002, at 180; G.D. Solis, *The Law of Armed Conflict: International Humanitarian Law in War*, Cambridge University Press, Cambridge 2010, at 523.

28 Dinstein, op. cit. n 5, at 116 Fenrick, op. cit. n 21, at 498. See the discussion regarding dual-use objects in 3.3.

29 See, for instance, R.A. Pape, *Bombing to Win: Air Power and Coercion in War*, Cornell Studies in Security Affairs, Cornell University Press, Ithaca, NY 1996, at 208–9.

Problematic cases 155

to result in definite military advantage? If harming civilian morale is the sole reason behind an attack on an object, then such an attack cannot result in military advantage *per se*, let alone a definite advantage. The experience of previous conflicts has shown that attacks aimed at civilian morale do not achieve the desired effect.[30]

A separate question arises if the destruction, capture or neutralization of the object could be expected to harm civilian morale to the extent that it would diminish civilian support for the war and the fighting disposition of the adversary. If the military's will to fight and wage war could be expected to deteriorate to the extent that this may lead to stopping the war, would not this amount to military advantage? The effect on civilian morale can only be *civilian* but, in theory, it may have some secondary impact on the adversary's will to fight. However, in practice such an effect has not been established with certainty.[31] Even if such an advantage can be considered *military*, the problem will be with establishing that it is *definite*.[32] Even if it were argued that civilian morale meets the requirement of advantage, the problem will remain with it satisfying the first element of the definition.

7.3 TV and radio broadcasting facilities

Contribution to military action is often invoked in the context of attacks on objects such as TV and radio broadcasting facilities, and is frequently subject to dispute. The determination of such objects' nexus to military operations is essential for their approval as lawful targets, as is evidence of what is being transmitted.

TV and radio stations may be used for military purposes in two forms. The station building may be used to house military infrastructure, or the broadcasting infrastructure may be used for military communications.[33] The communications could be purely military, or may involve the transmission of coded

---

30 *A contrario* to Fenrick, op. cit. n 21, at 497–8. See 2.1, 2.3 and 2.4.
31 Pape, op. cit. n 29, at 208–9.
32 See earlier discussion in 4.2. This will also create problems in satisfying other requirements, such as the proportionality test of 'direct'. This discussion is, however, outside the scope of this work. See 1.3.
33 The co-location of the infrastructure would mean it is likely to be incorporated into the military command, control and communications (C3) network. Sometimes such infrastructure is merely viewed as 'potential back-up' for military communications facilities. This is offered as justification in the absence of any evidence of actual use, or intended future use. Without having any other information, being a 'potential back-up' for military operations would probably not suffice to satisfy the test of effective contribution. An example of this approach can be found in J. Holland, 'Military Objective and Collateral Damage: Their Relationship and Dynamics', 7 *Yearbook of International Humanitarian Law* 2004, 35–78 at 63, and in US Department of Defense, *Conduct of the Persian Gulf War: Final Report to Congress*, 10 April 1992, Department of Defense Washington, DC, 1992, 1–418 at 127, and Appendix O, at O1–O36 [hereinafter: DOD Report].

156   *Military objective: concept and definition*

military messages in addition to normal civilian broadcasts.[34] Either of these military uses could be considered to contribute to military action, depending on the relevant facts. Stations may also issue innocuous broadcasts, merely rallying general support for the government, even if the government is not recognised as legitimate by the other parties in the conflict.[35] They may also be alleged to be involved in the incitement of crimes. Some such facilities appear to be likely targets due to their association with an alleged terrorist organisation.

In the 1990–1 Gulf War civil TV and radio stations appeared to be of interest to the Coalition because it was thought they could be used as back-up telecommunications facilities for military forces. Additionally, as the US Department of Defense's post-1990–1 Gulf War report revealed, this was because of their role in disseminating the Iraqi regime's propaganda.[36] Again, during operations in Afghanistan in 2001, attacks against the Afghan television and radio stations were defended as legitimate because these objects were believed to function as 'propaganda vehicles for the Taliban leadership'.[37] The attitude of another broadcaster, Al-Jazeera, could have been seen as antagonistic because the station had aired Osama bin Laden's occasional video statements. It is possible that for this reason, and because of a general suspected link to the al Qaeda organisation, the Al-Jazeera facilities were also targeted in 2001.[38] Interestingly, there are reports that other news agencies' bureaux in Kabul, including those of The Associated Press and the BBC, were also damaged by US strikes. US forces offered various explanations for these attacks, claiming weapons failure and collateral damage resulting from targeting other buildings nearby. They denied, though, intentionally targeting Western media facilities.[39.]

---

34 See n 53 and the accompanying text in Chapter 3.

35 It is worth noting that API offers special protection to journalists, who are considered to be civilians when they exercise their journalistic function during armed conflicts (Art 79). In parallel, one may infer that the normal journalistic functions of TV and radio broadcasting stations should also be civilian, which would suggest that such objects cannot be regarded as contributing to military action by nature. See the discussion in 3.1.

36 'The Saddam Hussein regime also controlled TV and radio and used them as the principal media for Iraqi propaganda. Thus, these installations also were struck.' DOD Report, op. cit. n 33; see also the discussion in 10.1.1.

37 C. Ponti, 'Air Operations against Afghanistan (2001–2)' in N. Ronzitti and G. Venturini (eds), *Current Issues in the International Humanitarian Law of Air Warfare*, Eleven International Publishing, Utrecht, 2005, at 307; Amnesty International, *Afghanistan: Accountability for Civilian Deaths*, Index No. ASA 11/022/2001 of 25 October 2001; R. Cryer 'The Fine Art of Friendship: Jus in Bello in Afghanistan', 7(1) *Journal of Conflict and Security Law* 2002, 37–83 at 55–6. See also the discussion in 10.1.3.

38 Committee to Protect Journalists, *Attacks on the Press 2001: Afghanistan*, available at: http://cpj.org/2002/03/attacks-on-the-press-2001-afghanistan.php (last accessed 1 May 2014).

39 Ibid.

Problematic cases   157

During the 2003 conflict in Iraq, Coalition forces again struck Iraqi State Television facilities in Baghdad and in Basra (both studios and broadcasting sites).[40] According to non-governmental organisation (NGO) reports, the Abu Ghraib Television Antennae Broadcast building was also destroyed.[41] Some reports indicated that all these objects were apparently integrated into the Iraqi command and communication system,[42] yet later official explanations cast doubt on the facilities' contribution to Iraqi military operations.[43] Referring to a telephone interview with a senior US Central Command official, Human Rights Watch questioned the status of the media installations, which they thought offered no clear-cut 'direct assistance to the Iraqi armed forces'. The official who was interviewed implied two potential reasons for the attacks. First, he alluded to the US's wish – outlined in official statements – to stop the spread of propaganda. He then implied a potential use of the installations by the Iraqi military forces to direct their forces, which apparently never materialised.[44]

The Al-Manar Television facilities in Lebanon were strongly associated with the adversary, the Hezbollah organisation.[45] In 2006 Israeli forces argued that the organisation was behind the 'incitement of acts of terrorism' and used the facility as a communication and recruitment centre,[46] either of which claims, according to the Israeli armed forces, turned the object into a military objective.[47] Yet the Al-Manar TV facilities in Beirut were not the only media facilities struck during the Lebanon conflict. A number of others, allegedly not linked to Hezbollah stations, were also attacked. These included the State-affiliated Lebanese Broadcasting Corporation (LBCI), Future TV, Al Jadeed TV (previously known as New TV Transmission) and the communication facilities of Télé Lumière. The Télé Lumière targets alone were at six different

---

40 Dinstein, op. cit. n 5, at 98; Human Rights Watch, *Off Target: The Conduct of the War and Civilian Casualties in Iraq*, December 2003, at 46 [hereinafter: HRW]. See also the discussion in 10.1.4.

41 HRW, op. cit. n 40, at 48.

42 Rogers, op. cit. n 5, at 83.

43 Although Iraqi TV and other media facilities could have been used to carry military communications, the actual use could not have been ascertained from the sources reviewed. It remains unclear whether an unequivocal intention of such use existed, and was known to the Coalition prior to the attacks, or whether the Coalition actions were based on the more distant possibility of such use. HRW, op. cit. n 40, at 49.

44 Ibid, at 48–9.

45 A. Exum, 'Illegal Attack or Legitimate Target? Al Manar, International Law and the Israeli War in Lebanon', *Arab Media and Society*, February 2007.

46 Ibid. Israel Ministry of Foreign Affairs, *Responding to Hizbullah Attacks from Lebanon: Issues of Proportionality*, Legal Background, 25 July 2006, available at www.mfa.gov.il/MFA/Government/Law/Legal+Issues+and+Rulings/Responding+to+Hizbullah+attacks+from+Lebanon-+Issues+of+proportionality+July+2006.htm (last accessed 1 May 2014).

47 Human Rights Council (HRC), Report of the Commission of Inquiry on Lebanon pursuant to Human Rights Council Resolution S-2/1, 23 November 2006, A/HRC/3/2, at 38 para 142 [hereinafter: HRC Report on Lebanon].

158 *Military objective: concept and definition*

locations throughout Lebanon. Their link to the Hezbollah military action, and overall qualification as military objectives, has been questioned.[48]

The most debated attack in this context was that against the Serbian Radio and TV broadcasting station (Radio Televisija Srbije, RTS) in Belgrade on 23 April 1999.[49] The RTS station appeared to have been designated as a target some time before the attack, which was allegedly made known in advance to the Serbian side.[50] The post-conflict US assessment report claimed that television and radio broadcasting facilities were generally considered to be used for both military and civilian purposes, and were therefore military objectives and considered part of the Serbian command, control and communications network.[51] Interestingly, however, the particular reference to the attack on the RTS station in Belgrade also stressed its use for propaganda.[52] A report to the Prosecutor of the International Criminal Tribunal for the former Yugoslavia (ICTY), published five months later than the above-mentioned Department of Defense Report to Congress, took exactly the same approach to the events analysed. This report to the Prosecutor relied on various NATO press releases and briefings, all but two of which were issued after the attack in question, and on an Amnesty International report, which was coincidentally published only a few days before the Report to the Prosecutor.[53]

There could be no doubt that members of the Coalition's political leadership and military forces perceived the Serbian radio and television stations as providing propaganda support to the regime. In the words of Air Commodore David Wilby, in a statement 12 days before the attack on RTS:

> Serb radio and TV is an instrument of propaganda and repression. It has filled the airwaves with hate and with lies over the years, and especially now. It is therefore a legitimate target in this campaign. If President Milosevic would provide equal time for Western news broadcasts in its programs without censorship, three hours a day between noon and 1800

---

48 Ibid, at 37 para 141 and at 38 para 143; Amnesty International, *Israel/Lebanon: Out of All Proportion – Civilians Bear the Brunt of the War*, AI Index: MDE 02/033/2006, November 2006, at 49.

49 Final Report to the Prosecutor by the Committee Established to Review the NATO Bombing Campaign Against the Federal Republic of Yugoslavia, 13 June 2000, 39(5) *International Legal Materials*, 1257–83 at 1279 [hereinafter: ICTY Report].

50 Ibid, para 77.

51 US Department of Defense Report to Congress, *Kosovo/Operation Allied Force, After-Action Report*, 31 January 2000, at 83.

52 Ibid, at A-8.

53 Amnesty International, 'Collateral Damage' or Unlawful Killings? Violations of the Laws of War by NATO during Operation Allied Force, AI Index: EUR 70/18/00, June 2000 [hereinafter: AI].

Problematic cases 159

and three hours a day between 1800 and midnight, then his TV could become an acceptable instrument of public information.[54]

This statement was issued on 12 April 1999, the day on which, allegedly, the attack was originally scheduled, but eventually postponed because of reported objections from the French and British authorities to the legitimacy of the target.[55] Some other statements of high-ranking politicians and military authorities were cited, emphasising the central role of the Serbian media as a powerful tool in spreading information aimed at boosting public support for the war effort.[56]

Following its initial line of argument, suggesting that the RTS was playing its role as an instrument of power in Milosevic's regime, NATO changed its official position and started putting stress on the object's military function. The Amnesty International report drew attention to initial assurances from the NATO spokesman, issued prior to the strikes, that television and radio transmitters would not be targeted directly, unless they were integrated into military facilities.[57] Notably, there was no mention of studio facilities in that statement. Only two weeks after the incident, NATO argued that the RTS station, together with the said studio facilities, were used to transmit instructions to troops in the field through a large, multi-purpose satellite communications dish.[58] Almost simultaneously, NATO attacked two electrical power transformer stations that were allegedly supplying power to air defence coordination networks, and generally providing power to the northern sector operations centre. All the objects, including the radio relay buildings, NATO claimed, constituted an interconnected system of communications, with its military and civilian uses indistinguishable from each other.[59]

This explanation was inferred from NATO press releases by the Committee preparing the report for the ICTY Office of the Prosecutor, without any further evidence being adduced in support of these claims. The Committee did not

---

54 Air Commodore David Wilby, quoted from an interview by Noah Adams, *All Things Considered*, National Public Radio, 12 April 1999, available at www.bu.edu/globalbeat/pubs/Pesic041299.html (last accessed 1 May 2014).

55 See the relevant discussion in Chapters 9 and 10 of this book. AI, op. cit. n 53, section 5.3; D. Priest, 'Bombing by the Committee: France Balked at NATO Targets', *Washington Post*, 20 September 1999; Human Rights Watch, *Civilian Deaths in NATO AIR Campaign*, Vol. 12, No. 1(d), February 2000, text attached to n 78, available at www.hrw.org/reports/2000/nato/ (last accessed 1 May 2014).

56 See HRW, op. cit. n 40; AI, op. cit. n 53, section 5.3; ICTY Report, op. cit. n 49, para 74; A. Laursen, 'NATO, Kosovo, and the ICTY Investigation', 17(4) *American University of International Law Review* 2001–2, 765–814 at 781.

57 AI, op. cit. n 53, section 5.3.

58 ICTY Report, op. cit. n 49, para 73.

59 Ibid, at paras 72–4.

160 *Military objective: concept and definition*

elaborate on what was supposed to be considered to be RTS's effective contribution to military action, but assumed that RTS satisfied the first element of the definition based on the limited and seemingly inconsistent NATO explanation. The intelligence on which NATO made its assessment is not in the public domain.[60]

The Committee also considered whether stopping Serbian propaganda was sufficient to make the attack lawful. In this context, the Committee distinguished between two substantive types of information that may be conveyed through television or radio facilities. These were (a) information inciting others to commit unlawful acts of violence and (b) information not intended to encourage such acts.[61] In the first case, messages would suggest the active taking up of arms against the perceived enemy, while the second type would result only in arousing general support for the war effort. This distinction was clearly derived from precedent – the 1946 case of the International Military Tribunal in Nuremberg against Hans Fritzsche, a senior official in the German Ministry of Propaganda and the head of its Radio Division.[62] Fritzsche was acquitted of incitement to war crimes because the Tribunal did not believe that his messages were intended to encourage the commission of violence. On the other hand, Julius Streicher was found guilty and sentenced for long-term and sustained anti-Semitic incitement. The incitement called for the active persecution of Jews through murder and extermination, and was found to amount to crimes against humanity.[63] It is important to underline that, in all these cases, the courts did not deal with the question of the legal status of the actual media facilities.[64]

---

60 The lack of detail as to the concrete military function was disputed not only in academic writing (e.g. Laursen, op. cit. n 56, at 789–90; O. Bring, 'International Humanitarian Law after Kosovo: Is Lex Lata Sufficient?', 71(1) *Nordic Journal of International Law* 2002, 39–54 at 43) but also in the various legal proceedings, most prominently in an application to the European Court of Human Rights instituted on behalf of the victims of the attack. See European Court of Human Rights, Decision as to the admissibility of Application no. 52207/99 of 12 December 2001 (Grand Chamber) in the case *Bankovic and Others v Belgium and 16 Other Contracting States* (Belgium, the Czech Republic, Denmark, France, Germany, Greece, Hungary, Iceland, Italy, Luxembourg, the Netherlands, Norway, Poland, Portugal, Spain, Turkey and the United Kingdom), 12 December 2001; also in the case before the Italian Court of Cassation, *Presidenza Consiglio Ministri c. Markovic e altri*, Cassazione (sez.un.), n. 8157 (ord.), 5 June 2002, in 85 RDI (2002), 800 *et seq.*
61 ICTY Report, op. cit. n 49, para 76.
62 *USA, France, UK and USSR v H. Goering at al.*, Judgment of the International Military Tribunal, Trial of [The] Major War Criminals, Nuremberg (1946), Vol. 1, at 79, 336–8.
63 Streicher was Fritzsche's co-accused in the same trial; see n 62 above, at 34, 77, 301–4.
64 The Committee also mentioned the case of the broadcasters in the Rwandan Radio *Télévision Libre Mille-Collines*, known as Hate Radio, who were prosecuted for airing instructions encouraging the commission of crimes against humanity, and genocide. This case will referred to in the context of the next subsection (*The Prosecutor v Ferdinand Nahimana, Jean-Bosco Barayagwiza, Hassan Ngeze*, ICTR-99-52-A International Criminal Tribunal for Rwanda (ICTR), Appeal Chamber, Judgment of 28 November 2007 and ICTR-99-52-T, Trial Chamber, Judgment of 3 December 2003).

Problematic cases 161

In these examples, though, the Committee concluded that if the RTS station was attacked only for its propaganda function, then some experts in the laws of armed conflict could question the attack's legitimacy.[65] The Committee suggested that averting propaganda, which did not amount to incitement to commit war crimes or other international crimes, was an incidental – albeit complementary – reason for the attack on RTS.

It is surprising to note that the Committee conceded that media stations seen as a 'nerve system that keeps a warmonger in power and thus perpetuates the war effort' may also fall within the limits of the definition.[66] The Committee indicated that such objects may become lawful targets, in accordance with the definition of military objectives, but did not elaborate how. There are commentators who nevertheless accept that exclusively State-controlled media, used by a State's political leadership directing the war effort to control the civilian population, could be considered legitimate military objectives.[67] Seemingly, the reference made to 'war effort' describes a kind of contribution that is much less specific than the one required by the definition, as explained in earlier discussion. There has to be a specific connection between the object's contribution and the conduct of hostilities for the object to meet the test.

It has been suggested that the use of media facilities, such as State-controlled TV and radio stations, to control the civilian population would turn them into military objectives.[68] This is debatable.[69] Whether such objects can be regarded as lawful targets, because their destruction or *neutralization* offers definite military advantage, will depend on their use. Some commentators have questioned the definite military advantage resulting from the destruction of the aforementioned RTS.[70] The Committee that reported to the Prosecutor of the ICTY inferred from various NATO press releases that the station constituted part of a wider, strategically significant network of radio relay stations contributing to the Serbian command and control network, and in particular to its air-defence system.[71] While the Committee did consider the station's possible contribution to military action, it did not address what the definite military advantage might have been.

Where a TV and radio broadcasting station is integrated into the military communication, command and control (C3) infrastructure, or used to house military infrastructure, then its destruction would offer a definite military

---

65 ICTY Report, op. cit. n 49, para 76.
66 Ibid, para 55.
67 Fenrick, op. cit. n 21, at 497.
68 Ibid.
69 It is unclear what is meant by 'control' and how stopping such control may be militarily advantageous to the adversary.
70 Bothe, op. cit. n 27, at 180; P. Rowe, 'Kosovo 1999: The Air Campaign – Have the Provisions of Additional Protocol I Withstood the Test?', 82(837) *International Review of the Red Cross* 2000, 147–65 at 149.
71 ICTY Report, op. cit. n 49, at 78.

162 *Military objective: concept and definition*

advantage. Similarly, the destruction of a station that transmits military communications, whether overt or coded messages during seemingly normal civilian broadcasts, could reasonably be expected to result in a definite military benefit. If, however, it broadcast only propaganda, and messages aimed at maintaining civilian support for the war, then there is a real difficulty in trying to determine the definite military advantage offered by its destruction.

The Committee also implied that an object could be attacked if it was a place from which international crimes of violence were being incited. If objects allegedly involved in incitement to violence can be considered lawful targets, whether in line with the law of armed conflict or other standards, then the question arises whether other objects involved in the commission of international crimes could also be justified in this context. This approach will be discussed next in a wider context of objects involved in commission of international crimes.

7.4 Objects involved in the commission of international crimes

The question of whether it is lawful to attack places where international crimes are being committed was raised, during and after the Second World War, in respect of Nazi concentration camps.[72] It was debated whether such sites should have been destroyed to prevent the future commission of crimes. There were arguments that even if it meant killing the victims of such crimes at the same time, attacks would prevent future victims being killed. If the rationale is to put an end to criminal human behaviour, would it be lawful to attack detention centres where individuals were known to have been killed?

Subsequently, it has been suggested that stopping such unlawful activity could avert the potential commission of war crimes in future, particularly if those crimes appeared to constitute part of an orchestrated military campaign in a specific armed conflict.[73] The question arises whether objects or places where international crimes are being committed may be considered lawful targets and, if so, whether that is based on the definition of military objective. It has been suggested that such objects could be targeted even if they do not meet the standard of military objectives.[74] If the law of armed conflict is applicable, there are likely to be difficulties in satisfying the military objective test, because the use to which the building is put may not contribute to military action and the assessment of definite military advantage may not be possible.

---

72 See for instance: D.S. Wyman, *The Abandonment of the Jews: America and the Holocaust*, Pantheon Books, New York 1984; D.S. Wyman and R. Medoff, *A Race Against Death: Peter Bergson, America, and the Holocaust*, New Press, New York 2004.

73 Laursen, op. cit. n 56, at 786.

74 Fenrick, op. cit. n 21, at 496.

Problematic cases   163

It is unclear whether permission to attack such objects would arise from the provisions of the law of armed conflict, or from other obligations relating to the general principles of State responsibility to prevent particular forms of international crimes, and/or international criminal law. The relevant distinction could be whether the behaviour in question involved the commission of war crimes and other international crimes, such as genocide or crimes against humanity.[75] As far as war crimes are concerned, permission to attack such objects may, arguably, be viewed either from application of Art 52.2 API or as arising from the general obligation of States to prevent war crimes.[76] One may also argue that, in principle, it is in the interest of all parties in an armed conflict to respect the rules. The underlying rationale of the laws of armed conflict is such that violations do not make military sense because their consequences are, if anything, counterproductive in long term.

One commentator has, correctly, noted that the connection between the use of a facility to commit war crimes, and the classification of that facility as a military objective, should not be treated as necessarily implied.[77] The reason why this presents a challenge is that the objects may well not contribute to the military action of the adversary. It would seem unreasonable to assume that the adversary may consider the torturing or killing of civilians to be militarily beneficial, and therefore to see the buildings where such criminal activity takes places as effectively contributing to (its own) military action. However, it may, paradoxically, contribute to the attacker's own military action. Take the example where State A has established concentration camps on its own territory, where numerous civilians of State B are kept sufficiently humanely and forced to work in A's factories. One may query, if such factories were to produce ammunition that A uses in the conduct of war, would this be considered an effective contribution to A's military action. This may not be the case if all they produced were dairy products for general consumption. If such camps were guarded by A's military personnel, this could

---

75 A separate question arises whether there is, in international law, the legal possibility of a State being able to put an end to the commission of crimes against humanity by military force and, if so, whether the law of armed conflict would have been of any relevance to such actions.

76 As far as grave breaches of GC are considered, one may infer a sense of obligation to stop the violence from Article 1, common to all GC, which requires States to 'ensure the respect' for the Conventions in all circumstances, as well as from Article 76 of API, which considers attacks against a civilian population as a grave breach of API. It is worth pointing out that while the obligation to prevent war crimes clearly applies to acts by one's own side, it is unclear whether it extends to the acts of other parties in the conflict. For further discussion, see F. Kalshoven, 'The Undertaking to Respect and Ensure Respect in All Circumstances: From Tiny Seed to Ripening Fruit', 2 *Yearbook of International Humanitarian Law* 1999, 3–61, available at http://journals.cambridge.org/action/displayAbstract?fromPage=online&aid= 4044608 – fn01 (last accessed 15 July 2014).

77 Fenrick, op. cit. n 21, at 496.

164　*Military objective: concept and definition*

constitute an effective contribution to B's military action due to A's diversion of military resources away from hostilities to guard such camps.[78]

As indicated earlier, the assessment of such objects may depend on whether the application of the laws of armed conflict would be appropriate, but if so, then determination of the object as a lawful target in accordance with Art 52.2 API would be required in relation to a State's obligation to prevent the commission of war crimes. Assuming, for the sake of analysis, that the definition of military objective were relevant, then the satisfaction of the definite military advantage requirement might, in theory, be possible but not by the attacker. Imagine, again, a situation in which State A runs concentration camps on its own territory where the citizens of B are being detained. These camps are managed and guarded by A's military personnel. It may be argued that this means that it is militarily beneficial for B to have A run the camps because it diverts the military effort. If they were destroyed, then attacking them would not be in the interest of State B because, after the attack, State A could divert the remaining militarily personnel to the battlefront. This could, paradoxically, be militarily advantageous to State A.

Separate questions arise whether objects other than places and buildings where crimes are commissioned can be considered in this context. Can the houses where the perpetrators reside be attacked?[79] Can the factory, which produces the equipment used in the commission of crimes? It would seem that it is considered lawful to attack places where the incitement to commission of unlawful violence takes place.[80] It is unclear if the laws of armed conflict would apply to such objects. In order to establish that war crimes were being committed through incitement, the precise content of the messages would have to be known. Even then, it is debatable whether the prevention of war crimes in itself could be considered as militarily advantageous, and could be anticipated from an attack. The Committee preparing the report to the ICTY Office of the Prosecutor, following the 1999 NATO intervention in Kosovo, concluded that if the RTS station was used in advocating the commission of violence akin to that in Rwanda, then according to the Committee, its

---

78 Caution has to be applied in considering such objects in international armed conflicts. If the war crimes involve harm being done to wounded, sick or shipwrecked members of the armed forces, prisoners of war and civilians, then attacks against such places cannot constitute belligerent reprisals.

79 The discussion regarding people as military objectives is outside the scope of this work. See 1.3.

80 The discussion of the TV and radio broadcasting stations in this context relates only to the consideration of their role in incitement to commission of unlawful violence and to what extent this may constitute a legitimate basis for attacking them. Other grounds were covered in the analysis in 7.3.

Problematic cases 165

destruction might have been justified.[81] The substance of the unlawful behaviour will be crucial in determining whether the law is being breached.[82]

The issue of attacks against objects allegedly involved in the incitement to commit unlawful violence arose in relation to the NATO attack against Libyan State Television (LST) in July 2011. NATO justified its attack on LST purely in terms of its incitement to violence against civilians.[83] NATO stressed that the facility was initially not regarded as a lawful target, as its broadcasts did not meet the threshold of 'incitement'. However, by early July 2011 the messages had apparently become more intense, calling for the commission of violence against civilians.[84] NATO claimed that stopping such incitement could have prevented the commission of any future acts.[85] It could be that the messages addressing the population as a whole encouraged the commission of violence amounting to war crimes.[86]

How does this relate to the destruction of LST offering a definite military advantage? The attack would, arguably, not give any military advantage to NATO. The potential victims of the war crimes, and the victims of the incitement, who would presumably benefit by the incitement being ended, might have viewed an attack on LST as advantageous – but not militarily so. It may be necessary, then, to assert that NATO's interests would be, in this case, coterminous with those of the victims.[87]

---

81 ICTY Report, op. cit. n 49, para 76. See also text attached to n 64 above.

82 The assessment of what is being incited can be quite complicated. For example, incitement will not always be unlawful; the determination will depend on what is being incited. There will be a difference between radio broadcasts encouraging national armed forces to kill enemy combatants and enemy civilians. The incitement to violence against civilians is prohibited, but incitement to kill the enemy is not. If the station were encouraging its own side's civilians to kill enemy combatants, then such incitement would not be unlawful. If, however, such incitement encouraged acts of violence against enemy civilians, then this could be considered in the context of crimes against humanity or genocide. The analysis may be affected by whether the broadcasting station was State-controlled or private.

83 NATO Letter to International Commission of Inquiry to investigate all alleged violations of international human rights law in the Libyan Arab Jamahiriya, OLA (2012) 006, 23 January 2012, at 6.

84 Ibid. Coincidentally, the attack on Libyan State Television was executed only after the International Criminal Court (ICC) had issued an indictment against Muammar Gaddafi and other senior members of the Libyan political structure (*The Prosecutor v Saif Al-Islam Gaddafi and Abdullah Al-Senussi*, ICC-01/11-01/11, 27 June 2011).

85 NATO press release: 'NATO Strikes Libyan State Satellite Facility', 31 July 2011.

86 In this example, the incitement was allegedly taking place in the context of non-international armed conflict, which in consequence means that non-international armed conflict war crimes are relevant. This example is used because it also involves international armed action undertaken under the auspices of NATO.

87 An alternative argument may be found in the claim that if the violence being incited was the cause of the war, then stopping the incitement might end the war. This, according to the Eritrea-Ethiopia Claims Commission, could be considered a significant military advantage. See discussion in 5.2.1.

166   *Military objective: concept and definition*

NATO implied that crimes against humanity, commissioned by Gaddafi and others accused by the International Criminal Court (ICC), corresponded with the criminal activity that the TV station had apparently been inciting.[88] NATO's remark regarding the ICC indictment suggests the Alliance might have felt compelled to attack the LST in relation to its broadcasting function, which encouraged the commission of serious international crimes based on a rationale not necessarily related to the laws of armed conflict.[89] This may suggest that the basis for attacks on objects from which criminal behaviour is incited may be found in areas of international law other than in the law of armed conflict, such as international human rights law.[90]

7.5 Conclusion

There are certain targets whose determination in accordance with the requirements of the definition is problematic. It is unclear whether the definition is at all applicable to some targets. These are objects that are involved in the commission of international crimes. It is unclear if the law of armed conflict framework is relevant in the consideration of such objects, or whether the justification of attacks on them could be found in other branches of international law. If the law of armed conflict is to be applied, then there are inherent problems with the application of the test to such objects, even if the factual situation is fairly clear.

Problems also arise in the analysis of objects associated with a political leadership. Here, the application of the test will depend very much on the question of the status of those exercising the State functions involved in the conduct of military operations. In the case of other targets, such as TV and radio stations, the problem will be associated with establishing a precise factual

---

88 It is striking that NATO did not provide any further justification of any connection to military operations, or indeed any further evidence of the claims regarding the 'inciting' function of the station.

89 Incitement is not addressed by the laws of armed conflict. As far as the laws of armed conflict are concerned, it is hard to see how NATO could have seen LST as satisfying an effective contribution to military action. If the incitement was aimed at encouraging civilian attacks on other civilians, then – bearing in mind that NATO's mandate for operations was limited to air strikes to protect Libyan civilians 'under the threat of attack' (UN Security Council Resolution 1973, 17 March 2011) – such incitement could, arguably, be considered to have contributed to Gaddafi's war effort. It would still be problematic, because the requirement of the definition is much more specific than war effort. See also n 82 above and NATO press release: 'NATO Strikes Libyan State Satellite Facility', 31 July 2011.

90 The incitement to unlawful violence could have been seen as contravening the explicit prohibition of the 'advocacy of national, racial or religious hatred that constitutes incitement to discrimination, hostility or violence' in Art 20 of the International Covenant on Civil and Political Rights. Art 20.2 of the International Covenant on Civil and Political Rights, 16 December 1966.

picture to which the law can be applied, and then drawing the appropriate legal conclusion.

This chapter concludes Part I of this study, which focused on the analysis of each element of the definition of military objectives. Part II looks at certain aspects of how the definition has been operationalised in armed conflicts since 1977. It also examines how military forces conceptualise military operations, and what problems arise involving interoperability between States when they make targeting decisions.

Part II

Operationalisation of the definition of military objective

Part I of this work considers the various phrases used in the definition of a military objective, their meaning and problems with their interpretation and practical application. The interpretation of law involves more than abstract analysis. It requires an insight into what States do, in addition to what they say. Looking at how States act can be beneficial in clarifying the meaning of the definition, but knowing how States act does not necessarily explain why they act in that way. A consideration of how military forces behave when they identify lawful targets would not, therefore, be complete without examining what factors might affect their behaviour.

Part II will examine how the definition works in practice. It will seek to identify what State practice can tell us about the interpretation of the definition, and the problems States may encounter when applying it.[1]

What States do during armed conflicts is shaped partly by military doctrine, and partly by law.[2] The law, however, is not the starting point in the process by which armed forces conceptualise their operations. Their starting point is to identify what they are trying to achieve. How they think about what they need to do to attain their goals will affect what they choose to target, and in what circumstances. Once the military goals are formulated, the armed forces will identify targets in line with military doctrine and the context of operations. This process is not determined by law, but by the manner in which the armed forces think of how to achieve their goals. The list of targets that they may have a military reason to attack may vary in different circumstances, and between operations or conflicts. When targets are identified, they are subject to legal scrutiny.

This process could affect the interpretation of the definition of military objective in practice. This might raise issues that would not be revealed by an

---

1 The majority of the examples in Part I, and the materials discussed in Part II, would strongly support the claim that the definition of military objective has attained customary status, particularly when combined with the statements of numerous States to that effect. As indicated in Chapter 1, this book will not examine the customary status of the definition, and it will not be discussed as a separate issue.

2 See also the discussion in 1.2.2 and 10.2 and 10.3.

170 *Operationalisation of the definition of military objective*

abstract legal analysis. The armed forces may identify a target they regard as desirable, but whose status as a military objective in accordance with the definition is arguable. These situations occur when the State is likely to approve what the armed forces want to target, not because the targets appear lawful, but because they are not clearly unlawful. If several States conduct attacks against similar targets, without the application of the definition being contested, then over time the interpretation is likely to be shaped by military doctrine rather than by legal considerations.[3]

Behaviour that constitutes State practice, in relation to the concept of military objective, is the result of a complex interaction between the targets identified through military thinking, which includes military doctrine and the law. In order to understand how the definition of military objective works in practice, one needs to understand how the law interacts with military doctrine.

One tool that helps determine the meaning of legal provisions is how a treaty is applied, as indicated by the Vienna Convention on the Law of Treaties.[4] It concerns any subsequent application of the Treaty 'which establishes the agreement of the parties regarding its interpretation'. The practice of States, in the context of the API definition of military objective, results not only from their view of the law, but also from how the military identify targets in line with military doctrine. The legal-military practice of each State forms that State's interpretation of the relevant legal provision, and contributes to treaty practice in general. 'General' treaty practice shapes the overall interpretation of all treaty provisions. Therefore, the international community's view of what a particular treaty provision means will be the aggregate of all treaty practice. This includes States where it is a product of targets identified through the application of military doctrine.[5]

Clearly, a State must see every object it decides to attack as a lawful target. However, it is not the case that all objects that States do not attack are unlawful targets. In other words, where the State does not target an object, it is not necessarily always because the State thinks the target does not meet the legal test. It is sometimes unclear why certain objects are not attacked. It may be that they are not proposed by the armed forces, and therefore not subject to legal scrutiny. Where targets are proposed for approval, their rejection may be based on legal concerns. It will not always be clear whether those legal concerns relate to the application of the definition of military objective, or some other legal obligation. It may be that there is a mixture of legal concerns, such

---

3 See, for instance, the progression of the attacks against media facilities in 7.3, and the discussion about the evolution of the international response to such attacks, especially after the 1999 attack on the Belgrade-based TV and radio broadcasting station, in Chapter 8.
4 Art 31 of the Vienna Convention on the Law of Treaties, Vienna, 23 May 1969, United Nations Treaty Series, vol. 1155, at 331 *et seq.*
5 Not all States engage in armed conflict at the same time.

Operationalisation of the definition of military objective 171

as the application of the definition, and precautions in attack. The basis for rejection might also be a combination of legal and non-legal concerns. Non-legal concerns could relate to military considerations, such as the nature of operations. They may also result from political imperatives, such as keeping a coalition together.

Even where the attacker can lawfully target an object but chooses not to do so, the reason may not be obvious or clear. It is thus not possible to draw legally significant conclusions about the views of States simply because a State does not attack a particular object. Such a decision is a product not only of the State's view of what is lawful or not; it can also be affected by several other factors.

Target lists are the product of conceptual thinking in three different layers connected to the organisation of military doctrine. In order to understand how they are created, it is necessary to understand the underlying principles and fundamental tenets of that doctrine.[6] While the principal interest of this work is the product, namely targets and military objectives, it will be necessary to elaborate on the doctrine, in particular its aspects pertaining to targeting.[7] If military doctrine shapes targeting, it is important to know whether States have the same or broadly similar military doctrines. If their doctrines are similar, but their behaviour in an armed conflict is different, that is possibly – but not necessarily – on account of their varying views on legal constraints. If the doctrines and behaviour that results in targeting questionable targets are similar, then it would appear that military doctrine may have an indirect impact on the interpretation of law. If, on the other hand, their doctrines differ, and only some States want to pursue particular objects, then the lawyers of those States that do not target the objects will not even get the chance to formulate a view of their lawfulness.

Part II also deals with coalition operations. When discussing issues relating to the terms used in the definition, a number of the examples given came from conflicts involving coalition operations. They were cited to illustrate or identify legal problems in respect of certain objects, such as the Al Firdus bunker discussed in Chapter 6. The examples discussed in Part II have a different function. They are used to emphasise the context of operations, and how this can affect the operationalisation of the concept of military objective.[8]

Considering coalition operations in this context is important for two reasons. First, unlike in conflicts involving one State against another, coalition operations involving numerous States give rise to greater scope for debate regarding some objects. If two States react differently in the same context in relation to the same obligation, the divergence in their views may be based

---

6 See 8.3–1.
7 See 8.5.1 and 8.6.1.
8 See 6.2 for a discussion of both the Al Firdus/Amariyah (Ameriyya) bunker and the role of context in the application of the term *circumstances ruling at the time*.

172   *Operationalisation of the definition of military objective*

on difference in interpretation of the legal obligation. If States have a problem with the definition itself, then each State will indicate as much. Where a State does not contest the definition, but interprets it in a particular way, then, once it is involved in a coalition, it may encounter other States that interpret the same obligation differently. That would not be a problem with the definition as such, but with the interpretation of it. Further differences in application of the definition may relate to States' view regarding some targets being unlawful either in principle or only in some circumstances. This is further complicated by the fact that non-legal reasons – such as military doctrine, domestic political constraints and policy imperatives – may also play a significant role in decision-taking.[9] All these reasons may result in tensions in targeting.

The second reason for the importance of coalition warfare relates to its 'context'. States may act differently when they are in coalition because they want to preserve the cohesion and unity of that coalition. Coalition members are normally aware of each other's legal obligations and views, particularly on strategic and politically sensitive issues.[10] This creates a situation in which the views of States are expressed in respect of their targeting choices.[11] However, problems may also arise with identifying practice in this context. States may decide against attacking certain targets not because of concerns regarding their lawfulness, and not even because of others' concerns about their lawfulness. It may, in fact, be because of other States' unwillingness to face the political implications of attacking such targets, which may affect the stability of the coalition. A State willing to engage such targets may decide they are not of sufficient importance to be worth 'trumping' the political considerations of other States.

Part II, then, discusses military doctrine and legal interoperability, aimed at clarifying the interpretation of the definition and post-ratification State practice. Chapter 8 focuses on the general and specific frameworks of military doctrine, as well as the relationship between the law and doctrine. Chapter 9 analyses interoperability problems identified in targeting certain objects in coalition operations after 1977.

---

9   See, for example, the highly restrictive United States Counterinsurgency (COIN) doctrine, which illustrates how armed forces may exercise restraint imposed by political constraints or, indeed, mission considerations. *Counterinsurgency Operations*, Joint Publication 3-24, Joint Chiefs of Staff, 5 October 2009.

10 See 9.2.

11 Generally speaking, coalition operations are sensitive for one reason or another. Issues that often give rise to a coalition may also cause sensitivities, e.g. the involvement of Arab States in the 1990–1 Gulf War. See the further discussion in 9.1.1.

8 Military doctrine and international law

This chapter contains a discussion of military doctrine. There are two main reasons why military doctrine is important when considering the application of the definition of military objective. First, military doctrine shapes how military forces are likely to conduct operations during armed conflicts, which in turn results in State practice. This practice assists in clarifying the interpretation of military objectives.

When planning and organising military operations, the armed forces apply their national military doctrine, which serves as a vehicle in conceptualising those operations. If the relevant military doctrine and the definition of military objectives are in conflict, that conflict may manifest itself in the subsequent practice. When that occurs, it is possible that pressure from the military operators may lead to a modification of the interpretation of the definition.

Second, doctrine plays a significant role in shaping the behaviour of the armed forces during an armed conflict. That being the case, it is expected that an analysis of doctrine will show how the law of armed conflict, and in particular the concept of military objective, is taken into account and/or incorporated into military thought and activity. Such an analysis should identify the situations where military doctrine may allow or even require the targeting of an object that might not be permitted by law. This may also expose situations in which military doctrine would advise against attacking an object, even if the law allowed it.

The presentation of the relevant military doctrine in this chapter is not intended to be exhaustive. The analysis of military doctrine is necessarily selective both in its scope and volume. It focuses on those aspects of doctrine that are primarily relevant to this study.[1] The doctrine referred to most often

---

1 Military forces involved in the execution of land operations may be involved in a number of different types of military activities. Not all would involve the existence of conventional international armed conflict. Such situations may arise in the context of other types of conflict, or they may not even amount to armed conflict, for example peace support or counter-insurgency operations. A discussion of the doctrine relevant to such operations is outside the scope of this study, and specifically this chapter, which is confined to an analysis of doctrine relevant to international armed conflicts.

174 *Operationalisation of the definition of military objective*

has been developed by the UK and US, as well as Australia, New Zealand, Canada and NATO. Where relevant, documents from other States, such as France, Spain, India or Germany, are considered.[2]

The area of doctrine most relevant to the concept of military objectives relates to concept of targets that result from the targeting process. In order to analyse the effect that doctrine may have on the identification of targets, and how the law is taken into account during targeting, it will be necessary to describe what these terms mean – and what targeting entails. Targeting is a military function that identifies and selects targets at the operational/tactical level of warfare. In order to understand its role at this level, it will first be necessary to explain the role that doctrine generally plays in the conduct of military operations. This chapter will consider the fundamental principles underpinning the broader framework of military doctrine.

This analysis will start with a brief presentation of the concepts developed by leading military theorists, whose work bears particular relevance to the targeting process, and the nature of targets in current armed conflicts. This will constitute section 1 of this chapter. Sections 2 and 3 will briefly present the fundamentals of higher-level doctrine, including the role of doctrine in military operations and doctrinal perspectives on operations. Section 3 concludes part A of this chapter. Part A is focused on the presentation of doctrine that is not expected to involve references to law.

Part B considers the relationship between doctrine and the law in general, with specific reference to the concept of military objective. Part B consists of three sections. Section 4 deals with the general relationship between the doctrine and the law. Section 5 analyses the targeting process, while section 6 discusses the concept of a target and its relevance to the definition of military objective.

Before continuing, two terms need to be explained. The term 'military advantage' has military and legal meanings, which were discussed in Chapter 5. In section 6 this term will be italicised where it is used in the legal sense. The term 'military objective' represents not only a legal concept, as discussed in Part I of this book. In military doctrine, it is also used to mean a goal of military operations.[3] In this chapter, it will be used in the military sense, interchangeable with the word 'goal'. Italics will be used to signal the difference in meaning where reference is made to the legal concept of military objectives.

---

2 This enumeration does not reflect the scope of the preliminary research, during which the relevant sources from other States were sought. The results of this research were limited as a number of States either appear not to have developed the relevant doctrine, or have chosen not to release it publicly. See also the discussion in 1.2.2.

3 *Manuel de Droit des Conflits Armés*, (French) Ministère de la Défense, Secrétariat Général Pour L'Administration, undated, at 50. See also 1.5.

PART A: MILITARY DOCTRINE

8.1 Fathers of modern targeting theories

Much of the modern understanding of the nature of conflict, and strategies for winning a war, rests on the groundwork of famous military thinkers such as Sun Tzu and Carl von Clausewitz. Sun Tzu is known for advocating a swift incapacitation of the enemy, who becomes 'helpless without fight' after the resource-consuming destruction of its military capacity by the adversary.[4] Clausewitz, a keen proponent of the annihilation of the enemy, distinguished between two types of war. The first is the ideal situation, in which the opponent is absolutely destroyed. The second is the 'real' state of affairs, in which such destruction is limited by political and military factors.[5] To Clausewitz, destruction was not necessarily physical. The enemy would have been 'destroyed' if it were no longer able or willing to fight. This could involve both its physical and psychological conditions.[6]

Examining Napoleonic conflicts on land, Clausewitz promoted a holistic approach to warfare. He said it should be consistent with the overall national goals and political-economic situations of the States involved. He focused on the mass and concentration of forces in space and time as the underlying features of warfare. Clausewitz attributed the mass of an adversary's combat power to their centre of gravity (COG), as well as to the commander's will or need to use it. Clausewitz suggested that, depending on the conflict, a nation's capital, a place for the accumulation of wealth, public opinion or national leadership could constitute the adversary's hubs of power. This allows the strengths and potential weaknesses of the enemy to be exploited at the same time.[7] Clausewitz's underlying belief in the inherent uncertainty of war led him and his followers into devising a certain intellectual method for conducting war. He insisted that commanders would be led to success by their knowledge and ability to have their thinking inspired or stimulated by military theory, rather than by following a rigid set of prescribed doctrinal rules.[8]

The works of two British First World War veterans further developed the underlying principles of modern strategic doctrine. John Fuller identified and categorised nine fundamental principles of warfare, all governed by the overarching law of economy of force.[9] In essence, he advocated the use of

---

4 Sun Tzu, *The Art of War*, trans. T. Cleary, Shambala Publications, Boston and London 1988, e.g. at 66–7, 72.
5 Carl von Clausewitz, *On War*, Wordsworth Editions, Ware 1997, Book I, Chapter II 'Ends and Means at War', at 25 *et seq.*
6 Ibid.
7 Ibid.
8 Ibid, Book II, Chapter II 'On the Theory of War', para 27.
9 In 1925 Fuller settled on nine principles: Objective, Offensive Action, Surprise, Concentration of Force, Distribution, Security, Mobility, Endurance and Determination. These principles are broadly incorporated into current military doctrine. J.F.C. Fuller, *The Foundations of the Science of War*, Hutchinson & Co., London 1925, Chapters XI–XIV in particular.

176 *Operationalisation of the definition of military objective*

minimum military effort to achieve maximum effect.[10] This concept, combined with his tripartite theory of war,[11] led Fuller to conclude that the decisive way to win a war was to destroy the adversary through a quick paralysis of the 'brain' of its military organisation, rather than by a drawn-out wearing down or destruction.[12] He called this the 'rendering inoperative of . . . power of command (brain warfare)'.[13]

Fuller witnessed technological developments that changed the understanding of military power, and the unprecedented potential of new weapons such as tanks and aircraft in place of machine guns. The rise of air power, in particular, led to the origins of the 'paralysis' idea, which is attributed to another British military theorist – the father of the Royal Air Force, Lord Trenchard.[14] Trenchard advocated the strategic bombardment of all transportation and communication nodes, as well as enemy military production centres.[15] He believed that pursuing military goals by attacking the 'vital centres' that sustained the war effort was the most effective and economical way of applying air power, rather than attacking the enemy's armed forces.[16] Another British strategist, Basil H. Liddell Hart, likened the enemy to the human body.[17] The paralysis of the enemy's nervous system would bring it to its knees, securing a swift victory in the most effective way. Liddell Hart viewed war on three levels, with an underlying focus on the psychological effects of hostilities.[18]

---

10 Fuller's law of economy of force stipulated that the winning side in a conflict would be better at economising its force in terms of both its quantity and quality. Fuller, op. cit. n 9, Chapter X.

11 Fuller viewed war in three simultaneous planes: physical (fighting power), mental (thinking power) and moral (endurance and will to sustain fighting). He based his theory on an analysis of the nature of men themselves, consisting of three elements: body, mind and soul, which direct or enable their actions and use of force (Fuller, op. cit. n 9, Chapter III). Note that Clausewitz also viewed society as consisting of three dimensions: armed forces, government and population. Armed forces corresponded with the physical sphere, while government and population corresponded with the structure's mental and moral aspects respectively.

12 Fuller, op. cit. n 9, Chapter XIII, section 21.

13 Ibid.

14 Strategic paralysis entails the systemic and irrevocable breakdown of the strategically important functions of the State, and critical infrastructure such as electricity, communication, and access to and distribution of petroleum, oil and lubricants (POL).

15 C. Webster and N. Frankland, *The Strategic Air Offensive Against Germany 1939–1945*, Vol. 4, Her Majesty's Stationery Office, London 1961, at 72.

16 Ibid, at 73–6.

17 Liddell Hart wrote: 'The analysis of war shows that while the nominal strength of a country is represented by its numbers and resources this muscular development is dependent on the state of its internal organs and nerve-system upon its stability of control, morale, and supply.' B.H. Liddell Hart, *Strategy of Indirect Approach*, Faber and Faber, London 1938, at 299.

18 Liddell Hart advocated that: '[A] strategist should think in terms of paralysing, not of killing. Even on the lower plane of warfare, a man killed is merely one man less, whereas a man unnerved is a highly infectious carrier of fear, capable of spreading an epidemic of panic. On a higher plane of warfare, the impression made on the mind of the opposing commander can nullify the whole fighting power that his troops possess. And on a still higher plane,

Military doctrine and international law 177

The capabilities of a third service, the air force, had a great impact on American military theorists. One leading theorist was Brigadier General 'Billy' Mitchell, who strongly believed in the idea of strategic paralysis. In 1930, he asserted:

> The advent of air power which can go straight to the vital centres and entirely neutralize and destroy them has put a completely new complexion on the old system of war. It is now realized that the hostile main army in the field is a false objective and the real objectives are the vital centres. The old theory that victory meant destruction of the hostile main army is untenable.[19]

In place of destruction, he promoted paralysing the 'enemy's nerve centres' as early in a conflict as possible. Such centres would include industrial complexes and other physical objects contributing to the waging of war. Mitchell forecast the ability to attack critical infrastructure from the air, deep inside enemy territory. This view influenced policy and teaching in the Air Corps Tactical School (ACTS) in the United States, which subsequently inspired modern theorists such as John Warden.

In the years leading to the Second World War, ACTS instructors believed in using air attack to strike at the enemy's strategic centres of power. They thought that targets related to the economic and industrial capacity to sustain war should be the centres of attention.[20] They felt that disrupting such targets would force the civilian population to endure increased hardship, thereby weakening morale.[21] Directly targeting civilian morale was not, however, supported as an effective and efficient method of achieving the objective, though disruption of day-to-day lives could weaken support for the war.[22] ACTS instructors realised that the destruction of only a few vital links might lead to the serious disruption of a network-based system, such as railways. Having reviewed the domestic vulnerabilities of national industrial structures, they further observed that social, economic, political and military 'divisions' of society could be affected separately, yet produce 'sympathetic disturbances' in others.[23]

---

psychological pressure on the government of a country may suffice to cancel all the resources at its command so that the sword drops from a paralysed hand.' Ibid, at 298.

19 W. Mitchell, *Skyways: A Book on Modern Aeronautics*, Lippincott, Philadelphia 1930, at 255.

20 S.D. West, *Warden and The Air Corps Tactical School: Déjà Vu?*, Thesis, School of Advanced Airpower Studies, Air University Press, Maxwell Air Force Base, AL 1999, at 6; US Air Force, *Intelligence Targeting Guide*, Air Force Pamphlet 14-210, Secretary of the US Air Force, 1 February 1998, at 131 [hereinafter: AFP14-210].

21 West, op. cit. n20, at 9.

22 Ibid, at 20; AFP14–210, op. cit. n 20.

23 West, op. cit. n 20, at 25.

178 Operationalisation of the definition of military objective

At the heart of this industrial theory lay the relationship between the means (air power) and the ends (achieving the ultimate aim of war, i.e. accepting the will of the victorious party through the weakening of the enemy's will, and its capacity to fight).[24] The economic capacity of the enemy was considered instrumental in achieving the war aim. Consequently, 'economic targets', such as production and industrial centres, as well as other targets such as lines of communication, transportation, and fuel and power supplies, became central in the industrial web theory.[25] In order to reduce the enemy's economic capacity and will to resist, the ACTS wanted to use strategic air bombardment as precisely as the technology of the time allowed.

The economy was an essential component of States' power and will to fight. There is no doubt that the ability of States to maintain a well-functioning economy, which would permit the hardships of war to be withstood, was considered vital. The 1940s Royal Air Force War Manual stressed that the resources of a nation, its vital centres, military potential and stock of food, raw materials and fuels, were potential targets of an air attack.[26] The post-Second World War edition of the same Manual described these features and assets as the 'war potential of a nation'.[27] It identified the resources of a nation as its willpower, industrial and economic strength, armed forces, the capacity for scientific research and development, and manpower.[28] The Manual highlighted that an adversary's 'military, industrial and economic system, the destruction or dislocation of which will contribute most effectively to the breakdown of his capacity to resist', would be the most crucial military objective in a conflict.[29]

One of the most influential military theorists in recent history is American Air Force Colonel John A. Warden III. Warden believed in the strategic application of air power in targeting the enemy leadership in order to end a conflict and make the adversary submit.[30]

Warden devised a model of analysing the enemy as a coherent system, consisting of five strategic entities. These entities form concentric rings consisting of sets of COGs. According to Warden, a specific COG represents

---

24 Ibid, at 7; AFP14–210, op. cit. n 20.

25 For more discussion regarding economic targets, see 4.3.

26 The Manual emphasised that the nation's morale, propaganda, finance and diplomacy, in addition to the targets mentioned earlier, contribute to its power of resistance. Royal Air Force War Manual, Air Ministry, Air Publication 1300, 2nd edn, February 1940, Chapter VIII, paras 8–31.

27 Royal Air Force War Manual, Air Ministry, Air Publication 1300, 3rd edn, January 1950, Chapter 1, para 10.

28 Ibid, paras 12–18.

29 Ibid, chapter 5, para 14.

30 Warden's inspiration came from Fuller, who originally promoted the idea of attacking the command and control component of the enemy's armed forces as a means of reducing its military capability. S. Fadok, *John Boyd and John Warden: Air Power's Quest for Strategic Paralysis*, Thesis, School of Advanced Airpower Studies, Air University Press, Maxwell Air Force Base, AL 1995, at 23.

Military doctrine and international law   179

the points at which 'the enemy is most vulnerable and . . . where an attack will have the best chance of being decisive'.[31] In this way, Warden acknowledged that COGs may be both centres of strength and points of weakness. In his theory, Warden thus appeared to have merged two concepts – centres of gravity and decisive points.[32]

The descending order of importance of COG, from the innermost to outermost ring, is: leadership (holding command and control over the system); 'system essentials' (production assets critical to the enemy's survival, such as power, i.e. petroleum, oil and lubricants (POL), and electricity); critical infrastructure (including lines of communication and transportation nodes); civilian population; and, finally, the armed forces in the field.[33] It is worth noting that Warden did not advocate the direct targeting of civilians, or even attempting to affect civilian morale. He considered this contrary to law and ethics, as well as plainly ineffective.[34] The 'civilian population' ring was nevertheless an important element of the enemy's system that Warden felt could be affected indirectly.

Warden believed the outermost ring of a State's military forces functioned chiefly to protect its own inner rings, and to attack the enemy targets constituting the relevant rings. When sufficiently damaged and feeling defenceless, the adversary might be compelled to make concessions.

When an enemy's most critical COG – the civilian and military leadership – is damaged, its armed forces might feel progressively isolated, and lose the drive to fight. Warden acknowledged that a direct attack on the enemy leaders and commanders might sometimes not be possible. However, as with the civilian population, he saw great scope for applying indirect pressure to induce the required change of policy.[35] Warden was adamant that the destruction of other outer rings might be sufficient to bring about such change and/or strategic paralysis.

The 'system essentials' ring comprises production facilities and production processes alike. Warden included in this power supplies, and industries such as electricity, petroleum, oil and gas, generated internally or imported.[36] He advised that even minor damage to this ring might impede or halt the enemy's use of certain weaponry and/or any potential military operations outside its own territory. This would induce the leadership to make substantive

---

31 J.A. Warden III, *The Air Campaign*, National Defence University Press, Washington, DC, 1988, at 9.

32 Jomini further expanded Clausewitz's analysis of COG by adding the concept of 'decisive' or 'objective' points to the operational doctrine. The idea of decisive points, sequenced along the line of an operation, is well known in modern military doctrine. See the further discussion of decisive points in n 123 below.

33 J.A. Warden III, 'The Enemy as a System', 9(2) *Airpower Journal* 1995, 40–55 at 47.

34 Ibid, at 49–50.

35 Ibid. See discussion regarding State and political leadership infrastructure and related considerations in 7.1.

36 More controversially, he also envisaged that food stocks and financial assets should be incorporated into this category. Warden, op. cit. n 33.

180   *Operationalisation of the definition of military objective*

concessions or cease fighting altogether, which would translate into the achievement of victory by the other side.

Warden called his third innermost ring the 'infrastructure', which consisted of transportation links and nodes including railway lines, airlines, roads, bridges, ports and airfields, as well as all other 'system essentials' industry. Warden, like the ACTS instructors, assumed in his analytical model that the enemy was the 'same as us', which meant an equally industrialised society. This, though, might not always be the case.

The fundamentals of Warden's theory were based on the systematic target analysis of the State's vital elements, and their subsequent selection and elimination. The destruction or neutralisation of each ring would destabilise the entire system; the extent of such destabilisation would depend on the significance of the ring and the nature of the conflict. The attacks should always be directed against 'the mind of the enemy command'.[37]Although primarily considered a strategic system, it was considered by Warden to be equally applicable to the identification of operational centres of gravity.[38]

Warden acknowledged that vulnerabilities may change through time and space.[39] The nature and characteristics of conflicts, and the adversaries involved in them, along with their specific societal structures, would determine which targets would be selected and attacked. Warden's concepts, in particular the five ring analysis, truly matured only after he had an opportunity to apply them during the 1990–1 Gulf War.

8.2 The role of doctrine in military operations

Military doctrine has been succinctly described as a bridge between thought and action.[40] Doctrine, 'a thought' or 'what is taught',[41] represents a body of

---

37 Warden, op. cit. n 31, at 50 and 54. In the advent of technological advancements, Warden embraced parallel attack – as opposed to serial attack – as the preferred approach in air warfare. Simultaneous attack was aimed at assisting the implementation of three types of military strategies, namely strategic paralysis or decapitation, coercion and finally destruction, which he found politically unviable in modern warfare. J.A. Warden III, 'Air Theory for the Twenty-first Century' in K.P. Magyar and Air University Press (eds), *Challenge and Response: Anticipating US Military Security Concerns*, Air University Press, Maxwell Air Force Base, AL 1996, at 8–14 and 327–9.

38 At the operational level, the innermost COG would be the commander and command, control and communications (C3). Its essentials would include logistics: fuel, weapons and ammunition, as well as food supplies, produced and delivered through the relevant infrastructure to the forces in the field. Warden, op. cit. n 31, at 53.

39 Ibid, at 51–2.

40 K. Homan, 'Doctrine' in A. Aldis and M. Drent (eds), *Common Norms and Good Practices of Civil Military Relations in the EU*, The Centre of European Security Studies, Groningen 2008, at 127.

41 Canadian Military Doctrine, Canadian Forces Joint Publication 01 (CFJP 01), B-GJ-005-000/FP-001, Canadian Forces Chief of Defence Staff, April 2009, at 1-1 para 0103 [hereinafter: CFJP 01].

Military doctrine and international law 181

knowledge accumulated from past experiences. Doctrine is not only forged from history and lessons learnt, it also codifies best practice.[42] It is shaped into a coherent set of 'fundamental principles by which military forces guide their actions in support of the objectives'.[43] It provides a concise, intellectually rigorous guide to principles and methods governing the conduct of military affairs.[44] Doctrine is supposed to inform and influence decision-making and action-taking by the armed forces. As an authoritative source of such direction, doctrine should be applied in any conflict with due judgement. Doctrine is not intended to provide a mathematical formula or solution that can be applied to all situations or decisions, but it provides ideas behind the ability to fight.[45]

Military doctrine – together with the principles of war, doctrinal writings, physical factors (manpower, training, equipment, logistics, etc.), moral considerations (for example: motivation, ethics) – forms the basis of 'military capacity', also known as fighting power or military power.[46] Military capacity means having a quantitative and qualitative ability to conduct military operations.

Military doctrine comprises three elements.[47] The first is the conceptual or theoretical component, which rests in the long-established philosophy and principles of war developed through the centuries. In this context, doctrine supplies analytical teachings of the fundamental tenets of warfare to the current and next generation of fighters.[48] Second, doctrine stipulates how these principles can best be applied to the present state of affairs.[49] The third component looks into the future. Using predictive analysis of the most recent conflicts, and any emergent social or technological developments relevant to military capability, it formulates recommendations as to how military force should best be used in short-term future operations. It also provides the basis for the training of any future cadre.[50]

---

42 See introductory comments to Part II and discussion at the beginning of this chapter.
43 NATO Glossary of Terms and Definitions (English and French), AAP-6 (2013); CFJP 01, op. cit. n 41, at 1–1 para 0104.
44 Foundations of New Zealand Military Doctrine, NZ DDP-D, New Zealand Defence Force, 2nd edn, November 2008, at 1-1 paras 1.2 *et seq.* [hereinafter: NZ DDP-D (2008)].
45 British Defence Doctrine, Joint Doctrine Publications 0-01 (JDP 0-01), Chief of Staffs, The Development, Concepts and Doctrine Centre, UK Ministry of Defence, 4th edn, 2011, at iv [hereinafter: British Defence Doctrine]; Army Doctrine Primer, UK Army Publication, AC 71954, May 2011, at 1-4 [hereinafter: Army Primer].
46 British Defence Doctrine, op. cit. n 45, Chapter 4, at 4-1 to 4-4 paras 401–6; CFJP 01, op. cit. n 41, at 2–3 paras 0210–11 and at 2–8 to 2–9 paras 0218–21; Army Primer, op. cit. n 45, at 1–4.
47 Homan, op. cit. n 40.
48 For instance, in Foundations of New Zealand Military Doctrine, NZ DDP-D, New Zealand Defence Force, February 2004, at 1-3 para 1.5 [hereinafter: NZ DDP-D (2004)].
49 For instance in NZ DDP-D (2004), op. cit. n 48, at 1–3 to 1–5 paras 1.8–14.
50 NZ DDP-D (2004), op. cit. n 48, at 1–3 paras 1.6–7; CFJP 01, op. cit. n 41, at 1–2 para 0105.

182 *Operationalisation of the definition of military objective*

Military doctrine is vital for all military forces, from top to bottom. It constitutes a shared framework of approach to warfare by each of the State's military forces. It influences how their behaviour is shaped on all levels of warfare.[51] Military doctrine provides military organisations with a common basis for understanding the nature of armed conflicts and its conduct, by which it encourages cohesion.[52]

8.2.1 Structure of the sources of doctrine

Military doctrine is divided into two levels. Higher-level doctrine encompasses the philosophy and the principles underlying the approach to military activity. Lower-level doctrine describes the practice and procedures related to the practical application of military force.[53]

Military doctrine is structured hierarchically.[54] It usually comprises a single document of joint military doctrine for all services, known as the 'capstone publication'.[55] A national joint doctrine publication, linking the doctrine to national strategy, is relevant to all aspects of military operations and takes precedence over other joint doctrine publications.

The joint doctrine publications also consist of the fundamental documents relating to key joint operational military activity, namely the planning and execution of campaigns. These are referred to as 'keystone' publications.[56] Below this level, joint tactical doctrine – known as tactics, techniques and procedures – primarily covers procedural aspects of military activity at unit level.[57] In addition to the joint operations doctrine, there are single service publications for specific environments (land, air and maritime). These are known as higher-level environmental doctrine publications, and provide functional guidance for joint and component commanders alike.[58] In this context, some overarching publications are regarded as capstone for a

---

51 *Doctrine for the Armed Forces of the United States*, Joint Publication 1, Joint Chiefs of Staff, 25 March 2013 at I-1, s 1(b) [hereinafter: USJP1]. See also the discussion in 4.2 and 5.3.

52 Army Primer, op. cit. n 45, at 2–1.

53 Ibid, at 3–1; British Defence Doctrine, op. cit. n 45, para 408.

54 CFJP 01, op. cit. n 41, at 1–4 para 0112; British Defence Doctrine, op. cit. n 45, para 408.

55 The following examples are considered to be capstone doctrine documents: British Defence Doctrine, op. cit. n 45; USJP1, op. cit. n 51; CFJP 01, op. cit. n 41; and Foundations of New Zealand Military Doctrine, NZ DDP-D, New Zealand Defence Force, 3rd edn, June 2012 [hereinafter: NZ DDP-D].

56 Joint operational practices for functional areas, such as intelligence or communication systems support or any other system relating to campaigning, provide an additional sub-layer of the joint operational doctrine.

57 This format is followed by the military forces of, for example, the United Kingdom, New Zealand, Canada and the United States. British Defence Doctrine, op. cit. n 45; NZ DDP-D, op. cit. n 55; CFJP 01, op. cit. n 41; USJP1, op. cit. n51.

58 CFJP 01, op. cit. n41, at 1–3 para 0107.

Military doctrine and international law   183

particular environment, for example the UK Air and Space Doctrine, and are supplemented by several keystone operational and tactical publications.[59]

Finally, apart from functional military doctrine, one can also distinguish thematic doctrine documents.[60] These are characterised by the inclusion in a single publication of all principles, procedures and practices relevant to the particular thematic area, such as type of campaign. This would include publications dealing with, for instance, multinational operations or multi-agency operations.

8.2.2 Doctrinal interoperability[61]

Conceptual coherence of the military doctrine between services of the same State, as well as between the forces of different States in multinational coalitions, is of tremendous practical importance. NATO Allied doctrine, the most influential international source of unified military thinking, asserts that:

> common NATO doctrine is essential to enhance interoperability, both at the intellectual level, allowing commanders from different nations to have a common approach to operations, and at the procedural level.[62]

States usually ensure their own doctrine is allied with the doctrinal tenets of the international organisations or other States with which they associate themselves. The doctrine of Canadian forces, in particular, prioritises key doctrines of NATO, the US, the UK, Australia and New Zealand to ensure compatibility while carrying out allied/multinational and combined operations.[63] British doctrinal documents are closely linked to NATO doctrine, and

---

59   *UK Air and Space Doctrine*, Joint Doctrine Publication JDP-030 (formerly AP 3000), UK Chiefs of Staff, The Development, Concepts and Doctrine Centre, Ministry of Defence, July 2013.
60   Functional doctrine is organised according to the discrete functions of military activity, for instance campaigning or targeting.
61   Flowing from the requirement of unity of effort, interoperability is defined as 'the ability to operate in synergy in the execution of assigned tasks' (US DOD, *Dictionary of Military and Associated Terms*, Joint Publication, JP 1-02, 8 November 2010 with amendments as of March 2014). Doctrinal interoperability provides a common conceptual platform, enabling the synergic execution of tasks between services, units and formations, as well as between the foreign forces in an alliance or coalition. (See also USJP1, op. cit. n 51, at II-7 s 7(b); *Unified Action Armed Forces*, Joint Publication JP 0-2, US Joint Chiefs of Staff, 10 July 2001, at I-10 s 10(b) and at III-17 para 13(d) [hereinafter: USJP 0-2]; CFJP 01, op. cit. n 41, at 1–4 paras 0113–14 and at 6–5 to 6–6 paras 0617–19).
62   NATO Allied Joint Doctrine, AJP-01 (D), December 2010, para 0104 [hereinafter: AJP-01 (D)].
63   CFJP 01, op. cit. n 41, at 1–4 paras 0113–14 and at 6–6 para 0620. See also *The Tactical Commander's Guide to Command and Control in Operations*, FT-05 (Eng.), Armée de Terre, Centre de doctrine d'emploi des forces, Ministère de la Défense, November 2011, at 12–13 [hereinafter: FT-05].

184 *Operationalisation of the definition of military objective*

are represented in the Allied Joint Publications with caveats relevant to British interests. The European setting of the UK would require UK doctrine to be aligned with European Union Security and Defence Policy, which is also based on NATO doctrine. Strategic military forums involving forces of various States such as ABCA, or the Multilateral Interoperability Programme, promote the development of a coherent doctrine among Member States.[64] Some States may choose to adopt other States' doctrine below the capstone level.[65]

8.3 Doctrinal perspectives on levels of warfare

A three-tier framework for the command and control of operations and analysis provides a convenient way of systematising military activity.[66] The three main accepted categories of warfare are strategic (national and military), operational and tactical. These will be discussed in more detail below.

The direction of any military effort comes from the military-strategic level, while the planning and execution of operations is rooted in operational and tactical level activities.[67] Although often viewed in the context of command and control functions, the categories are not necessarily directly linked to a particular level of command, size of unit or type of force.[68] They are, in effect, distinguished according to their effects, or their contribution towards achieving specified objectives.[69] Military engagements can, in practice, produce effects across the three categories. Therefore, a strict delineation of these categories could often be frustrated.[70]

It should be recognised at this point that military activity is also conceptually organised according to a hierarchy. At the highest level, the military contribution to the achievement of a national strategic aim is translated into

---

64 The ABCA organisation comprises members of American, British, Australian, Canadian and New Zealand forces. The Multilateral Interoperability Programme is an interoperability organisation established to facilitate use of command and control (C2) systems in a multinational or coalition environment. AUSCANNZUKUS is a naval command, control, communications and computers (C4) interoperability organisation that involves Australia, Canada, New Zealand, the UK and the US.

65 The New Zealand Defence forces, for instance, apply on a case-by-case basis the Australian Defence Force's joint operational and application level publications, while retaining their own strategic and joint or single-force tactical doctrine. NZ DDP-D (2008), at 4.3–4.4 paras 4.7–10.

66 The framework permits a clearer view of military activity before, during and after the conduct of military operations. British Defence Doctrine, op. cit. n 45, para 220; Indian Army Doctrine, Headquarters Army Training Command, October 2004, para 3.2; USJP1, op. cit. n 51, s 5(a) at I-7.

67 AJP-01 (D), op. cit. n 62, para 0113; NZ DDP-D, op. cit. n 55, paras 2.05–6.

68 *Joint Operations*, Joint Publication JP 3-0, US Joint Chiefs of Staff, 11 August 2011, at I-12 s 6(a) [hereinafter: USJP3-0].

69 Ibid.

70 AJP-01 (D), op. cit. n 62, para 0117; NZ DDP-D, op. cit. n 55, at 17–18 para 2.10; British Defence Doctrine, op. cit. n 45, para 220.

Military doctrine and international law 185

a campaign's end-state. A 'campaign' encompasses 'military operations' that are directed towards the achievement of one or more campaign objectives.[71] Military operations consist of a series of synchronised 'military actions' directed at the accomplishment of the commander's objectives, and their supporting effects.[72] Operations have a unifying theme that gives them an underlying purpose, such as major combat operations, security and stabilisation or peace support. Military actions, in turn, comprise tactical activities undertaken as part of Joint Action.

8.3.1 Strategy and strategic military doctrine

At the strategic level, top-level governing bodies determine the national strategic aim, strategic objectives and guidance through their policies.[73] The military contribution to the achievement of a national strategic aim is thus reflected in the military strategic end-state, expressed through several military strategic objectives supporting the theatre/campaign strategic planning.[74]

The maintenance of, and control over, the overarching national interests of security, territorial integrity, political independence and stability constitute the central concerns of the grand (or national) strategy. This grand strategy represents the highest level of planning for the comprehensive and coherent use of all means of national power to secure national interests.[75] The national security strategy may include both a national defence strategy as well as a foreign relations policy.[76]

Military strategy focuses on the development and use of military forces.[77] Military strategic level doctrine therefore addresses 'the military aspects of

---

71 *Campaign Planning*, Joint Doctrine Publication 01 (JDP 05), UK Chiefs of Staff, The Development, Concepts and Doctrine Centre, UK Ministry of Defence, 3rd edn, July 2013, at 2-09 Fig. 2.3 and at 2-11 [hereinafter: JDP 05]; *Joint Operation Planning*, Joint Publication JP 5-0, US Joint Chiefs of Staff, 11 August 2011, at III-20–1 [hereinafter: USJP5-0]; NZ DDP-D, op. cit. n 55 para 2.09.

72 NZ DDP-D, op. cit. n 55, at 17.

73 A national strategic aim is the government's (or president's) declared purpose in a given situation. A strategic objective is a goal to be achieved by one or more instruments of national power to meet the national strategic aim. JDP 05, op. cit. n 71, paras 202–10; Indian Army Doctrine, op. cit. n 66, para 3.3.

74 USJP3–0, op. cit. n 68, at I-13 s 6(b); JDP 05, op. cit. n 71, at 2–7 para 211.

75 The instruments of power encompass various diplomatic, economic or, indeed, military tools to seize and maintain control of an opposing party, or to eliminate a perceived threat, whether internal or external to the State (national security policies). CFJP 01, op. cit. n 41, at 3–2 para 0301 and at 2–1 para 0201; *Campaigning*, Joint Doctrine Publication 01 (JDP 01), UK Chiefs of Staff, The Development, Concepts and Doctrine Centre, UK Ministry of Defence, 2nd edn, December 2008, at 2–3 para 212 [hereinafter: JDP 01].

76 For instance in USJP 0-2, op. cit. n 61, at I-2 s 2(a) and (b); US Department of Defense, *Dictionary of Military and Associated Terms*, op. cit. n 61, at 182–3.

77 JDP 01, op. cit. n 75, at 2–6 para 220; USJP1, op. cit. n 51, at xii.

186 *Operationalisation of the definition of military objective*

planning and direction of conflict'.[78] Accordingly, this requires having a clear idea of the desired military end-states, and how they are to be achieved.[79] The rationale of the military strategy must correspond with the objectives enshrined in the grand (national) strategy.[80] The military strategy links the political desires of the governing bodies, which provide a rationale for military operations,[81] to the operational power of military forces and other instruments of national power.[82] Military considerations may have an impact on shaping defence policy, which should not demand what is militarily impossible.[83] The military strategy's main focus is on the organisation and effective allocation of military resources – for both current and long-term operational demands – in order to achieve the government's political and military objectives.[84]

Military strategy is used to support the development and application of military power towards the achievement of the strategic end-states. This skill is known as strategic art. It governs the relationship between 'ends' (objectives), 'ways' (representing strategic direction and guidance) and 'means', namely resources.[85] Strategic commanders provide the guidance and direction for all military operations, including contributions to multinational campaigns. In particular campaigns and operations, they focus on identifying and defining the strategic military goals consistent with national security strategy. They also bear a responsibility towards identifying the desired strategic effects, and the best course of action elaborated through campaign-planning.[86]

Military goals, also known as military objectives, are 'clearly defined, decisive, and attainable goal(s) toward which every military operation should be directed'.[87] These are military strategic and operational goals consistent with

---

78 NZ DDP-D, op. cit. n 55, at 15 para 2.05; British Defence Doctrine, op. cit. n 45, paras 116–17.

79 The military end-state is usually a point in time or circumstances/conditions, beyond which the military instrument of national power is no longer necessary to accomplish the remaining national strategic objectives. USJP5-0, op. cit. n 71, III-7 s 4.b.(2) and at III-19 s 6(b); NZ DDP-D, op. cit. n 55, at 16 paras 2.05–6.

80 JDP 01, op. cit. n 75, at 2–5 para 219.

81 British Defence Doctrine, op. cit. n 45, at 216 para 118.

82 British Defence Doctrine, op. cit. n 45, paras 115–17; similarly in AJP-01 (D), op. cit. n 62, para 0404.

83 Liddle Hart, op. cit. n 17; JDP 01, op. cit. n 75, at 2–6 para 221. Defence policy does not necessarily deal with the same issues as military strategy, although the two appear closely related. While strategy is concerned primarily with the political outcomes of the threat or use of force, defence policy provides the objectives of the strategy and shapes military capability (British Defence Doctrine, op. cit. n 45, paras 110–14).

84 British Defence Doctrine, op. cit. n 45, para 115; CFJP 01, op. cit. n 41, at 3–2 para 0303; USJP1, op. cit. n 51, at xiii, I-8, s 5(b).

85 JDP 01, op. cit. n 75, at 2–5 para 216 and 3–8 and 3–9 para 321; Indian Army Doctrine, op. cit. n 66, para 3.3.

86 CFJP 01, op. cit. n 41, at 3–3 para 0308; USJP3-0, op. cit. n 68, at I-7 s 4(d); JDP 01, op. cit. n 75, at 3–9 to 3–11 paras 322–4.

87 See the introduction to this chapter for clarification regarding the term military objective. USJP5-0, op. cit. n 71, Appendix A, at A-1 s 2(a).

Military doctrine and international law 187

a mission's purpose. Objectives help to maintain the focus of military action and unity of effort.[88] Military strategic objectives concentrate on the role of military forces in attaining national strategic aims.[89] In support of this, strategic commanders designate the means, comprising a spectrum of military resources, principal financial arrangements, and command and communication responsibilities.[90]

In safeguarding national security goals, the armed forces are guided by the imperatives of deterrence and coercion. Coercion attempts to induce opponents into behaviour that they may not have otherwise chosen to display, for example by compelling them to take certain positive action.[91] Deterrence, on the other hand, is aimed at dissuading a potential opponent from adopting a course of action that would threaten defence and other national interests.[92] There could be direct (violent) and non-direct (non-violent) means of coercion or deterrence.[93] The application of military force, through the 'deliberate use and orchestration of available military capabilities to realise the effects needed to secure a favourable outcome', will affect the enemy's ability to understand the situation and to make informed and effective decisions.[94] The application of such means may produce three main strategic military effects – the disruption, defeat and destruction of the opponent.[95]

88 USJP 0-2, op. cit. n 61, at I-6 s 5; Indian Army Doctrine, op. cit. n 66, para 4.24; *General Tactics*, FT-02 (Eng.), Armée de Terre, Centre de doctrine d'emploi des forces, Ministère de la Défense, July 2010, at 32 [hereinafter: FT-02].
89 USJP5-0, op. cit. n 71, at III-1 s 1(b) and III-7 s 4(b)(1); Indian Army Doctrine, op. cit. n 66, para 4.4.
90 CFJP 01, op. cit. n 41, at 3–3 para 0308; USJP1, op. cit. n 51, at III-11 Fig. II-1 and III-9, s 14; USJP5-0, op. cit. n 71, at IV-31 s 6(b)(1). Security strategies and defence policies may favour coalition operations over autonomous actions. In such cases, any issues of interoperability, the allocation of joint military resources and guidance regarding command, coordination and communications solutions need to be enshrined in the relevant military strategic documents. (USJP1 op. cit. n 51, at II-7 s 7(b)).
91 These are known as compellance operations. Compellance operations are associated with the threat or use of lethal force to establish control and dominance, to induce a change in behaviour, or to enforce and maintain compliance of the opponent with agreements, mechanisms, mandates, etc. USJP1 op. cit. n 51, at I-13 s 9(3).
92 British Defence Doctrine, op. cit. n 45, paras 153–60; CFJP 01, op. cit. n 41, at 2–2 para 0207; USJP5-0, op. cit. n 11, at xxiv, Appendix E at E-2 s 2 and GL-9; USJP3-0, op. cit. n 68, at xx.
93 British Defence Doctrine, op. cit. n 45, para 161; CFJP 01, op. cit. n 41, at 2–3 para 0208.
94 British Defence Doctrine, op. cit. n 45, para 155. US Forces doctrine defines such force application as interdiction (USJP3-0, op. cit. n 68, at III-22 s 4(a) and III-24 s 4).
95 Disruption is the least destructive effect, diminishing the opponent's physical and moral capabilities. Defeat implies the comprehensive disruption and/or partial destruction of the enemy's capability, so he can no longer be perceived to be an effective threat. (British Defence Doctrine, supra op. cit. n 45, para 162; Indian Army Doctrine, supra op. cit. n 66, para 3.11).

188　*Operationalisation of the definition of military objective*

8.3.1.1 Principles of war

The principles of war provide a foundation for all military activity, including combat operations. British Defence Doctrine cautions that the principles should be adhered to with reasoned 'judgement, common sense and intelligent interpretation', as their relevance is subject to the broader context of the situation, including other legal, political, moral and ethical considerations.[96] Which principles of war States adopt will vary from State to State, although some rules are common to most of them.[97] These standards include the selection and maintenance of aims or objectives, known as the 'master principle'[98], surprise, security and the maintenance of morale, cooperation/unity of effort (unified action), flexibility and sustainability.[99]

A unified action principle requires effective interoperability and acting in a joint and expedient manner, from planning and executing operations through to training and exercises.[100] Concentration of force, known as mass,[101] as well as economy of force, in particular, relate to the application of fighting power in order to achieve planned effects.[102] The principle of economy opposes the wasteful allocation of resources that do not contribute to achieving and upholding the primary objectives.[103] In compliance with the economy of force principle, a commander is expected to identify and apply 'the best tool, in the right place, at the right time, leading to the right result'.[104]

Identifying clearly defined, simple and accepted campaign objectives is fundamental to the prosecution of all military actions to attain the anticipated

---

96　British Defence Doctrine, op. cit. n 45, paras 205, 407.

97　See a comparative outline of the principles upheld by the UK, the Netherlands and the Czech Republic in Homan, op. cit. n 40; see also NZ DDP-D, op. cit. n 55, at 36–41 paras 4.12–27; CFJP 01, op. cit. n 41, at 2–4 to 2–6 paras 0212–14; FT-02, op. cit. n 88, at 30–6.

98　NZ DDP-D, op. cit. n 55, at 36 para 4.17.

99　Some States also uphold the principle of offensive action, designed to gain, seize and retain the initiative and advantage. British Defence Doctrine, op. cit. n 45, paras 206–15; NZ DDP-D, op. cit. n 55, at 37–8 para 4.19; CFJP 01, op. cit. n 41, at 2–5 para 0212(c); Indian Army Doctrine, op. cit. n 66, s 6.

100　USJP1 op. cit. n 51, at xiii, xv and II-13 s 9(b); Indian Army Doctrine, op. cit. n 66, para 4.24; USJP3-0, op. cit. n 68, Appendix A at A-2 s 2(c).

101　Field Manual 3-0, United States Department of Army, 27 February 2008 incorporating change of February 2011, at A-2 paras A-6 to A-9 [hereinafter: FM 3-0]; Indian Army Doctrine, op. cit. n 66, para 2.29.

102　Concentration of force stresses the need for the decisive and synchronised application of force in order to realise the intended goal in a specific time and space. Economy of force or effort demands the most effective use of resources to achieve the required aims. AJP-01 (D), op. cit. n 62, para 0118(e); British Defence Doctrine, op. cit. n 45, paras 206–15; NZ DDP-D, op. cit. n 55, at 39 para 4.23; CFJP 01, op. cit. n 41, at 2–5 para 0212(f); FM 3-0, op. cit. n 101, at A-2 para A-10.

103　This means that in situations or areas of lower priority, it would not be necessary to employ all the available forces, or all forces equally, to achieve the desired primary outcome. NZ DDP-D, op. cit. n 55, at 38–9 para 4.24; CFJP 01, op. cit. n 41, at 2–5 para 0212(g); Indian Army Doctrine, op. cit. n 66, para 2.31; FT-02, op. cit. n 88, at 33.

104　British Defence Doctrine, op. cit. n 45, para 212.

Military doctrine and international law 189

end-state.[105] When the objective is set as a 'main effort', all joint activity should be directed towards achieving that objective.[106] Each phase of a conflict, and even each operation, may have a separate aim, whether strategic, operational or tactical. Subordinate aims are often more limited, but more concrete than the higher-level aims. Most importantly, they should be consistent with each other.[107] Developing and agreeing common military goals is particularly important in multinational operations.[108] One of the sources of 'mission creep' is a situation in which additional tasks are adopted that may not conform to the original purpose of the mission, as well as potentially being in conflict with the political and military interests of some States inside the coalition.[109] 'Mission creep' may lead to the collapse of the coalition if not contained.

8.3.1.2 Limitations

In addition to identifying the strategic goals and campaign objectives (end-states) in particular conflicts, military strategists need to analyse any political, financial or legal limitations when considering the use of force.[110] Political decisions may restrict or widen the nature and scope of military goals, which, as already emphasised, should be clearly defined prior to the campaign.[111]

Operations should be planned and undertaken with a clear understanding of the relevant national and international law.[112] Law, as much as policy decisions, influences what targets are legitimate as well as defining the boundaries of lawful military activities.[113]

---

105 AJP-01 (D), op. cit. n 62, paras 0118(a) and (b). It is worth noting that some tactical military objectives, also referred to as military targets, mean specific physical objects or capabilities (i.e. physical objectives) that become subject to seizure, damage, destruction or neutralisation if such action is required to fulfil the commander's plans (USJP5-0, op. cit. n 71, at III-11 s 7(b)(2)). The physical objective should not be confused with the military aim. The former contributes to attaining the latter, though the two terms may sometimes overlap (USJP 0-2, op. cit. n 61, at I-6 s 5).

106 Joint activity includes the collaboration of military forces and other agencies and organisations, as well as other States if they are contributing. AJP-01 (D), op. cit. n 62, para 0118(a); Indian Army Doctrine, op. cit. n 66, para 4.22; British Defence Doctrine, op. cit. n 45, para 206.

107 NZ DDP-D, op. cit. n 55, at 6-12, para 4.16.

108 CFJP 01, op. cit. n 41, at 6–7 para 0627; USJP3-0, op. cit. n 68, at I-8 to I-11 s 5(c) and (d) and Appendix A, at A-2 s 2(f).

109 AJP-01 (D), op. cit. n 62, para 0512(b); CFJP 01, op. cit. n 41, at 6–7 para 0629.

110 CFJP 01, op. cit. n 41, at 2–14, paras 0233–4; USJP1, op. cit. n 51, at II-21 s 11(a)(3–4).

111 British Defence Doctrine, op. cit. n 45, paras 166, 171; CFJP 01, op. cit. n 41, at 2-14 para 0234; Indian Army Doctrine, op. cit. n 66, paras 3.3 and 4.2.

112 The relation between the law and doctrine will be further explored in part B of this chapter. British Defence Doctrine, op. cit. n 45, paras 167, 171–2, IB5.

113 There is an intricate relationship between policy and law. The State may abide by the provisions of a treaty, even if it is not formally bound to it as a matter of law, if such policy decisions are predicted to improve cooperation and cohesion in allied/coalition operations.

190 *Operationalisation of the definition of military objective*

8.3.2 Operational level framework

The planning, execution and maintenance of campaigns and major operations within the theatre and other operational areas are undertaken only at the operational level of warfare.[114] Military doctrine coined the term 'operational art' to describe processes and methods involved in matching actions and appropriate resources to accomplish strategic objectives.[115] These objectives are translated into more specific operational objectives through the design, organisation and conduct of strategies, campaigns and other major operations and battles.[116] Operational context or design is expected to contain a thorough analysis of the situation, including the cultural and historical context of the enemy nation or society,[117] the potential points of engagement and the adversary's operational centres of gravity (COG).[118] An operational commander's functions include further refining the theatre strategy and the campaign plans received from his or her superior authority, and allocating appropriate resources.[119] Operational commanders are in charge of directing the military effort in coordinated and sustained operations, and do so by issuing orders to tactical leaders.[120]

In devising an operational strategy, operational commanders should consider a variety of combat tools, usually in combination.[121] Depending on

114 JDP 01, op. cit. n 75, at 2–1 para 203; USJP3-0, op. cit. n 68, at I-13 s 6(c); Indian Army Doctrine, op. cit. n 66, para 3.4; FT-02, op. cit. n 88, at 69; British Defence Doctrine, op. cit. n 45, para 218.
115 JDP 05, op. cit. n 71, at 2–4 and 205, paras 205–6; USJP3-0, op. cit. n 68, at II-3 to II-4 s 3(a)–(c). Strategic commanders issue strategic guidance that translates the political, strategic direction into the objectives necessary to achieve clearly stipulated end-states, i.e. what amounts to a success or victory, allocated military resources and capabilities, and the method of achieving the end-states and objectives. Operational art 'integrates Ends, Ways and Means across the levels of warfare'. USJP5-0, op. cit. n 71, at xix, xxv, I-5 s 4 and at Chapter III throughout; USJP3-0, op. cit. n 68, at xiii, II-3 to II-5 s 3; JDP 01, op. cit. n 75, at 3–8 para 321; Indian Army Doctrine, op. cit. n 66, para 3.4 and para 4.2; FT-02, op. cit. n 88, at 69; USJP1, op. cit. n 51, at I-8 s 5(c).
116 NZ DDP-D, op. cit. n 55, at 37 para 4.16; JDP 01, op. cit. n 75, at 3–6 para 315; USJP3-0, op. cit. n 68, at II-4 s 3(c).
117 British Defence Doctrine, op. cit. n 45, paras 225–304, 403–4; JDP 01, op. cit. n 75, at 3–18 paras 342–3.
118 Centre of gravity is 'a characteristic, capability to influence from which a nation, an alliance, a military force or other civil or militia grouping draws its freedom of action, physical strength, cohesion or will to fight' (JDP 01, op. cit. n 75, at Lexicon-7). The notion of COGs will be crucially important to the process of targeting. It will therefore be discussed in more detail in 8.3.1. USJP3-0, op. cit. n 68, GL-6; JDP 01, op. cit. n 75, at 1-5 to 1-6 para 115 and 3-22 para 351; Indian Army Doctrine, op. cit. n 66, para 3.7; USJP5-0, op. cit. n 71, at III-22 s 6(e).
119 AJP-01 (D), op. cit. n 62 paras 0115, 501–9; NZ DDP-D, op. cit. n 55, at 41–2 paras 4.32 to 4.35; CFJP 01, op. cit. n 41, at 1-3 para 0106; USJP1, op. cit. n 51, at V-6 and V-7 s 3(c); Indian Army Doctrine, op. cit. n 66, para 3.4; FT-05, op. cit. n 63, at 10–11.
120 AJP-01 (D), op. cit. n 62, para 0503; USJP5-0, op. cit. n 71, at III-7 s 4(b)(1); FT-05, op. cit. n 63, at 14.
121 JDP 01, op. cit. n 75, at 3-21 paras 348 *et seq.*

Military doctrine and international law   191

the nature of the goals, these may include Joint Operation/Action,[122] Fires[123] (the use of physical means or force to create primarily physical effects[124]), Manoeuvre[125] and Influence Activities consisting of some kind of potential to affect the behaviour of others.[126] Manoeuvre is defined as a coordinated activity aimed at gaining an advantage within the position (time and space),[127] with the main focus on exhausting the enemy's cohesion and will to fight.[128] It involves using or threatening to use force though violent and non-violent means.[129] Manoeuvre at the operational level is regarded as a means of concentrating forces to affect the COG, or focusing on the decisive points (relative to enemy COG)[130] to achieve psychological effects and surprise, as well as the physical effects and momentum necessary to attain the ultimate goals. When opponents become vulnerable, they can be further affected through direct firepower/attack on their COGs, and through interdiction operations. Interdiction is a method that seeks to divert, disrupt/neutralise and destroy the enemy's surface military power before it can be used against friendly forces.[131]

---

122 AJP-01 (D), op. cit. n 62, paras 0505–8; British Defence Doctrine, op. cit. n 45, para 518.

123 Fires involves using physical means to cause primarily physical effects (JDP 01, op. cit. n 71, at 3-14 para 332) and encompasses offensive attack, including precision strikes against enemy COGs by air, missile, special or any other linear or non-linear operation. Non-linear operations involve engagements beyond the designated forward lines of operations, indicating a greater focus on objectives rather than geographical position or direction (FT-02, op. cit. n 88, at 22–4).

124 British Defence Doctrine, op. cit. n 45, para 518 and attached footnotes.

125 American spelling: Maneuver. USJP3–0, op. cit. n 68, at GL-12, xv, III-28 and III-29 s 5(c).

126 British Defence Doctrine, op. cit. n 45, para 518 and attached footnotes.

127 British Defence Doctrine, op. cit. n 45, para 518 and attached footnotes; CFJP 01, op. cit. n 41, at 6-13 and 6-14 paras 0642 and 0644; FT-02, op. cit. n 88, at 54; NZ DDP-D, op. cit. n 55, at 41 paras 4.29 and 4.31.

128 JDP 01, op. cit. n 75, at 3-12 para 328; CFJP 01, op. cit. n 41, at 6-14 para 0643; FT-02, op. cit. n 88, at 54.

129 The manoeuvrist approach puts great emphasis on the defeat or neutralisation of the enemy through indirect means. British Defence Doctrine, op. cit. n 45, paras 521–3; CFJP 01, op. cit. n 41, at 6-13 to 6-14 paras 0642–4; AJP-01 (D), op. cit. n 62, para 0611. See the operational aspect of the manoeuvrist approach called 'Engage' in JDP 01, op. cit. n 75, at 3-16 para 335, and 'Shape' in JDP 01, op. cit. n 75, at 3-15 para 334.

130 Decisive points are geographical spots/positions, key events, critical factors or functions, which would be attacked due to their ability to provide leverage against the enemy COCs (at the operational level) and/or directly contribute to the accomplishment of the objective (at a tactical level). The application of combat power against a number of decisive points, but avoiding a direct attack on COGs, is known as an indirect approach. USJP3–0, op. cit. n 68, GL-8; USJP5-0, op. cit. n 71, at III-26 s 6(f) *et seq.*; CFJP 01, op. cit. n 41, at 6-14 para 0645; Indian Army Doctrine, op. cit. n 66, para 4.9; FT-02, op. cit. n 88, at 39–42.

131 See the operational aspects of 'Engage' and 'Exploit' of the manoeuvrist approach in JDP 01, op. cit. n 75, at 3-16 paras 335–6, and more comprehensively discussed in, for instance, *Joint Interdiction*, Joint Publication JP 3-03, US Joint Chiefs of Staff, 14 October 2011 [hereinafter: JP 3-03].

192   *Operationalisation of the definition of military objective*

Commanders may also choose to employ an approach known as attrition.[132] This involves a constant and incremental wearing down of opponents, with a view to weakening their military capability.[133] Accompanying attrition would be a surgical 'strategic attack' against military, economic or political targets selected to help achieve national and military strategic objectives. Attacking such targets would not necessarily need to contribute to the achievement of operational objectives.[134]

Some of these techniques or tactics will be more relevant than others, or employed more frequently by one of the services.[135] The operational commander's task would be to integrate and synchronise the appropriate elements.[136]

8.3.3 Tactical level of warfare

The level at which units, formations and individuals confront an opponent is known as tactical warfare.[137] The tactical level is where fighting actually takes place, where battles and engagements are fought under the direction of component commanders.[138] It is, therefore, focused mainly on the execution of military tasks and activities in a localised dimension.[139]

Tactics determine the ways in which formations, small units or even individuals or weapons systems are deployed in order to achieve desirable objectives.[140] The three services (sea, air and land), as well as special forces,

---

132 Attrition means a reduction in or weakening of the effectiveness of military capability by loss of *matériel* or personnel. Australian Defence Force Publication 04.1.1 – Glossary, ADFP 04.1.1 (101).

133 R.E. Simpkin, *Race to the Swift: Thought on Twenty-First Century Warfare*, Brassey's, London 1994, at 96–7; Indian Army Doctrine, op. cit. n 66, para 4.12.

134 US military doctrine purports that such attacks could be conducted independently from the overall conduct of the military campaign. USJP3-0, op. cit. n 68, at III-22 s 4(a)(5); JP 3-03, op. cit. n 131, at II-12 s 2(a); *Annex 3-70 Strategic Attack*, US Air Force Doctrine, 12 June 2007, at 2, 5 and 7.

135 For example, South Africa upholds both attrition and manoeuvre methods in addition to the indirect approach. Republic of South Africa, *Joint Warfare Manual (JWM) 91: The Levels of War*, Department of Defence, March 1998, at A-1, cited in E. Jordaan and F. Vrey, 'Operational Strategy and the South African Way of War: The Way Forward', 28(1) *Strategic Review for Southern Africa* 2006, 30–62 at n 26.

136 AJP-01 (D), op. cit. n 62, para 0531; JDP 01, op. cit. n 75, at 4-7 para 415.

137 British Defence Doctrine, op. cit. n 45, para 219; Indian Army Doctrine, op. cit. n 66, para 3.5.

138 Battles consist of a set of related engagements that last longer and may involve a greater number of forces than engagements. An engagement is defined as a tactical conflict and short-duration action between opposing forces. USJP3-0, op. cit. n 68, at GL-9; FT-02, op. cit. n 88, at 39, 68.

139 USJP1, op. cit. n 51, at I-8 s 5(d) and I-9 s 6(a).

140 Tactics focus on the use and composition of forces in relation to each other. FM 3-0, op. cit. n 101, at D-2 para D-7.

Military doctrine and international law 193

assets and enablers, are used to produce effects contributing to the successful accomplishment or gaining of military objectives, whether specific to the particular mission or to the concrete strategic and operational goals of the campaign.[141] Combat forces are employed in an ordered sequence and with specified functions or tasks to perform controlled manoeuvres.[142] Tactical art, which is applied at the level of confrontation, and often in chaotic combat circumstances, is regarded as one of the most fundamental skills that service-men and women must master.

In addition to tactics, numerous techniques, procedures and technical instructions have been developed to address the specific aspects of the required behaviour or performance, such as accomplishing a mission, tasks and functions. Techniques serve as a primary means of passing on the lessons learnt in previous operations.[143] Procedures, on the other hand, being inherently prescriptive, provide detailed guidance in the form of simple and clear steps required for the successful completion of an assignment or support of combat operations, e.g. an effective operation or maintenance of equipment.[144]

Some of the targets that the grand military theoreticians identified as being of significant interest could cause problems in the application of the test for lawful targets. Some of their ideas found their way into strategic and operational military doctrine through the identification of strategic, opera-tional and tactical targets. Targets associated with the ability to wage war – such as command, control and communications – include operational targets as 'governmental control' objects.[145] These, on the tactical level, comprise 'governmental administrative ministries' as well as TV and radio facilities.[146] Military thinking clearly translates into doctrine, which asserts the identification of targets to which the application of the definition could be problematic. This requires a consideration of the relationship between military doctrine and the law, which follows next.

---

141 AJP-01 (D), op. cit. n 62, para 0115; NZ DDP-D, op. cit. n 55, at 16 para 2.08; CFJP 01, op. cit. n 41, at 1-3 para 0106; Indian Army Doctrine, op. cit. n 66, para 3.5; USJP1 op. cit. n 51, at I-8 s 5(e).
142 USJP3-0, op. cit. n 68, at III-22 s 5; USJP 0-2, op. cit. n 61, at IV-5 s 4(a).
143 FM 3-0, op. cit. n 101, at D-2 para D-8.
144 Ibid, at D-2 para D-9.
145 AFP14-210, op. cit. n 20, at 44; see also 8.6.1.
146 Ibid.

194 *Operationalisation of the definition of military objective*

PART B: THE RELATIONSHIP BETWEEN MILITARY DOCTRINE AND THE LAW

The military doctrine discussed so far has, perhaps unsurprisingly, contained only two brief indications that the law is a consideration in military activity. The mention of law was noted in the context of higher-level doctrine, which stresses that law is one of the limitations that commanders must take into account when planning and executing operations.[147] The aim of this part of the chapter is to look more closely at the presence of the law in military doctrine, in particular targeting doctrine, as well as in non-doctrinal sources relevant to the law of armed conflict. The general discussion regarding the law and doctrine is in section 4, while a more specific discussion in the context of targeting is presented in section 5. After establishing the nature of the relationship between law and doctrine, section 6 will discuss specific issues arising from any possible tensions in that relationship, which may affect how the definition of military objective is interpreted.

8.4 The recognition of law in doctrine

There is no doubt that the military doctrine discussed so far implies that armed forces are conscious that they need to take the law into account when they act. It appears clear that the law is not incorporated *in toto* into doctrine; instead, it is viewed as a separate source of obligation. Figure 8.1, used by US forces, illustrates this approach.[148]

Policy and legal delineations are normally set out in the Rules of Engagement (ROE), which contain a mixture of political, military and legal considerations. They are regarded as lawful orders in the context of a specific campaign.[149] They are issued to ensure that soldiers' actions are consistent with the law, national policy, and military goals and regulations.[150] The ROE, which regulate the use of armed force, should take into account

---

147 See discussion in 8.3.2.2. For the reminder of this chapter the term *military objective* will be used in its legal sense.

148 Operational Law Handbook, JA 422, International and Operational Law Department, The Judge Advocate General's Legal Center and School, 1997 edn, at 8-1 [hereinafter: Operational Law Handbook 1997]; *Air Force Operations and the Law: A Guide for Air, Space and Cyber Forces*, US Air Force, The Judge Advocate General's School 2002, at 270.

149 CFJP 01, op. cit. n 41, at 2-16 para 0241.This refers to mission or operation-specific ROE; there are also more general Conflict ROE. See also D. Mandsager (ed.), *Rules of Engagement Handbook*, International Institute of Humanitarian Law, Sanremo, November 2009 and G.D. Solis, *The Law of Armed Conflict: International Humanitarian Law in War*, Cambridge University Press, Cambridge 2010, at 491 *et seq.*

150 USJP1 op. cit. n 51, at I-4 s 3(b); FM 3-0, op. cit. n 101, at 1-19 para 1-85; JDP 01, op. cit. n 75, at 4-21 para 450. See also J.-M. Veyrat, 'The Commanders Indispensible Freedom of Action', 4 *Doctrine: The Legal Environment for Ground Forces*, Ministère de la Défense, General Military Review, September 2004, 5–7.

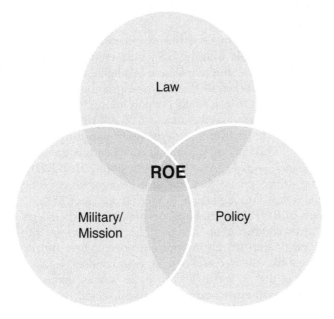

Figure 8.1 Legal, political/policy and military considerations in Rules of Engagement (ROE).

all the above.[151] They vary between operations, and may change during a campaign. In multinational operations, the States involved would normally agree a common set of ROE, which would not preclude them from retaining potentially different interpretations of various rules.[152] Differences in interpretation of the same ROE might also occur, and could be dictated by specific legal obligations, policy or customary practice. In NATO-led operations, efforts are made to issue a single set of ROE applicable to all allied forces. However, national contingents may issue their own national ROE to

151 British Defence Doctrine, op. cit. n 45, para 172; *Joint Targeting*, Joint Publication JP 3–60, US Joint Chiefs of Staff, 31 January 2013, at A-2 s 3(b) [hereinafter: JP 3–60]. In this context, force entails both kinetic (hard-kill actions) and non-kinetic (soft-kill activities) capabilities. AJP-01 (D), op. cit. n 62, para 0520. See also F. Martineu, 'The Rules of Engagement in Ten Questions', 4 *Doctrine: The Legal Environment for Ground Forces*, Ministère de la Défense, General Military Review, September 2004, 18–20 and B.O. Matthias von Lepel, 'Overseas Operations of the Bundeswehr in the Light of International and Constitutional Law' 4 *Doctrine: The Legal Environment for Ground Forces*, Ministère de la Défense, General Military Review, September 2004, 24–7 at 26–7.
152 Alternatively, State forces would operate under two sets of ROE – coalition and national ones – that would reflect these divergences. See the further discussion in Chapter 9 in general.

196 *Operationalisation of the definition of military objective*

their troops.[153] National ROE may differ from NATO rules, but should not be more permissive.[154]

The US Air Force targeting doctrine document, issued in 2006, appears to be compatible in principle with the US joint targeting doctrine (JP 3–60).[155] As discussed in Chapter 4, this publication highlights, among other things, the intricate relationship between ROE and law of armed conflict (LOAC).[156] With regard to targeting, ROE essentially contain information on the delineation of how and when targets may be attacked.[157] It further confirms that ROE may only be more restrictive, and never more permissive, than the law of armed conflict.[158] This implies, in principle, that compliance with ROE should ensure compliance with LOAC. It is worth noting that ROE are not all-encompassing, which means they may not incorporate references to all the relevant legal obligations applicable to specific operations.[159]

In addition to ROE, the armed forces also rely on their legal advisers to ensure the lawful conduct of operations.[160] Legal advisers in British forces are involved in every step of the targeting process. Their function is purely advisory.[161] Just like the decision-making commanders, legal advisors must be fully aware of the potential differences in policies, national ROE, legal obligations and/or interpretations of the same legal concepts among the

153 Non-member forces may be guided by a separate set of national ROE, as well as by the operation-specific NATO ROE, if agreed with NATO before the campaign began. AJP-01 (D), op. cit. n 62, para 0521.
154 Matthias von Lepel, op. cit. n 151, at 27.
155 *Targeting*, US Air Force Doctrine Document AFDD 2-1.9, 8 June 2006 [hereinafter: AFDD 2-1.9].
156 See the discussion in 4.3.
157 AFDD 2-1.9, op. cit. n 155, at 93.
158 NATO doctrine specifies that targeting policy may only be more restrictive – and never more permissive – than what is regarded as lawful conduct (NATO, Allied Joint Doctrine for Joint Targeting, AJP-3.9, May 2008, at 1-6 para 0112 [hereinafter: AJP-3.9])
159 AFDD 2-1.9, op. cit. n 155, at 94. ROE are not to be treated as comprehensive reflections of policy or law.
160 Campaign Execution (Joint Doctrine Publication 3-00 (JDP 3-00), UK Chiefs of Staff, The Development, Concepts and Doctrine Centre, UK Ministry of Defence, 3rd edn, October 2009, at 3B-1 para 3B4 [hereinafter: JDP 3-00]; FT-05, op. cit. n 63, at 14; see also J. Cario, 'Legal Advice Supporting Command', 20 *Doctrine: Command in Operations*, Ministère de la Défense, General Military Review, 2011, 55–6; and K.W. Watkin and Z. Drebot, 'The Operational Lawyer: An Essential Resource for the Modern Commander', Office of the Judge Advocate General, copy on file with author.
161 *Legal Support to Joint Operations*, Joint Doctrine Publication 3-46 (JDP 3-46), UK Chiefs of Staff, The Development, Concepts and Doctrine Centre, UK Ministry of Defence, 2nd edn, August 2010, at 2-5 para 211 and 2-7 para 215 [hereinafter: JDP 3-46]; *Targeting*, Australian Defence Doctrine Publication 3.14, Department of Defence, 2nd edn, 2009, 2 February 2009, para 3.33 [hereinafter: ADDP 3.14]. Consider also *Legal Support to Military Operations*, US Joint Chiefs of Staff, Joint Publication, JP 1-04, August 2011. Boothby also suggests that UK legal advisors provide a legal contribution to the development of military doctrine (W.H. Boothby, *The Law of Targeting*, Oxford University Press, Oxford 2012, at 480).

Military doctrine and international law 197

contributing nations in multinational operations.[162] In particular, they advise component targeting boards on the lawfulness of the nominated targets.[163] At the heart of the legal advisers' contribution lies the task of bringing the attention of the targeting planners and decision-makers to the importance of not relying on 'assumptions, outdated information or superficial reports'.[164]

Finally, the law is used as part of teaching for a new cadre. This may be part of the training in military doctrine, mission-specific or legal training, particularly at an operational/tactical level.[165] In some States, the teaching of military doctrine reflects the respect for the basic tenets of the law of armed conflict, even it is not labelled as such. For example, when teaching how to undertake an ambush, the armed forces are taught of the need to protect civilians from harm, which is consistent with legal standards.

8.4.1 Law and the conduct of operations

All military operations must be conducted in compliance with the law, including domestic regulations, a State's own standards, those of the host State, and international conventional and customary law. The application of specific regulations will depend on the nature of the conflict or crisis. In relation to international law, the process of targeting in most armed conflicts will be governed by the LOAC or international humanitarian law.[166] British forces, for instance, are bound to apply Additional Protocol I to the 1949 Geneva Conventions, as well as relevant customary law rules, when targeting in an international armed conflict.[167] As a matter of policy, however, they may decide to apply the same standards to targeting in non-international armed conflicts.[168] The US obligations applicable to the conduct of hostilities would depend

---

162 JDP 3-46, op. cit. n 161, at 2-8 para 216(c) and 2-10 para 222. Their efforts should be seen as an enabling factor rather than an obstacle in reducing the risk of unlawful conduct.

163 Ibid, at 2-6 para 213.

164 Ibid, at 2-7 para 214.

165 Ibid, at 1-10 paras 124–5.

166 This includes international armed conflicts, but may also apply to the conduct of hostilities authorised by the UN, and potentially some internal conflicts. British Defence Doctrine, op. cit. n 45, para 1B1; JDP 01, op. cit. n 75, at 4-21 para 450; see also JP 3-60, op. cit. n 151, at II-29 s 3, and in general *Legal Considerations in Targeting*, Appendix A to JP 3-60, op. cit. n 151; ADDP 3.14, op. cit. n 161, para 3.1; JDP 3-00, op. cit. n 160, at 3B-1 and 3B-2 para 3B4; Matthias von Lepel, op. cit. n 151, at 26–7; FT-02, op. cit. n 88, at 50–1; FT-05, op. cit. n 63, at 15; *Operations Law for RAAF Commanders*, Royal Australian Air Force, AAP 1003, 2nd edn 2004, at 47–55.

167 Each member of the British armed forces, before deployment to the zone of operations, is provided with a copy of the eight-page leaflet *Aide Mémoire on the Law of Armed Conflict*. This contains the essence of legal rules addressed to junior soldiers, marines and airmen, and to senior officers, in parts B and C respectively. *Aide Mémoire on the Law of Armed Conflict*, Joint Service Publication 381 (JSP 381). The author's copy is undated.

168 JDP 3-46, op. cit. n 161, at 1-14 para 130.

198 *Operationalisation of the definition of military objective*

on the customary laws of armed conflict, applicable in international armed conflicts.[169]

8.4.2 Operational law and LOAC manuals

An overview of the LOAC considerations in doctrine would not be complete without a reference to the publications that pertain to the law applying to military operations and military legal practice. Operational law is not a doctrinal source. Operational law is generally considered to comprise the domestic and international law relevant to military operations.[170] It includes many legal issues, such as the laws of war. The US Judge Advocate Corps, for example, issues on an annual basis the Operational Law Handbook.[171] This provides guidelines on how and where commanders may obtain the necessary legal advice and support in operations. The Operational Law Handbook combines practical and legal information, including the appropriate references and interpretation of law. The US service-specific publications, including compilations such as *The Law of Land Warfare*, Army Field Manual 27-10[172] and the Navy/ Marine Corps/ Coast Guard, *Commander's Handbook on the Law of Naval Operations*,[173] both referred to in Chapter 4, also reflect the law applicable to US military operations.[174]

---

169 The US default policy position was – and still is – that the binding laws of armed conflict apply to any military operations in which the US takes part, no matter how they are characterised. United States Department of Defense, Directive 2311.01E, Law of War Program, 9 May 2006.

170 *Operations Law for RAAF Commanders*, op. cit. n 166, at 1; *Manual de Derecho Operacional*, FF. MM 3-41, El Comando General de las Fuerzas Militares, Republic of Colombia, 2009; *Law of Armed Conflict*, Australian Defence Doctrine Publication, ADDP 06.4, May 2006, at 1.53 [hereinafter: ADDP 06.4]. See also Watkin and Drebot, op. cit. n 160, at 4–5; M.L. Warren, 'Operational Law: A Concept Matures', 152 *Military Law Review* 1996, 33–73 at 33 *et seq.*

171 Operational Law Handbook, JA 422, International and Operational Law Department, The Judge Advocate General's Legal Center and School, 2013 edn.

172 *Law of Land Warfare*, Field Manual FM 27-10, US Department of Army, 18 July 1956 with subsequent amendments of 15 July 1976. The Manual is also included in the supplement to the Operational Law/Law of War Handbooks *Law of War Documentary Supplement*, International and Operational Law Department, The US Judge Advocate General's Legal Center and School, 2007, see ns 175 and 176 below.

173 US Navy, Marine Corps and Coast Guard, *Commander's Handbook on the Law of Naval Operations*, Department of Navy, Office of the Chief of Naval Operations, Headquarters, US Marine Corps, Department of Transportation, US Coastal Guard, NWP 1-14M, MCWP 5-2.1, COMDTPUB P5800.7 (formerly known as Naval Warfare Pub. No. NWP 9 (Rev. A)/FMFM 1-10, 1989), 2nd edn, May 1995 superseded by the third and current version of July 2007. The Handbook is supported by the *Annotated Supplement*, which should not be regarded as reflecting the official policy or position of the US government or its forces. A.R. Thomas and J.C. Duncan (eds), *Annotated Supplement to the Commander's Handbook on the Law of Naval Operations*, Vol. 73, Navy War College, International Law Studies, Newport, RI 1999, Introductory Note.

174 The operational LOAC regarding the definition of military objectives was extensively reviewed in 4.3.1 of this book. The reflections in this section are provided only to highlight the more general function of the relevant documents.

Military doctrine and international law 199

Some States issue separate LOAC manuals.[175] Such manuals present the State's interpretation of the overall LOAC obligations with the relevant legal references. The US *Law of War Handbook* is a guide for Judge Advocates practising the law of war.[176] The information about the relevant application of LOAC in Air Force operations is currently in the operational law-oriented publication *Air Force Operations and the Law*, as well as being reinforced in the Air Force guide on law for military commanders, *The Military Commander and the Law*.[177]

8.5 Legal considerations in the selection of targets

Targeting is the part of military doctrine where the application of the legal concept of military objectives becomes particularly relevant as it is applied to the identified desirable targets. This is where the armed forces propose which targets they want to pursue, and where the LOAC, in particular the definition of military objective, is taken into account. This is achieved through the targeting process, which will be introduced in the next section.

---

175 ADDP 06.4, op. cit. n 170; Humanitarian Law in Armed Conflicts – Manual (Eng.), The Federal Ministry of Defence of The Federal Republic of Germany, ZDv 15/2 VR II 3, August 1992; The Manual of the Law of Armed Conflict, UK Ministry of Defence, JSP 383, Oxford University Press, Oxford 2004; *Manuel de Droit des Conflits Armés*, (French) Ministère de la Défense, Secrétariat Général Pour L'Administration, undated; *Orientaciones. El Derecho de los Conflictos Armados*, OR7–004, Ministry of Defence of Spain, 2nd edn, 2007; *Manual De Derecho Internacional De Los Conflictos Armados*, Ministry of Defence of Argentina, 2010; *Law of Armed Conflict at the Operational and Tactical Levels*, Joint Doctrine Manual B-GJ-005-104/FP-021, Office of the Judge Advocate General, Canadian National Defence, 13 August 2001, at 4-1 and 4-2 para 406(2). Extensive review of the numerous LOAC military manuals from other States can be found in M. Henckaerts and L. Doswald-Beck (eds), *Customary International Humanitarian Law*, Cambridge University Press, Cambridge 2005, Vol. I (Rules) with supplementary evidence in Vol. II (Practice), which was extensively referred to in previous chapters of this study.
176 *Law of War Handbook*, JA 423, International and Operational Law Department, The US Judge Advocate General's Legal Center and School, annual edition. The Handbook is supplemented by *Law of War Documentary Supplement*, JA 42, International and Operational Law Department, The US Judge Advocate General's Legal Center and School, 2007.
177 US Air Force's Pamphlet 110–31 (*International Law – The Conduct of Armed Conflict and Air Operations*), 19 November 1976, was in force until it was rescinded in 2006; R.L. Bridge, 'Operations Law: An Overview', 37 *Air Force Law Review* 1994, 1–4; H. DeSaussure, 'The Conduct of Armed Conflict and Air Operations. By US Air Force (Pamphlet 110–31, 19 November 1976)'. Review, 72(1) *American Journal of International Law* 1978, 174–6 at 174–5; *Air Force Operations and the Law, A Guide for Air, Space and Cyber Forces*, US Air Force, The Judge Advocate General's School, 2nd edn, 2009. See also n 148 above; *The Military Commander and the Law*, US Air Force, The Judge Advocate General's School, 11th edn, 2012.

200 *Operationalisation of the definition of military objective*

8.5.1 Targeting process

The body of doctrine addressing targeting is relatively new and still evolving at international and national levels. The *NATO Allied Joint Targeting* publication (AJP-3.9) was finalised as recently as May 2008.[178] The US Forces' principal *Joint Targeting* document (JP 3–60) was first issued in April 2007 and was updated in 2013.[179] The Australian targeting-specific publication was first published in 2006 and updated in 2009.[180] UK joint targeting publications were completed in 2005. They were followed by subsequent versions of the *UK Joint Targeting Policy* (JSP 900),[181] and supplemented by a specific annex to the 2009 keystone operational doctrine publication *Campaign Execution* (JDP 3-00).[182] The latter flows directly from the capstone publication *Campaigning* (JDP 01)[183] and, together with *Campaign Planning* (JDP 5–00), represents the UK authority for the conduct of deployed joint operations.[184] Similarly, the US *Joint Targeting* doctrine addresses the operational-level considerations for combatant commands and joint task forces, and the subordinate commands of specific components.[185] It further indicates that, in multinational operations, the military command should follow multinational doctrine and procedures ratified by the US, or – if not ratified – the doctrine and procedures consistent with US law and doctrine.[186]

In NATO's multinational military doctrine, targeting is described as the operational and component level command function aimed at the identification and coordination of the lethal and non-lethal actions necessary to achieve the

178 AJP-3.9, op. cit. n 158, which is linked directly to capstone publication AJP-01 (D)(op. cit. n 62) and other keystone joint doctrine documents. See also G.S. Corn and G.P. Corn, 'The Law of Operational Targeting: Viewing the LOAC through an Operational Lens', 47(2) *Texas International Law Journal* 2012, 337–80 at 349 *et seq.*

179 JP 3–60, op. cit. n 151. US services also issue their own targeting publications such as (Army) *The Targeting Process*, FM 3-60 (FM 6-20-10), US Army Headquarters, 26 November 2010 and (Air Force) *Annex 3-60 Targeting*, US Air Force Doctrine, 10 January 2014.

180 ADDP 3.14, op. cit. n 161.

181 UK *Joint Targeting Policy and Battle Damage Assessment Policy Paper*, endorsed by the Vice Chief of Defence Staff in September 2005, is mentioned in *Campaign Execution* (JDP 3-00), op. cit. n 160, at 3-11 n 11. It is unclear if it has been updated or changed. The first version of British Defence Doctrine (JWP0-01), 1996 also contained references to targeting in the context of the Laws of Armed Conflict (Annex B, at B.6).

182 See Annex 3B 'Joint Action Targeting Process' as well as the selected paragraphs in the main text (e.g. paras 327–9 at 3-10 and 3-11), which replaced the corresponding statements previously found in Annex 2E 'The Joint Operations Support Activities' and Appendix 2E1 'Joint Fires Aspect of Targeting' to *Joint Operations Execution*, Joint Warfare Publication 3-00, UK Chiefs of Staff, The Development, Concepts and Doctrine Centre, UK Ministry of Defence, 2nd edn, March 2004 [hereinafter: JWP 3-00).

183 JDP 01, op. cit. n 75.

184 JDP 3-00, op. cit. n 160, at v para 1.

185 JP 3-60, op. cit. n 151, at ix, I-1, sec. 1 and II-1 sec. 1(a).

186 Ibid, at i s 3 (Application).

Military doctrine and international law 201

commanders' designated operational objectives, and the desired effects in consideration of all available means.[187] Targeting is therefore appropriately conducted at the most centralised and practical level, that is the operational level.[188] Following strategic direction and authority, commanders have to synchronise and merge the relevant tactical activities and events[189] with the operational and strategically directed activities.[190] Targeting is a complex process. It focuses on the coordination, selection and prioritisation of targets, as well as matching the best response in the context of operational needs and capabilities.[191] Targeting links intelligence, planning and the execution of operations across all levels of warfare.[192]

The doctrine takes into account two general types of targets that may require different types of planning. Pre-planned targets are identified during a 'deliberate' targeting process. Deliberate targeting is aimed at prosecuting scheduled targets or targets that were planned but engaged only when requested or required (on call).

Targets that were not previously identified (unknown, unexpected or unanticipated targets) or that were identified but not detected, located or selected in time to be included in a deliberate targeting cycle (anticipated targets) are subject to a dynamic targeting process.[193] Dynamic targeting may thus involve targets about which only partial information was available at the time the targeting took place. These are the anticipated dynamic targets that the planners identified, but for which they require more specific information, such as their location, to be able to schedule an attack.

The importance of any potential targets may change in accordance with the rapidly changing circumstances of the conflict. The targets may become militarily more valuable and offer an opportunity for achieving greater military advantage. They will require an immediate response because they pose or may soon pose a threat to friendly operations, or are highly valuable.[194] Known also as targets of opportunity, such targets are more likely dealt with by the

---

187 AJP-3.9, op. cit. n 158, at 1-1 paras 0102 and 0104.
188 Ibid, at 4-1, para 0401.
189 The execution of an action against a target, consistent with the operational objectives, is regarded as a tactical activity. AJP-3.9, op. cit. n 158, at 1-1 para 0102.
190 JDP 3-00, op. cit. n 160, at 3-10 para 328.
191 NATO Glossary, op. cit. n 43; JDP 01, op. cit. n 75, at 3-33 para 376; JP 3-60, op. cit. n 151, at I-1 s 1.
192 JP 3–60, op. cit. n 151, at I-8 to I-9 s 6(b); ADDP 3.14, op. cit. n 161, para 1.2.
193 AJP-3.9, op. cit. n 158, at 1-2 para 0106; ADDP 3.14, op. cit. n 161, paras 1.10–15; JP 3–60, op. cit. n 151, at II-1 to II-2 s 2. British military doctrine refers to accelerated targeting, comprising time-sensitive and dynamic targets prosecution. Such targets are those the adversary can least afford to lose. JDP 3-46, op. cit. n 161, at 2-6 para 212. See also JP 3–60, op. cit. n 151, at II-2 s 2(a)(2).
194 Time-sensitive and critical targets are regarded as 'high-payoff' targets, which constitute a part of high value targets. AJP-3.9, op. cit. n 158, at 1-3 para 0107; JP 3-60, op. cit. n 151, at I-8 and I-9 s 6(b)–(d).

202 *Operationalisation of the definition of military objective*

dynamic targeting process.[195] In order to be successful, the doctrine indicates that the processing of such targets will require a considerable amount of intense preparation and planning in a relatively short period of time, possibly involving disrupting scheduled operations.[196]

As far as the law is concerned, the deliberate targeting process does not give rise to significant problems. The most important point to note in this context is that doctrine envisages for the law to be taken into account during the selection of the targets. This is illustrated in the context of NATO's deliberate targeting framework, entitled 'Joint Targeting Cycle'. NATO targeting doctrine indicates that the process consists of six phases, conducted mostly at the operational and tactical levels.[197] Phase 2 Target Development, Validation, Nomination, and Prioritisation represents the crucial stage of the process, where the application of international law and, in particular, the legal concept of military objective becomes most relevant.

The overall military strategic targeting direction is presented in the targeting annex or appendix to the strategic-level Operation Plan, created by the Strategic Commander, based on the military mission-defining North Atlantic Council's (NAC) Initiating Directive.[198] In addition, the Strategic Commander would be tasked by the NAC to develop the target sets and categories, later approved by the NAC and also included in such an annex. Target sets/categories comprise the groups of target categories, or targets considered to be of military significance and serving the same function, or being part of the adversary's network, such as command, control and communication centres,[199] lines of communications or transportation, weapons of mass destruction, petroleum industry sites, political leadership or media facilities.[200]

Preferred targets drawn from the NATO integrated database[201] are listed in a consolidated Joint Target List (JTL), which is an initial list of unapproved targets.[202] The JTL also incorporates restricted and prohibited targets, collated

---

195 See also 6.2.2.
196 It is thus recommended that it is undertaken only in respect to a very limited number of targets. JP 3–60, op. cit. n 141, at I-9 s 6(d)(1).
197 See AJP-3.9, op. cit. n 158, Chapter 2 'Joint Targeting Cycle'. The American and Australian targeting framework of the targeting cycle is largely consistent with that of NATO. JP 3-60, op. cit. n 151, Chapters 2 and 3; ADDP 3.14, op. cit. n 161, Chapter 4.
198 This targeting annex or appendix should include all the relevant guidance from the NAC, including any national targeting constraints and caveats. AJP-3.9, op. cit. n 158, at 3-1 para 0301, 3-2 para 0306, and 3-4 para 0312.
199 The US equivalent of target sets or categories is CTL, which stands for Candidate Target List (JP 3-60, op. cit. n 151, at II-11 s 3(d)(5)(b)).
200 AJP-3.9, op. cit. n 158, at 3-2 para 0306; see also examples of NATO target sets in Annex A to AJP-3.9, op. cit. n 158, at A-13.
201 Ibid, at 4-7-2 paras 0415–16.
202 Ibid, at 1-3 para 0108.

Military doctrine and international law 203

respectively in Restricted Target List(s) and Non-Strike List(s),[203] and, as far as possible, anticipated targets that are time-sensitive[204]. All these groups of targets are subject to consideration in the light of political guidance and the goals of the military mission.[205]

The processes described occur during Part 1 of Phase 2 of the Joint Targeting Cycle, entitled *Target Development*. *Target Development* builds on the overall Operational Plan and tasking order by identifying the adversary's strengths, weaknesses and centres of gravity.[206] After this step, targets are subject to *Validation* through assessing whether they comply with the military goals of the operation, strategic guidance, intent, policies and international law.[207] Only after the targets have been validated can they be nominated to be approved and prioritised. The Joint Targeting Coordination Board is responsible for preparing the Joint Prioritised Target List (JPTL), consisting of the strategic and operational targets vetted against the military goals, guidance, intent and law.[208]

---

203 Ibid, at 3-4 para 0311 and at 4-9 paras 0422–3. The British equivalent of JTL derives from the overall Master Target List, which includes targets generally designated to be engaged, and the Non-Strike List, which includes targets that are particularly sensitive, whether legally, politically or for any other reason, and that are thus protected from attack at any point. Restricted targets, although they may constitute legitimate military targets, are temporarily protected from attack because of the potential adverse effects their disruption may cause to other military activities (JDP 3-46, op. cit. n 161, at 2-4 para 210 and JDP 3–00, op. cit. n 160, at 3B-4 para 3B9 and 3B-5 para 3B12). See also JP 3–60, op. cit. n 151, at II-13 s 7(c)(2).

204 Time-sensitive targets require an immediate response because of the danger they pose to friendly operations, or because they 'are highly lucrative, fleeting targets of opportunity' (AJP-3.9, op. cit. n 158, at 1-3 para 0107, as well as in chapter 5 AJP-3.9) or constitute a 'fleeting opportunity of tactical advantage' (JP 3-60, op. cit. n 151, at I-8 s 6(b)(3)). They cannot be processed in the normal joint targeting cycle because of limited time, and require a fast-track procedure. See the relevant comments below in this section of the chapter.

205 AJP-3.9, op. cit. n 158, at 3-3 paras 0307–8 and at 3-8, para 319.

206 This is where the 'Ends, Ways and Means' method converges with the effect-based approach in targeting such centres and achieving the required operational goals. While it is commonly understood that COGs consist of points of strength, the Manoeuvrist approach assumes that points of weakness can also represent COGs.

207 AJP-3.9, op. cit. n 158, 2-2 para 0203(b); JP 3–60, op. cit. n 151, at II-11 s 3(d)(5)(b) and II-29 s 3(g)(4)(d)(3).

208 AJP-3.9, op. cit. n 158, at 4-8 paras 0418–19. The JPTL combines targets from the master JTL, the Restricted Target List(s) and targets nominated or proposed for restriction by subordinate commanders (AJP-3.9, op. cit. n 158, at 1-3 para 0108). British doctrine uses the terms Joint Integrated Target List(s) and Joint Integrated Prioritized Target List(s) to set out the equivalent groups of targets (JDP 3-46, op. cit. n 161, at 2-4 para 210). It would appear that, in US doctrine, the Joint Target List contains targets developed, vetted and validated, while the Joint Integrated Prioritized Target List represents all targets selected by components from JTL and compiled into Target Nomination Lists, which are subsequently combined, validated and prioritised (JP3-60, op. cit. n 151, at II-12 s 3(d)(7)(a)(4)).

204 *Operationalisation of the definition of military objective*

Just like deliberate targets, any time-sensitive targets analysed in a dynamic targeting process must comply with the military goals, guidance and intent, as well as with policy and law. The dynamic targeting cycle usually consists of six steps. One of these steps requires the vetting of any targets against the ROE and the restricted/prohibited targets lists.[209] At this stage, time-sensitive targets receive their final approval before they are tasked for engagement by the relevant components of the joint force.[210]

8.5.2 The application of law

LOAC requires that those who plan and execute attacks must ensure they target legitimate objects.[211] This means that legal scrutiny should be applied in all targeting processes.[212] Military commanders, bearing the primary responsibility for targeting decisions both in planning and carrying out attacks, are under an obligation to apply the relevant legal provisions during operations.[213] Commanders would ideally be supported at every stage of the process by specialist legal advisers, who play a vital role in ensuring that proposed targets comply with the legal rules.[214] In multinational operations, the varying national policy positions and legal obligations of the national contingents, as well as potential differences in the interpretation of the same LOAC concepts among different nations, must be recognised.[215]

In the framework of NATO's deliberate targeting process, some legal scrutiny will already have been performed during the initial phase of the targeting cycle when the target set/categories are prepared, together with a list of prohibited or restricted targets. These are all contained in a separate attachment to the Operational Plan.[216] Full legal screening, however, appears

---

209 AJP-3.9, op. cit. n 158, at A-5 and A-6 para 0506; JP3-60, op. cit. n 151, at ix and II-21 s 3(g)(4).

210 Time-sensitive targets that do not fit into the NAC designated target sets or categories are forwarded by the Joint Forces Command to the NAC with a recommendation for approval. AJP-3.9, op. cit. n 158, at A-7 and A-8 para 0507.

211 Art 57 API (Protocol Additional to the Geneva Conventions of 12 August 1949, and Relating to the Protection of Victims of International Armed Conflicts (Protocol I), Geneva, 8 June 1977, reprinted in D. Schindler and J. Toman (eds), *The Laws of Armed Conflict*, 4th edn, 2004, Martinus Nijhoff, Leiden 2004, at 711 *et seq.* [hereinafter: API]). Discussion of issues related to provisions regulating the manner in which attacks are undertaken is outside the scope of this work. See 1.3.

212 AJP-3.9, op. cit. n 158, at 4-3 para 0404(b); JDP 01, op. cit. n 75, at 3-33 para 376.

213 JDP 3-46, op. cit. n 161, at 2-7 para 215.

214 AJP-3.9, op. cit. n 158, at 1-6 para 0112; JDP 3-00, op. cit. n 160, at 3B-1 para 3B4; JDP 3-46, op. cit. n 161, at 2-7 para 215; JP 3-60, op. cit. n 161, at A-7 s 9; ADDP 3.14, op. cit. n 161, paras 3.32, 3.34 and 3.35.

215 JDP 01, op. cit. n 75, at 3-33 para 376, 4-22 para 450(c) and 4A-5 para 4A18(c); JDP 3-00, op. cit. n 160, at 3-10 paras 327–8.

216 Similarly, US military doctrine stresses that legal considerations would already have been taken into account in the preparation of the theatre strategic concepts. USJP3-0, op. cit. n 68, at III-23 s 4(b)(5); USJP5-0, op. cit. n 71, at III-9 s 4(c)(5)(e).

Military doctrine and international law   205

to be undertaken only in Phase 2, during validation of the targets nominated for the JPTL.[217] Additionally, component commanders, when acting upon the Joint Forces Command-approved JPTL, must ensure that all target orders sent to lower echelon formations and units for execution, which are compiled in the daily Target Nomination Lists, must be law- and ROE-compliant.[218] This does not relieve tactical commanders from their continuing obligation to ensure that the targets they are about to engage meet the appropriate legal requirements.[219] Similar to the NATO model, British contingent or component commanders must clear targets in the theatre at the time of an attack, despite having them approved at the higher level.[220]

Compliance with the underlying principles of LOAC – such as distinction, military necessity, proportionality and humanity – is seen not just as a legal obligation, but also a reflection of ethical considerations.[221] The principle of distinction requires that all targeting decisions distinguish between legitimate targets and the civilian population and objects.[222] Doctrine highlights the relationship between the implementation of the principles of distinction and proportionality, and the timely conduct of operations. It stresses that the assessment of the anticipated military advantage and the status of the target must be undertaken at the time the attack is authorised.[223] The attack will normally be authorised some time after the targets are verified at higher levels of authority.[224] Thus, a further double-check in the light of 'current situation and information' appears essential to fulfil the legal requirements.[225]

There is no doubt that the definition of military objective has to be applied to every target under consideration. The law does not provide different standards for different objects. However, in practice there could be situations in which the application of the test may vary in different contexts. As far as pre-planned and anticipated dynamic targets are concerned, the application of the definition is likely not to be problematic. In regard to anticipated dynamic targets, a legal problem may well arise with regard to the risk of collateral casualties. In the case of unanticipated dynamic targets, there will be less information, and certainly less time to gather or corroborate information on the basis of which a target's lawfulness is evaluated. This may suggest that if the test were applied in the same way as with pre-planned or anticipated dynamic targets, then fewer targets would pass the legal test. It is unclear if this is indeed the case.

---

217 See the discussion in 8.4. AJP-3.9, op. cit. n 158, at 4-8, paras 0417–18.
218 AJP-3.9, op. cit. n 158, at 4-3 para 0404 and 4-4 para 0405(f).
219 Ibid, at 3-1 para 0301 and 4-3 para 0404(b).
220 JDP 3-46, op. cit. n 161, at 2-7 para 214.
221 British Defence Doctrine, op. cit. n 45, para 1B5; FT-02, op. cit. n 88, at 50.
222 AJP-3.9, op. cit. n 158, at 1-6 para 0113(c).
223 Ibid.
224 Ibid.
225 See the discussion in 6.2.

206 *Operationalisation of the definition of military objective*

Certain targets might need special strategic and/or political approval because of the potential ramifications stemming from their engagement, including increased collateral damage or other adverse legal, economic or political consequences.[226] Interestingly, *Air Force Operations and the Law* stresses that not all restrictions having an impact on targeting may be specified in the ROE themselves. There may also be differences between the ROE in a coalition environment, particularly in regard to 'certain sensitive targets such as leadership, weapons of mass destruction'.[227] The sensitivity around such targets does not have to result from their nature or particular characteristics. Instead, US or coalition forces may believe that attacking such targets – or failing to do so – may result in adverse consequences, including potential political repercussions.[228] Such sensitive targets should not be confused with the 'time-sensitive' targets mentioned earlier in this chapter, which are prosecuted because they are critical to the operation. All types of targets, whether pursued during the deliberate or dynamic targeting process, must be scrutinised in accordance with LOAC.[229] Even an electronic attack during an armed conflict must be directed against targets that satisfy the requirements of the definition of military objectives.[230]

8.6 The concept of military objective and targets

One aspect of military doctrine may put the definition of military objective under considerable strain. It is linked to the perception of the enemy in modern conflicts. How the enemy is perceived will impact upon which targets are proposed for attack. In order to understand how this may occur, it is important to elaborate further on what the term 'target' means, and what its role is in military operations.

8.6.1 Targets

Targets encompass a broad spectrum of people, objects, places and even concepts. NATO Targeting Doctrine defines a target as a 'selected geographic area, object, capability, person or organisation including their will, under-standing and behaviour, which can be influenced as part of a military

---

226 AJP-3.9, op. cit. n 158, at 1-8 para 0117; JDP 3–00, op. cit. n 160, at 3-10 para 328.
227 *Air Force Operations and the Law*, op. cit. n 177, at 252. See also 3.1.3 and 7.1.
228 *Air Force Operations and the Law*, op. cit. n 177, at 254.
229 Ibid, at 254, 257 and 260.
230 Ibid, at 367. Electronic attack is defined in the guide as action involving 'the use of electromagnetic energy, directed energy or anti-radiation weapons to attack personnel, facilities, or equipment'. This definition is consistent with the US joint operational doctrine publication *Electronic Warfare*, Joint Publication JP 3-13.1, US Joint Chiefs of Staff, 8 February 2012, at I-4 s 3(b).

Military doctrine and international law 207

contribution to a political end-state'.[231] American targeting doctrine succinctly describes it as an 'entity (person, place or thing) considered for possible engagement or action to alter or neutralize the function it performs to the adversary', with many examples of what a target could be: an area; a complex or installation; a capability; a function; an individual; or an entire force, system or behaviour as well as virtual entity.[232]

The doctrine further describes five types of characteristics that define a target, namely physical, functional, cognitive, environmental and temporal[233] ones.[234] Physical characteristics focus on what the target *is* (e.g. shape, location, number, nature, structural design and mobility).[235] The functional features describe the target's function (i.e. what it *does*, and how, and its ability to reconstitute itself), its importance within the enemy's strategic structure – such as a cultural or geopolitical role – and its vulnerability.[236] Cognitive characteristics relate to the target's ability and capability to think and process information, as well as to its control functions.[237] Environmental factors analyse the effects of the environment on the target, such as atmosphere, terrain, physical relations, and any dependency on energy, water, raw materials or command/control.[238]

Air Force Operations and the Law specifies a three-tier selection of potential targets in accordance with the doctrinal levels of warfare. In respect of strategic targets, the publication identifies reserve forces, military bases, command and control, communication and transportation, as well as industrial infrastructure and significant geographic points. In addition, the publication indicated that political targets, such as 'governmental agencies that support war effort' could be regarded as strategic targets. Air defence systems, weapons and ammunition storage areas, lines of communication and mobile forces are all regarded as examples of operational targets. Finally, tactical targets would generally encompass the adversary's deployed forces.[239]

A target's importance rests in its potential contribution towards the adversary's critical vulnerability, and to the creation of the effects required by the achievement of the military objectives[240] and end-states identified by

---

231 AJP-3.9, op. cit. n 158, at 1-1 para 0103.
232 JP 3–60, op. cit. n 151, at I-1 s 2(a).
233 American doctrine links time-sensitivity to the rapidly rising importance of targets in the context of the dynamic nature of the battlespace environment. Ibid, at I-5 s 3(e).
234 Ibid, at I-2, s 3(a); ADDP 3.14, op. cit. n 161, para 1.8.
235 JP 3-60, op. cit. n 151, at I-2 s 3(b); ADDP 3.14, op. cit. n 161, para 1.8.
236 JP 3-60, op. cit. n 151, at I-2 and I-3 s 3(b).
237 Ibid, at I-3 s 3(c); ADDP 3.14, op. cit. n 161, para 1.8.
238 JP 3–60, op. cit. n 151, at I-4 s 3(d).
239 However, the document stressed that all targets must satisfy the requirements of the legal definition of military objectives before they can be lawfully engaged. *Air Force Operations and the Law*, op. cit. n 177, at 248. See also 3.1.1 and 7.1.
240 AJP-3.9, op. cit. n 158, at 1-1 para 0103; ADDP 3.14, op. cit. n 161, para 1.7; JP 3–60, op. cit. n 151, at I-1 s 2(a).

208 *Operationalisation of the definition of military objective*

the Joint Force Commander.[241] In other words, while the objectives prescribe the goals, the effects describe the behaviour of the system in the operational environment. Effects should be measurable and clearly distinct from objectives. Effects should not be intended to replace objectives, but should be designed to contribute to achieving the goals, that is desired effects.[242] Effects-based operations, in general, put greater emphasis on understanding the adversary's capabilities, intentions and objectives. They allow the use of more streamlined operations against key points of strength and weakness using a wider spectrum of capabilities, from lethal physical force to sophisticated influence, electronic and psychological operations.[243]

The targeting process in effects-based operations concentrates on the selection of targets designed to bring about certain desired effects. The targets are selected in direct correlation with the nature or characteristics of the effects.[244] Targets that facilitate the use of weapons of mass destruction, or strategic command and control facilities, would be regarded as enabling or affecting the opponent's long-term military capacity and strategic decision-making, together with its stability and potential will to sustain the war.[245] Some lines of communication, air defence systems and energy storage facilities, which all directly support the adversary's military capacity, would be considered as yielding operational effects.[246] Finally, tactical effects are associated with targets that affect the military forces' ability to engage on a relatively localised basis.

US targeting doctrine defines 'effect' as a physical and/or behavioural state or condition[247] of the system that results from an action, a set of them, or another effect inflicted by lethal or non-lethal means. Desired effects are viewed as those that support the achievement of the planned objective, while undesired effects can hinder such an outcome.[248] Effects can be divided into direct and indirect effects, as well as cumulative and cascading effects.[249] They can all embody any number of the results of military action, both direct

---

241 JP 3-60, op. cit. n 151, at II-4 s 3(c)(1) and II-7 s 3(b); ADDP 3.14, op. cit. n 161, paras 1.17–18; FT-02, op. cit. n 88, at 39–40.
242 USJP5-0, op. cit. n 71, at III-20 s 6(a)–(d).
243 AJP-3.9, op. cit. n 158, at 1-9 para 0119.
244 JP 3-60, op. cit. n 151, at ix, xi, I-2 s 2(b) and I-5 s 4(a).
245 *Legal Support to Joint Operations*, Joint Warfare Publication 3-46 (JWP 3-46), UK Chiefs of Staff, The Development, Concepts and Doctrine Centre, UK Ministry of Defence, April 2005, at 2-12 para 223. (This publication is no longer in use. It has been superseded by the second edition of the relevant doctrinal document, JDP 3-46, op. cit. n 161.)
246 Ibid.
247 Similarly distinguished in CFJP 01, op. cit. n 41, at 6-5 para 0616; ADDP 3.14, op. cit. n 161, para 1.19.
248 JP 3-60, op. cit. n 151, at xiii and II-33 s 5(a); see also USJP5-0, op. cit. n 71, at xxi and III-20 to III-21 s.6(c)–(d); ADDP 3.14, op. cit. n 161, para 1.19.
249 ADDP 3.14, op. cit. n 161, para 1.21.

Military doctrine and international law 209

and indirect.[250] Effects must be seen in the context of the system, described as a complex 'whole', consisting of functionally, physically or behaviourally related groups of elements, like nodes and links between them, representing the relationships between the nodes.[251] The adversary is seen as a system or set of associated systems, be they military, political, economic, information, social or infrastructural.

Some key nodes critical to the functioning of the system could well be in a number of systems that do not have to be affected by military capabilities but by other instruments of national power.[252] Actions against specific nodes will often be undertaken in order to sever the intertwined links between them, rather than merely to neutralise this concrete node. Full understanding of the characteristics, capabilities and vulnerabilities of the systems, and their interactions with the military system and other operational systems mentioned earlier, would support the COG analysis and the determination of the best options to affect the COG.[253]

COGs comprise points of 'exploitable vulnerabilities' based on the broad spectrum of intelligence research.[254] They are regarded as representing sources of moral and physical strength, and centres of power and movement, including the freedom to act. These are the points towards which all efforts should be concentrated. COGs might be physical or virtual, material or cognitive. Both strategic and operational COGs are crucial to targeting, as they identify points that may bring about the enemy's defeat most efficiently.[255] The main strategic COG is the will and motivation to fight, both on one's own side and that of the enemy. It might also be the military alliance in itself. Operational COGs are predominantly physical vulnerabilities related to the ability to wage war and military capability.

Additional to the critical capabilities and vulnerabilities analysis is the *strategic ring* model. This depicts the adversary as an 'organism' divided into a set of systems based on their functionality, or contribution to the overall 'organism'. Such a model's features encompass, for instance, infrastructure, leadership or defence, and fighting capabilities. Strategic ring technique has

---

250 Both direct and indirect effects can be physical and behavioural. JP 3-60, op. cit. n 151, at II-35 to II-36 s 5(e)(1)–(3).
251 Nodes represent tangible elements within the system that can be targeted for action. USJP5-0, op. cit. n 71, at III-22 s 6(d)(4); JP 3-60, op. cit. n 151, at II-5 s 3(d)(2)(a).
252 All nodes associated with a COG will be regarded as key nodes. USJP5-0, op. cit. n 71, at III-26 s 6(f).
253 USJP5-0, op. cit. n 71, at III-24 s 6(e)(5); FT-02, op. cit. n 88, at 39–42.
254 AJP-3.9, op. cit. n 158, at 2-2 para 0203(a); FT-02, op. cit. n 88, at 40–2. In the US targeting cycle, the identification of COG is undertaken in Phase 1 of the targeting process (JP 3-60, op. cit. n 151, at II-5 s 3(c)(1)), while the *Development* stage focuses on studying the target systems, their connections (nodal analysis) and the selection of targets that, when engaged, have the greatest potential to create the desired effects (JP 3-60, op. cit. n 151, at II-5 s 3(d); USJP5-0, op. cit. n 71, at III-22 s 6(e)).
255 USJP5-0, op. cit. n 71, at III-22 s 6(e)(1).

210   *Operationalisation of the definition of military objective*

several variations. The two most common include the five-ring model, and the seven-ring elements of national value. The five-ring model, championed by Warden, consists of five concentric systems representing national facets including political leadership, economic systems, infrastructure, population and military forces.[256] It is believed that Warden's theory shaped not only the targeting decisions in the 1990–1 Coalition operations against Iraq,[257] but also in the subsequent 1999 Kosovo intervention.[258]

8.6.2 Military objectives and targets

The overarching political goals of war, and the strategic military objectives consistent with these, shape the choice and priority of theatre targets. While the war aims in conflicts vary, one fundamental aim is common to all of them. This is to reduce or eliminate the enemy's capacity or ability to wage war, at the time of the conflict or in the future. Degrading the enemy's capacity may be achieved directly – by destroying its military potential – or indirectly, by attacking targets that may influence its behaviour and decision-making processes.

An adversary's ability to wage war depends on its military and non-military power. Depending on the economic, political and cultural context of a conflict, an opponent's leadership may encompass military potential or war-fighting capability; leadership-owned or controlled localities, buildings and vehicles, including private residences as well as the ruling party headquarters; and State-owned or ruling party-owned financial businesses, assets and resources.[259] Some of these objects, such as TV and radio stations, could be regarded as supporting the broader war effort by helping to keep the leadership in power.[260] The ability to wage war is often supplemented by a focus on the 'will' to wage war, which relates to the psychological aspects of an opponent's overall capacity.

The adversary's economic resources and power base are recognised in military thinking as key targets.[261] An adversary's ability to stay in power and function as a government requires control over its territory, political coherence and the ability to protect its territory and population from outside threats. Political hubs of power comprise governmental structures and assets, and

---

256 See discussion in 8.1.
257 J.W. Crawford, 'The Law of Noncombatant Immunity and the Targeting of National Electrical Power Systems', 21(2) *Fletcher Forum of War Affairs* 1997, 101–19 at 101 *et seq.*
258 W.J. Fenrick, 'Targeting and Proportionality during the NATO Bombing Campaign against Yugoslavia', 12(3) *European Journal of International Law* 2001, 489–502 at 491 *et seq.*
259 See the discussion relating to the political leadership infrastructure in 3.1.1 and 7.1.
260 See the discussion relating to 3.1.3 and 7.1.
261 See the discussion relating to economic targets in 4.3.

Military doctrine and international law 211

control over the media. Economic sources of power range from State-owned or controlled enterprises, industry and infrastructure, to private businesses and property. For example, the generation and supply of electric power constitute an important nation-building consideration. Economic and industrial targets, as described in Chapter 4, were closely linked to an opponent's military potential, and/or its ability to wage war in general.

Examples of American military thinking that sees both the broadly perceived economic capacity of the adversary, and its political leadership, as valuable targets include General Sherman's views that led to the destruction of cotton during the American Civil War,[262] the industrial web theory developed by the ACTS, and Warden's strategic rings theory.[263] These theories are used in practice. Warden's theory was applied and tested during the 1990–1 Gulf War, and to some extent in the 1999 NATO intervention in Kosovo and the 2003 conflict in Iraq.[264]

Taking as an example the four international conflicts that will be examined in Chapter 9, it is clear that war effort is no longer confined to 'weakening the military forces' of the adversary. The destruction of Iraq's overall capacity to wage war, as well as targeting the Republican Guard ground forces, degrading and damaging Serbia's capacity to wage war and to continue the violence in Kosovo, and weakening the Taliban's military and political potential, were all strategic and military goals in the respective Coalition campaigns.[265] Industrial military-economic infrastructure and lines of communication were subject to extensive attacks in the 1990–1 Gulf War and the 1999 Kosovo conflict. The majority of such targets were not attacked during the 2001–2 conflict in Afghanistan and in 2003 in Iraq, but not because they were seen as without a value to the enemy. They were seen as more valuable to the Coalition, who felt it should preserve such infrastructure.[266] Biddle observed, for example, that the 2003 Coalition ground advance in Iraq was dependent on the ability to use a series of bridges over the Euphrates River, which meant they were not going to be destroyed prior to the ground offensive.[267]

---

262 See the discussion in 4.3.2.
263 See the earlier discussion in 8.1.
264 See 9.1.
265 See n 19 above and the accompanying text, and also further discussion regarding these conflicts in 9.1.
266 ROE contained a recommendation that critical infrastructure and some economic targets are not to be attacked unless this is unavoidable. See the further discussion in Chapter 9.
267 Biddle also noted that the speed with which the Coalition was securing infrastructure sites, such as oilfields, ports and bridges, in Iraq in 2003 was in response to Saddam Hussein's threats of 'scorched earth', namely destroying such sites before Coalition forces could get to them. He also noted that such threats were never carried out. S. Biddle, 'Iraq, Afghanistan and American Military Transformation' in S. Hopkins (ed.), *Asymmetry and Complexity*, Land Warfare Studies Centre, Study Paper No. 308, Canberra 2007, at 80–4, 94–9.

212 *Operationalisation of the definition of military objective*

Facilities associated with Saddam Hussein and the Ba'ath Party in Iraq, Slobodan Milosevic and the Socialist Party in Serbia, and the Taliban regime in Afghanistan, were all subjected to direct and indirect attacks. As discussed in Part I of this work, it is not clear which, if any, of the objects associated with leadership may in fact be regarded as satisfying the first element of the definition.[268] This may also be true, to some extent, with regard to some economic targets.[269]

In all these conflicts, the enemy leadership – together with broadly perceived economic targets – was clearly a crucial COG. Commanders and military planners focus their efforts on all COGs that they consider to be militarily advantageous. Consequently, the pool of COGs that military forces can aim to affect would be wider and more varied than the COGs that are eventually pursued. The choice of targets that a commander considers may potentially help to achieve the military objectives could be substantially wider than the choice of targets that would contribute to the advancement of the goals.

Tension may arise between what armed forces identify as militarily advantageous, and what could be *militarily advantageous* in a legal sense, as required by the definition of military objective. The latter must be definite, military and expected in the circumstances ruling at the time. Not all COG and the targets associated with them will always be able to fulfil this requirement.

Military theorists, including Warden, focused on looking at which of an opponent's assets are useful for it to prosecute war, and which are useful for its survival. Their denial or neutralisation is expected to damage the opponent enough to force a change in its behaviour, and bring an end to hostilities. To interpret *definite military advantage* as resulting from the end of the entire conflict is, however, too broad.[270]

Additional pressure to pursue controversial targets comes from the doctrinal concepts of strategic attack and effect-based operations. According to the basic principles of effect-based operations, striking targets other than those expected to produce certain effects is unnecessary and wasteful. Strategic targets are regarded as including military bases, C3 facilities, transport and industrial infrastructure, and political targets include elements of the government supporting the 'war effort'. Therefore, if a strategic objective is to eliminate a threat from the opponent's leadership, the objects associated with such leadership would become prima facie strategic COG, and subject to legal validation as military objectives.[271] As was highlighted in Part I, an assessment

---

268 See also discussions in 3.1 and 7.1.

269 See discussion in 4.3.

270 *A contrario* to Eritrea-Ethiopia Claims Commission *obiter* in the Hirgigo case. See the discussion in 5.2.4.

271 *Annex 3-70 Strategic Attack*, op. cit. n 134, at 18, 46–7.

Military doctrine and international law 213

of the legality of political leadership infrastructure targets is problematic.[272] The problems may arise in respect of both elements of the definition.

Paralysing the enemy does not necessary entail its destruction, but it does require reducing its strength to the point where it loses the will to fight. In effect-based operations, only targets that could be expected to produce certain desired effects would be attacked. This would mean that only some elements of the system or network of which a target forms a part would have to be attacked. It therefore appears more likely that military methods such as 'surgical' attacks against key targets would be employed during effect-based operations rather than as part of classic attrition operations. While seemingly aiding economy of force, such a method of warfare may pose certain problems in the context of assessment of lawful targets. The *military advantage* offered by strategic attack may appear less tangible and less immediate. *Military advantage* required by the definition must be *definite* in the circumstances ruling at the time.

In regard to the concept of strategic attack, several targets, not necessarily related to the operational goals, could be engaged. US military doctrine recommends that such targets may be military, political or economic and linked to the strategic COG. Strategic COGs are believed to be linked not only to an enemy's ability to wage war, but also to its will or motivation to fight. Affecting them can bring about the defeat of the enemy in a most effective way. Considering such targets as military objectives in accordance with law may be problematic.

While general US military doctrine might promote identifying such problematic targets, specific joint targeting doctrine appears to bring targets in line with the law. The *effective contribution to military action* is viewed in this document in the context of contribution to military or war-fighting capability or effort. This, as mentioned in Chapter 4, may well be consistent with the meaning of the terms used in the definition of military objective.[273] What is striking is that the both documents relevant to the conduct of armed forces that contain the controversial phrase 'war-sustaining effort', apparently reflecting the US interpretation of the first element of the test, are contained in joint doctrine and two operational law handbooks – for navy and land forces. This permits two observations. First, there could be a broader scope of objects that the US and its coalition partners may want to target, because the military doctrine encourages this. Second, unlike lawyers in other States, US operational lawyers are more likely to regard such objects as lawful targets based on their interpretation of the definition.

272 See the relevant discussion in 3.1 and 7.1.
273 See 4.3.

214 *Operationalisation of the definition of military objective*

8.7 Conclusion

Unlike military doctrine, which can specifically address various types of operation, the law has to be flexible enough to suit every kind of operation. The law does not advise what is desirable, sensible or what should be targeted. This is the role of military doctrine. Inevitably, military doctrine may promote concepts that put the law under pressure. In the context of the definition, military doctrine encourages the selection of targets that may not always offer a definite military advantage, and some that may not contribute to military action (or it is unclear how they do so). The doctrine recognises that destruction is not the only method of affecting targets, and that targeting decisions depend on the variety of information and other factors available in the given circumstances.

Doctrine emphasises the importance of strategic targets connected to the most critical or vulnerable COG, which pose the greatest threat and whose neutralisation or destruction would result in the greatest damage to the enemy's war effort. Such targets may not be confined to military targets, but may also include economic assets or political leadership. These may represent points of contention between what military doctrine promotes as desirable targets and what the law views as permissible ones.

There is no doubt that military forces take the law into account when conducting operations. There are mechanisms to ensure that the military behaviour dictated by the doctrine is compliant with the relevant law. Specifically, the legal scrutiny of proposed targets is part of the targeting process, in which an important role is played by legal advisers who participate in the vetting of targets. Their contribution to the process is vital, and particularly so when dealing with strategic targets linked to strategic COGs. These targets may display significant problems with regard to their compliance with the requirements of the definition. Their assessment should be approached with greater care by military lawyers and commanders. The latter, being more exposed to military doctrine, may be under greater pressure to pursue such targets unless they are told that they are unlawful objects. The lawyers need to comprehend military doctrine to understand a commander's intentions. It is possible that US operational lawyers, unlike their counterparts in other States, would be prepared to consider such targets as lawful. Where the application of military doctrine results in behaviour that becomes State practice, there is a risk that this will appear to others as a manifestation of the legal interpretation of the definition of military objective.

Military doctrine is not the only factor that may affect how States conduct hostilities. The next chapter considers other potential factors that could have had an impact on targeting decisions in Coalition operations in four conflicts: the 1990–1 Gulf War, the 1999 NATO intervention in Kosovo, combat operations in Afghanistan in 2001–2, and the 2003 war in Iraq.

9 Problems of legal interoperability in relation to the identification of lawful targets[1]

Law undoubtedly plays a role in the execution of military operations. Chapter 8 illustrated how current national and international doctrine demands adherence to the relevant standards and rules at all levels of warfare. Modern warfare doctrine is not arrived at arbitrarily. Rather, its fundamentals come from years of experience and a multitude of previous engagements. This chapter will subject these military operations to closer scrutiny. Looking at military conduct during military operations of a specific type, namely coalition operations, may give a specific insight into the interpretation of the definition of military objectives.

The identification of targets in coalition operations may provoke debate among coalition partners.[2] Some States may be bound by additional restrictions on what they can attack. Others may object to certain targets being attacked in the specific circumstances, while others may object to certain targets in principle. Why this is so is not always clear. Following a NATO intervention, one US commander observed:

> We need to understand going in the limitations that our coalition partners will place upon themselves and upon us. There are nations that will not attack targets that my nation will attack. There are nations that do not

---

1 Interoperability concerns the ability of forces involved in the same coalition or alliance to operate together coherently, effectively and efficiently (NATO Allied Joint Doctrine, AJP-01 (D), December 2010, para 0314). Doctrinal interoperability is a type of procedural interoperability. Legal interoperability would fall between procedural and human (related to language or terminology) interoperability, in accordance with the distinctions made by the NATO doctrine.

2 As mentioned in the Introduction to Part II and in Chapter 8 (in particular 8.5.2 and 8.6.2), the discussion of disputed targets may arise only if these specific targets were designated through an application of military doctrine, and subject to subsequent validation. If certain objects are never considered as targets, they will not be scrutinised during the targeting process.

216 *Operationalisation of the definition of military objective*

share with us a definition of what is a valid military target, and we need to know that up front.[3]

When referring to the various limitations, General Short singled out the legal considerations that coalition partners should take into account. The problem is that there are three different kinds of legal consideration. First, there could be a difference in the treaty obligations between the coalition partners, as some States may not have ratified the relevant treaties or provisions. There is then a separate problem where some States take a different view of the substantive content of the relevant customary law. Finally, legal differences may result from different interpretations of the relevant legal obligations.

In addition to legal considerations, there are also non-legal factors that need to be taken into account. Some States' conduct might be dictated by national political constraints or military considerations. As far as political factors are concerned, some political pressures will only affect particular States within a coalition, while others are likely to have an impact on all the coalition partners. If at the national political level it is not acceptable for the State to be involved in an 'armed conflict', the State may assert that the situation it is in is not an armed conflict, which will have legal consequences even if this assertion is prompted by national political constraints. It may also be that increased civilian and/or military casualties are regarded as sensitive due to domestic political pressures. There are, additionally, military factors that may have an impact on targeting decisions. Military factors are shaped by military doctrine, strategy or culture. As explained in Chapter 8, doctrine is likely to impact on the State's concept of operations. It may be that different States will have different doctrines that they apply to the same type of situation. As a result, different doctrines are applied to the same operation. Problems could also occur if there are differences in how States characterise operations. Even if different States' doctrines are in harmony, one State may see the situation differently and, as a result, may use different parts of its doctrine. Finally, considerations of military culture are reflected through issues such as a willingness to take greater risks to avoid civilian casualties, some of which may already be incorporated into the doctrine. Such limitations and considerations could well have an operational impact. For instance, there might be a refusal to grant over-flight rights or to take part in planning the relevant missions.[4]

---

3 Lieutenant General Michael Short, USAF, Commander of Allied Air Forces, Southern Europe, quoted in Amnesty International, NATO/FRY, *'Collateral Damage' or Unlawful Killings? Violations of the Laws of War by NATO During Operation Allied Force*, AI Index: EUR 70/18/00, June 2000, available at http://reliefweb.int/sites/reliefweb.int/files/resources/84AF11F7520D41B3C12575A100460CE7-Full_Report.pdf (last accessed 1 May 2014) [hereinafter: Amnesty Report].

4 *Air Force Operations and the Law: A Guide for Air, Space and Cyber Forces*, US Air Force, The Judge Advocate General's School, 2nd edn, 2009, at 310 [hereinafter: *Air Force Operations and the Law*].

Any such disruption could potentially hamper the success of the operation, and the achievement of the overall military goals.

Differences in levels of available intelligence will inevitably affect the outcome of the legal and policy assessment of a target. The standards relating to the sufficiency, volume and quality of information needed to make targeting decisions may vary between States. Some States may require more information, or information of a different type, before they find the target lawful. This may have an operational impact on the execution of operations. Lack of intelligence-sharing might also be a significant impediment to multinational targeting. Differences leading to divergent evaluations could, in principle, be lessened or even avoided if forces could exchange collated intelligence between themselves. Sometimes this will be impaired by confidentiality issues.[5] The question then arises whether a State would be comfortable relying on the assessment of its coalition partners. The problem might be further complicated where the initial assessment is carried out by third parties.[6]

A focus on the behaviour of States in recent international armed conflicts determined the choice of conflicts analysed in this chapter. There are four major Coalition operations post-1977.[7] These are the 1990–1 Gulf War, the 1999 NATO intervention in Kosovo, the 2001–2 international conflict in Afghanistan and the 2003 war in Iraq. The consideration of the conflicts in Afghanistan and Iraq will only examine the high-intensity combat phase of these operations.[8] The subsequent sections of this chapter examine the issues potentially affecting how the concept of military objective is applied in the identification of targets in Coalition operations. The first section focuses on identifying any disagreements regarding particular targets between the Coalition members in the four conflicts, together with the basis for them. If such differences result from legal obligations, one has to ascertain whether the problem stems from the scope of the rules or their interpretation. The discussion then expands to how Coalition members have dealt with any legal differences, in particular the methods known as the 'red card' and 'lowest common denominator'.

---

5 *Air Force Operations and the Law*, op. cit. n 4, at 309.

6 See the further discussion in 9.1.3.

7 During this period, US forces took part in a number of armed conflicts involving multinational forces. The exception was its 1989 Operation Just Cause in Panama, which was carried out by US forces alone. As part of multinational forces, the US engaged in the 1999 NATO intervention in Kosovo.

8 The combat phase of these conflicts can be indisputably described as international armed conflicts, which is consistent with the essential limitation on the scope of this work (see 1.2.3). Looking at the issues raised in the context of targeting in coalition warfare will require a discussion of some types of targets or even individual objects. Unlike the examples used in Part I, which were used to identify problems with the definition of military objectives, the specific examples in this chapter are used because of the context in which they arose. See also the Introduction to Part II.

218 *Operationalisation of the definition of military objective*

9.1 Targeting in Coalition operations

The following section will trace some of the interoperability issues that have arisen in four Coalition conflicts since 1977. They will be analysed in accordance with the following framework. The analysis starts with brief comments regarding the origins and the claimed authority for initiation of the conflict, the Coalition partners and their contributions to the operations. This will be followed by an indication as to the Coalition partners' legal obligations at the time, in particular whether they had ratified Additional Protocol I to the 1949 Geneva Conventions, which is most relevant to this work.[9] Finally, the chapter will present a brief overview of the targeting process and the targets that were attacked, particularly those which provoked a debate.

9.1.1 1990–1 Gulf War

From the mid-1980s, the US Central Command, concerned by Iraq's growing demands towards its neighbours,[10] was devising a provisional plan of operations in the event of an Iraqi invasion of Saudi Arabia and Kuwait.[11] Rising tensions in the Middle East led eventually to the Iraqi assault on Kuwait. The Iraqi attack began on 2 August 1990.[12] There had been, at that point, serious concerns in the US about the safety of more than 2,000 American embassy staff in the Kuwaiti capital. The United States also held significant economic interests in the region, relating to its oil supplies.[13]

The Coalition of 'willing' States started forming after the UN Security Council's decision to impose economic sanctions and a trade embargo on Iraq.[14] In November 1990, the Security Council adopted a Resolution that authorised the 'use of all necessary means' by UN members to restore peace

---

9 Protocol Additional to the Geneva Conventions of 12 August 1949, and Relating to the Protection of Victims of International Armed Conflicts (Protocol I), Geneva, 8 June 1977, reprinted in D. Schindler and J. Toman (eds), *The Laws of Armed Conflict*, 4th edn, 2004, Martinus Nijhoff, Leiden 2004, at 711 *et seq.* [hereinafter: API].

10 The Iraqis pressed for a reduction in oil production to the levels established by the Organization of the Petroleum Exporting Countries, the annulment of Iraqi debts and compensation for pumping oil from Iraq's part of the Rumayla field.

11 The plan was coded Operations Plan 1002–90. T.A. Keaney and E.A. Cohen, *Gulf War Air Power Survey Summary Report*, US Department of Air Force, US Government Printing Office 1993, Volume II, at 11 [hereinafter: GWAPS II].

12 P.D. Jamieson, *Lucrative Targets: The U.S. Air Force in the Kuwaiti Theatre of Operations*, Air Force History and Museums Program, US Air Force, Washington, DC 2001, at 1.

13 Ibid, at 2.

14 UN SC Res. 661, UN Doc. S/RES/0661 of 6 August 1990, which followed initial Res. 660 of 2 August 1990 condemning the Iraqi invasion of Kuwait and demanding the withdrawal of its troops. These were followed by the US with the institution of a blockade on 9 August 1990 (Jamieson, op. cit. n 12, at 4). By the end of August 1990, the UN Security Council had further instituted a naval blockade to enforce the economic sanctions against Iraq (UN SC Res. 665, UN Doc.S/RES/0665 of 25 August 1990).

Legal interoperability in targeting 219

and security in the region, if Iraqi troops failed to withdraw from Kuwait by 15 January 1991, as requested by earlier Security Council resolutions.[15] Eventually, 39 States joined the Coalition, including prominent Arab nations.[16] The US and UK, and Saudi Arabia and Egypt from Arab League, provided the biggest contribution to Coalition forces. Only ten States engaged in the air campaign: the US, UK, Saudi Arabia, Bahrain, France, Italy, Canada, Kuwait, the United Arab Emirates and Qatar. British, American, French and Kuwaiti forces took part in the land offensive leading to the liberation of Kuwait.[17]

Members of the Coalition with some of the largest contingents, such as the US, the UK and France, were not parties to API during the 1990–1 Gulf War.[18] The Coalition members that had ratified API when the conflict started included Italy, Bahrain, Canada, Kuwait, Saudi Arabia and the United Arab Emirates. It is worth pointing out that all these States took part in the combat air operations in 1991, while the UK, US, France and Kuwait also engaged in the subsequent ground offensive. In December 1990 Canada had just ratified API, but the treaty had not yet entered into force for Canadian forces before the 1991 hostilities took place. It was decided as a matter of policy that API would be applied to this conflict, but it remains unknown if the application of API caused any legal interoperability problems for the Canadians.

In early August 1990 US Colonel Warden, who was air staff deputy director of planning, sensed that US military and political leaders were anticipating some kind of confrontation in an effort to stabilise the situation in the Middle East. He took the initiative to build a planning team, tasked with designing an air campaign aimed at expelling the Iraqis from Kuwait.[19] As the situation in the Persian Gulf region was deteriorating rapidly, US General Norman Schwarzkopf asked Warden to present his team's operational concept and plan both to himself and other commanders.

Warden's initial plan, named 'Instant Thunder', was strikingly different to the concept employed in the air campaign in Vietnam.[20] The operational

---

15 UN SC Res. 678, UN Doc. S/RES/0678 of 29 November 1990. See also n 14 above.
16 The participation of Arab States was considered a political imperative in the conduct of Coalition operations.
17 For a more elaborate discussion regarding the Gulf War, see US US Department of Defense, *Conduct of the Persian Gulf War: Final Report to Congress*, 10 April 1992, Department of Defense Washington, 1992 [hereinafter: DOD Report].
18 It is worth noting that Iraq was not bound by API at the time of Gulf War. Iraq ratified API only in April 2010.
19 See discussion of Warden's strategic rings theory in 7.1. GWAPS II, op. cit. n 11, at 21–2; Jamieson, op. cit. n 12, at 23–6.
20 Note that the US Tactical Air Command, as well as the US Navy, also devised separate strategies for air operations, which followed quite substantively the unsuccessful Vietnam concept of a gradual escalation of attacks, and were not further developed. GWAPS II, op. cit. n 11, at 25–6.

220 *Operationalisation of the definition of military objective*

concept foresaw an intense application of massive air power, designed to destroy Iraqi strategic centres of gravity, or aimed at Iraq's vulnerabilities – including those of its military forces, its political system and elements of its economy.[21] The underlying objective of Warden's team was to attack and incapacitate the Iraqi leadership, in a bid to remove Saddam Hussein from power.[22] In order to achieve that, the plan envisaged strikes against 84 interrelated targets believed to be vital to the regime.

Warden's focus on the Iraqi leadership lay at the heart of the planned air campaign. This target set comprised command, control and communications centres, the telephone network, and radio and TV facilities.[23] Oil and electricity production and supply sites constituted other key targets. It was hoped that attacking electricity supply networks would not only directly affect the leadership, and military communications and facilities dependent on computers, but would also create discontent within the Iraqi population with the conduct of the war. In turn, it was hoped this would put pressure on the Iraqi leadership to cease fighting. Warden's list of 84 targets, organised into 10 target sets, had expanded to 481 targets by mid-January 1991.[24] The overarching strategic centre of gravity was the Iraqi military potential, whose destruction was viewed as critical to ensuring long-term stability in the region.[25] Within this framework, the planners selected targets whose damage or annihilation would produce significant, cascading effects on other parts of the enemy system.[26]

The actual combat operations – codenamed 'Operation Desert Storm' by the American planners, 'Operation Granby'[27] by the British authorities and the 'Mother of All Battles' by the Iraqi leadership – began in the early hours

---

21 See also the discussion of Warden's strategic ring theory in 8.1 and 8.6.2. GWAPS II, op. cit. n 11, at 22.

22 GWAPS II, op. cit. n 11, at 22.

23 Ibid, at 24. See also GWAPS, op. cit. n 11, Vol. IV, at 181 *et seq.* [hereinafter: GWAPS IV].

24 The additional targets were also divided into sets in the following categories: leadership; command, control and communications; strategic air defences; airfields; nuclear, biological and chemical research and production facilities; naval forces and port facilities; military storage and production; railways, rail bridges and road bridges. GWAPS II, op. cit. n 11, at 38–9.

25 Ibid, at 32. See also 8.6.1.

26 It was expected, for example, that the attack on the electricity supply network would further disrupt the communications and control system nodes, which were to be attacked simultaneously. Iraq's communications and control networks were linked to integrated and centralised air defences. Jamieson, op. cit. n 12, at 33. For more on the concept behind effect-based operations, see D.A. Deptula, *Effect-Based Operations: Change in the Nature of Warfare*, Aerospace Education Foundation, Arlington 2001.

27 For the overall official assessment of British operations in the 1990–1 Persian Gulf War, see United Kingdom House of Commons, Defence Committee, *Preliminary Lessons of Operation Granby*, Tenth Report, Her Majesty's Stationery Office, London 1991 [hereinafter: UK Tenth Report], and *Implementation of Lessons Learnt From Operation Granby*, Fifth Report, Her Majesty's Stationery Office, London 1994 [hereinafter: UK Fifth Report].

Legal interoperability in targeting 221

of 17 January 1991.[28] The Coalition theatre objectives were consistent with the operational plan of attacking the Iraqi leadership and command and control sites, the destruction of the Republican Guard forces, and cutting off and destroying supply lines while gaining and maintaining air superiority.[29] Pursuing these objectives was expected to lead to the liberation of Kuwait City through the ground offensive, and the annihilation of Iraqi military forces in the Kuwaiti Theatre of Operations (KTO).

The British component, guided by the fundamental aim of attacking the 'Iraqi war machine so that it no longer cast a shadow over Kuwait',[30] took part in the attacks against Iraqi airfields, air defences, and the command and communications network.[31] In Phase II of the operations, the Royal Air Force's main task was to break the military supply routes to and from Kuwait by attacking the bridges along them. UK troops also took part in the ground offensive in this phase.[32]

On the first day of the campaign, the Coalition hit several clearly military targets, as well as the presidential palace and several electricity generating sites around Baghdad, and Saddam's private residence in Tikrit.[33] At the end of the first day of operations, most of Baghdad had been deprived of electricity, Iraqi air defences had disintegrated, and several military command and control nodes had ceased to operate effectively – or at all.[34] On this second day, the US air Force bombarded more targets in Baghdad including the Internal Security Agency, Military Intelligence headquarters, the Ba'ath Party head-quarters and the Ministry of Information.[35] Most of these objects were valued as prominent symbols of the regime, and it was thought that attacking them would produce political as well as military effects.[36] In the second week of air

28 GWAPS II, op. cit. n 11, at 120.
29 Ibid, at 115.
30 United Kingdom, Letter to UN Security Council, UN Doc. S/22156, 28 January 1991.
31 Ibid, and in UK Fifth Report, op. cit. n 27, at xx.
32 UK Tenth Report, op. cit. n 27, at G43–G45.
33 The military targets included the Baghdad Air Force headquarters, Air Defence Operating Centre, the Tallil Sector Operations Centre and the Salman Pak Intercept Operations Centre. It is possible that the presidential palace mentioned had also potentially included command and control facilities as number of such palaces did (GWAPS II, op. cit. n 11, at 124, 126). Additional command and control facilities, surface to air missile (SAM) launch sites and radars were struck, as well as the Al Taqaddum airfield taxiways and runways, and the Habbaniya Petroleum Storage Facility (GWAPS II op. cit. n 11, at 126–7, 134, 143; GWAPS IV, op. cit. n 23, at 203). Late in the day, the Tawakalna Division of the Republican Guard and the airfield, bridges and petroleum complex around Basra were subjected to strikes (GWAPS II, op. cit. n 11, at 144; Jamieson, op. cit. n 12, at 45).
34 GWAPS II, op. cit. n 11, at 137; Jamieson, op. cit. n 12, at 42.
35 The second 24 hours of the air campaign brought more attacks against chemical and biological warfare facilities, the airfields and air bases at Balul and Jaliba, and more SAM sites (GWAPS II, op. cit. n 11, at 148–51). The American Navy also interdicted the bridges along the Euphrates in an attempt to deprive Republican Guard forces of supply routes and the possibility of retreating across the river (GWAPS II, op. cit. n 11, at 169–70, 202).
36 GWAPS II, op. cit. n 11, at 176.

222   *Operationalisation of the definition of military objective*

operations, the Coalition destroyed the Ministry of Defence computer centre, major power plants and 11 out of 12 major Iraqi oil refineries.[37]

As time progressed, several operational command and control nodes were eliminated, which required the Iraqi commanders to identify new, active facilities to replace them. By mid-January Coalition intelligence had identified 25 bunkers that could potentially be used in such a way, and that were not believed to have been active at the start of the campaign. As discussed elsewhere, by 13 February 1991 at least one of them, the Al Firdus/Amariyah (Ameriyya) bunker in Baghdad, appeared to have become operational.[38] The subsequent attack on this facility resulted in substantial civilian casualties. The most comprehensive commentary so far of Operation Desert Storm, the Gulf War Air Power Survey (GWAPS), suggested strongly that the attackers were absolutely unaware that the Al Firdus/Amariyah (Ameriyya) bunker was being used as a civilian shelter at the time.[39]

The political pressure and public outcry following the destruction of the bunker in effect stopped any potential Coalition attacks in downtown Baghdad.[40] The GWAPS authors observed that, for the Coalition air campaign to have succeeded on its own in forcing the collapse of Saddam Hussein's regime, it would have had to focus on targets directly related to the political structure.[41] Such targeting, however, as exemplified by the Al Firdus/Amariyah (Ameriyya) bunker incident, carried a much higher risk of increased civilian casualties.

There is relatively little information available about legal interoperability during the 1990–1 Gulf War. It is, nonetheless, possible that, as with other operations of this type, each contributing State sets its own limits on operational conduct, while still being guided by the ROE. French military forces, for

---

37 Some 600 bunkers were used by the Iraqis primarily as aircraft shelters, such as the one at Qalat Salih airfield, or the super-hardened shelters at Balad and Al-Asad airfields. Jamieson, op. cit. n 12, at 47.

38 See the discussion in 6.2.

39 GWAPS II, op. cit. n 11, at 206. Human Rights Watch alleges that failure in verification of the evidence before the strike might have resulted in the alleged lack of knowledge regarding civilian use. Middle East Watch (Human Rights Watch), *Needless Deaths in the Gulf War: Civilian Casualties During the Air Campaign and Violations of the Laws of War*, Human Rights Watch, New York 1991, in chapter 4 [hereinafter: Needless Deaths].

40 Subsequent to the bunker attack, further strikes on the bridges over the Tigris River and on the Baghdad targets were cancelled. The latter apparently included a statue of Saddam Hussein and the victory arches erected in commemoration of the Iran–Iraq war. J.D. Reynolds, 'Collateral damage on the 21st Century Battlefield: Enemy Exploitation of the Law of Armed Conflict, and The Struggle For a Moral High Ground', 56 *The Air Force Law Review* 2005, 1–108 at 34–5.

41 The GWAPS concluded that if the Coalition had wanted to conduct the air campaign only against the military potential, the political regime could not have been changed unless the air operations were followed by the occupation of Iraq. GWAPS II, op. cit. n 11, at 206–8.

Legal interoperability in targeting   223

instance, were willing to operate only in the KTO, while the Saudi Arabian contingent preferred not to contribute to the ground offensive at all.[42] The solution to the constraints imposed by national policy was therefore to separate the Coalition forces, geographically or functionally.

As far as targeting was concerned, each State's forces could, in principle, opt out of engaging in an attack if they had concerns about the legality of the targets.[43] Each Coalition force was responsible for providing legal advice and guidance regarding the targets assigned to it; this included limited participation from Canada.[44] It is unclear if such advice had much practical impact, as target selection and validation appeared to be very much in US hands.[45]

If the selection and validation of targets was controlled by US forces, with no specific objections from other contributing States – particularly those engaged in active combat and bound by API – it may be reasonable to conclude that the relevant legal standard in this operation was the customary definition of military objectives.[46] However, it is uncertain whether the US decided to adopt a customary standard resembling API, or whether it applied a broader or narrower interpretation. The US might not have wanted to apply a broader interpretation because it did not want to create tensions that could have affected the stability of the Coalition. This would be a political reason.

Using the available official sources, it is not possible to conclude whether there were any disagreements regarding the assessment of targets for air operations among Italy, Saudi Arabia, Kuwait, Bahrain and Syria, who were all bound by API at the time, and if there were, how the differences were resolved.[47] It appears, however, that on at least two occasions British air forces refused to engage certain targets because of concerns about the possible malfunction of a weapon, which would increase the risk of collateral

---

42 *United States and NATO Military Operations Against the Federal Republic of Yugoslavia*, Hearing before United States House of Representatives Committee on Armed Services, 106th Congress, 28 April 1999, H.A.S.C. No. 106–12, at 77.

43 R.L. Bridge, 'Operations Law: An Overview', 37 *Air Force Law Review* 1994, at 3.

44 K. Watkin and Z. Drebot, 'The Operational Lawyer: An Essential Resource for the Modern Commander', undated, on file with author.

45 US military command, or US CENTCOM, held general authority over the choice of targets until the attack on the Al Firdus/Amariyah (Ameriyya) bunker, when the US Department of Defense reportedly took over the targeting process, presumably due to an increased concern about collateral damage. S. Myrow, 'Waging War on the Advice of Counsel: The Role of Operational War in the Gulf War', 7 *US Air Force Academy Journal of Legal Studies* 1996–7, 131–58 at 139–41; DOD Report, op. cit. n 17, chapter V, 83–116; A.L. DeSaussure, 'The Role of Law of Armed Conflict During the Persian Gulf War: An Overview', 37 *The Air Force Law Review* 1994, 41–68 at 58 n 97.

46 DOD Report, op. cit. n 17, Appendix O, at O-10.

47 It is unclear whether these Coalition members engaged in vetting the targets at all. See also Watkin and Drebot, op. cit. n 44.

224 *Operationalisation of the definition of military objective*

damage.[48] Air Vice Marshal Wratten, who mentioned those occasions, implied that the targets in question were not fundamentally important to the achievement of victory. This may suggest that although the status of these 'unknown' targets was not disputed, the manner in which the attack was going to be conducted might have resulted in disproportionate civilian casualties.[49]

A number of targets associated with the political leadership, TV stations and Iraqi economic industrial installations were attacked during the 1990–1 Gulf War. Some of these attacks, especially against 'dual-use' infrastructure such as the power grid, caused controversy in the mass media, which often involved non-governmental organisations such as Human Rights Watch questioning the lawfulness of some of the strikes.[50] The problem was that the assessment of such attacks was based on the limited information gathered and evaluated in hindsight.[51] The reason for targeting oil tankers might have been attributed to the flawed method of tracking Scud missile launchers, and not a reflection of the Coalition's view as to the lawfulness of the attacks.[52] The subsequent US government report addressed some of the concerns raised. It explained, for example, that the bridges over the Euphrates contained fibre-optic cables that provided secure communication links, in addition to their role in transportation and Iraqi military logistics.[53] The report also indicated that TV and radio stations were hit because they were controlled and used by Saddam's regime as the 'principal media for Iraqi propaganda'.[54] It is unclear whether that was the only basis of such attacks. If so, this reason would have not satisfied the definition of military objective.[55] Similarly, a number of attacks on State and political leadership facilities were conducted, but received only limited attention.[56]

---

48 W.J. Wratten, Comments to United Kingdom House of Commons Defence Committee, Tenth Report, op. cit. n 27, para 274. See also T. Stein, 'Coalition Warfare and Differing Legal Obligations of Coalition Members under International Humanitarian Law' in A.E. Wall (ed.), *Legal and Ethical Lessons of NATO's Kosovo Campaign*, Vol. 78, US Naval War College International Law Studies, Newport, RI 2002, at 326–7.

49 This might be a reflection of the potential specific military consideration regarding the weapons malfunction, the legal constraint related to the application of proportionality, or a more general political sensitivity regarding the collateral casualties and damage following the attack on the Al Firdus/Amariyah (Ameriyya) bunker.

50 Needless Deaths, op. cit. n 39, for example chapter 4.

51 See also the discussion in 6.2 and 10.4.

52 It has been suggested that an attack on oil-carrying trucks on the way to Jordan might, in fact, have been attributed to the frantic SCUD missile pursuit as the trucks emitted an infrared signature resembling the traces produced by the mobile launchers. GWAPS II, op. cit. n 11, at 189.

53 DOD Report, op. cit. n 17, at 178 and 210, and Appendix O, at O-11.

54 Ibid, at 148.

55 These attacks have not created much debate even in the report of non-governmental organisations. See discussion in 7.3.

56 See the discussion in the text attached to n 35 above. See also the discussion in 3.1.2 and 7.4.

Legal interoperability in targeting 225

9.1.2 1999 NATO intervention in Kosovo

Following almost a year of diplomatic efforts to avert the increasing violence against the Kosovo Albanians, NATO decided to initiate military operations against the Serbian President, Slobodan Milosevic, on 24 March 1999. The NATO air campaign, codenamed 'Operation Allied Force', lasted 78 days, from 24 March to 10 June.[57] The Serb forces finally withdrew from Kosovan territory on 20 June.

'Operation Allied Force' was NATO's largest military operation since 1945, and its second in the Balkans region.[58] Out of the then 19 NATO member States, 14 contributed aircraft, with the US committing the majority.[59] Twelve States ultimately participated in combat operations.[60] Although this was predominantly an air operation, it also involved supporting British and US naval units and assets.[61]

The UK ratified API on 28 January 1998, and was therefore bound by the treaty during the intervention in Kosovo and subsequent operations.[62] France ratified API only in April 2001.[63] The legal position of the US in the conflicts analysed in this chapter was different to that of its Coalition partners. As mentioned in Chapter 4, the US generally accepts the Art 52.2 API definition as reflecting customary law and, to this extent, is bound by it.[64] However, the

---

57 Strictly adhering to the doctrinal definitions, some commentators rejected Operation Allied Force as an 'air campaign', which is defined as a number of connected operations, not as one continuous, coercive effort (see, for instance: B.S. Lambeth, *NATO's Air War for Kosovo: A Strategic and Operational Assessment*, RAND, Santa Monica 2001, at 20 n 10 and 196). The narrow operational perception of the NATO intervention did not affect its legal qualification as an armed conflict and, as such, being subject to the laws of war.

58 NATO had already been present in the region from 1992 onwards, in a peacekeeping role. During 1994–5 it also conducted a number of offensive air strikes against Bosnian Serb forces and military objects, in line with UN Security Council Resolution 816 (UN Doc. S/RES/0816 of 31 March 1993).

59 *Kosovo Air Operations, Need to Maintain Alliance Cohesion Resulted in Doctrinal Departures*, United States General Accounting Office, Report to Congressional Requesters, GAO-01-784, July 2001, at 3 [hereinafter: *Kosovo Air Operations*].

60 Lambeth, op. cit. n 57, at 20.

61 Ibid.

62 In line with the Former Republic of Yugoslavia (FRY)'s commitment to abide by the international obligations of the former Federal Republic of Yugoslavia, FRY was bound by API due to its ratification in 1979.

63 Even though France was not formally a member of the NATO military alliance at that time, as a member of NATO it retained a political power of veto. France rejoined the military alliance in 2009. See information at: www.nato.int/cps/en/natolive/topics_52044.htm (last accessed 1 May 2014).

64 The US is a State signatory of API. *Legal Lessons Learned from Afghanistan and Iraq, Volume I, Major Combat Operations (11 September 2011 to 1 May 2003)*, Center for Law and Military Operations, United States Army, The Judge Advocate General's Legal Center and School, Charlottesville, VA, 1 August 2004, at 123 [hereinafter Centre for Law and Military Operations (CLAMO) 2004]; *Forged in the Fire: Legal Lessons Learnt During Military Operations 1994–2008*, Center for Law and Military Operations, United States Army, The Judge

226　*Operationalisation of the definition of military objective*

US interprets certain provisions of it in quite a particular way.[65] At the time of the Kosovo intervention, there appears to have been some uncertainty about the scope of the definition within US legal circles.[66] This would imply one of two things: either those inside the legal circles were not sufficiently informed about the official US interpretation of the customary definition, or there was disagreement in this area. The latter appears more likely. This could mean that, by 1999, the US interpretation of the customary law definition of military objectives had not yet fully crystallised.

The Alliance engaged in operational planning for nearly 12 months prior to the intervention, from spring 1998.[67] In essence, the plans envisaged a five-phase operation.[68] Phases 1 and 2 focused on the Kosovo area and certain targets south of 44 degrees north latitude. Phase 1 was aimed at achieving air superiority, and degrading command and control and integrated air defence objects in both areas. Phase 2 was aimed at attacking other military objectives and Yugoslav forces in Kosovo, as well as forces south of 44 degrees that were supporting Serbian operations in Kosovo. An expansion of air operations against strategic or high value targets throughout the then Federal Republic of Yugoslavia was anticipated in Phase 3. Phase 4 provided for the possibility of the redeployment of forces. Initially, a ground offensive was also envisaged. However, by the time air operations had begun, it was agreed that this campaign alone would be the optimal action.[69]

This vision of operations was transformed shortly before the start of the intervention. The new plan comprised an initial two-day strike on targets in the territory of the then Former Republic of Yugoslavia. This plan was accompanied by a developed set of targets that were intended to compel the authorities in Belgrade to withdraw their forces and to end the violence in Kosovo.[70]

When this two-day attack did not attain the required military goals, the air campaign continued incrementally for the following 76 days. During the initial two days, Phase 1 targets were engaged. On 27 March 1999, in the light

---

Advocate General's Legal Center and School, Charlottesville, VA, September 2008, at 350 [hereinafter: CLAMO 2008]. See also DOD Report, op. cit. n 17, at 127.

65　See also the discussion in 4.3.

66　*Military Operations in Kosovo 1999–2001: Lessons Learned for Advocates*, Report, Center for Law and Military Operations, Judge Advocate General's School, United States Army, December 2001, at 52 [hereinafter: CLAMO 2001].

67　*Kosovo / Operation Allied Force After Action Report*, Report to Congress, US Department of Defense, January 2000, at 8 [hereinafter: *Kosovo After Action*]; Ministry of Defence, *Kosovo Lessons from the Crisis*, UK DCCS Media Publications, London 2000, para 8.1 [hereinafter: *Kosovo Lessons from the Crisis*].

68　The five-phase plan included Phase 0, which provided for a deployment of air force assets to the European Theatre prior to the commencement of hostilities.

69　Phase 5 envisaged the possibility of ground forces being deployed, which in substance was considered only towards the end of the conflict in May 1999.

70　*Kosovo Lessons from the Crisis*, op. cit. n 67, para 3.4.

Legal interoperability in targeting 227

of the lack of Serbian concessions, targets related to Phase 2 objectives were authorised for attack.[71] In the next two days NATO moved towards attacking strategic objects, as envisaged in Phase 3.[72] Commentators indicated that Phases 1 to 3 were implemented in an accelerated and concentrated way simultaneously.[73]

A few of the command and control facilities that were attacked were believed to have been empty or unused. This prompted some criticism as to whether attacking these targets had any effect on averting the humanitarian crisis.[74] A similar argument was put forward in respect of attacks on tanks. Kosovo Albanians were not killed by tanks, but by rifles and other small arms. Thus, focusing effort on the destruction of tanks did not seem to advance the primary political and military aim.[75] Having said that, there was some value in attacks against such objects. The Serbian intention was to utilise tanks and other heavy armour against the Kosovo Liberation Army (KLA) once Kosovo had been 'cleared' of ethnic Albanians. Therefore, NATO strikes on tanks would have given some military advantage to the KLA.[76]

71 In total, some 40 targets were pursued during this initial stage, including police and military barracks, munitions stores and weapons production sites, the majority of which were outside Kosovo. According to official reports on 25 March 1999, the target list was expanded to include forces in Kosovo, and further fixed military facilities outside Kosovo. Lambeth, op. cit. n 57, at 21–4.

72 Note that there is an ambiguity as to a formal recognition of moving to another phase of the operational plans, which, short of such formal acknowledgement, came to be known as Phase 2A. United Kingdom House of Commons, Committee on Defence, *Lessons of Kosovo*, Fourteenth Report, HC 347-I, Her Majesty Stationery Office, London, October 2000, paras 97–9, available at www.publications.parliament.uk/pa/cm199900/cmselect/cmfaff/28/2802.htm (last accessed 17 July 2014) [hereinafter: UK Fourteenth Report].

73 Ibid, para 84; *Kosovo: Operation 'Allied Force'*, UK House of Commons, Research Paper, 99/48, 29 April 1999, at 16 [hereinafter: *Kosovo: Operation 'Allied Force'*]; and Lambeth, op. cit. n 57, at 28.

74 Dispersed, light and mobile Serbian units did not need sophisticated communications infrastructure to conduct atrocities in Kosovo. Additionally, if they had needed any fixed quarters, they could easily have seized civilian buildings. A.H. Cordesman, *The Effectiveness of the NATO Tactical Air and Missile Campaign against the Serbian and Ground Forces in Kosovo*, A Working Paper, Center for Strategic and International Studies, August 2000, at 3. A question arises whether the humanitarian nature of the operations and the related concept of operations in military doctrine, could have an effect on the narrowing the scope of the objects that can be targeted. It is unclear if this would be a policy restriction or a legal restriction. See also n 30 in Chapter 9. Such argument was proposed by M. Bothe, 'The Protection of the Civilian Population and NATO Bombing on Yugoslavia: Comments on a Report to the Prosecutor of the ICTY', 12(3) *European Journal of International Law* 2001, 531–55 at 535 and was met with criticism from K. Watkin, 'Canada/United States Military Interoperability and Humanitarian Law Issues: Land Mines, Terrorism, Military Objectives and Targeted Killing', 15(2) *Duke Journal of International and Comparative Law* 2005, 281–314 at 306.

75 General Shelton, cited in Cordesman, op. cit. n 74, at 48, and General Ralston and others, cited in Lambeth, op. cit. n 57, at 134.

76 This raises an interesting question regarding the issue of towards whose military action the objects were contributing, and whose military operations benefited from their destruction. In the context of these operations, the attacks appear to have been advantageous possibly

228 *Operationalisation of the definition of military objective*

Consistent with the aims of the campaign, NATO simultaneously pursued two distinct strategies. One was of denial, and the other of inducing compliance. Attention shifted between the two, depending on which targets had been given the seal of approval, and what was happening in Kosovo at any given time. The aim of degrading the capabilities of the Serbian military and security forces through denial was pursued throughout the remainder of campaign, in parallel with the coercive objective aimed at inducing compliance.[77] The latter objective encompassed strategic targets, the destruction or neutralisation of which would have influenced the ruling elite – including the Serbian leader. It would also have had a general impact on the Serbian civilian population, aimed at changing its attitudes towards the government-sponsored violence in Kosovo.[78]

The attacks against broadly perceived, strategic coercive objectives caused concern not only among the public, media and politicians, but also among military commanders themselves.[79] Several issues were raised. Strategic coercive targets were aimed at striking Serbian decision-makers at their most vulnerable centres of gravity (COG). NATO believed these weak points comprised the following pillars of power: police and security forces, media outlets, and the industrial infrastructure and businesses sustaining the leadership – or the war – financially.[80] At a glance, the targets associated with such assets and symbols tend to be civilian in nature. If also used for military purposes, they are likely to carry higher levels of collateral damage due to their location and their use by civilians. It is unsurprising, therefore, that once NATO had embarked on attacks against several such objects, doubts were raised as to the legality of these objectives and, sometimes, of the proportionality of such attacks. One can recall attacks against the headquarters of the Socialist Party and Belgrade's TV and radio broadcasting station, as well as some State-owned manufacturing plants such as a cigarette factory or the Zastava car plant.[81] The strikes against the Sloboda vacuum cleaner production facility were also criticised, but NATO maintained the facility was also used for tank servicing and repairs. One commentator in Belgrade suggested that NATO's efforts in general had a limited effect, if any, on the Serbian population.[82]

---

not to one State or even the whole Coalition, but to third-party forces. See the discussion in 1.2 and 5.2.1.

77 Lambeth, op. cit. n 57, at 28.

78 These objects were approved on 28 March. Strikes against them began on 30 March, and escalated from 3 April. Attacks on Belgrade's Defence and Interior Ministry headquarters, as well as against the transport and communication infrastructure elsewhere in Serbia, took place before 1 April (Lambeth, op. cit. n 57, at 29).

79 UK Fourteenth Report, op. cit. n 72, paras 89 and 91.

80 Ibid, para 90; *Kosovo: Operation 'Allied Force'*, op. cit. n 73, at 19, 22, 24–5; Lambeth, op. cit. n 57, at 39–43.

81 See 3.1, and 7.1 and 7.3.

82 UK Fourteenth Report, op. cit. n 72, paras 257–58.

Legal interoperability in targeting 229

One military commander reflected on the limited effectiveness of other attacks. In the context of petroleum, oil and lubricants (POL) facilities, where NATO claimed to have destroyed or damaged all Yugoslav oil refineries, and more than 50 per cent of its petroleum reserves,[83] he noted that new POL supplies had been delivered by sea through Montenegro.[84] This demonstrated how much the political decision not to impose an oil embargo or naval blockade in time had influenced the effectiveness of theatre operations.[85] Additionally, one commentator observed that cutting off the POL supply lines was likely to have resulted in the increased seizure by Serbian forces in Kosovo of stores of petrol from the Kosovars. This would have contributed to the worsening of the refugee crisis.[86]

The Kosovo intervention Coalition differed from others inasmuch as it was not based on an *ad hoc* agreement between 'willing' States, but rooted in the pre-existing North Atlantic Alliance. This inevitably affected how targeting would be conducted. The identification, selection and approval of strategic targets were all considered to be operational problems.[87] Most of the proposed targets originated from the US, flowing from its intelligence capabilities, though other States also nominated targets.[88] The proposed targets were collated at NATO command, and first vetted by the US leadership. If approved, they were handed to other NATO Member States for approval.[89] However, only the US, UK and France engaged in the clearance of individual targets, while all Member States took a vote on the adding of target sets when moving from one phase to another.[90] The French leadership wanted, in principle, a greater control over, and input into, clearing the targets.[91] Subsequently, the French authorities engaged in the process quite extensively.[92]

---

83 *Kosovo Lessons from the Crisis*, op. cit. n 67, para 7.16.
84 General Wesley Clark cited in UK Fourteenth Report, op. cit. n 72, para 125; *Kosovo: Operation 'Allied Force'*, op. cit. n 73, at 29.
85 General Wesley Clark cited in UK Fourteenth Report, op. cit. n 72, at 261.
86 Cordesman, op. cit. n 74, at 2 and 8.
87 It has been noted, for instance, that parallel US and NATO command structures frustrated smooth operational planning and command unity. Enhancing interoperability between NATO and its members became one of the most important objectives after the Kosovo intervention. *Kosovo After-Action*, op. cit. n 67, at 20; *Kosovo Lessons from the Crisis*, op. cit. n 67, chapter 5 *in toto*; Lambeth, op. cit. n 57, at 207–18; W.K. Clark, *Waging Modern War*, Public Affairs, Oxford 2001, at 226; P.C. Spedero, *Time Sensitive Targeting – The Operational Commander's Role*, Naval War College, Newport, RI, 9 February 2004, at 5.
88 Lambeth, op. cit. n 57, at 186; Clark, op. cit. n 87, at 180, 226.
89 CLAMO 2001, op. cit. n 66, at 50; Spedero, op. cit. n 87, at 5.
90 Lambeth, op. cit. n 57, at 187.
91 J. Hoekema, *NATO Policy and NATO Strategy in Light of the Kosovo Conflict*, Draft General Report, NATO Defense and Security Committee, 6 October 1999, s III B, para 21.
92 Even though France was not formally a member of the NATO military alliance, as a member of the NATO organisation it retained a political power of veto.

230   *Operationalisation of the definition of military objective*

As the campaign developed, US approval of certain targets was delegated to lower levels of command.[93] Other States' legal officers could have taken part in the operational-level assessment of the targets assigned to their national forces.[94] The forces whose States did not approve certain targets were excluded from undertaking attacks against these targets.[95] There was a suggestion that certain targets were indeed considered unlawful, which led to the cancelling of planned attacks against them, but it is unclear which targets they were. It is unclear if they were regarded as unlawful in principle or in the specific circumstances. This would appear to suggest a disagreement about the determination of some objects as military objectives.[96]

A review of any individual targets by each Alliance member's political leadership, with the effective ability to veto any targets, significantly slowed the targeting process.[97] Even though NATO delegated the clearance of operational and tactical targets to military commanders, they were limited to giving validation only to 'safe' fixed military objects with low anticipated levels of collateral damage.

Significantly, all the NATO States had an opportunity to engage in vetting the targets, with the right to veto. It is unclear whether the States that did not take that opportunity agreed with the targeting choices. It could be that they were uncomfortable with them, but found practical ways round this by not permitting their troops to engage in the attacks. Such measures could have covered what may otherwise have been disquiet over some targets. There have been various reports of countries that impeded US aircraft, for example by denying airspace, because they had not approved the targets to be struck. This was true in the case of the UK: General Michael Short, then Commander of the Allied Air Forces, gave testimony to this effect when he spoke at the US Naval War College.[98] The Australian authorities adopted a similar stance.[99]

---

93 CLAMO 2001, op. cit. n 66, at 50.

94 British domestic regulations demanded, for example, that any targets engaged by UK-based aircraft had to be approved by British lawyers. Canadian legal officers reviewed every target assigned to the Canadian Task Force.

95 M. Short, 'Operational Allied Force from the Perspective of the NATO Air Commander' in A.E. Wall (ed.), *Legal and Ethical Lessons of NATO's Kosovo Campaign*, Vol. 78, US Naval War College International Law Studies, Newport, RI 2002, at 26.

96 Ibid, at 25.

97 R. Grant, 'Reach-Forward', *Air Force Magazine*, October 2002, at 45; *Kosovo Lessons from the Crisis*, op. cit. n 67, para 7.2; *Kosovo After-Action*, op. cit. n 67, at 51; Hoekema, op. cit. n 91, s III B, para 22. The Center of Naval Analysis report, cited in one of the post-conflict studies, indicated that some 64 per cent of all fixed targets required vetting by higher-level authorities. The process thus suffered significant delays. Reportedly, some 150 out of 778 fixed objects were still awaiting such approval after the operation ceased (*Kosovo Air Operations*, op. cit. n 59, at 8).

98 Short, op. cit. n 95, at 26; also mentioned in Clark, op. cit. n 87.

99 K. Cochrane, *Kosovo Targeting – A Bureaucratic and Legal Nightmare: The Implications for US/ Australian Interoperability*, Aerospace Centre, Paper No. 3, June 2001, at 7.

Legal interoperability in targeting 231

Consequently, several US missions were either cancelled or turned around when aircraft were en route to their destinations.[100]

Only the French leadership appeared actually to exercise a 'total veto'. This meant that if they failed to approve a target, it could not then be attacked by other States. General Wesley Clark suggested that there was a possibility he might have been ordered to engage such targets, despite the absence of approval from the French authorities.[101] This, however, did not appear to constitute unusual practice: according to Colonel Michael Kelly of the Australian military forces, most of the targets that were not approved by other States were subsequently attacked by the American component of NATO forces.[102]

The NATO operation was riddled with the complexities of various political, legal and operational considerations that had to be balanced in order to maintain cohesion and unity.[103] Some proposed strategic targets provoked particular concern among the Allies and the public. Television and media facilities, infrastructure and the national grid caused most controversy.[104]

Certain bridges were considered highly sensitive objects as their military significance was in doubt.[105] NATO attached a particular strategic significance to the bridges over the River Danube, whose position cut the country in half. NATO believed that the destruction of these bridges, even though they were far from Kosovo, would hinder the movement of Serbian forces and supplies across the country.[106] French forces refused to participate in the attacks against the bridges, allegedly because of the unclear anticipated military advantage,[107] though admittedly these targets' contribution to the military action was also questioned.[108]

---

100 M. Kelly, 'Legal Factors in Military Planning for Coalition Warfare and Military Interoperability: Some Implications for the Australian Defence Force', 2 *Australian Army Journal* 2005, 161–72 at 163.

101 Clark, op. cit. n 87, at 276.

102 Unsurprisingly, certain frictions can arise between the members of a coalition, often resulting in additional and impromptu operational measures being taken. Kelly, op. cit. n 100, at 163.

103 UK Fourteenth Report, op. cit. n 72, para 61.

104 Attacks on marshalling yards were unapproved by American political leadership due to concerns about the weaponry to be used. Clark, op. cit. n 87, at 319.

105 Ibid, at 251.

106 General Sir Charles Guthrie statement on 27 April 1999, as cited in *Kosovo: Operation 'Allied Force'*, op. cit. n 73, at 26.

107 N. Quenivet, 'Report of the Prosecutor of the ICTY Concerning NATO BOMBING against the FRY: A Comment', 41(3) *Indian Journal of International Law* 2001, 478–94 at 484.

108 M. Bothe, 'Targeting' in A.E. Wall (ed.), *Legal and Ethical Lessons of NATO's Kosovo Campaign*, Vol. 78, US Naval War College International Law Studies, Newport, RI 2002, at 179; M.N. Schmitt, 'The Law of Targeting' in E. Wilmshurst and S. Breau (eds), *Perspectives on the ICRC Study on Customary International Humanitarian Law*, Cambridge University Press, Cambridge 2007, at 147.

232 *Operationalisation of the definition of military objective*

It has been noted that attacks against some other bridges might not have been effective in stopping the movement of troops and supplies. Cordesman, in his extensive study of the targets struck in Kosovo, observed that the relatively light forces of the kind deployed to Kosovo, that is infantry, could have bypassed destroyed or severely damaged bridges using boats and pontoons within 48 hours.[109] In this context, one could question the military advantage that was anticipated from neutralising such objects.[110]

Sources in the public domain appear to suggest that the most controversial targets of the Kosovo intervention were contested due to concerns about collateral damage rather than their lawfulness as military objectives.[111] General Wesley Clark, in his memoirs, recalled that the US leadership, in the early stages of the campaign, invalidated certain bridges – as well as petroleum storage sites in Kosovo – apparently due to proportionality concerns.[112] Reportedly, Canadian lawyers tasked with validating potential military objectives – particularly those serving both military *and* civilian functions – encountered difficulties because of a lack of relevant, appropriate or sufficient information about these objectives. It is unclear whether the Canadians were unable to determine whether the target was a lawful military objective, or whether the lack of information concerned the precautions in attack.[113] This suggests a different consideration that relates to the standard of information required to make a legal determination.[114]

Some sources suggest the British and French authorities questioned the lawfulness of specific television and media targets not only because of the risk of collateral damage, but also because of their lawfulness as military objectives.[115] Although the French leadership gave their approval to strike one

---

109 Cordesman, op. cit. n 74, at 3 and 8.

110 Another author suggested that attacks around the capital, for instance, were aimed at isolating the centre of power from its industrial base, which was concentrated in the northern province of Vojvodina. This meant that the railways and bridges connecting the two locations were attacked. S.W. Belt, 'Missiles over Kosovo: Emergence, *Lex Lata*, of a Customary Norm Requiring the Use of Precision Munitions in Urban Areas', 47 *Naval Law Review* 2000, 115–75 at 134.

111 This would suggest legal concerns, but considerations related to proportionality also very often result from political pressure. Spedero gives an example of a denied strike against a Serbian Armoured Personnel Carrier parked near a civilian tractor. He claims denial was based on potential collateral damage to the tractor. Spedero, op. cit. n 87, at 6.

112 Clark, op. cit. n 87, at 227.

113 Radio relay stations were highlighted as examples of such 'dual-use' objects. Other objects engaged by Canadian pilots included bridges, tunnels, petroleum, oil and lubricant (POL) facilities, and industrial sites. J.S.T. Pitzul, 'Operational Law and the Legal Professional: A Canadian Perspective', 51 *Air Force Law Review* 2001, 311–22 at 319.

114 Ibid. One source suggested that in the context of operations in Afghanistan and Iraq, each Coalition member should make an assessment according to the information it possessed (CLAMO 2004, op. cit. n 64, at 123. See the discussion in 9.1.1 and 9.1.2, 6.2 and 9.4.

115 Clark, op. cit. n 87, at 251; Hoekema, op. cit. n 91, s III B, para 25; M. Ignatieff, *Virtual War: Kosovo and Beyond*, Metropolitan Books, Henry Holt, New York 2000, at 194–5, 207.

Legal interoperability in targeting 233

television transmitter, this was subsequently withdrawn. Instead, a green light was given to attacks on the Serbian Socialist Party headquarters and the Belgrade television station facilities.[116]

Electricity supply targets also divided opinion among the allies: General Clark claimed that the American authorities were keen for NATO to strike the electricity network targets, but it was not until the end of April 1999 that the French authorities managed to validate attacks against certain components of that system.[117] The electricity supply grid was also mentioned in this context, as well as lines of communication with both military and civilian functions.[118] Even though Serbian civilian structures linked to the adversary's political leadership were attacked, there is not much information, other than the late French approval of some of these targets, to suggest they were viewed as contentious.

9.1.3 2001–2 conflict in Afghanistan

The US-led military campaign in Afghanistan was directed against the *de facto* Taliban administration, which permitted the presence of the al Qaeda organisation's members, supporters and infrastructure. This, according to the US authorities, led to the 9/11 terrorist attacks on US soil.[119]

On 7 October 2001, invoking the right to self-defence, the US and other Allied countries engaged in military operations in Afghanistan.[120] The US

---

116 See also the discussion of TV and radio broadcasting stations in 3.3 and 7.3. Clark, op. cit. n 87, at 266.
117 Clark, op. cit. n 87, at 276.
118 CLAMO 2001, op. cit. n 66, at 52.
119 The analysis in this section is confined to the initial phase of the conflict, leading up to the overthrow of the Taliban regime and the establishment of a new, recognised Afghan Interim Authority in December 2001 to early 2002. The UN supported this authority in its Security Council Resolution 1386, where it also authorised the creation of the International Security Assistance Force (ISAF) designed to assist the nascent Afghan government (UN SC Res. 1386, UN Doc. S/RES/1386 (2001), 20 December 2001). ISAF initially had a limited mandate, which was then expanded, particularly following NATO's assumption of the command of these forces from 2003 onwards (compare: B. Koenders, 'Afghanistan and the Future of the Alliance', NATO Parliamentary Assembly, Annual Report 174 PC 06 E, 2006). It is worth noting that, alongside ISAF, there has been a continuing operation undertaken as part of Operation Enduring Freedom (OEF). After 2006 most of the former OEF forces were, however, moved under ISAF command (T. Noetzel and S. Scheipers, *Coalition Warfare in Afghanistan: Burden Sharing or Disunity?*, Chatham House, Asian and International Security Programmes, ASP/ISP BP 07/01, October 2007, at 6).
120 This was the first time NATO invoked Article 5 of the Washington Treaty (see S.L. v. Gorka, 'Invocation in Context', available at www.nato.int/docu/review/2006/issue2/english/art1.html, last accessed 1 May 2014). See also UN Security Council Resolution 1368, UN Doc. S/RES/1368 of 12 September 2001; 'Operation *Enduring Freedom* and the Conflict in Afghanistan: An Update', United Kingdom, House of Commons, International Affairs and Defence Section, Research Paper 01/81, 31 October 2001, at 9–10 [hereinafter: HoC Research Paper].

234 *Operationalisation of the definition of military objective*

forces codenamed this military action 'Operation Enduring Freedom' (OEF).[121] The British military planners' codename was 'Veritas',[122] while the Canadian military officials' codename was 'Apollo'. The main political objective of the operation was counter-terrorism, with al Qaeda members and affiliates being considered the prime enemies. The military action in line with this objective was aimed at severely weakening the Taliban's military potential, as well as ensuring that Afghan soil was no longer used as a base for the al Qaeda network.[123] A change in the country's leadership, to enable Afghanistan's reintegration into international society, was also envisaged.[124]

In the initial stage of the conflict, key American, Canadian, Australian and British forces engaged in air operations,[125] while other Allied States provided non-combat forms of support.[126] Less than two weeks into the air campaign, some ground forces, although limited in number, were deployed to Afghan territory.[127] These consisted primarily of US Special Forces and intelligence experts, including possibly non-military State actors. These operatives concentrated on liaising with local leaders of the United Front (Northern Alliance) and other associated anti-Taliban militias.[128]

All the Coalition members that engaged in combat operations, with the exception of the US, were bound by the provisions of API. As mentioned, Canada ratified API in 1990 and the UK in 1998. Australia had been bound by API since June 1991.

The initial air operations focused on targets in and around Kabul, Jalalabad and Kandahar. They concentrated on al Qaeda forces and training infrastructure, as well as numerous Taliban military complexes and targets.[129]

---

121 Operation Enduring Freedom (OEF) represents part of a wider counter-terrorism campaign known as the 'Global War on Terror', initiated by the US in or after 2001. OEF comprises a number of combat and non-combat operations in various regions of the world.

122 *Operations in Afghanistan: Background Briefing*, UK Ministry of Defence, on file with author [hereinafter: MOD Operations].

123 Longer-term aims included the eradication of terrorism, including the deterrence of State-sponsored terrorism. United States Department of Defense, News Briefing, Secretary General Rumsfeld and Gen. Myers, 7 October 2001.

124 'Defeating International Terrorism: Campaign Objectives', United Kingdom Ministry of Defence, Dep 01/1460, 16 October 2001; see also MOD Operations, op. cit. n 122, at 11–13.

125 HoC Research Paper, op. cit. n 120, at 26–7 and 31–2.

126 Other contributors to the initial Coalition included, among others, Denmark, France, Germany, the Netherlands, Italy, Japan, New Zealand, Norway and Turkey. Ibid, at 31.

127 DOD News Briefing, Secretary General Rumsfeld and Gen. Myers, 20 October 2001.

128 At that time the Northern Alliance forces were not well equipped, and struggled to secure reliable supply routes. Only with effective Coalition air support were they able to push the front line forward, particularly in the first half of November, when the Alliance increased its control over some 50 per cent of the territory. HoC Research Paper, op. cit. n 120, at 34–5; DOD News Briefing, Secretary General Rumsfeld and Gen. Myers, 31 October 2001.

129 They included 'missile, vehicle and armour maintenance and storage sites; airfields; troop deployment and garrison areas, command and control facilities' (DOD News Briefing,

In some statements, the American leadership referred to 'concentrations of military capabilities', which was presumed to denote the relevant ground forces.[130] According to US military sources, some 85 per cent of the initial set of 31 targets had been damaged in the first three days of air strikes, yet a number were attacked again to cause more substantial damage.[131]

In the following days, Coalition planes conducted raids against the Taliban and al Qaeda fighter positions, and equipment stored in the network of mountain caves. As Taliban and al Qaeda fighters moved through Afghanistan, the air strikes expanded towards other areas of the country, divided into separate engagement zones.[132] This seemed to indicate an increasing preparedness for the growing volume of emerging targets.[133] A transformation from pre-briefed targets to targets of opportunity followed in subsequent weeks. By mid-December 2001 the intense air campaign came to a halt. The operational focus shifted to ground operations, with close air support working with special operations teams and ground forward air controllers. These tactics proved to be more successful in tracking down Taliban and al Qaeda forces in both this specific terrain and in the increasingly dynamic war environment.

The specific context of the conflict in Afghanistan further shaped the targeting decisions. Prior to the 2001 attack, Afghanistan had been war-torn for two decades, resulting in little industrial infrastructure and a crippled economy. The pre-campaign targeting process identified targets including the airports at Kabul, Jalalabad and Kandahar, as well as government buildings and residences used by Taliban leaders in and around Kabul and Kandahar.[134] It is worth noting that, prior to 2001, Afghanistan's electricity and communications networks were rudimentary and reserved for a small part of the population. Electricity was a commodity used only by the ruling political elite. The road network was elementary, and was composed of highways linking the airports and cities of Kabul, Kandahar, Herat and Jalalabad, as well as links

Secretary General Rumsfeld and Gen. Myers, 18 October 2001; see also DOD News Briefing, Secretary General Rumsfeld and Gen. Myers, 12 October 2001), SAM/anti-aircraft defence sites (DOD News Briefing, Secretary General Rumsfeld and Gen. Myers, 9 and 12 October 2001) and airfield and barracks facilities (DOD News Briefings of 11, 12 and 16 October 2001).

130 See, for example, DOD News Briefing, Secretary of Defence Donald Rumsfeld, 11 October 2001.

131 All 31 targets were linked to the military capacity of the Taliban authorities and al Qaeda facilities such as training bases, SAM sites and airfields. DOD News Briefing, Secretary General Rumsfeld and Gen. Myers, 9 October 2001; also in B.S. Lambeth, *Airpower Against Terror: America's Conduct of OEF*, National Defense Research Institute, RAND, Santa Monica 2005, at 88.

132 See, for example, Lambeth, op. cit. n 131, at 89–90, 92–3, 99, 110, 112, 149 *et seq.*

133 Ibid, at xvi–xvii, 93 *et seq.*

134 Ibid, at 55, 78 and 81.

236 *Operationalisation of the definition of military objective*

to Pakistan.[135] The rail network comprised of just two maintained short cross-border rail lines, extending to Uzbekistan and Turkmenistan. Finally, Afghanistan has no access to the sea.

The initial air campaign concentrated on Taliban/al Qaeda affiliated positions and infrastructure, as well as their supply lines and lines of communication.[136] The Afghan air defences, as well as the small Afghan Air Force, were not considered to be significant threats.[137] Coalition air supremacy was achieved early in the campaign, and no Afghan aircraft ever took off to oppose the US.[138] The Coalition attacks rendered almost all the airfields unusable in the first two days of air operations,[139] yet they were not damaged beyond repair.[140] Unlike the airfields already mentioned, where an effort was made to preserve some of the infrastructure for post-Taliban operations, aircraft and helicopters were relentlessly destroyed – especially after air supremacy had been achieved.[141] This was in line with the overall efforts to reduce the Taliban's ability to fly, while preserving the core infrastructure.[142]

From the outset, all available lines of communication and transportation centres became strategically valuable targets. Afghanistan's fixed infrastructure was not extensive, which partially contributed to the rapid completion of the air campaign.[143] The other reason behind the seemingly constrained air attacks may have been another goal of the entire intervention – namely, the provision of humanitarian aid and post-conflict long-term support in reconstructing the country. This meant that the extensive destruction of targets that could facilitate the fulfilment of this longer-term goal would have been counterproductive. Such targets would include the scarce lines of

---

135 The strategic value of the limited road network in Afghanistan was relatively much higher than that of lines of communication in more developed States, where the terrain and infrastructure provides a wealth of alternative transportation routes.
136 It is open to discussion whether targeting the al Qaeda training facilities was operationally, as opposed to politically, advantageous. Some commentators have suggested that these compounds, as well as some Taliban military depots, were abandoned shortly after the terrorist attacks on the US in September 2001 and thus offered no definite military advantage. Lambeth, op. cit. n 131, at 122.
137 The two biggest air bases were located in and around Kandahar and Bagram, while the two others were at Dehdadi and Shindand. Kandahar airfield in southern Afghanistan had been, and still is, regarded as one of the most strategically important military transport hubs. At the time of the conflict, the Bagram and Shindand facilities, as well as the Jalalabad airfield, performed purely military functions, while the other airfields also served civilian purposes. Lambeth, op. cit. n 131, at 76–7; see also R. Grant, 'An Air War Like No Other', *Air Force Magazine*, November 2002, at 33.
138 Lambeth, op. cit. n 131, at 84.
139 Lambeth, op. cit. n 131, at 60; DOD News Briefing, Secretary General Rumsfeld and Gen. Myers, 12 October 2001.
140 DOD News Briefing, Secretary of Defence Donald Rumsfeld, 11 October 2001.
141 Ibid.
142 Ibid.
143 Tarmac roads, for instance, were few and far between, and many other roads were merely tracks. Lambeth, op. cit. n 131, at 73–4.

Legal interoperability in targeting 237

communication and transportation, as well as the electricity supply network.[144] Capturing Mazar-i-Sharif, for instance, was strategically and operationally beneficial, as it enabled the opening of the land transport route to Uzbekistan, dramatically cutting the logistical costs of supplies and fuel shipments.[145]

This two-pronged concept of operations may have contributed to the internal friction in the US command as to the application of the most appropriate military doctrine.[146] The American central command, CENTCOM, favoured attrition-oriented air operations, followed by the deployment of sizeable ground forces to achieve the war goals. This approach initially required the destruction of fixed 'lucrative' objects, enemy forces and their assets, regardless of how each of them might contribute to the accomplishment of the war objectives. In effect, a high success rate in engaging specific targets was prioritised above studying the actual impact of the effects on enemy behaviour and their connection to the overall desired objectives.

Air force operational commanders, on the other hand, believed that the destruction of targets was not necessary for the realisation of their military goals. Bearing in mind the policy and legal restrictions, they thought it might be counter-productive to the mission aims and to the economy of the military force applied. They believed that the special operations units, in collaboration with local opposition militiamen and with appropriate air support, could achieve the goal of removing the Taliban from power. It was alleged that the full extent of the Allies' air capabilities remained unrecognised by CENTCOM, who assumed the ground offensive would follow.[147] Eventually, a combination of both approaches led to the advance of the Allied forces and the defeat, however temporary, of the Taliban and al Qaeda fighters.

A distinctive feature of the initial war effort was the close synergy of air and land forces, which produced more verified and accurate outcomes, particularly at the tactical level.[148] Such collaboration also permitted more precise and faster-response attacks against enemy units that were on the move. One such attack used laser-guided missiles to kill a Taliban unit taking cover under a bridge, without damaging the structure itself.[149] In addition to utilising human

144 Ibid, at 60 and 123.
145 Ibid, at 122.
146 The operational commander, General Tommy Franks, was said to prefer first fully utilising all the available air power, while the Defense Secretary, Donald Rumsfeld, appeared to favour sending in Special Forces for ground assaults. It seems that the overall vision and direction of the campaign lacked a certain degree of clarity, except for the simultaneous application of all available means and methods to fight the enemy. See DOD News Briefing, Secretary General Rumsfeld and Gen. Myers, 22 October 2001; see also HoC Research Paper, op. cit. n 120, at 25.
147 Lambeth, op. cit. n 131, at 298–9, 302–3, 349, 354, 358–9.
148 Ibid, at 259–60, 362–5; Spedero, op. cit. n 87, at 9–10.
149 V. Loeb, 'Afghan War Is a Lab for U.S. Innovation: New Technologies Are Tested in Battle', *The Washington Post*, 26 March 2002, available at www.highbeam.com/doc/1P2-334756.html (last accessed 1 May 2014).

238 *Operationalisation of the definition of military objective*

intelligence on the ground, the greater use of satellite and aerial surveillance undoubtedly contributed to an improved awareness of the situation. However, while operators on the ground effectively identified targets, the question arises as to whether they also made the relevant legal assessments of such targets. It is unclear whether such assessments made by operators including non-military US State actors, such as employees of the Central Intelligence Agency, and non-Coalition forces, such as the Northern Alliance, were relied upon when attacks were approved and, if so, to what extent. One commentator suggested that, at least on one occasion, Northern Alliance forces identified target – a Taliban military outpost – as military objective and called on US forces to provide airpower.[150]

In stark contrast to the subsequent NATO-led International Security Assistance Force operations, hindered by national caveats on the use of force, the US-led high-intensity combat operations in Afghanistan were marked by a relative unity of effort.[151] Minimising civilian casualties and damage to civilian objects was one of the main goals of the ROE, and the authorities involved gave approval judiciously for targets considered 'high-risk'.[152] Another important tenet related to infrastructure targets. As a matter of policy, attacks on what was loosely termed 'critical infrastructure' were expressly avoided.[153] Such 'infrastructure' included lines of communication, such as bridges and railways, and economic objects benefiting from ROE protection.[154] The reasons were two-fold: the first was to avoid antagonising the Afghan civilian population and neighbouring States, which would secure continued support for the Coalition. The second reason was to enable the delivery of humanitarian aid to the Afghan population. Preserving infrastructure would also help Coalition forces establish a ground presence later on.

---

150 Grant, op. cit. n 137, at 36. It has been indicated that one of the States currently contributing to ISAF requires a confirmation that the forward air controller is indeed from a State that is bound by Additional Protocol II to 1949 Geneva Conventions before it delivers munitions as requested by such controller (Lt.-Col. M. Dakers, *Presentation on Legal Interoperability*, International Society of Military Law and Law of War, Quebec, 3 May 2012, point 7). A separate question arises in respect of the State responsibility in regard to attacks conducted by Coalition air forces based on the determinations made by such operators. See also n 128 above and the text accompanying it.

151 Noetzel and Scheipers, op. cit. n 119; V. Morelli and P. Belkin, *NATO in Afghanistan: A Test of the Transatlantic Alliance*, Congressional Research Service, Report for Congress, United States, 3 December 2009; House of Commons, Defence Committee, Fifth Report: *The UK Deployment to Afghanistan*, Her Majesty Stationery Office, London, 28 March 2006.

152 Consequently, numerous potential targets, particularly time-sensitive and mobile ones, were not engaged due to proportionality constraints. Lambeth, op. cit. n 131, at XXX, 314–15, 322–3.

153 Point 1(e), ROE Card, Appendix B-1 in CLAMO 2004, op. cit. n 64.

154 *Targeting*, Newsletter No. 03-27, Operation Outreach, US Center for Army Lessons Learnt, October 2003.

Legal interoperability in targeting 239

Several previously controversial targets were attacked during this conflict, such as TV and radio stations, or infrastructure objects associated with the political leadership of Afghanistan.[155] Yet there does not seem to be much evidence of specific disagreements between Coalition members in relation to such targets.[156] The British leadership, as in Kosovo, insisted on vetting at ministerial level any targets assigned to it, as well as any targets designated for attack by US planes stationed at Diego Garcia, a British-owned island in the Indian Ocean. Reportedly, the British forces used a 'red card' on some time-sensitive human targets.[157] There were other reasons behind objections to the approval of some objects. Certain targets, in particular those subject to dynamic targeting, were not approved simply because of a lack of accurate intelligence.[158]

9.1.4 2003 war in Iraq

By the end of 2002, in defiance of the terms of the 1991 ceasefire and the subsequent UN Security Council Resolution 687, and despite pressure from the international community in the following years, Iraq was suspected of having continued its nuclear, chemical and biological (NCB) weapons development programmes, and therefore of remaining a serious threat to the stability of the region. The US was preparing politically and militarily for another conflict, in which it hoped to remove Saddam Hussein from power, and to secure or destroy suspected NCB weapons facilities and stock. It is conceivable, though, that existing long-term economic interests played a role in the US determination to intervene.

The existence of a legal basis for the ensuing invasion remains a controversial issue to this day. This time, there was no explicit authority from a UN Security Council Resolution. Many US allies in the previous Gulf War considered the actions unlawful and/or illegitimate. The initial Coalition of the 'willing' principally included support from three troop-contributing States: the UK, Australia and Poland.[159] There was a smaller contribution from two other

---

155 See the further discussion regarding the political leadership infrastructure in 1.1 and 7.1. See the discussion of the TV and radio stations in 7.3.

156 Grant recalled a situation in which a permission to attack a convoy suspected of carrying Taliban spiritual leader Mullah Omar was not granted by US CENTCOM Commander Tommy Franks himself. It is likely, though uncertain, that concern over collateral damage was the reason for the lack of approval. Grant, op. cit. n 137, at 34.

157 Lambeth, op. cit. n 131, at 317.

158 See also the discussion in 6.2 and 10.4, and CLAMO 2008, op. cit. n 64, at 331–2.

159 The Polish contingent's most significant engagement in the initial phase of the conflict, together with their British and American counterparts, was to secure port facilities in Umm Qasr.

240 *Operationalisation of the definition of military objective*

States: Portugal and Denmark. Eventually, more than 30 other countries joined the Coalition in the aftermath of the initial combat operations. The US-led forces were also supported by numerous Iraqi Kurdish militia units. The Coalition members involved in the initial hostilities were all parties to API, except for the US.[160] Iraq was not bound by API.[161]

The 'shock and awe' invasion of Iraq lasted approximately six weeks before Coalition forces asserted control over the majority of Iraqi territory. George W. Bush, the US President, issued a declaration on 1 May 2003 indicating that the combat phase of Operation Iraqi Freedom (OIF)[162] had been completed,[163] though signs of major combat operations coming to an end were already present by mid-April 2003.[164] UN Security Council Resolution 1483, adopted on 22 May 2003, provided a political recognition of the conflict moving into an occupation phase.[165]

From the spring and summer of 2002, military planners in the US, UK and Australia were drafting contingency plans for potential military action in Iraq.[166] Australia retained control over its own forces, which meant that any targets allocated to its forces had to be vetted in accordance with Australia's own legal obligations and policy.[167] In general, the British land, air and navy contingents operated under the tactical command and control of the relevant US Component Commanders, while British command retained the national strategic and operational direction of UK forces.[168] This arrangement allowed for UK commanders to ensure that their troops were engaged only in tasks approved by the UK. In terms of targeting, the UK contributed to the

---

160 See n 64 above and the attached text.

161 Even though Iraq had not ratified API at that time, this treaty was applicable to all parties who, at that time, were bound by it. Y. Sandoz, C. Swinarski and B. Zimmermann (eds), *Commentary on the Additional Protocols of 8 June 1977 to the Geneva Conventions of 12 August 1949*, ICRC, Geneva, and Martinus Nijhoff, The Hague 1987, paras 47–55.

162 Operation Iraqi Freedom is an official name for the military operations carried out by US forces in Iraq in 2003. The United Kingdom uses the codename Operation Telic (www.nao.org.uk/wp-content/uploads/2003/12/030460.pdf, last accessed 1 May 2014) and Australia uses Operation Falconer (*The War in Iraq, Australian Defence Operations in Middle East in 2003*, Australian Ministry of Defence, at 5 *et seq.* [hereinafter: ADF Report]). For the purposes of this book, the US codename will be used.

163 'President Bush Announces Combat Operations in Iraq Have Ended', White House, 1 May 2003.

164 Pentagon Spokesman Statement on 14 April 2003 reported in S. Loughlin, 'Pentagon: "Major combat" over, but smaller fights remain', available at www.cnn.com/2003/US/04/14/sprj.irq.pentagon/index.html (last accessed 1 May 2014).

165 UN SC Res. 1483, UN Doc. S/RES/1483 of 22 May 2003.

166 ADF Report, op. cit. n 162, at 8–9; UK Ministry of Defence, *Operations in Iraq: First Reflections*, DCCS Media Publications, London, July 2003, at 4 [hereinafter: MOD First Reflections].

167 ADF Report, op. cit. n 162, at 13.

168 UK Ministry of Defence, *Operations in Iraq: Lessons for the Future*, DCCS Media Publications, London, December 2003, at 9 [hereinafter: MOD Lessons for the Future].

Legal interoperability in targeting 241

development of a list of more than 900 potential targets for the Coalition.[169] When tasked with the execution of attacks using their own platforms or assets, the UK ensured appropriate vetting of the designated targets. In addition, British commanders reportedly assisted the US command in planning specific attacks undertaken by US forces.[170]

The war broke out on 19 March 2003 with an attempted attack on Saddam Hussein, who was believed to have been visiting the al-Dora farm on the outskirts of Baghdad.[171] The attack was a prelude to the start of hostilities on the following day. This was the first of many attacks on leadership 'targets of opportunity'.[172] This colloquial term described emerging, fleeting targets such as mobile weapons launchers or, in this case, enemy leaders moving in vehicles, that required an immediate response.

In line with the underlying, although officially unstated, political objective of regime change, the central strategic COG of the air campaign was undoubtedly the Iraqi leadership, with Saddam Hussein at the very top of the target list.[173] The Allied air forces concentrated on pursuing further pre-planned military objects, as well as the emerging time-sensitive targets in a predominantly urban environment. These tactics led to increased civilian casualties, for which the Coalition was widely criticised.[174]

In contrast to the 1991 conflict, the invasion in 2003 proceeded with simultaneous air operations and a ground assault. The initial air attacks were conducted against the Iraqi defence systems and government facilities in the capital, Baghdad. Air supremacy was established, and while targets in Baghdad remained a priority in the first few days, the Republican Guard divisions and several telecommunication facilities in and around the city were also subjected to sustained attack. Baghdad airport had been captured by 3 April, by which time the Allied air forces' attention was on targets related to the ongoing ground offensive. The Australian Air Force attacked the Republican Guard, Iraqi intelligence facilities and numerous military objects such as tanks, artillery,

---

169 Ibid, at 28.
170 Ibid. See also 8.2 and 8.5.1.
171 See the discussion regarding the political leadership infrastructure in 2.1 and 7.1.
172 This first attack was known as a 'decapitating' strike that aimed to remove the very core of the Iraqi command and control mechanism. It is unclear whether the person or building was targeted, as this complex was known to contain command and control facilities.
173 Spedero, op. cit. n 87, at 10–11. The US Central Intelligence Agency and the armed forces and military forces pre-prepared 'Black List' of high-value targets included 52 top Iraqi officials in a form of playing cards.
174 To add to public discontent, none of the 50 strikes executed against such targets yielded any substantial results. This failure was attributed mainly to flawed or inadequate intelligence, and to an unreliable targeting method based on tracking signals emitted by the satellite phones used by some Iraqi officials. Human Rights Watch, *Off Target. The Conduct of the War and Civilian Casualties in Iraq*, December 2003, at 22–39 [hereinafter: HRW].

242 *Operationalisation of the definition of military objective*

ammunition storage sites and anti-aircraft defence system objects.[175] Other units were deployed in western Iraq, with the strategic aim of securing weapons of mass destruction (WMD) facilities and thereby reducing the threat they posed.[176] Overall, the capturing and securing of major Iraqi cities such as Nasiriyah, Najaf, Basra and Kirkuk were considered to be of strategic importance to the entire operation. The fall of Baghdad in mid-April 2003 symbolised the achievement of one of the main objectives of OIF, namely the collapse of the Iraqi regime, and depriving Saddam Hussein of power.

Coalition ground troops played a crucial role in securing the Iraqi oil infrastructure. Rather than damaging this infrastructure through air attacks, as in the previous conflict, Coalition troops focused on the speedy seizure of such sites with a minimum of damage. One of the first major strategic goals was to capture the Al Faw peninsula and secure the Rumailah and Az Zubayr oil fields.[177]

In 2003 the preservation of essential infrastructure, respect for religious and cultural sites, and the avoidance of the excessive collateral damage were all key features of the US ROE.[178] Lines of communication, such as bridges and railways, economic objects and even military objects such as abandoned vehicles, also benefited from ROE protection.[179] The ROE stated that such objects could be targeted in self-defence or when ordered by the commander, but otherwise the aim should be to neutralise rather than destroy.[180] The ROE aimed at protection of the infrastructure was warranted by both political and military considerations. It is possible that this reduced the number of controversies that arose, because fewer potentially questionable targets were attacked.[181]

Although the need for all Coalition members to be aware of each other's different constraints regarding the use of force was widely recognised, interoperability during the high-intensity combat phase still showed scope for

---

175 ADF report, op. cit. n 162, at 13 and 27–8; F. Walker, 'Our Pilots Refused to Bomb 40 Times', *Sydney Morning Herald*, 14 March 2004.

176 ADF Report, op. cit. n 162, at 21.

177 ADF Report, op. cit. n 162, at 18; MOD Lessons for the Future, op. cit. n 168, at 11–12.

178 The Human Rights Watch report indicated that the written ROE might have differed from the verbal ROE guidance during the high-intensity combat phase of operations, particularly in respect of the 'positive identification of target' standard. HRW, op. cit. n 174, at 101-01; compare with CLAMO 2008, op. cit. n 64, Appendix E: Rules of Engagement for US Military Forces in Iraq, Points c, d and e. See also CLAMO 2004, op. cit. n 64, Appendix B-1, at 314; M. Warren, 'The "Fog of Law": The Law of Armed Conflict in Operation Iraqi Freedom' in M.D. Carsten (ed.), *International Law and Military Operations*, Vol. 84, US Naval War College International Law Studies, Newport, RI 2008, at 169–71.

179 *Targeting*, op. cit. n 154.

180 Ibid.

181 This may have explained the fewer debates regarding 'infrastructure' targets, but it would not be helpful in an analysis of the attacks against other questionable objects such as TV and radio broadcasting stations. See also 7.3, n 74 *et seq.* and the accompanying text.

Legal interoperability in targeting   243

improvement. British and Australian forces underwent rather different experiences during their involvement in targeting processes during the 2003 operations in Iraq. The early involvement of British planners in ROE development and the targeting process, alongside the harmonised targeting doctrine, improved interoperability between US and British forces. British military officers were involved in both the nomination and selection of the pre-planned targets.[182] The UK reserved the right to vet the targets against which British assets were deployed, as well as those against which foreign assets or platforms utilising British facilities or locations were used.[183] Furthermore, the British political leadership at the Ministry of Defence retained authority to approve selected targets,[184] though there is insufficient information available to ascertain which targets were subject to this higher-level approval. Reflecting on the issues of interoperability experienced during the high-intensity combat phase, British military lawyers felt the differences in national legal obligations were not significant, particularly in respect of pre-planned attacks on fixed objects.[185]

Australian defence forces encountered problems during the early stages of their engagement in Iraq. The available commentaries attribute this to the lack of full Coalition-coordinated military doctrine and ROE.[186] This apparently resulted in a seemingly 'new' legal environment for Australian combat operations.[187] One has to bear in mind, though, that Australia had participated in an earlier Coalition in Afghanistan, and had been bound by API since 1991.[188] The impact of this legal situation was most commonly mentioned in the context of the disputes relating to the assessment of the legality of attacks against targets associated with potentially excessive collateral damage.[189] It remains unclear whether any concerns were raised in relation to the definition

---

182 House of Commons, Defence Committee, Third Report: *Lessons of Iraq*, Her Majesty Stationery Office, London, 16 March 2003, para 94 [hereinafter: UK Third Report]; MOD First Reflections, op. cit. n 166, para 2.4.

183 UK Third Report; MOD First Reflections.

184 UK Third Report; MOD First Reflections; MOD Lessons for the Future, op. cit. n 168, para 6.3.

185 N. Brown, 'Issues Arising from Coalition Operations: An Operational Lawyer's Perspective' in M.D. Carsten (ed.), *International Law and Military Operations*, Vol. 84, US Naval War College International Law Studies, Newport, RI 2008, at 227.

186 Kelly, op. cit. n 100, at 165. Note that other sources imply ROE compatibility and the early involvement of the Australian legal contingent in interoperability during the Iraq conflict. See CLAMO 2008, op. cit. n 64, at 344 and Warren, op. cit. n 178, at 172.

187 Kelly, op. cit. n 100, at 164.

188 It is possible that the Australian forces had already experienced interoperability problems during the 2001–2 conflict in Afghanistan, and they simply remained unresolved by the time Australia joined the Coalition in Iraq.

189 T. Cook, 'Australian Pilots aborted US-assigned bombing raids during Iraq War', World Socialist Web Site, 23 March 2004, available at www.wsws.org/en/articles/2004/03/raaf-m23.html (last accessed 1 May 2014). It is unclear whether the concerns were solely based on the precautions in attack or whether the lawfulness of the targets was also in question. See n 37 and the accompanying text in Chapter 10.

244 *Operationalisation of the definition of military objective*

of military objectives. Media reports indicate that, owing to inaccurate intelligence, there were numerous occasions when Australian forces refused to attack the designated targets.[190] This was not apparently limited to Australian forces, and also affected British conduct.[191]

9.2 Methods of resolving the legal interoperability problems

During coalition operations individual Member States have to reconcile their own policies on targeting with those of their partners. There are various ways to deal with legal interoperability problems in targeting. A State might express its objection to a specific target by using its veto power, or a 'red card' mechanism. Some States prefer to adopt a practical solution instead of flashing a red card. One possibility is that a coalition policy decision, such as not targeting dual-use infrastructure, will have the incidental effect of reducing targeting disagreements. A second way of avoiding potential disagreement would be the use of coalition ROE. However, agreeing on coalition ROE could be difficult in practice. Where available, the interpretation of the same ROE by different States may also be a source of problems.[192] In recognition of a coalition partner's differing interpretations of its obligations, the coalition armed forces may design matrices to reflect this.

Finally, a coalition may adopt an approach that allows it to avoid application of veto, red cards and other mentioned measures, and to keep the coalition stable. This may occur if all of the members of the coalition agree to apply one legal standard to all attacks. This approach appears to have acquired the label 'lowest common denominator'. This approach, and some of the other measures mentioned, will be discussed next.

During the Kosovo intervention there were many reports of disagreements when NATO partners attempted to identify targets. Undoubtedly, the frequent lack of approval of targets was attributable to the law, though one must bear in mind that other factors were applied in the decision-making process. Decisions were sometimes dictated by political interests, or resulted from differences among Member States over what strategy should be used in operations.[193] If the reason was a legal one, the main consideration was usually the possibility of civilian casualties and damage to civilian property, particularly

---

190 It is unclear whether in the reported examples the problem was the insufficiently corroborated information or wrong intelligence. Walker, op. cit. n 175; Cook, op. cit. n 189.
191 Walker, op. cit. n 175. There is a difference between the comments of Brown (see op. cit. n 185) relating to lack of problems resulting from the differences in legal obligations and this situation, where the problem concerns specific information of about the target. The problems with information may, however, affect how the definition is applied in practice. See also 10.4.
192 See also the discussion in 8.4.
193 Clark, op. cit. n 87, at 238–9, 317–19; Ignatieff, op. cit. n 115, at 170, 206.

Legal interoperability in targeting 245

if the proposed target also performed a civilian function. Other legal restrictions related to the proposed use of certain weapons.

All the members of NATO were able to use a 'veto card' system to resolve differences of opinion. NATO is based on consensus. A practical consequence of this was the fact that, during military operations in Kosovo, the only targets that were attacked were those that had been agreed by all States. In practice, as stated earlier, only the UK, US and France were effectively involved in the approval of targets. General Short, however, suggested that the German leadership might also have undertaken some high-level scrutiny of selected proposed targets.[194] Does this mean that even though only a handful of NATO States actually engage in the targeting process at the operational level, all States have to declare their view on particular targets at the strategic political-military level?[195] It could be that the standard adopted was, in fact, 'lack of expressed objection' rather than 'expressed approval'. This difference would be important in ascertaining State practice regarding certain targets. The lack of any clear disassociation by States not approving these controversial targets may be interpreted as their tacit approval of the position regarding their lawfulness. This way, all these non-objecting Member States might be viewed as contributing to overall State practice, which would be relevant in an analysis of the interpretation of the legal provisions of the treaty.[196]

The Australians dealt with the 2003 conflict in Iraq, when their legal obligations were different to those of Americans, in two ways. The first was to adopt the 'red card' mechanism, and the second was to develop matrices reflecting the different interpretations of obligations by Australia and other Coalition States. All the targets received by Australian forces from the US-developed strike-list were checked for compliance with Australia's legal obligations. Some of the target categories, including those carrying an increased risk of collateral damage, required prior ministerial approval.[197] If the proposed targets were inconsistent with Australian legal obligations and policy, the Australians could – and frequently did – refuse to participate in missions. This is the 'red card' mechanism.[198]

---

194 Short, op. cit. n 95, at 24–5. In many cases a double approval mechanism continued to be applied in NATO targeting. The double approval mechanism involves first receiving NATO approval for the strike and then, separately, a national approval. Dakers, op. cit. n 150, point 5.

195 See 10.3.

196 This may also suggest that the type of legal responsibility in these two types of operations may be different. In coalitions of 'the willing', only the State may be responsible for its own actions, whereas in alliances the responsibility of each member may encompass the actions of every other member, unless they clearly disassociate themselves from a specific action.

197 ADF Report, op. cit. n 162, at 13; V. McConache, 'Coalition Operations: A Compromise or an Accommodation' in M.D. Carsten (ed.), *International Law and Military Operations*, Vol. 84, US Naval War College International Law Studies, Newport, RI 2008, at 244; CLAMO 2004, op. cit. n 64, at 124.

198 Kelly, op. cit. n 100.

246 *Operationalisation of the definition of military objective*

In order to resolve interpretational differences, two matrices were developed to assist commanders with planning and decision-making. One covered all the areas of law dealing with armed conflict (which involved potentially different obligations for each Coalition member). The second matrix provided a similar overview, but for the rules of engagement of the various Coalition partners.[199] The Australian ROE were developed, for whatever reason, only when combat operations had already begun. The delay of the Australians in developing ROE had a markedly negative impact on the way in which they, as well as their Coalition partners, executed operations.

Sometimes, a State might prefer not to use the 'red card' mechanism to avoid being involved in an attack of which it disapproved. This involves situations where it refuses to be involved in a specific attack, or any attacks at a specific time. This was apparently the case for British forces during the Kosovo intervention.[200]

Relatively little is known about the approach in dealing with legal differences known as the 'lowest common denominator'. This approach appears to have been mentioned in the context of the 1999 Kosovo intervention and the 2003 conflict in Iraq.[201] It involved identifying a standard shared by, or acceptable to, all parties. The adjective 'lowest', though, conveys a potentially misleading impression. It might appear to imply a minimum level of legal obligation when, in fact, the level upon which all parties agree will be higher than that which would be adopted by certain parties acting on their own. In practice, such a standard may be more restrictive and result in a greater level of protection for civilians. If the customary rule containing a definition of military objective reflects the codified definition, then the same standard will effectively apply. In addition to there being a legal reason for adopting the 'lowest common denominator' approach, there may also be political considerations.

If only one State advocates a different, possibly broader interpretation of a certain legal concept, it might decide to abandon its own position if it seems counter-productive to its political and military interests. By adopting a widespread but possibly narrower legal standard, such a State would support the cohesion and unity of the coalition military effort. This would not mean that such a State would be precluded from applying its broader interpretation in situations not involving multinational military operations.

It is unclear how this approach is applied in practice. Presumably, whether a single 'common denominator' can be identified will depend on the members of a particular coalition, and their legal obligations and national and/or

---

199 McConache, op. cit. n 197, at 244.
200 See n 98 above and the accompanying text.
201 Kelly, op. cit. n 100, at 168; see also comments by Gen. Naumann referring to the pace and intensity of operations being determined by such a denominator, as cited in the UK Fourteenth Report, op. cit. n 72, para 68.

Legal interoperability in targeting 247

international political constraints. Each coalition partner has to comply with the national standard by which it is bound.

In relation to the US, for example, this could mean that a 'lower' common legal standard would be potentially – but not necessarily – more restrictive. For the US to impose on itself a more constraining obligation would take the issue from the legal realm into that of policy. The US might, therefore, decide not to apply its own interpretation of military objectives when acting as a member of multinational and combined combat operations. This would not depend on a pre-existing legal requirement,[202] but on a policy decision. One may recall, in this context, the policy restriction issued in Iraq and Afghanistan on attacks against infrastructure, which clearly elevated the standard to a more restrictive level.

9.3 Conclusion

The 1999 NATO operations in Kosovo represented a very different multinational operation compared with the three other coalitions. Operations during the Gulf War, in Afghanistan and then in Iraq, were all coalitions of 'willing' States, while the NATO operations were undertaken under the umbrella of a pre-existing security organisation. In addition, two of the coalitions of the 'willing' included far fewer States than the NATO operation.

How States behave in a coalition will depend on various factors. This may be dictated by political considerations, such as during the 1990–1 Gulf War. Here, it was politically vital to include Arab States in Coalition operations. States' behaviour in coalition warfare will also be driven by military doctrine, political considerations (both domestic and international) and legal obligations.

When States operate together, they know they have to be aware of each other's legal obligations. Many of the coalition partners are, in fact, bound by the same obligations, resulting from treaty or customary law. There may be differences in the interpretation of certain provisions. Separately, when engaging in a military operation they may devise a set of coalition ROE that take account of the law as much as other considerations.[203] If a difference of opinion regarding particular targets occurs, States will apply a veto when acting as part of a consensus-based military alliance, or use a 'red card' system when operating within a coalition of the 'willing'. In the first situation, one would expect that targets designated through an application of military doctrine, and

---

202 Contrary to the assertion proposed in S.C. Breau, 'A Single Standard for Coalitions: Lowest Common Denominator or Highest Standards?' in M. Odello and R. Piotrowicz (eds), *International Military Missions and International Law*, Martinus Nijhof, Leiden 2011, at 73–97.

203 Each coalition partner is likely to have its own national ROE applicable in the conflict. Some coalition partners may adopt a mission-specific ROE in specific circumstances. See the discussion regarding ROE in 8.4.

248 *Operationalisation of the definition of military objective*

subsequently vetoed, would not be further engaged.[204] In coalitions of the 'willing', targets that one State was unwilling to attack would simply be passed to forces that would be willing to attack them. That may not be true in other operations, such as those involving a permanent alliance.

Little information is available regarding the specific reasons why States object to attacks on particular targets. If one can establish that a legal consideration is behind a State's view, one also needs to determine whether that legal concern is about the lawfulness of the target, in line with the requirements of the definition of military objective. If this can be established, it is not necessarily clear that disagreements indicate a general problem with the definition for all States, or with its interpretation for some States only. What seems to be clear is that, in all four conflicts, there were problems with the standard of information used to determine whether targets were lawful. These problems were primarily related to the gathering of information and its quality and quantity; in some cases there may have been a problem with sharing of information. The standard of required information may vary between States. This will have a direct impact on the application of the definition of military objective to the facts, and also, in coalition operations, on legal interoperability.

It is striking that some types of targets triggered more discussion than others. These are the TV and radio broadcasting stations, objects linked to the political leadership and other political entities such as the facilities of political parties. These types of targets appear to have been struck in all four conflicts, but the lawfulness of these attacks was seemingly debated by Coalition States only during the 1999 NATO intervention in Kosovo. In other Coalition operations, attacks against such targets appear to have been questioned by the media and public opinion, rather than by the States concerned. This could mean that, since 1999, such targets are viewed as military objectives by States engaged in such attacks, or they may have been viewed as military objectives only in the specific circumstances of the individual attacks.

In all these conflicts, the enemy leadership was the focus of attention for the attacking forces. Saddam Hussein and the Ba'ath Party elite in Iraq, Slobodan Milosevic and the ruling Socialist Party in Serbia, and the Taliban regime in Afghanistan were all subjected to attacks. Most controversy was generated by the strikes against objects associated with such structures, which did not appear to serve any military function or contribute to the military action of the adversary. The continuing engagement of such targets suggests that the States in question regard them as lawful. It is not clear whether this is because they regard such targets in principle as military objectives, or

---

204 This was not, apparently, the case during the Kosovo intervention, where sources indicated that US forces conducted attacks against targets previously rejected by other States (see text attached to ns 101 and 102 above). It is unclear whether objections were raised to such US practice, and whether such practice would affect the liability of the States for such an act undertaken in the name of the alliance.

because a ruling party is perceived as a tool in the hands of a dictator, whether elected or not.[205] This would indicate an evolving interpretation of the definition that expands the understanding of its terms beyond their ordinary meaning, which requires a nexus to military action. This may be a result of the pressure of military doctrine focusing on leadership targets as the most important centre of gravity, and thus one of the fundamental targets.

---

205 If certain objects can be targeted if they are perceived as 'tools in the hands' of repressive regimes, this may give rise to questions regarding the alleged impartiality, neutrality and even-handedness of LOAC.

10 Conclusion

It is 35 years since the concept of military objective was formally defined. There is clear and strong support for the definition among States, but has it stood the test of time?

This work has examined the definition of the concept, its background and its components. The analysis presented in Part I suggests there could be problems with the interpretation of some of its elements, or with applying the requirements of the definition to the facts. The relevant findings will be reflected upon in 10.1 and 10.2. Part II examined the subsequent application of API, and specifically the definition of military objectives enshrined in Art 52.2. This analysis highlighted not only specific factors that can influence how the definition is put into operation, but also the inherent difficulty in attempting to examine subsequent practice, which may be shaped by legal or non-legal considerations. 10.3 will reflect on these issues. One question that emerged in the course of this research was a general legal issue that is not specific to the law of armed conflict (LOAC), but that will arise whenever people apply the law to the facts. This issue relates to the quantity, quality and sufficiency of evidence in determining whether something is lawful. This, as the analysis in both parts of this work has indicated, may also impact on how the definition is applied in practice, and how State practice in this area may be assessed. Section 4 will address this problem.

10.1 The definition

As was shown in Chapter 2, the adoption of the definition of military objective in 1977 was marked by apparent agreement among the negotiating States.[1] A flexible definition was preferred, in place of lists of categories of objects that it was considered permissible to attack. The definition consists of two key elements, qualified by additional terms. The elements are connected by the

---

1 See 2.5.

252   *Conclusion*

conjunction 'and' – with the exception of the Spanish version of the original text, which suggests that both key elements must be satisfied at the time an object is assessed – as mentioned in Chapter 5.[2]

Substantively, both key elements must show a military nexus. For the first element, this nexus is found through an object's *effective contribution to military action* in accordance with any of the four criteria: *nature, location, use* or *purpose*. As seen in Chapter 3, the *nature* criterion is very different to the other three.[3] It is permanent, not contextual and does not change according to circumstances. The objects considered to satisfy this criterion are often 'presumed' in practice to satisfy all the elements of the definition in all circumstances. This, together with the fact that States tend to refer to objects they think satisfy this condition in the form of categories and lists, is a matter of concern, because such a practice may lead to the inclusion of objects whose eligibility are context-specific. Very often, commentators agree that an object is a military objective, but they disagree about which criterion of the four describes its contribution.[4]

A separate issue arises as to whether the object fulfils the requirement of *effective contribution to military action*. Objects that are targeted on account of their impact on civilian morale, or on the economic welfare of the adversary, do not necessarily contribute at all, let alone effectively, to the war-related conduct of military forces *per se*.[5] The most problematic objects in this regard appear to be those that facilitate the commission of international crimes, such as concentration camps, or means by which violence against the civilian population is incited.[6] Objects that are used for such purposes do not appear to contribute to the military action of the adversary. Such places or objects may involve the diversion of military effort to manage them. As mentioned in Chapter 5, the potential *definite military advantage* resulting from the destruction, capture or *neutralization* of such objects is also difficult to ascertain in line with the requirements of the definition. This raises a genuine problem of applicability of LOAC standards to such objects. A more appropriate basis for attacks against such objects may need to be found in other branches of international law.

As far as the second key element – *definite military advantage* – is concerned, a difficulty is posed by targets whose destruction, capture or neutralization would offer an economic or psychological advantage believed to lead to the achievement of strategic political and military goals. Such a justification was envisaged by the Eritrea-Ethiopia Claims Commission, as mentioned in

---

2 See 5.1.
3 See 3.1.
4 See Conclusion to Chapter 3.
5 See 4.2 and 4.3.2.
6 This is relevant to situations in which such objects do not have any other relevant military function. See 7.4.

Conclusion   253

Chapter 5, but this needs to be approached with great caution.[7] If attacks on such objects are justified on this basis, it could lead to the justification of the strikes against Hiroshima and Nagasaki, which were hoped would end the Second World War.[8]

It appears that the definition itself has not been regarded as problematic. No State seems to have opposed the use of the formula enshrined in Art 52.2 in any international armed conflict. It is striking that parties that have not ratified API, such as the United States and Israel, use that formula and regard themselves as bound by it. However, even if the agreed formula is not contested, there may be differences in opinion regarding the interpretation of the terms used in the definition.

10.2 The interpretation of the definition

While States appear to agree on the definition, they may disagree on interpretation of its terms. This disagreement could be one of principle or it could concern an application of interpretation to what is generally seen as a target of questionable lawfulness.

The first situation is quite clearly represented by the US-specific interpretation of the first key element of the definition, namely *effective contribution to military action*.[9] The US interpretation covers *war-fighting* and *war-sustaining efforts (capabilities)*. It is unclear whether this interpretation is relevant only to 'economic targets', as suggested in some of the documents, and, if so, what is meant by economic targets.[10] Questions arise over the targeting of objects that generate resources that a State needs in order to continue fighting, or that generate economic resources that are not vital for fighting, but that might be used to sustain war. Even though the US uses two terms in its interpretation, they appear to cover a spectrum of targets. Clearly, targets that directly assist military effort – such as munitions factories – would contribute both to military action and war-fighting effort. Targets such as natural resources, and places associated with their extraction and processing to generate the power needed to sustain the military effort, would be seen as linked to the conduct of hostilities. Such power could be produced from resources such as gas, oil, coal or water. Power does not have to be used solely for military purposes. Very often, it will also serve civilian needs (dual-use object).[11] Industrial plants involved in the manufacture of resources essential to produce military

---

7 See 5.3.
8 A.D. Coox, 'Strategic Bombing in the Pacific 1942–5' in R.C. Hall (ed.), *Case Studies in Strategic Bombardment*, US Air Force History and Museums Program, Washington, DC 1998, at 356, 362–6.
9 See 4.3 and 8.6.2 and Conclusion to Chapter 8.
10 See 2.3, 4.3 and 8.1 and 8.6.
11 See 3.3.

254   *Conclusion*

equipment – such as steel or aluminium plants, or military-grade computer chips factories – could also be regarded as directly linked to military effort. Similarly, raw materials used for military purposes might also be destined for civilian use.[12] These targets could be seen as falling within the remit of the definition because of their link to military activity, whether they were defined as war-fighting or contributing to military action.

There are also resources that generate economic wealth that is then utilised to sustain the war, for example exports of produce such as wine and fruit, or exports of natural resources such as diamonds.[13] They do not have any link to the conduct of hostilities or military activity, but the assets they generate may be used to finance the continuation of war, for instance through the purchase of weapons. If the term *war-sustaining effort (capability)* is intended to denominate such resources and assets, then it is likely to be outside the scope of the definition. The assessment may be further complicated in the case of natural resources such as oil, which may either be exported for financial gain or utilised for domestic military purposes.

There is confusion and uncertainty as to what the US regards as economic targets and what it interprets as war–fighting and/or war sustaining effort (capability).[14] It is not clear whether other States define these terms in the same manner. The US may refer to objects as 'economic targets' because they carry a significant economic value, without thereby addressing the association of the objects with military action or war-fighting effort. In general, it appears that States are more likely to accept that objects involved in the generation of power, or resources that directly assist military activity, could come within the interpretation of the definition.[15] The likely opposition is to be found in respect of targets that generate economic resources that could potentially be used to sustain the war effort.

The other situation that may impact on how the definition is interpreted may occur where the application of the definition to particular types of objects is uncertain. Two such types of objects were identified in this work – the infrastructure targets associated with a political leadership, and TV and radio

---

12 Ibid.

13 The problem in relation to such targets is not only confined to the interpretation of the definition, but may also impact on the application of the definition. The Eritrea-Ethiopia Claims Commission, as observed in Chapter 5, envisaged the possibility that the economic dislocation of the adversary, resulting from attacks on particular targets, may be permissible as a means of ending the war. This author disagrees with that position, as there is no such possibility provided for in law. See 5.2.1.

14 The relevant discussion regarding how the contemporary US experience in the Tanker War has possibly influenced the US Navy in formulating the original position in this area is contained in 4.3.2. This position was then reproduced, in some cases only partially, in various US resources, which led to the situation in which the US position appears to be unclear.

15 See 4.3.2.

Conclusion 255

broadcasting stations. These two groups have two things in common. Both types of targets were subject to attack in the post-1977 international armed conflicts analysed here, and their assessment as lawful targets will depend on how their function is to be interpreted.

When considering objects linked to a political leadership, it is necessary to note that it is not always clear whether such objects are indeed the actual targets.[16] It may be that such buildings and places are damaged as a result of an attack on the people in them. The discussion of attacks against the people is clearly outside the scope of this work. Where the buildings themselves are targeted, this may be because they are used or associated with people whose functions are relevant to the conduct of war. This may include, for example, buildings used by the commander-in-chief. It is far less certain whether any other individuals exercising some functions relevant to the conduct of armed conflict would be targetable and, if so, whether the buildings, places and objects associated with them could also be lawful targets. The determination of the status of such people will have knock-on effects on how the objects connected to them will be assessed. In other words, the reasoning related to such objects will depend on the reasoning attached to the functions of the individuals. If, however, some people are not targetable, there will be no grounds for attacking the buildings associated with them, unless those building are used to perform military functions. In regard to such functions, the distinction between executive authority and political party functions could be useful.[17] This distinction can be further complicated, or may not exist, in single-party States where the State structure is in the hands of a repressive leader.[18] In recent coalition operations, some targets linked to the political process in a wider sense, in particular the ruling political party, were attacked – such as the Ba'ath party facilities during both the 1990–1 Gulf War and the 2003 conflict in Iraq.[19] It is not certain whether this reflects a view that such targets should be considered as satisfying the requirements of the definition, either at all or in certain circumstances, and if so, which.

Media facilities, especially TV and radio broadcasting stations, have controversially been attacked during armed conflicts.[20] Their classification as military objectives will depend on the activity they facilitate. It would be legitimate to consider an attack against a station that transmits military messages; when its infrastructure is used for military communications; or even when the military infrastructure is merely co-located in the broadcasting

---

16 See 1.1.3 and 7.1.
17 The executive infrastructure of the State relates to functioning governmental bodies, whereas political infrastructure relates to political entities such as political parties. See 3.1.3 and 7.1.
18 See also discussion in Chapter 9 throughout.
19 See 9.1 and 7.1.
20 See 7.3 and 9.1.

256   *Conclusion*

station.[21] It would not be acceptable to consider targeting a station that is merely used for journalistic functions or propaganda. Any assessment of such targets is linked to the advantage that their destruction or *neutralization* may offer. This, quite clearly, cannot be purely political or psychological.[22]

Interestingly, the first attacks on broadcasting stations sparked intense debate about their legitimacy in the media, and among Coalition members.[23] The same cannot be said about the attacks against such targets during more recent conflicts such as in 2003 in Iraq, in 2006 in Lebanon and during the NATO engagement in Libya in 2011. NATO, as mentioned in Chapter 4, argued that the attack on Libyan State Television facilities was legitimate because the broadcaster was involved in the incitement of violence against civilians.[24] NATO was therefore using the argument that the facilities were associated with the commission of international crimes. There does not seem to be any evidence of objections to the attack on this station, or of it provoking anything like as much a debate as the attack on the Serbian TV and radio broadcasting station in Belgrade.

Economic targets, including war-sustaining assets and resources, political leadership infrastructure, media facilities and all the objects identified in Part I of this work as being problematic in regard to the interpretation of the definition, share one significant feature. All have been identified and prioritised as strategic targets in military doctrine, as viewed in the context of the enemy as a system.[25] The continued pattern of attacks on such targets constitutes a part of military practice that possibly shapes the interpretation of the definition.

Military doctrine attaches more importance to some targets because affecting them may assist in achieving military goals. Such targets include the political leadership, resources and assets including economic targets, and civilian morale. Civilian morale may certainly be perceived as a target as defined in Chapters 1 and 7, but it cannot be seen as a military objective in the legal sense of this phrase.[26] Civilian morale was identified as one of the problematic targets in Part I, as there are difficulties in ascertaining its contribution to military action as well as whether it gives definite military advantage.[27] If the armed forces want to affect civilian morale, they would have to identify more specific objects that they think may contribute to such an effect, and then subject these objects to legal scrutiny in line with the requirements of the definition.

---

21 See 7.3.
22 See 5.2.1.
23 See 9.1.2.
24 See 7.47.
25 In Part I these objects were identified as legally problematic. It should be noted that they are promoted by military doctrine, but not because they are legally questionable. See 8.6 and 9.1.
26 See 1.5 and 8.1 and 8.6.
27 See 7.2.

10.3 The subsequent practice in the application of the treaty

The subsequent practice in the application of the treaty is relevant in interpreting a treaty obligation as set out in the Vienna Convention on the Law of Treaties.[28] One of the most significant findings about practice, relevant to the application of the Art 52.2 definition, is the recognition of its complexity and uncertainty. It is difficult to know how to identify and evaluate such practice.

Law requires that States attack only objects that are military objectives. When a State attacks certain objects, it presumably thinks they are lawful targets. This may not necessarily be true in the case of questionable targets, whose assessment may be arguable. Chapter 8 examined the possible impact of military doctrine on the targets identified as desirable by the armed forces. The potential legal implications of military doctrine on other LOAC provisions regulating the means and methods of fighting could also usefully be explored more widely and not just in connection to the definition of military objective.[29] At the practical level, the greater involvement of lawyers in the articulation of military doctrine should be considered. If objects are identified by armed forces as valuable targets, the risk could be that they may be approved not because they are lawful, but because they are not clearly unlawful. The pattern of such targets being attacked in numerous conflicts may give the impression that this is an accepted interpretation of the definition. In Part I and in Chapter 9, it was shown that targets relating to the political leadership, as well as TV and radio broadcasting stations, are regularly attacked. Even where such a trend exists, the context of the attacks is not always the same.

A separate question arises whether the nature of operations aimed at the protection of civilians and averting the crisis may have a narrowing impact on both the identification of targets and on application of the definition in practice. It is possible that objects that contribute to military action by *purpose* might be the most affected in such operations.[30]

The other issue with the identification of the relevant practice relates to situations where States do not attack particular objects. Targets that are not identified and proposed for attack, in line with military doctrine, will not be legally scrutinised during the targeting process. When possible targets are proposed by military forces, they are subject to verification and validation, which may lead to their rejection. The reasons for rejection could be military considerations arising out of the nature of the operations, limitations

---

28 Art 31 of the Vienna Convention on the Law of Treaties, Vienna, 23 May 1969, United Nations Treaty Series, vol. 1155, at 331 *et seq*. See also 1.2.2 and the Introduction to Part II.

29 A study of the impact of doctrine on the interpretation of Arts 51.4, 51.5, 57.2.a.ii, 57.2.a.iii and 57.2.b of API could be particularly interesting in this context.

30 See n 74 and the accompanying text in Chapter 9 and 3.1.4.

258 *Conclusion*

(e.g. a lack of suitable resources for the attack), military culture, political reasons resulting from national politics or executive policies, or reasons related to the law. It is not clear which factors play the prevailing role, and in what circumstances. It may be a combination of all these factors. Even if we could identify that the target was rejected for legal reasons, it may not be evident that the problem was linked to the definition of military objective.[31]

One specific environment that should seemingly offer greater opportunities for States to express their positions regarding a particular target is coalition warfare.[32] Here too, however, one is faced with the problem of knowing why States may have disagreed. The reasons behind such disagreements could be attributed to political imperatives, related both to coalition affairs and to domestic legal considerations and military concerns.[33] Where there seems to be a legal reason involved, it is not certain that it relates to the legal assessment of the proposed targets. Some overt disagreements about particular objects have been identified in this work, predominantly during the 1999 Kosovo intervention. It is striking that in subsequent NATO operations there appear to be progressively fewer disagreements. It is not completely clear why this is so, but one can imagine that a group of States that tend to engage in military operations together would find ways to resolve any potential problems in legal interoperability. Evidence for that can be found in the mechanisms that participating States have devised to prevent these legal differences having a negative impact on operations.[34] That does not mean that problems cease to exist. The measures adopted often permit States to circumvent such problems, in effect masking rather than resolving them. It remains unclear if these problems are related to the interpretation of or the application of the definition of military objectives.

One problem in the evaluation of practice arises in the case of a member of a coalition or alliance that does not make its views known.[35] When a disagreement regarding particular objects occurs, one might expect States to give their reasons for that disagreement. Does a State's silence mean it tacitly supports the position adopted by the others?[36] When evaluating the subsequent

---

31 Other relevant legal considerations in this context may include the principle of proportionality or precautions in attack, all of which are outside of the scope of this work. See 1.3.
32 See Chapter 9 throughout.
33 Ibid.
34 See 9.2.
35 See the discussion in 9.2.
36 Analogous problems can be found with the formation of customary rules, where States need to object to emerging rules if they do not want to be affected by them (with exception to *jus cogens* norms). Their acquiescence will otherwise be taken as their consent. Consult, for example: I.C. MacGibbon, 'Customary International Law and Acquiescence', 33 *British Yearbook of International Law* 1957, 115–45, and a more recent source, A.E. Roberts, 'Traditional and Modern Approaches to Customary International Law: A Reconciliation', 95(4) *American Journal of International Law* 2001, 757–91 at 757 *et seq.*

practice, does the behaviour of the silent State reinforce the view taken by others in the coalition or alliance? It is also unclear how this should be evaluated in respect of permanent military alliances, such as NATO. Every member of NATO presumably accepts what is done under the organisation's auspices, even if it is not a member of the particular fighting coalition. Not taking a clear position may have consequences beyond the definition of military objective. This might also affect a State's responsibility, particularly when acting as part of an integrated military alliance. It is possible that States that do not disassociate themselves from a position advocated by others may be held responsible for an attack executed by the State or States whose view prevailed.

All these issues make the identification of subsequent practice a very difficult process. There is, however, a further issue relating to the evaluation of relevant practice. It concerns access to relevant information by third parties, and the inability to evaluate aspects of practice that are not made known publicly.

As stated numerous times in this work, States tend to avoid sharing relevant information with the wider public.[37] They do not readily indicate their view on if, and how, particular targets fit the requirements of the definition. States tend not to indicate clearly if they support or object to other States' positions regarding particular targets. If they do disagree, it is hard to establish the reasons in the absence of a more detailed explanation from the States involved.

When explaining why a particular State did not take part in an operation against a particular target, the explanation given may relate superficially to the issue of collateral damage. It is often not clear whether the State is certain that a target was a military objective and only objected to the risk of excessive casualties, or whether the formula was also used to cover situations where both the status of the target was in doubt and some risk of collateral damage existed.[38]

It is understandable that some information might be kept confidential during and even after a conflict. The absence of any information regarding controversial attacks may add to speculation generated by media and non-governmental organisations reporting on the attacks. Only limited information can be found in military manuals or handbooks, post-operation military 'lessons learnt' studies, and parliamentary debates or inquiries. While these documents may contain some information as to States' understanding of the terms, they do not explain why a specific target was selected, how it fulfilled the definition and what information was used in the targeting decision. Even post-conflict inquiries, such as the one commissioned by the ICTY Office of the Prosecutor into the conduct of hostilities by NATO in 1999 in Kosovo,

---

37 See, for example, the discussion in 4.3.

38 This could also be a reflection of military or political concerns in the context of the given operation, in which any, let alone excessive civilian casualties would be undesirable rather than unlawful. See also n 188 and the accompanying text in Chapter 9.

260   *Conclusion*

did not reveal any specific evidence about the basis on which NATO members targeted particular objects. The welcome exception in this context is the NATO response to the UN Commission of Inquiry examining NATO's conduct during the 2011 conflict in Libya.[39]

A difficulty in enforcing the law of armed conflict is that the violation of the rule does not depend on the result or even on information available to the victim of the attack. It depends on the information available to the party that executed the attack.[40]

Sometimes when an explanation is volunteered, it may not be expressed in a way that is helpful in an examination of the elements of the definition. A State may simply indicate that the object was 'militarily significant', or describe it as a 'command and control centre'. As observed in Chapter 3, this may, to some extent, be a reflection of operational efficiency in the application of the definition.[41] States may, for instance, attach importance to establishing whether the target fulfils the necessary requirements of the definition, and not so much on whether this is on account of its *nature, location, purpose* or *use.* Use of the object may be concealed and not obvious to others, especially to those who examine the attack *ex post facto*.[42] The issue of access to relevant information could affect the perception of whether and how the rule is being enforced. Where the targeting of a particular object as a military objective is challenged, it would be useful if States expressed not only whether they supported or objected to the choice of target, but also explained their reasoning for this decision.

10.4 Problems of information

Research has revealed two further kinds of problems associated with information that may have an impact on the application of the definition. One relates to an absence of information-sharing, while the other relates to the quality of the information on which States determine whether targets are military objectives.

10.4.1 Absence of information-sharing

The problem connected to the sharing of information arises in the context of coalition warfare, and may affect whether particular targets can be determined

---

39 NATO Letter to the International Commission of Inquiry to investigate all alleged violations of international human rights law in the Libyan Arab Jamahiriya, OLA (2012) 006, 23 January 2012.

40 See more detailed information in 6.2.

41 See Conclusion to Chapter 3.

42 See, for example, 3.3, 4.3 and 6.2.

as military objectives. It is unclear how the process of sharing information is undertaken during operations. If intelligence is not shared, it may mean that one State would need to accept other States' evaluation of the information. This may suggest a potentially significant operational problem, where some coalition or alliance members are unable to make their own assessments of the targets they are asked to attack. This could also have legal implications in regard to a State's responsibility for attacks undertaken on the basis of someone else's assessment. This problem may not only occur between the forces of different States but also between the armed forces of one State, where, for example, the air force is involved in an attack that relies on a prior evaluation undertaken by land forces. Similar problems may arise if such an evaluation is undertaken by non-military forces such as the US Central Intelligence Agency, or local opposition groups fighting on the ground that are supported by the air forces of a foreign State or coalition of States.[43]

10.4.2 Standard of information on the basis of which a decision is made

A separate problem arises when States do share information about targets in coalition warfare. The forces of the State tasked with the execution of attacks against particular objects will, most likely, undertake their own legal scrutiny of the proposed targets. As part of such an analysis, they will have to apply the definition of military objective to the facts, which will be based on the available information. One State may view that information as sufficiently reliable and accurate to make a legal assessment, while another may require more information, or information of a different type. If members of one State's armed forces feel there is a problem with the information supplied, then they may not be able to reach a conclusion that would permit the lawful execution of the attack. It may be that they require further or different information to be able to determine whether the specific requirements of the definition are satisfied. Problems with information or intelligence-sharing between coalition members were first seen in the context of the NATO intervention in Kosovo. Here, Canadian lawyers encountered problems in the assessment of targets designated for attack by Canadian forces based on the information provided to them.[44]

This raises a more profound question relating to the standard of information on which the determination of a target as a military objective is made. If there are different standards of information on which States make their decisions, what are they?

---

43 See 9.1.2.
44 See 9.1.2.

262   *Conclusion*

There is no doubt that the information available to a commander at the time a decision about a target is reached will be a relevant consideration in assessing the legality of such a decision.[45] Very little is known about what standard States require when they apply the definition to the facts. How much information is required? What quality and nature of information must be found or should be sought? Should States look for opposing or corroborating information? How reliable, accurate or recent must the information be? Does it have to be verified by more than one source? How much weight is to be given to one type of source, and how much to another?

The standard might be that commanders should consider the information from all the sources reasonably available to them at the relevant time, as mentioned in Chapter 6. This still does not explain what quality, quantity or type of information is expected for commanders to make their decision. Some crucial considerations in this context involve determining what the decision-makers knew, what they thought they knew, or what they ought to have known at the time they made their decision. Different standards may be applied in targeting deliberate and anticipated dynamic targets in comparison to the unanticipated dynamic targets.[46]

The standard of information required in the application of the definition to the facts arose as a new and separate issue in this work. It is a significant issue in the operation of the definition, yet does not appear to be addressed in international law. Presumably the standard of sufficiency of evidence applied would, at least, be in conformity with the standard applied by the International Court of Justice.[47] It is likely that the legal standard of evaluation of evidence will be different in civilian and criminal proceedings. If this problem can affect the conduct of operations, especially coalition warfare, then perhaps it should also be addressed in coalition or joint military doctrine as well as in the training of military cadre involved in evaluating the information.

10.5 Final thought

> *Tout est extrêmement lié.*[48]

The analysis in this work has showed how various considerations, legal and non-legal, may be relevant in understanding the concept of military objective and how it is operationalised. It has also highlighted that these considerations are closely linked together, which on occasion may frustrate drawing clear-cut conclusions.

---

45 See 6.2.1.
46 See the more detailed discussion in 1.5 and 8.4.1.
47 See also A. Riddell and B. Plant, Evidence Before the International Court of Justice, British Institute of International and Comparative Law, London, February 2009.
48 Montesquieu, *De L'esprit de lois*, Norph Nop, 2012, Livre XIX, Chapitre XV.

Bibliography

1 Legal sources

International treaties, declarations and instruments

Treaty between Great Britain and The United States for the Amicable Settling of All Causes of Difference between the Two Countries, Washington, 8 May 1871.

Project of an International Declaration Concerning the Laws and Customs of War, Brussels, 1874.

The Laws of War on Land, Manual of Institute of International Law, Oxford, 9 September 1880.

Convention No. II Respecting the Laws and Customs of War on Land and its Annex: Regulations Concerning the Laws and Customs of War on Land, The Hague, 29 July 1899.

Convention (IV) Respecting the Laws and Customs of War on Land and its Annex: Regulations Concerning the Laws and Customs of War on Land, The Hague, 18 October 1907.

Convention (IX) Concerning Bombardment by Naval Forces in Time of War, 18 October 1907.

Rules concerning the Control of Wireless Telegraphy in Time of War and Air Warfare, drafted by a Commission of Jurists at The Hague, 11 December 1922–17 February 1923.

Protocol for the Prohibition of the Use of Asphyxiating, Poisonous or Other Gases, and of Bacteriological Methods of Warfare, Geneva, 17 June 1925.

Draft Convention for the Protection of Civilian Populations Against New Engines of War, International Law Association, Amsterdam, 3 September 1938.

Protection of Civilian Populations Against Bombing from the Air in Case of War, Resolution of the League of Nations Assembly, 30 September 1938.

General Directive No. 5 (S.46368/111. D.C.A.S), 14 February 1942.

Charter of the United Nations, United Nations, 24 October 1945, 1 UN Treaty Series 14.

Convention (I) for the Amelioration of the Condition of the Wounded and Sick in Armed Forces in the Field, Geneva, 12 August 1949.

Convention (II) for the Amelioration of the Condition of Wounded, Sick and Shipwrecked Members of Armed Forces at Sea, 12 August 1949.

Convention (III) Relative to the Treatment of Prisoners of War, 12 August 1949.

264 Bibliography

Convention (IV) Relative to the Protection of Civilian Persons in Time of War, Geneva, 12 August 1949.

Convention for the Protection of Cultural Property in the Event of Armed Conflict, The Hague, 14 May 1954.

Draft Rules for the Protection of the Civilian Population from the Dangers of Indiscriminate Warfare, International Committee of the Red Cross, 1955.

Draft Rules for the Limitation of the Dangers Incurred by the Civilian Population in Time of War, International Committee of the Red Cross, 1956.

International Covenant on Civil and Political Rights, 16 December 1966.

Vienna Convention on the Law of Treaties, Vienna, 23 May 1969.

The Distinction between Military Objectives and Non-Military Objectives in General and Particularly the Problems Associated with Weapons of Mass Destruction, Institute of International Law, Edinburgh, 9 September 1969.

Protocol Additional to the Geneva Conventions of 12 August 1949, and Relating to the Protection of Victims of International Armed Conflicts (Protocol I), Geneva, 8 June 1977, entered into force 7 December 1978.

Protocol Additional to the Geneva Conventions of 12 August 1949, and Relating to the Protection of Victims of Non-International Armed Conflicts (Protocol II), Geneva, 8 June 1977, entered into force 7 December 1978.

Convention on Prohibitions or Restrictions on the Use of Certain Conventional Weapons which May Be Deemed to Be Excessively Injurious or to Have Indiscriminate Effects, 10 October 1980.

Protocol on Prohibitions or Restrictions on the Use of Mines, Booby-Traps and Other Devices (Protocol II to the 1980 Convention), 10 October 1980.

Protocol on Prohibitions or Restrictions on the Use of Incendiary Weapons (Protocol III to the 1980 Convention), 10 October 1980.

Amended Protocol on Prohibitions or Restrictions on the Use of Mines, Booby-Traps and Other Devices (Amended Protocol II to the 1980 Convention), 3 May 1996.

Second Protocol to the Convention for the Protection of Cultural Property in the Event of Armed Conflict, The Hague, 14 May 1954, The Hague, 26 March 1999.

International cases and decisions

American Military Tribunal

United States v W. List et al. (Case no. 7), American Military Tribunal, Nuremberg Military Tribunals, Nuremberg 1950.

European Court of Human Rights

Bankovic and Others v Belgium and 16 Other Contracting States (Belgium, the Czech Republic, Denmark, France, Germany, Greece, Hungary, Iceland, Italy, Luxembourg, the Netherlands, Norway, Poland, Portugal, Spain, Turkey and the United Kingdom), 12 December 2001, Decision as to the admissibility of Application no. *52207*/99 of 12 December 2001 (Grand Chamber).

Bibliography 265

Eritrea-Ethiopia Claims Commission

Partial Award: Western Front, Aerial Bombardment and Related Claims Eritrea Claims 1, 3, 5, 9–13, 14, 21, 25 and 26 between The State of Eritrea and The Federal Democratic Republic of Ethiopia, The Hague, 19 December 2005.

International Court of Justice

Legality of the Threat or Use of Nuclear Weapons, Advisory Opinion of 8 July 1996, 1996 ICJ Reports 226.
North Sea Continental Shelf Cases, Judgment, 20 February 1969, ICJ Reports 1969.

International Criminal Court

The Prosecutor v Saif Al-Islam Gaddafi and Abdullah Al-Senussi, ICC-01/11-01/11, 27 June 2011.

International Criminal Tribunal for Former Yugoslavia

Prosecutor v Blaskic, Judgment of 3 March 2000, Trial Chamber, ICTY No. IT-95-14-T.
Prosecutor v Galic, Judgment and Opinion of 5 December 2003, Trial Chamber, ICTY No. IT-98-29-T.
Prosecutor v Kordic and Cerkez, Judgment of 3 March 2000, Trial Chamber, ICTY No. IT-95-14-T.
Prosecutor v Kordic and Cerkez, Judgment of 17 December 2004, Appeals Chamber, ICTY No. IT-95-14/2A.
The Prosecutor v Kupreskic (et al.), Judgment of 23 October 2001, Appeals Chamber, ICTY No. IT-95-16-A.
Prosecutor v Rajic, Judgment of 8 May 2006, Trial Chamber, ICTY No. IT-95-12-T.
Prosecutor v Strugar, Judgment of 31 January 2005, Trial Chamber, ICTY No. IT-01-42-T.

International Criminal Tribunal for Rwanda

The Prosecutor v Ferdinand Nahimana, Jean-Bosco Barayagwiza, Hassan Ngeze, ICTR-99-52-A (ICTR), Appeal Chamber, Judgment of 28 November 2007 and ICTR-99-52T, Trial Chamber, Judgment of 3 December 2003.

International Military Court

USA, France, UK and USSR v H. Goering et al., Judgment of the International Military Tribunal, Trial of [The] Major War Criminals, Nuremberg (1946).

Special Court for Sierra Leone

The Prosecutor v Fonfana and Kondewa, Judgment of 2 August 2007, Trial Chamber, Special Court for Sierra Leone, Case no. SCSL-04-14-J.

266   *Bibliography*

The Prosecutor v Fonfana and Kondewa, Judgment of 28 May 2008, Appeals Chamber, Special Court for Sierra Leone, Case no. SCSL-04-14-A.

Other international governmental documents

European Union

Independent International Fact-Finding Mission on the Conflict in Georgia, Report of September 2009.

UN Human Rights Council

Report of the Special Rapporteur on extrajudicial, summary or arbitrary executions, Philip Alston; the Special Rapporteur on the right of everyone to the enjoyment of the highest attainable standard of physical and mental health, Paul Hunt; the Representative of the Secretary-General on human rights of internally displaced persons, Walter Kälin; and the Special Rapporteur on adequate housing as a component of the right to an adequate standard of living, Miloon Kothari, Mission to Lebanon and Israel, 2 October 2006, A/HRC/2/7.

Report of the Commission of Inquiry on Lebanon pursuant to Human Rights Council Resolution S–2/1, UN Doc. A/HRC/3/2, 23 November 2006.

Report of the United Nations Fact-Finding Mission on the Gaza Conflict, UN Doc. A/HRC/12/48, 25 September 2009.

UN Security Council

Study of the Battle and Siege of Sarajevo, Annex VI, part 1, Final report of the United Nations Commission of Experts established pursuant to Security Council Resolution 780 (1992), S/1994/674/Add. 2 (Vol. II), 27 May 1994.

UN SC Resolution 660, UN Doc. S/RES/0660 of 2 August 1990.

UN SC Resolution 661, UN Doc. S/RES/0661 of 6 August 1990.

UN SC Resolution 665, UN Doc. S/RES/0665 of 25 August 1990.

UN SC Resolution 678, UN Doc. S/RES/0678 of 29 November 1990.

UN SC Resolution 816, UN Doc. S/RES/0816 of 31 March 1993.

UN SC Resolution 1368, UN Doc. S/RES/1368 of 12 September 2001.

UN SC Resolution 1386, UN Doc. S/RES/1386 of 20 December 2001.

UN SC Resolution 1483, UN Doc. S/RES/1483 of 22 May 2003.

National documents and national cases

Argentina

Manual De Derecho Internacional De Los Conflictos Armados, Ministry of Defence of Argentina, 2010.

Bibliography   267

Australia

Operations Law for RAAF Commanders, Royal Australian Air Force, Air Power Publication AAP 1003, 2nd edn, 2004.
Law of Armed Conflict, Australian Defence Doctrine Publication, ADDP 06.4, May 2006.

Canada

Law of Armed Conflict at the Operational and Tactical Levels, Joint Doctrine Manual B-GJ-005-104/FP-021, Office of the Judge Advocate General, Canadian National Defence, 13 August 2001.

Columbia

Manual de Derecho Operacional, FF. MM 3-41, El Comando General de las Fuerzas Militares, Republic of Colombia, 2009.

France

Manuel de Droit des Conflits Armés, (French) Ministère de la Défense, Secrétariat Général Pour L'Administration, undated.

Germany

Directive No. 1, *Directives for the Conduct of War*, The Supreme Commander of Armed Forces, 31 August 1939, in *Fuehrer Directives and other Top-Level Directives of the German Armed Forces 1939–1941*, ATO Press, Washington, DC 1948, at 49–50.
Directive No. 9*: Principles for the Conduct of War Against the Enemy's Economy*, The Supreme Commander of Armed Forces, 29 November 1939, in *Fuehrer Directives and other Top-Level Directives of the German Armed Forces 1939–1941*, ATO Press, Washington, DC 1948, at 73–5.
The Basic Law for the Federal Republic of Germany (*Grundgesetz für die Bundesrepublik Deutschland*), 8 May 1949.
Humanitarian Law in Armed Conflicts –Manual (Eng.), The Federal Ministry of Defence of The Federal Republic of Germany, ZDv 15/2 VR II 3, August 1992.

Israel

Israel Ministry of Foreign Affairs, *Responding to Hizbullah Attacks from Lebanon: Issues of Proportionality*, Legal Background, Jerusalem 25 July 2006, available at www.mfa. gov.il/mfa/aboutisrael/state/law/pages/responding%20to%20hizbullah%20attack s%20from%20lebanon-%20issues%20of%20proportionality%20july%202006.aspx.
Israel Ministry of Foreign Affairs [IMFA], *The Operation in Gaza – Factual and Legal Aspects; 27 December 2008–18 January 2009*, 29 July 2009, available at www.jewishvirtual library.org/jsource/Peace/GazaOpReport0709.pdf.

268   *Bibliography*

The Second Lebanon War – One Year Later, Israel Ministry of Foreign Affairs, 12 July 2007, available at www.mfa.gov.il/mfa/foreignpolicy/issues/pages/the%20second%20 lebanon%20war%20-%20one%20year%20later%20-%20july%202007.aspx.

Israel Ministry of Foreign Affairs, *Gaza Operation Investigations: An Update*, January 2010.

Italy

Italian Court of Cassation, *Presidenza Consiglio Ministri c. Markovic e altri*, Cassazione (sez.un.), n. 8157 (ord.), 5 June 2002, in 85 RDI (2002).

Japan

R. *Shimoda et al. v The State*, Tokyo District Court, 7 December 1963, translated in 8 *Japanese Annual of International Law* 1964; 32 *International Law Review* 1964, 626–42.

Spain

Orientaciones. El Derecho de los Conflictos Armados, OR7–004, Ministry of Defence of Spain, 2nd edn, 2007, Vol. I.

United Kingdom

Aide Mémoire on the Law of Armed Conflict, Joint Service Publication 381 (JSP 381), undated.

Air Ministry, *Instructions and Notes on the Rules to be Observed By the Royal Air Force in War* and a covering note of 22 August 1939, A.H. Self (Air Ministry) to Air Officer Commanding-in-Chief, Bomber Command, in AIR 14/249, National Archives of the United Kingdom.

Air Ministry, *Instructions Governing Naval and Air Bombardment*, 5 June 1940, in AIR 14/249, National Archives of the United Kingdom.

Directive to the Appropriate British and US Air Force Commanders to Govern the Operation of British and US Bomber Commands in the United Kingdom, approved by the Combined Chiefs of Staff at their 65th meeting on 21 January 1943.

House of Commons, Defence Committee, *Preliminary Lessons of Operation Granby*, Tenth Report, Her Majesty's Stationery Office, London, 1991.

Letter to UN Security Council, UN Doc. S/22156, 28 January 1991.

House of Commons, Defence Committee, *Implementation of Lessons Learnt From Operation Granby*, Fifth Report, Her Majesty's Stationery Office, London, 1994.

Kosovo: Operation 'Allied Force', UK House of Commons, Research Paper, 99/48, 29 April 1999.

House of Commons, Foreign Affairs Committee, Fourth Report on Kosovo, 7 June 2000.

House of Commons, Committee on Defence, *Lessons of Kosovo*, Fourteenth Report, HC 347-I, Her Majesty Stationery Office, London, October 2000. Available online at www.publications.parliament.uk/pa/cm199900/cmselect/cmfaff/28/2802.htm.

Ministry of Defence, *Kosovo Lessons from the Crisis*, UK DCCS Media Publications, London 2000.

'Operation *Enduring Freedom* and the Conflict in Afghanistan: An Update', United Kingdom, House of Commons, International Affairs and Defence Section, Research Paper 01/81, 31 October 2001.

Bibliography 269

House of Commons, Defence Committee, Third Report: *Lessons of Iraq*, Her Majesty's Stationery Office, London, 16 March 2003.

Ministry of Defence, *Operations in Iraq: First Reflections*, DCCS Media Publications, London, July 2003.

Ministry of Defence, *Operations in Iraq: Lessons for the Future*, DCCS Media Publications, London, December 2003.

The Manual of the Law of Armed Conflict, UK Ministry of Defence, JSP 383, Oxford University Press, Oxford 2004.

House of Commons, Defence Committee, Fifth Report: *The UK Deployment to Afghanistan*, Her Majesty Stationery Office, London, 28 March 2006.

United States

Instructions for the Government of Armies of the United States in the Field, promulgated as General Orders no. 100, 24 April 1863.

Mrs. Alexander's Cotton, US Supreme Court, 69 U.S.2 Wall. (1864).

War Department, *The War of the Rebellion: a Compilation of the Official Records of the Union and Confederate Armies*, US Government Printing Office, 1880–1901, 24 December 1864, Series I, Vol. XLIV, Part 1.

Military Division of the Mississippi, Special Field Orders No. 120, 9 November 1864.

Lamar v Browne, US Supreme Court, 92 U. S. (1875).

Young v United States, 97 U.S. 39 (1877).

Ford v Surget, US Supreme Court, 97 U.S. (1878).

Basic Field Manual Rules of Land Warfare of 1914, 1934 and 1940.

The Tokyo Raid Report, Informational Intelligence Summary (Special) No. 20, US Army Air Forces, Director of Intelligence Service, C-426, AF, 5 October 1942.

Law of Land Warfare, Field Manual 27-10, US Department of Army, 18 July 1956 with subsequent amendments of 15 July 1976.

Department of Air Force, *International Law – The Conduct of Armed Conflict and Air Operations* (AFP 110–31), 19 November 1976.

US Department of Defense, *Conduct of the Persian Gulf War: Final Report to Congress*, 10 April 1992, Department of Defense Washington, 1992

Law and Military Operations in the Balkans 1995–1998: Lessons Learned for Advocates, Report, Center for Law and Military Operations, Judge Advocates General's School, United States Army.

Department of Navy, *Annotated Supplement to the Commander's Handbook on the Law of Naval Operations*, US Naval War College, Newport, RI, 1997.

Operational Law Handbook, JA 422, International and Operational Law Department, The Judge Advocate General's Legal Center and School, 1997 edn.

United States and NATO Military Operations Against the Federal Republic of Yugoslavia, Hearing before United States House of Representatives Committee on Armed Services, 106th Congress, 28 April 1999, H.A.S.C. No. 106–12

Kosovo/Operation Allied Force After-Action Report, Report to Congress, US Department of Defense, January 2000.

Kosovo Air Operations, Need to Maintain Alliance Cohesion Resulted in Doctrinal Departures, United States General Accounting Office, Report to Congressional Requesters, GAO-01-784, July 2001.

Military Operations in the Kosovo 1999–2001: Lessons Learned for Advocates, Report, Center for Law and Military Operations, Judge Advocate General's School, United States Army, December 2001.

270   *Bibliography*

US Air Force, *Air Force Operations and the Law: A Guide for Air, Space and Cyber Forces*, US Air Force, The Judge Advocate General's School, 2002.

Department of Defense Instructions for the US Military Commission at Guantanamo Bay, Military Commission Instructions No. 2, Crimes and Elements for Trials by Military Commission, 30 April 2003.

Legal Lessons Learned from Afghanistan and Iraq, Volume I, Major Combat Operations (11 September 2011 to 1 May 2003), Center for Law and Military Operations, United States Army, The Judge Advocate General's Legal Center and School, Charlottesville, VA, 1 August 2004.

Law of War Handbook, JA 423, International and Operational Law Department, The Judge Advocate General's Legal Center and School, 2004 and 2005 edns.

Military Commissions Act, 10 U.S.C §§948a–950w, 30 September 2006.

Department of Defense, Directive 2311.01E, Law of War Program, 9 May 2006.

US Air Force's Pamphlet 110–31 *(International Law – The Conduct of Armed Conflict and Air Operations)*, 19 November 1976, in force until it was rescinded in 2006.

Law of War Handbook, JA 423, International and Operational Law Department, The US Judge Advocate General's Legal Center and School, annual edition; supplemented by *Law of War Documentary Supplement*, JA 42, International and Operational Law Department, The US Judge Advocate General's Legal Center and School, 2007.

US Navy, Marine Corps and Coast Guard, *Commander's Handbook on the Law of Naval Operations*, Department of the Navy, Office of the Chief of Naval Operations, Headquarters, US Marine Corps, Department of Transportation, US Coastal Guard, NWP 1-14M, MCWP 5-2.1, COMDTPUB P5800.7 (formerly known as Naval Warfare Pub. No. NWP 9 (Rev. A)/FMFM 1-10, 1989), 1987, 2nd edn 1995, 3rd edn 2007.

Forged in the Fire: Legal Lessons Learnt During Military Operations 1994–2008, Center for Law and Military Operations, United States Army, The Judge Advocate General's Legal Center and School, Charlottesville, VA, September 2008.

US Air Force, *Air Force Operations and the Law: A Guide for Air, Space and Cyber Forces*, US Air Force, The Judge Advocate General's School, 2nd edn, 2009.

US Air Force, *The Military Commander and the Law*, The Judge Advocate General's School, 11th edn, 2012.

US Operational Law Handbook, JA 422, International and Operational Law Department, The Judge Advocate General's Legal Center and School, 1997edn, 2009 edn, 2013 edn.

Conference records

Report on the Work of the Conference, Conference of Government Experts on the Reaffirmation and Development of International Humanitarian Law Applicable in Armed Conflicts (Geneva 24 May–12 June 1971), ICRC, Geneva 1971.

Report on the Work of the Conference, Conference of Government Experts on the Reaffirmation and Development of International Humanitarian Law Applicable in Armed Conflicts (Second Session Geneva 3 May–3 June 1972), ICRC, Geneva 1972.

Bibliography 271

Official Records of the Diplomatic Conference on the Reaffirmation and Development of International Humanitarian Law Applicable in Armed Conflicts, Geneva (1974–7), Berne 1978, volumes I–XVI.

Books (monographs and collections of essays)

Best G., *Humanity in Warfare*, J.W. Arrowsmith, Bristol 1983.

Best G., *War and Law since 1945*, Clarendon Press, Oxford 1994.

Boothby W.H., *The Law of Targeting*, Oxford University Press, Oxford, 2012.

Bothe M., Partsch K. and Solf W., *New Rules for Victims of Armed Conflict: Commentary on the Two 1977 Protocols Additional to the Geneva Conventions of 1949*, Martinus Nijhoff, The Hague 1982.

Cassese, A., *International Law*, Oxford University Press, Oxford 2001.

Cherif Bassiouni M., *Crimes Against Humanity in International Criminal Law*, Kluwer Law International, The Hague 1999.

Dinstein Y., *The Conduct of Hostilities under the Law of International Armed Conflict*, Cambridge University Press, Cambridge 2004.

Dinstein Y., *The Conduct of Hostilities under the Law of International Armed Conflict*, 2nd edn, Cambridge University Press, Cambridge 2010.

Doswald-Beck L. (ed.), *San Remo Manual on International Law Applicable to Armed Conflicts at Sea*, Cambridge University Press, Cambridge 1995.

Fleck D. (ed.), *Handbook of Humanitarian Law in Armed Conflict*, Oxford University Press, Oxford 2008.

Green L.C., *The Contemporary Law of Armed Conflict*, Melland Schill Studies in International Law, 3rd edn, Manchester University Press, Manchester 2008.

Heintschel von Heinegg W. and Epping V. (eds), *International Humanitarian Law Facing New Challenges*, Springer Publishers, Berlin 2007.

Henckaerts J.M. and Doswald-Beck L., *Customary International Humanitarian Law, Volume I: Rules, International Committee of the Red Cross*, Cambridge University Press, Cambridge 2005.

Henckaerts J.M. and Doswald-Beck L., *Customary International Humanitarian Law, Volume II: Practice, International Committee of the Red Cross*, Cambridge University Press, Cambridge 2005.

Henderson I., *The Contemporary Law of Targeting*, Martinus Nijhoff, Leiden 2009.

Kalshoven F., *Reflections on the Law of War: Collected Essays*, International Humanitarian Law Series 17, Brill, Leiden 2008.

Meyer M. (ed.), Armed Conflict and the New Law, British Institute of International and Comparative Law, London 1989.

Montesquieu, *De L'esprit de lois*, Norph Nop, 2012 (e-book).

Olasolo H., *Unlawful Attacks in Combat Situations: From the ICTY's Case Law to the Rome Statute*, Martinus Nijhoff, Leiden, 2008.

Perry C. (ed.), *The Consolidated Treaty Series*, Oceana Publications, Dobbs Ferry 1977, Vol. 143.

Primoraz I. (ed.), *Civilian Immunity in War*, Oxford University Press, Oxford 2007.

Riddell A. and Plant B., Evidence Before the International Court of Justice, British Institute of International and Comparative Law, London, February 2009.

Rogers A.V.P, *Law on the Battlefield*, Melland Schill Studies in International Law, 3rd edn, Manchester University Press, Manchester 2012.

272 *Bibliography*

Ronzitti N. and Venturini G. (eds), *Current Issues in the International Humanitarian Law of Air Warfare*, Eleven International Publishing, Utrecht, 2005.

Rowe P. (ed.), *The Gulf War 1990–1991 in International and English Law*, Routledge, London 1993.

Royse M.W., *Aerial Bombardment and the International Regulation of Warfare*, Harold Vinal, New York 1928.

Sandoz Y., Swinarski C. and Zimmermann B. (eds), *Commentary on the Additional Protocols of 8 June 1977 to the Geneva Conventions of 12 August 1949*, ICRC, Geneva, and Martinus Nijhoff, The Hague 1987.

Schindler D. and Toman J. (eds), *The Laws of Armed Conflict*, 4th edn, Martinus Nijhoff, Leiden 2004.

Schmitt M.N. (ed.), *Tallinn Manual on The International Law Applicable to Cyber Warfare*, Cambridge University Press, Cambridge 2013.

Solis G.D., *The Law of Armed Conflict: International Humanitarian Law in War*, Cambridge University Press, Cambridge 2010.

Spaight J.M., *Air Power and War Rights*, 3rd edn, Longmans, Green, London 1947.

Thomas A.R. and Duncan J.C. (eds), *Annotated Supplement to the Commander's Handbook on the Law of Naval Operations*, Vol. 73, Navy War College, International Law Studies, Newport, RI 1999.

Wilmshurst E. and Breau S. (eds), *Perspectives on the ICRC Study on Customary International Humanitarian Law*, Cambridge University Press, Cambridge 2007.

Wippman D. and Evangelista M. (eds), *New Wars, New Laws? Applying the Laws of War in 21st Century Conflicts*, Transnational, Ardsley, NY 2005.

Contributions

Bothe M., 'Targeting' in A.E. Wall (ed.), *Legal and Ethical Lessons of NATO's Kosovo Campaign*, Vol. 78, US Naval War College International Law Studies, Newport, RI 2002.

Breau S.C., 'A Single Standard for Coalitions: Lowest Common Denominator or Highest Standards?' in M. Odello and R. Piotrowicz (eds), *International Military Missions and International Law*, Martinus Nijhoff, Leiden 2011.

Brown N., 'Issues Arising from Coalition Operations: An Operational Lawyer's Perspective' in M.D. Carsten (ed.), *International Law and Military Operations*, Vol. 84, US Naval War College International Law Studies, Newport, RI 2008.

Dinstein Y., 'Discussion', comments in A.E. Wall (ed.), *Legal and Ethical Lessons of NATO's Kosovo Campaign*, US Naval War College International Law Studies, Vol. 78, Newport, RI 2002.

Doswald-Beck L., 'The Value of the 1977 Protocols' in M.A. Meyer (ed.), *Armed Conflict and the New Law. Aspects of the 1977 Geneva Protocols and the 1981 Weapons Convention*, Vol. 1, British Institute of International and Comparative Law, London 1989.

Dunlap C.J., 'Targeting Hearts and Minds: National Will and Other Legitimate Objectives of Modern War' in W. Heintschel von Heinegg and V. Epping (eds), *International Humanitarian Law Facing New Challenges*, Springer, Berlin 2007.

Garrett S.A., 'Airpower and Non-Combatant Immunity' in I. Primoraz (ed.), *Civilian Immunity in War*, Oxford University Press, Oxford 2007.

Greenwood C., 'Customary International Law and the First Geneva Protocol of 1977 in the Gulf Conflict' in P. Rowe (ed.), *The Gulf War 1990–1991 in International and English Law*, Routledge, London 1993.

Bibliography 273

Greenwood C., 'The Law of War (International Humanitarian Law)', Chapter 25 in M.D. Evans (ed.), *International Law*, Oxford University Press, Oxford 2003.

Haines S., 'The United Kingdom and Legitimate Military Objectives: Current Practice ... and Future Trends?' in W. Heintschel von Heinegg and V. Epping (eds), *International Humanitarian Law Facing New Challenges*, Springer, Berlin 2007.

Hampson F.J., 'Means and Methods of Warfare in the Conflict in the Gulf' in P. Rowe (ed.), *The Gulf War 1990–1991 in International and English Law*, Routledge, London 1993.

Hays Parks W., 'Asymmetries and the Identification of Legitimate Military Objectives' in W. Heintschel von Heinegg and V. Epping (eds), *International Humanitarian Law Facing New Challenges*, Springer, Berlin 2007.

Heintschel von Heinegg, W., 'Commentary' in A.E. Wall (ed.), *Legal and Ethical Lessons of NATO's Kosovo Campaign*, Vol. 78, US Naval War College International Law Studies, Newport, RI 2002.

Heintschel von Heinegg W., 'The Law of Armed Conflict at Sea' in D. Fleck (ed.), *The Handbook of Humanitarian Law in Armed Conflicts*, 2nd edn, Oxford University Press, Oxford 2008.

Heintschel von Heinegg, W., 'The Law of Military Operations at Sea' in T. Gill and D. Fleck (eds), *The Handbook of International Law of Military Operations*, Oxford University Press, Oxford 2010.

Lowe V. and Tzanakopoulos A., 'Economic Warfare' in R. Wolfrum (ed.), *Max Planck Encyclopaedia of Public International Law*, Oxford University Press, Oxford 2012.

McConache V., 'Coalition Operations: A Compromise or an Accommodation' in M.D. Carsten (ed.), *International Law and Military Operations*, Vol. 84, US Naval War College International Law Studies, Newport, RI 2008.

Marauhn T. and Kirchener S., 'Target Area Bombing' in N. Ronzitti and G. Venturini (eds), *Current Issues in the International Humanitarian Law of Air Warfare*, Eleven International Publishing, Utrecht, 2005.

Oeter S., 'Comment: Is the Principle of Distinction Outdated?' in W. Heintschel von Heinegg and V. Epping (eds), *International Humanitarian Law Facing New Challenges*, Springer, Berlin 2007.

Oeter S., 'Methods and Means of Combat' in D. Fleck (ed.), *The Handbook of Humanitarian Law in Armed Conflicts*, 2nd edn, Oxford University Press, Oxford 2008.

Ponti C., 'Air Operations against Afghanistan (2001–2)' in N. Ronzitti and G. Venturini (eds), *Current Issues in the International Humanitarian Law of Air Warfare*, Eleven International Publishing, Utrecht, 2005.

Roberts A., 'Air Power, Accuracy and the Law of Targeting: Why No Brave New World?' in R.B. Jaques (ed.), *Issues in International Law and Military Operations*, Vol. 80, Naval War College, International Law Studies, Newport, RI 2006.

Sassoli M., 'Targeting: The Scope and Utility of the Concept of "Military Objectives" for the Protection of Civilians in Contemporary Armed Conflicts' in D. Wippman and M. Evangelista (eds), *New Wars, New Laws? Applying the Laws of War in 21st Century Conflicts*, Transnational, Ardsley 2005.

Sassoli M. and Cameron L., 'The Protection of Civilian Objects – Current State of the Law and Issues *de lege ferenda*' in N. Ronzitti and G. Venturini (eds), *Current Issues in the International Humanitarian Law of Air Warfare*, Eleven International Publishing, Utrecht, 2005.

274 *Bibliography*

Schmitt M.N., 'War and the Environment: Fault Lines in the Prescriptive Landscape' in J.E. Austin and C.E. Bruch, *The Environmental Consequences of War*, Cambridge University Press, Cambridge 2000.

Schmitt M.N., 'Fault Lines in the Law of Attack' in S.C. Breau and A. Jachec-Neale (eds), *Testing the Boundaries of International Humanitarian Law*, British Institute of International and Comparative Law, London 2006.

Schmitt M.N., 'The Law of Targeting' in E. Wilmshurst and S. Breau (eds), *Perspectives on the ICRC Study on Customary International Humanitarian Law*, Cambridge University Press, Cambridge 2007.

Schmitt M.N., 'Targeting and International Humanitarian Law in Afghanistan' in M.N. Schmitt (ed.), *The War in Afghanistan: A Legal Analysis*, Vol. 85, US Naval War College International Law Studies, Newport, RI 2009.

Short M., 'Operational Allied Force from the Perspective of the NATO Air Commander' in A.E. Wall (ed.), *Legal and Ethical Lessons of NATO's Kosovo Campaign*, Vol. 78, US Naval War College International Law Studies, Newport, RI 2002.

Stein T., 'Coalition Warfare and Differing Legal Obligations of Coalition Members under International Humanitarian Law' in A.E. Wall (ed.), *Legal and Ethical Lessons of NATO's Kosovo Campaign*, Vol. 78, US Naval War College International Law Studies, Newport, RI 2002.

Warren M., 'The "Fog of Law": The Law of Armed Conflict in Operation Iraqi Freedom' in M.D. Carsten (ed.), *International Law and Military Operations*, Vol. 84, US Naval War College International Law Studies, Newport, RI 2008.

Watkin K.W., 'Coalition Operations: A Canadian Perspective' in M.D. Carsten (ed.), *International Law and Military Operations*, Vol. 84, US Naval War College International Law Studies, Newport, RI 2008.

Articles and research papers

Aquila, 'Air Power in Economic Warfare, A Comparison with Naval Blockade', 94(576) *Royal United Services Institute Journal* 1949, 572–5.

Belt S.W., 'Missiles Over Kosovo: Emergence, *Lex Lata*, of a Customary Norm Requiring the Use of Precision Munitions in Urban Areas' 47 *Naval Law Review* 2000, 115–75.

Benvenuti P., 'The ICTY Prosecutor and the Review of the NATO Bombing Campaign against the Federal Republic of Yugoslavia', 12(3) *European Journal of International Law* 2001, 503–30.

Bill B.J., 'The Rendulic "Rule": Military Necessity, Commander's Knowledge, and Methods of Warfare', 12 *Yearbook of International Humanitarian Law* 2009, 119–55.

Blank L.R., 'The Application of IHL in the Goldstone Report: Critical Commentary', 12 *Yearbook of International Humanitarian Law* 2009, 347–402.

Boivin A., 'The Legal Regime Applicable to Targeting Military Objectives in the Context of Contemporary Warfare', Research paper 02/2006, Geneva Academy of International Humanitarian Law and Human Rights.

Bothe M., 'The Protection of the Civilian Population and NATO Bombing on Yugoslavia: Comments on a Report to the Prosecutor of the ICTY', 12(3) *European Journal of International Law* 2001, 531–55.

Bridge R.L., 'Operations Law: An Overview', 37 *Air Force Law Review* 1994, 1–4.

Bring O., 'International Humanitarian Law after Kosovo: Is Lex Lata Sufficient?' 71(1) *Nordic Journal of International Law* 2002, 39–54.

Bibliography 275

Cario J., 'Legal Advice Supporting Command', 20 *Doctrine: Command in Operations*, Ministère de la Défense, General Military Review 2011, 55–6.

Carnahan B.M., 'The Law of Air Bombardment in its Historical Context', 17(2) *The Air Force Law Review* 1975, 39–60.

Carnahan B.M., 'Protecting Civilians Under the Draft Geneva Protocol: A Preliminary Inquiry', 18(4) *Air Force Law Review* 1976, 32–69.

Cochrane K., *Kosovo Targeting – A Bureaucratic and Legal Nightmare: The Implications for US/Australian Interoperability*, Aerospace Centre, Paper No. 3, June 2001.

Colby E., 'Aerial Law and War Targets', 19(4) *American Journal of International Law* 1925, 702–15.

Corn G.S. and Corn G.P., 'The Law of Operational Targeting: Viewing the LOAC through an Operational Lens', 47(2) *Texas International Law Journal* 2012, 337–80.

Crawford J.W., 'The Law of Noncombatant Immunity and the Targeting of National Electrical Power Systems', 21(2) *Fletcher Forum of World Affairs* 1997, 101–19.

Cryer R., 'The Fine Art of Friendship: Jus in Bello in Afghanistan', 7(1) *Journal of Conflict and Security Law* 2002, 37–83.

Dakers M. Lt.-Col., *Presentation on Legal Interoperability*, International Society of Military Law and Law of War, Quebec, 3 May 2012.

De Mulinen F., Report on the Question 'What Is Military and What is Civilian?', Meeting of the Committee for the Protection of Human Life in Armed Conflict, 39 *Revue de droit pénal militaire et de droit de la guerre* 2000, 401–5.

DeSaussure A.L., 'The Role of Law of Armed Conflict During the Persian Gulf War: An Overview', 37 *The Air Force Law Review* 1994, 41–68.

DeSaussure H., 'The Conduct of Armed Conflict and Air Operations. By US Air Force (Pamphlet 110–31, 19 November 1976)' Review, 72(1) *American Journal of International Law* 1978, 174–6.

DeSaussure H., Commentator, The American Red Cross–Washington College of Law Conference: International Humanitarian Law, 11–12 March 1982 proceedings, 31 *American University Law Review*, 1981–2.

Dinstein Y., 'Legitimate Military Objectives Under the Current *Jus in Bello*' 31 *Israel Yearbook on Human Rights* 2002, 1–34.

Doswald-Beck L, 'San Remo Manual on International Law Applicable to Armed Conflicts at Sea', 89 *American Journal of International Law* 1995, 192–208.

Dunlap, C.J., Jr., 'The End of Innocence: Rethinking Non-combatancy in the Post-Kosovo Era', 28(3) *Strategic Review* 2000, 9–17.

Elliott H.W., 'Open Cities and (Un)defended Places', *Army Lawyer*, April 1995.

Exum A., 'Illegal Attack or Legitimate Target? Al Manar, International Law and the Israeli War in Lebanon', *Arab Media and Society*, February 2007.

Fenrick W.J., 'Legal Aspects of Targeting in the Law of Naval Warfare', 29 *Canadian Yearbook of International Law* 1991, 238–82.

Fenrick W.J., 'Targeting and Proportionality during the NATO Bombing Campaign against Yugoslavia' 12(3) *European Journal of International Law* 2001, 489–502.

Fuchs J., 'Shot in the Dark: International Law of Targeting in Theory and State Practice', 3 *Acta Societatis Martensis* 2007/2008, 21–38.

Goda P.J., 'The Protection of Civilians from Bombardment by Aircraft: The Ineffectiveness of the International Law of War', 33 *Military Law Review* 1966, 93–113.

276 Bibliography

Greenwood C., 'Current Issues in the Law of Armed Conflict: Weapons, Targets and International Criminal Liability', 1 *Singapore Journal of International and Comparative Law* 1997, 441–67.

Hampson F.J., 'Proportionality and Necessity in the Gulf War', 86 *American Society of International Law Proceedings* 1992, 45–54.

Hanke H.M., 'The 1923 Hague Rules of Air Warfare', 292 *International Review of the Red Cross*, Jan–Feb. 1993, 12–44.

Hays Parks W., 'Linebacker and the Law of War', 34 *Air University Review*, Jan.–Feb. 1983, 2–30.

Hays Parks W., 'Air War and the Law of War', 32 *Air Force Law Review* 1990, 1–225.

Hays Parks W., 'The Protection of Civilians from Air Warfare' 27 *Israel Yearbook on Human Rights* 1997, 65–111.

Holland J., 'Military Objective and Collateral Damage: Their Relationship and Dynamics', 7 *Yearbook of International Humanitarian Law* 2004, 35–78.

Jordaan E. and Vrey F., 'Operational Strategy and the South African Way of War: The Way Forward', 28(1) *Strategic Review for Southern Africa* 2006, 30–62.

Kalshoven F., 'Reaffirmation and Development of International Humanitarian Law Applicable in Armed Conflicts: The Diplomatic Conference, Geneva, 1974–1977', 9 *Netherlands Yearbook of International Law* 1978, 107–71.

Kalshoven F., 'The Undertaking to Respect and Ensure Respect in All Circumstances: From Tiny Seed to Ripening Fruit', 2 *Yearbook of International Humanitarian Law*, 1999, 3–61, available at http://journals.cambridge.org/action/displayAbstract?from Page=online&aid=4044608 – fn01.

Kelly M., 'Legal Factors in Military Planning for Coalition Warfare and Military Interoperability: Some Implications for the Australian Defence Force', 2 *Australian Army Journal* 2005, 161–72.

Kunz, J.L., 'The Laws of War', 50(2) *The American Journal of International Law* 1956, 313–37.

Laursen A., 'NATO, Kosovo, and the ICTY Investigation', 17(4) *American University of International Law Review* 2001–2, 765–814.

Lewis M.W., 'The Law of Aerial Bombardment in the 1991 Gulf War', 97(3) American *Journal of International Law* 2003, 481–509.

MacGibbon I.C., 'Customary International Law and Acquiescence', 33 *British Yearbook of International Law* 1957, 115–45.

Martineu F., 'The Rules of Engagement in Ten Questions', 4 *Doctrine: The Legal Environment for Ground Forces*, Ministère de la Défense, General Military Review, September 2004, 18–20.

Matheson M.J., 'The United States Position on the Relation of Customary International Law to the 1977 Protocols Additional to the 1949 Geneva Conventions' 2(2) *American University Journal of International Law and Policy* 1987, 419–31.

Matthias von Lepel B.O., 'Overseas Operations of the Bundeswehr in the Light of International and Constitutional Law', 4 *Doctrine: The Legal Environment for Ground Forces*, Ministère de la Défense, General Military Review, September 2004, 24–7.

Medenica O., 'Protocol I and Operation Allied Force in Kosovo: Did NATO Abide by Principle of Proportionality?', 23(3) *The Loyola of Los Angeles International* and *Comparative Law Review* 2001, 329–426.

Bibliography 277

Melson D.A., 'Targeting War-Sustaining Capability at Sea: Compatibility with Additional Protocol I', *The Army Lawyer*, Department of the Army Pamphlet 27–50–434, July 2009.

Meyer J.M., 'Tearing Down the Facade: A Critical Look at the Current Law on Targeting the Will of the Enemy and Air Force Doctrine' 51 *Air Force Law Review* 2001, 143–82.

Meyrowitz H., 'Buts de Guerre et Objectifs Militaires', 1–2 *Revue de droit pénal militaire et de droit de la guerre* 1983, 95–113.

Myrow S., 'Waging War on the Advice of Counsel: The Role of Operational War in the Gulf War', 7 *US Air Force Academy Journal of Legal Studies* 1996–7, 131–58.

Pitzul J.S.T., 'Operational Law and the Legal Professional: A Canadian Perspective', 51 *Air Force Law Review* 2001, 311–22.

Prugh G.S., 'Conduct of combat and risks run by the civilian population', 21 *Revue de droit pénal militaire et de droit de la guerre* 1982, 281–4.

Quenivet N., 'Report of the Prosecutor of the ICTY Concerning NATO Bombing against the FRY: A Comment', 41(3) *Indian Journal of International Law* 2001, 478–94.

Quindry F.E., 'Aerial Bombardment of Civilian and Military Objectives', 2 *Journal of Air Law and Commerce* 1931, 474–509.

Rauch E., 'Attack Restraints, Target Limitations and Prohibitions or Restrictions of Use of Certain Conventional Weapons', 18 *Revue de droit pénal militaire et de droit de la guerre* 1979, 51–72.

Rauch E., 'Conduct of Combat and Risks Run by the Civilian Population', 21 *Revue de droit pénal militaire et de droit de la guerre* 1982, 66–72.

Reynolds J.D., 'Collateral Damage on the 21st Century Battlefield: Enemy Exploitation of the Law of Armed Conflict, and The Struggle For a Moral High Ground', 56 *The Air Force Law Review* 2005, 1–108.

Roberts A.E., 'Traditional and Modern Approaches to Customary International Law: A Reconciliation', 95(4) *American Journal of International Law* 2001, 757–91.

Robertson H.B., 'The Principle of the Military Objective in the Law of Armed Conflict' 8 *US Air Force Academy Journal of Legal Studies* 1997–8, 35–69.

Rogers A.P.V., 'Armed Forces and Development of the Law of War', 21 *Revue de droit pénal militaire et de droit de la guerre* 1982, 293–317.

Rogers A.P.V., 'Conduct of Combat and Risks Run by the Civilian Population' General Report 21(1–2–3–4) *Revue de droit pénal militaire et de droit de la guerre The Military Law and Law of War Review* 1982, 293–317.

Rosenblad E., 'Area Bombing and International Law' 15(1–2) *The Military Law and Law of War Review/Revue de droit pénal militaire et de droit de la guerre* 1976, 53–111.

Rowe P., 'Kosovo 1999: The Air Campaign – Have the Provisions of Additional Protocol I Withstood the Test?' 82(837) *International Review of the Red Cross* 2000, 147–65.

Sassoli M., 'Legitimate Targets of Attacks Under International Humanitarian Law', International Humanitarian Law Research Initiative Background Paper 2004, 1–10.

Schachter O., 'United Nations Law in the Gulf Conflict', 85(3) *American Journal of International Law* 1991, 452–73.

Shotwell C.B., 'Economy and Humanity in the Use of Force: A Look at the Aerial Rules of Engagement in the 1991 Gulf War', 4 *United States Air Force Academy Journal of Legal Studies* 1993, 15–58.

Shue H. and Wippman D., 'Limiting Attacks on Dual-Use Facilities Performing Indispensable Civilian Functions' 35(3) *Cornell International Law Journal* 2002, 559–79.

278 *Bibliography*

Skarsted C.-I., 'Conduct of combat and risks run by the civilian population', 21 *Revue de droit pénal militaire et de droit de la guerre* 1982, 230–31.

Solf W.A., 'Protection of Civilians against the Effects of Hostilities under Customary International Law and under Protocol I' 1(1) *American University International Law Review* 1986, 117–35.

Spaight J.M., 'Air Bombardment', 4 *British Yearbook of International Law* 1923–4, 21–33.

Veyrat J.-M., 'The Commanders Indispensible Freedom of Action', 4 *Doctrine: The Legal Environment for Ground Forces*, Ministère de la Défense, General Military Review, September 2004, 5–7.

Warren M.L., 'Operational Law: A Concept Matures', 152 *Military Law Review* 1996, 33–73.

Watkin K., 'Assessing Proportionality: Moral Complexity and Legal Rules', 8 *International Yearbook of International Humanitarian Law* 2005, 3–53.

Watkin K., 'Canada/United States Military Interoperability and Humanitarian Law Issues: Land Mines, Terrorism, Military Objectives and Targeted Killing', 15(2) *Duke Journal of International and Comparative Law* 2005, 281–314.

Watkin K. and Drebot Z., 'The Operational Lawyer: An Essential Resource for the Modern Commander', 2005 [no page numbers].

Watkin K. and Drebot Z., 'The Operational Lawyer: An Essential Resource for the Modern Commander', Office of the Judge Advocate General, undated.

Yihdego Z., 'Gaza Mission: Implications for International Humanitarian Law and UN Fact-Finding', 13(1) *Melbourne Journal of International Law* 2012, 158–216.

Other reports, manuals and studies

Amnesty International, *'Collateral Damage' or Unlawful Killings? Violations of the Laws of War by NATO during Operation Allied Force*, AI Index: EUR 70/18/00, June 2000, available at http://reliefweb.int/sites/reliefweb.int/files/resources/84AF11F7520D 41B3C12575A100460CE7-Full_Report.pdf.

Amnesty International, *Afghanistan: Accountability for Civilian Deaths*, Index No. ASA 11/022/2001 of 25 October 2001.

Amnesty International, *Israel/Lebanon: Deliberate Destruction or Collateral Damage?*, AI Index: MDE 18/007/2006, August 2006.

Amnesty International, *Israel/Lebanon: Out of All Proportion – Civilians Bear the Brunt of the War*, AI Index: MDE 02/033/2006, November 2006.

Final Report to the Prosecutor by the Committee Established to Review the NATO Bombing Campaign Against the Federal Republic of Yugoslavia, 13 June 2000, 39(5) *International Legal Materials* 1257–83.

Human Rights Watch, *Civilian Deaths in NATO AIR Campaign*, Vol. 12, No. 1(d), February 2000, available at www.hrw.org/reports/2000/nato/.

Human Rights Watch, *International Humanitarian Law Issues in a Potential War in Iraq*, February 2003.

Human Rights Watch, *Off Target: The Conduct of the War and Civilian Casualties in Iraq*, December 2003.

Human Rights Watch, *Up in Flames*, 23 January 2009.

Manual on International Law Applicable to Air and Missile Warfare, Program on Humanitarian Policy and Conflict Research, Harvard University, 15 May 2009, with the associated Commentary.

Bibliography 279

Middle East Watch (Human Rights Watch), *Needless Deaths in the Gulf War: Civilian Casualties During the Air Campaign and Violations of the Laws of War*, Human Rights Watch, New York, 1991, available at www.hrw.org/legacy/reports/1991/gulfwar/index. htm#TopOfPage.

NATO Letter to the International Commission of Inquiry to investigate all alleged violations of international human rights law in the Libyan Arab Jamahiriya, OLA (2012) 006, 23 January 2012.

Targeting Military Objectives, Report on Expert Meeting, University Centre for International Humanitarian Law, 12 May 2005.

2 Military doctrine (non-legal)

Australia

Australian Defence Force Publication 04.1.1 – Glossary, ADFP 04.1.1.(101).

Targeting, Australian Defence Doctrine Publication 3.14, Department of Defence, 2nd edn, 2009, 2 February 2009.

Canada

Canadian Military Doctrine, Canadian Forces Joint Publication 01 (CFJP 01), B-GJ-005-000/FP-001, Canadian Forces Chief of Defence Staff, April 2009.

France

General Tactics, FT-02 (Eng.), Armée de Terre, Centre de doctrine d'emploi des forces, Ministère de la Défense, July 2010.

The Tactical Commander's Guide to Command and Control in Operations, FT-05 (Eng.), Armée de Terre, Centre de doctrine d'emploi des forces, Ministère de la Défense, November 2011.

India

Indian Army Doctrine, Headquarters Army Training Command, October 2004.

NATO

NATO Allied Joint Doctrine for Joint Targeting, AJP-3.9, May 2008.

NATO Allied Joint Doctrine, AJP-01 (D), December 2010.

NATO Glossary of Terms and Definitions (English and French), AAP-6 (2013).

New Zealand

Foundations of New Zealand Military Doctrine, NZ DDP-D, New Zealand Defence Force, February 2004.

Foundations of New Zealand Military Doctrine, NZ DDP-D, New Zealand Defence Force, 2nd edn, November 2008.

Foundations of New Zealand Military Doctrine, NZ DDP-D, New Zealand Defence Force, 3rd edn, June 2012.

280   *Bibliography*

South Africa

Republic of South Africa, *Joint Warfare Manual (JWM) 91: The Levels of War*, Department of Defence, March 1998.

United Kingdom

Royal Air Force War Manual, Air Ministry, Air Publication 1300, 2nd edn, February 1940.

Royal Air Force War Manual, Air Ministry, Air Publication 1300, 3rd edn, January 1950.

British Airpower Doctrine AP 3000, 3rd edn, UK Ministry of Defence, 1999.

UK Joint Air Operations, Interim Joint Warfare Publication, IJWP 3-30, UK Ministry of Defence, 2003.

Joint Operations Execution, Joint Warfare Publication 3-00, UK Chiefs of Staff, The Development, Concepts and Doctrine Centre, UK Ministry of Defence, 2nd edn, March 2004.

Legal Support to Joint Operations, Joint Warfare Publication 3-46 (JWP 3-46), UK Chiefs of Staff, The Development, Concepts and Doctrine Centre, UK Ministry of Defence, 1st edn, April 2005, and 2nd edn, August 2010.

Joint Targeting Policy and Battle Damage Assessment Policy Paper, September 2005.

British Defence Doctrine, Joint Warfare Publication (JWP0-01), UK Ministry of Defence, 1996, 3rd edn August 2008.

Campaigning, Joint Doctrine Publication (JDP 01), UK Ministry of Defence, 2nd edn, December 2008.

Campaign Execution, Joint Doctrine Publication 3-00 (JDP 3-00), UK Chiefs of Staff, The Development, Concepts and Doctrine Centre, UK Ministry of Defence, 3rd edn, October 2009.

Legal Support to Joint Operations, Joint Doctrine Publication 3-46 (JDP 3-46), UK Chiefs of Staff, The Development, Concepts and Doctrine Centre, UK Ministry of Defence, 2nd edn, August 2010.

British Defence Doctrine, Joint Doctrine Publications 0-01 (JDP 0-01), Chief of Staffs, The Development, Concepts and Doctrine Centre, UK Ministry of Defence, 4th edn, 2011.

Army Doctrine Primer, UK Army Publication, AC 71954, May 2011.

Campaign Planning, Joint Doctrine Publication 01 (JDP 05), UK Chiefs of Staff, The Development, Concepts and Doctrine Centre, UK Ministry of Defence, 3rd edn, July 2013.

UK Air and Space Doctrine, Joint Doctrine Publication JDP-030 (formerly AP 3000), UK Chiefs of Staff, The Development, Concepts and Doctrine Centre, Ministry of Defence, July 2013.

United States

US Air Force, *Intelligence Targeting Guide*, Air Force Pamphlet 14-210, Secretary of the US Air Force, 1 February 1998. This document superseded AFP 200-17, 23 June 1989 and AFP 200-18, Volumes I and II, 1 October 1990.

Air Force Doctrine Document 2-1.2, *Strategic Attacks*, 20 May 1998.

Bibliography   281

Unified Action Armed Forces, Joint Publication (JP 0-2), US Joint Chiefs of Staff, July 2001.

Targeting, Newsletter No. 03-27, Operation Outreach, US Center for Army Lessons Learnt, October 2003.

US Air Force Basic Doctrine: Document 1, 17 November 2003.

Targeting, US Air Force Doctrine, Document AFDD 2-1.9, 8 June 2006.

Annex 3-70 Strategic Attack, US Air Force Doctrine, 12 June 2007.

Counterinsurgency Operations, Joint Publication (JP 3-24), Joint Chiefs of Staff, 5 October 2009.

The Targeting Process, FM 3-60 (FM 6-20-10), US Army Headquarters, 26 November 2010.

Field Manual FM 3-0, United States Department of Army, 27 February 2008 incorporating change of February 2011.

Legal Support to Military Operations, Joint Publication (JP 1-04), US Joint Chiefs of Staff, August 2011.

Joint Operations, Joint Publication (JP 3-0), US Joint Chiefs of Staff, 11 August 2011.

Joint Operation Planning, Joint Publication (JP 5-0), US Joint Chiefs of Staff, 11 August 2011.

Joint Interdiction, Joint Publication (JP 3-03), US Joint Chiefs of Staff, 14 October 2011.

Electronic Warfare, Joint Publication (JP 3-13.1), US Joint Chiefs of Staff, 8 February 2012.

Joint Doctrine for Targeting, US Joint Chiefs of Staff, Joint Publication 3-60, 17 January 2002, superseded by Joint Publication JP-03-60, *Joint Targeting*, 13 April 2007 and 31 January 2013.

Doctrine for the Armed Forces of the United States, Joint Publication (JP 1), Joint Chiefs of Staff, 25 March 2013.

Joint Doctrine for Multinational Operations, Joint Publication (JP 3-16), US Joint Chiefs of Staff, 7 March 2007, updated as of 16 July 2013.

Annex 3-60 Targeting, US Air Force Doctrine, 10 January 2014.

Dictionary of Military and Associated Terms, Joint Publication (JP 1-02), US Department of Defense, 8 November 2010 with amendments as of 15 March 2014.

3 Other documents

Books, studies and presentations

Biddle S., 'Iraq, Afghanistan and American Military Transformation' in S. Hopkins (ed.), *Asymmetry and Complexity*, Land Warfare Studies Centre, Study Paper No. 308, Canberra 2007.

Butler S., 'Acquisition Support to the Operational Arena', presentation for the 11th International Command and Control Research and Technology Symposium, available at www.dodccrp.org/events/11th_ICCRTS/html/presentations/Butler_Acquisition_Support.pdf.

Catton B., *This Hallowed Ground: The Story of the Union Side of the Civil War*, Wordsworth Editions, Ware 1998.

Catton B., *The Civil War*, First Mariner Books, Houghton Mifflin, Boston, MA 2004.

Clark W.K., *Waging Modern War*, Public Affairs, Oxford 2001.

Clausewitz C. von, *On War*, Wordsworth Editions, Ware 1997.

282 *Bibliography*

Committee to Protect Journalists, *Attacks on the Press 2001: Afghanistan*, available at http://cpj.org/2002/03/attacks-on-the-press-2001-afghanistan.php.

Cordesman A.H., *The Effectiveness of the NATO Tactical Air and Missile Campaign against the Serbian and Ground Forces in Kosovo*, A Working Paper, Center for Strategic and International Studies, August 2000.

Cordesman A.H. and Al-Rodhan K.R., *Gulf Military Forces in an Era of Asymmetric Warfare: Saudi Arabia*, Center for Strategic and International Studies, Washington, DC 2007.

Coox A.D., 'Strategic Bombing in the Pacific 1942–1945' in R.C. Hall (ed.), *Case Studies in Strategic Bombardment*, US Air Force History and Museums Program, Washington, DC 1998.

'Defeating International Terrorism: Campaign Objectives', United Kingdom Ministry of Defence, Dep 01/1460, 16 October 2001.

Denning D.E., 'Activism, Hacktivism, and Cyberterrorism: The Internet as a Tool for Influencing Foreign Policy' in J. Arquilla and D. Ronfeldt (eds), *Networks and Netwars: The Future of Terror, Crime, and Militancy*, RAND, Santa Monica, CA 2001.

Denning D.E., 'A View of Cyberterrorism Five Years Later' in K.E. Himma (ed.), *Internet Security: Hacking, Counterhacking and Society*, Jones and Bartlett, Sudbury, MA 2007.

Deptula D.A., *Effect-Based Operations: Change in the Nature of Warfare*, Aerospace Education Foundation, Arlington, TX 2001.

Evans S.A., 'Defining Dual-Use: An International Assessment of the Discourses around Technology', Presentation given to the ESCR New Directions in WMD Proliferation Seminar, 27 February 2006.

Fadok S., *John Boyd and John Warden: Air Power's Quest for Strategic Paralysis*, Thesis, School of Advanced Airpower Studies, Air University Press, Maxwell Air Force Base, AL 1995.

Fuller J.F.C., *The Foundations of the Science of War*, Hutchinson & Co., London 1925.

Grant R., 'Reach-Forward', *Air Force Magazine*, October 2002.

Grant R., 'An Air War Like No Other', *Air Force Magazine*, November 2002.

Hall R.C. (ed.), *Case Studies in Strategic Bombardment*, US Air Force History and Museums Programme, Special Studies, Washington, DC 1998.

Hattaway H. and Jones A., *How the North Won: A Military History of the Civil War*, University of Illinois Press, Urbana, IL 1983.

Hermes W.G., *United States Army in the Korean War: Truce Tent and Fighting War*, Center of Military History, US Army, Washington, DC 1992.

Hoekema J., *NATO Policy and NATO Strategy in Light of the Kosovo Conflict*, Draft General Report, NATO Defense and Security Committee, 6 October 1999.

Homan K., 'Doctrine' in A. Aldis and M. Drent (eds), *Common Norms and Good Practices of Civil Military Relations in the EU*, The Centre of European Security Studies, Groningen, 2008.

Hone T.C., 'Strategic Bombing: Korea and Vietnam' in R.C. Hall (ed.), *Case Studies in Strategic Bombardment*, US Air Force History and Museums Program, Washington, DC 1998.

Ignatieff M., *Virtual War: Kosovo and Beyond*, Picador, Metropolitan Books, Henry Holt, New York 2000.

Jacobs W.A., 'The British Strategic Air Offensive Against Germany in World War II' in R.C. Hall (ed.), *Case Studies in Strategic Bombardment*, US Air Force History and Museums Program, Washington, DC 1998.

Bibliography   283

Jamieson P.D., *Lucrative Targets: The U.S. Air Force in the Kuwaiti Theatre of Operations*, Air Force History and Museums Program, US Air Force, Washington, DC 2001.

Keaney T.A. and Cohen E.A., *Gulf War Air Power Survey* Operations and Effects and Effectiveness, US Department of Air Force, US Government Printing Office 1993.

Kennett L., *Marching through Georgia: The Story of Soldiers and Civilians During Sherman's Campaign*, HarperCollins, New York 1995.

Koenders B., 'Afghanistan and the Future of the Alliance', NATO Parliamentary Assembly, Annual Report 174 PC 06 E, 2006.

Lambeth, B.S. *NATO's Air War for Kosovo: A Strategic and Operational Assessment*, RAND, Santa Monica, CA 2001.

Lambeth, B.S. *Airpower Against Terror: America's Conduct of OEF*, National Defense Research Institute, RAND, Santa Monica, CA 2005.

Liddell Hart B.H., *Strategy of Indirect Approach*, Faber & Faber, London 1938.

Luttwak E.N., *The Grand Strategy of the Roman Empire from the First Century AD to the Third*, The Johns Hopkins University Press, Baltimore, MD 1976.

McFarland S.L. and Newton W.P., 'The American Strategic Air Offensive Against Germany in World War II', in R.C. Hall (ed.), *Case Studies in Strategic Bombardment*, US Air Force History and Museums Programme, Special Studies, Washington, DC 1998.

Maeda T., 'Strategic Bombing of Chongqing by Imperial Japanese Army and Naval Forces' in Y. Tanaka and M.B. Young (eds), *Bombing Civilians: Twentieth Century History*, The New Press, New York, 2009.

Mandsager D. (ed.), *Rules of Engagement Handbook*, International Institute of Humanitarian Law, Sanremo, November 2009.

Mitchell W., *Skyways: A Book on Modern Aeronautics*, Lippincott, Philadelphia 1930.

Morelli V. and Belkin P., *NATO in Afghanistan: A Test of the Transatlantic Alliance*, Congressional Research Service, Report for Congress, United States, 3 December 2009.

Noetzel T. and Scheipers S., *Coalition Warfare in Afghanistan: Burden-Sharing or Disunity?*, Chatham House Security Programmes, ASP/ISP BP 07/01, October 2007.

North B., 'UK Space Capability Development', Presentation for Defense iQ Military Satellites, 12 July 2010.

Operation Falconer, The War in Iraq, Australian Defence Operations in Middle East in 2003, Australian Ministry of Defence.

Operations in Afghanistan: Background Briefing, UK Ministry of Defence, on file with author.

Overview by The US Cyber Consequences Unit of the Cyber Campaign Against Georgia in August 2008, US-CCU Special Report, August 2009.

Pape R.A., *Bombing to Win: Air Power and Coercion in War*, Cornell Studies in Security Affairs, Cornell University Press, Ithaca, NY 1996.

Pope J.R., 'U.S. Marines in Operation Desert Storm' in C.D. Melson, E.A. Englander and D.A. Dawson, *U.S. Marines in the Persian Gulf, 1990–1991: Anthology and Annotated Bibliography*, US Marines Corps Headquarters, Washington, DC 1992.

'Saudi Arabia Outsources Training and Support to Northrop Grumman', Defense Update Business Report, January 2010, available at defense-update.com/newscast/0110/businessnews_0110.html.

Simpkin R.E., *Race to the Swift: Thought on Twenty-First Century Warfare*, Brassey's, London 1994.

Spedero P.C., *Time Sensitive Targeting – The Operational Commander's Role*, Naval War College, Newport, RI, 9 February 2004.

284 *Bibliography*

Sun Tzu, *The Art of War*, trans. T. Cleary, Shambala Publications, Boston and London 1988.

Tavani H.T., *Ethics and Technology: Controversies, Questions, and Strategies for Ethical Computing*, 3rd edn, John Wiley & Sons Publishers, Hoboken, NJ 2009.

v. Gorka S.L., 'Invocation in Context', available at www.nato.int/docu/review/2006/issue2/english/art1.html.

What Is NATO? An Introduction to the Transatlantic Alliance, NATO Public Diplomacy Division, Brussels 2012.

Warden J.A. III, *The Air Campaign*, National Defence University Press, Washington, DC, 1988.

Warden J.A. III, 'The Enemy as a System', 9(2) *Airpower Journal* Spring 1995, 40–55.

Warden J.A. III, 'Air Theory for the Twenty-first Century' in K.P. Magyar and Air University Press (eds), *Challenge and Response: Anticipating US Military Security Concerns*, Air University Press, Maxwell Air Force Base, AL 1996.

Webster C. and Frankland N., *The Strategic Air Offensive Against Germany 1939–1945*, Vols. 1 and 4, Her Majesty's Stationery Office, London 1961.

West S.D., *Warden and The Air Corps Tactical School: Déjà Vu?*, Thesis, School of Advanced Airpower Studies, Air University Press, Maxwell Air Force Base, AL 1999.

Wyman D.S., *The Abandonment of the Jews: America and the Holocaust*, Pantheon Books, New York 1984.

Wyman D.S. and Medoff R., *A Race Against Death: Peter Bergson, America, and the Holocaust*, New Press, New York 2004.

Zanini M. and Edwards S.J.A., 'The Networking of Terror in the Information Age' in J. Arquilla and D. Ronfeldt (eds), *Networks and Netwars: The Future of Terror, Crime, and Militancy*, RAND, Santa Monica, CA 2001.

Press releases and press articles

Adams N., *All Things Considered*, National Public Radio, 12 April 1999, available at www.bu.edu/globalbeat/pubs/Pesic041299.html.

Amos J., 'UK Skynet: Not to Be Confused with The Terminator', 10 March 2010, BBC Spaceman Blog, available at www.bbc.co.uk/blogs/thereporters/jonathan amos/2010/03/uk-skynet-not-to-be-confused-w.shtml.

British Broadcasting Corporation Online Archive, available at www.bbc.co.uk/history/ww2peopleswar/timeline/factfiles/nonflash/a1132921.shtml.

Cook T., 'Australian Pilots Aborted US-assigned Bombing Raids during Iraq War', World Socialist Web Site, 23 March 2004, available at www.wsws.org/en/articles/2004/03/raaf-m23.html.

'Fog of War: Q&A with Lt. Gen. Charles Horner', *The Washington Post*, July 1998.

Loeb V., 'Afghan War Is a Lab for U.S. Innovation: New Technologies Are Tested in Battle', *The Washington Post*, 26 March 2002.

NATO, 'NATO Strikes Libyan State Satellite Facility', 31 July 2011.

'President Bush Announces Combat Operations in Iraq Have Ended', White House, 1 May 2003.

Priest D., 'Bombing by the Committee: France Balked at NATO Targets', *Washington Post*, 20 September 1999.

Shanker, T. and Sanger, D., 'NATO Says it Is Stepping Up Attacks on Libya Targets', *The New York Times*, 26 April, 2011.

United States Department of Defense, News Briefing, Secretary General Rumsfeld and Gen. Myers of 7, 9, 11, 12, 16, 18, 20, 22, 31 October 2001.

US CENTCOM, *U.S. Marines Destroy Ba'ath Party Headquarters*, Press Release No. 03-03-105 of 31 March 2003.

Walker F., 'Our Pilots Refused to Bomb 40 Times', *Sydney Morning Herald*, 14 March 2004.

Walsh D., 'Pakistani Army Fights Street by Street to Banish Taliban from Swat Valley', *The Guardian*, 24 May 2009.

Index

10 Downing Street, London 151
1863–1922 history 16–19
1923 Hague Rules of Air Warfare
19–23

Abu Ghraib Television Antennae
Broadcast building 157
Abyssinia 23
ACTS *see* Air Corps Tactical School
Additional Protocol I (API): 1977
definitions 32–42; applicability 34–5;
concept 2–3, 7–8, 15, 32–42;
customary status of a rule 37–9;
definite military advantage 112, 114,
115, 120, 124–7; definition 2–3,
32–42; effective contribution 86–8,
101–4; flexibility 40–2; international
crimes 164; latitude 40–2; legal
interoperability 219, 223, 225–6,
234; location criterion 63–4; military
advantage 134, 139; nature criterion
55–6; use criterion 66–7
Additional Protocol II (APII) 34–5
Additional Protocol III (APIII) 34–5
advantage *see* military advantage
advisers, legal 196, 232
aerial warfare: broadcasting facilities
156; effective contribution 108;
legal interoperability 230–1, 234–5,
241–2; military advantage 140–1;
pre-1923 treaty law 18–19, *see also*
Hague Rules of Air Warfare
aerodromes 52
Afghanistan 1, 156, 212, 233–9
Air Corps Tactical School (ACTS)
177–8, 211

Air Force Operations and the Law 103–4,
199, 206, 207
Air and Missile Warfare (AMW):
definite military advantage 122–3;
nature criterion 49–54, 57; purpose
criterion 77
airports 56, 133–4, 235, 241
Alabama Commission 98, *see also*
Claims Tribunal of Arbitration
Albanian army *see* Kosovo
Al Firdus/Amariyah (Ameriyya) bunker
76, 140–1
Al-Jazeera broadcasting facilities 156
Allied Air Forces 230–1, 241
Allied Joint Publications 183–4
Allied Joint Targeting 101–4, 106, 114,
200
Al-Manar Television facilities 157
al Qaeda/Taliban 156, 233–9
America *see* United States
Amnesty International 57
AMW *see* Manual on International
Law Applicable to Air and Missile
Warfare
*Annotated Supplement to the Commander's
Handbook* 100
anti-Semitism 160
APCs *see* armoured personnel carriers
API *see* Additional Protocol I
APII *see* Additional Protocol II
APIII *see* Additional Protocol III
area-bombing 19
Argentina 113–14
Armed Conflict, Law of 127
armoured personnel carriers (APCs)
51

Index 287

arteries of transport *see* lines of communication and transportation
The Associated Press 156
atomic bombs 22, 28
attack/attacker: available intelligence 137–42; definite military advantage 120–4; definitions 10
attrition 192
Australia 105, 230–1, 239–42, 246

Ba'ath Party 61, 151–3, 212, 221–2, 248–9
Baghdad 55, 140–1, 157
barracks 47–8
Basra broadcasting facilities 157
battlefield concepts 20
BBC *see* British Broadcasting Corporation
Beirut International Airport 133–4
Belgrade 150, 228, 232–3
Berlin 27–8
biological (NCB) weapons 239
blitz of London 28
bombardments: broadcasting facilities 156; effective contribution 108; Hague Rules of Air Warfare 19–23; post-Second World War 29–30, *see also* aerial warfare
bombs 134
Bosnia 64–5, 68
Bosnian Muslims 56
Bosnian Serb Army 121
Bothe, M. 54–5
bridges: legal interoperability 238; military advantage 138, 143; nature criterion 52, 54–5
Britain *see* United Kingdom
British Broadcasting Corporation (BBC) 58, 156
British Joint Theatre Forces 72
British prime minister 151
broadcasting facilities 57–8, 71–2; legal interoperability 228, 232–3, 239; problematic cases 155–62
bunkers 76, 140–1

C3 centres *see* command, control and communications centres
Campaign Planning 200

Canada 120, 232
capability *see* war-fighting effort
capture: military advantage 131–2, *see also* destruction, capture or neutralization
carpet-bombing 19
Casablanca Directive 26–7
CENTCOM (American central command) 237
Central Intelligence Agency (CIA) 238
centres of gravity (COGs): legal interoperability 228, 241; operational level frameworks 190–1; target concepts 209, 212, 213; targeting theory 175, 178–9
Chamberlain, Neville 24
changing circumstances 142–3
chemical and biological (NCB) weapons 239
chemical industries 74
CIA *see* Central Intelligence Agency
CiC *see* commander-in-chief
circumstances ruling at the time 115–16, 128–9, 131, 136–44
Civil War 98, 211
civilian buildings, use criterion 67–8
civilian morale 153–5
Claims Tribunal of Arbitration 98, *see also* Alabama Commission
Clark, General Wesley 231, 232
Clausewitz, Carl von 175
clock tower sniper positions 67–8
cluster weapons 64
coalition operations: Afghanistan 233–9; doctrine 206, 211; Gulf war 218–24; Iraq 239–44; Kosovo 225–33, *see also* United Kingdom; United States
coercion 187
Colombia's Operational Law Manual 114
command, control and communications (C3) centres 57–8
commander-in-chief (CiC) 60–1, 149–52
Commander's Handbook on the Law of Naval Operations 100, 104, 198
Commission *see* European Commission

288 *Index*

Committee of Imperial Defence 23
common denominator methods *see*
lowest common denominator
methods
communication and transportation
(LOC) 52–3, 54–8, 238
communication, command and control
(C3) infrastructure 161–2
communications networks 57–8, 71–2,
161–2, *see also* lines of communication
and transportation
computers 71–2
Convention on the Law of Treaties 3,
112, 170
Cormorant network 72
cotton, destruction of 98, 211
creep, mission 189
criminal courts 121
Croatia 65, 68, 122
Croatian Defence Council Military
Police headquarters 68
customary status of a rule 37–9

dairy farms 94–5
defended targets 16–19
definite military advantage 111–28;
definition 111–16; doctrine 212, 213;
pursuit of 116–24
deliberate targeting 11, 201–2, 204
democracy 60–1
Denmark 239–40
Department of Defense 100–1
Desert Storm (operation) 220–1
destruction: broadcasting facilities 161;
military advantage 130–1
destruction, capture or neutralization:
1977 definition 36; concept and
definition 2; military advantage,
methods 129; nature criterion 48–9;
practice 4; problematic cases
151–2
deterrence 187
developing industrial centres 18–19
Dinstein, Y. 36, 37; definite military
advantage 122; location criterion 62;
nature criterion 47–8, 51–3, 55;
problematic cases 150; purpose
criterion 75, 77, 79; use criterion 66
direct coercion 187

Directives for the Conduct of War 25
doctrine 173–214; international law
194–213; interoperability 183–4;
modern targeting theory 175–80;
operational level frameworks 190–2;
role of 180–4; source structure
182–3; strategic military doctrine
185–9; tactical warfare 192–3;
warfare levels 184–93
Draft Rules 30–2; nature criterion 52,
57; use criterion 72
Dresden 27
dual use objects 67–71, 74
Dubrovnik (Croatia) 65, 122
dynamic targeting 11, 201–2, 204–6,
239, 262

EC *see* European Commission
economic warfare 18–19, 92–5; doctrine
178; legal interoperability 238
effective contribution 2, 83–110; 1977
definite military advantage 111–16;
definition 36, 83–4; doctrine 213;
economic warfare 92–5; problems
92–109; war-fighting/sustaining
effort 95–109
electrical infrastructure/supply 73–4,
89–91, 117–19, 134–5
Enduring Freedom (Operation)
233–4
energy supply 73–4, 89–91, 117–19,
134–5
engineering industries 74
Eritrea 70, 89–91, 117–19
Ethiopia 70, 89–91, 117–19
Euphrates River 55, 211
European Commission (EC) 70, 89–91,
117–19

Federal Department of Defence, Civil
Protection and Sports (FDCPS) 59
fighter jets 137
First World War 18, 20
food, destruction/denial of 94, 96–8
France: effective contribution 85–6;
legal interoperability 219, 222–3,
229, 232–3, 245
Fritzsche, Hans 160
Fuller, John 175–6

Index 289

Gaza 94, 150–1
Geneva Conventions (GC) 29, *see also* Additional Protocols
Germany: definite military advantage 123; effective contribution 93; First World War 18; Hague Rules of Air Warfare 23, 25, 26–8; Ministry of Propaganda 160
governmental control objects 193
Granby (operation) 220–1
graphite bombs 134
Great Britain *see* Britain
Greenwood, C. 151
Guantanamo Bay 100–1
Gulf War 76, 124; broadcasting facilities 156; doctrine 211; military advantage 138, 140–1
Gulf War Air Power Survey (GWAPS) 222

Hague Convention on Cultural Property 52–3
Hague Regulations: historical origins 16–17; military advantage 130
Hague Rules Concerning the Control of Wireless Telegraphy in time of War and Air Warfare 15, 19–29
Hamas party 150–1
Hamburg 27
Hampson, F.J. 54
Hart, Basil H. Liddell 176
Henderson, I. 64
Herat 235–6
Herzegovina 64–5
Hezbollah 57, 94–5
Hirgigo power station 89–91, 117–19
Hiroshima 22, 28, 119, 252–3
history: 1863–1922 history 16–19; 1923 Hague Rules of Air Warfare 19–29; 1977 definitions 32–42; post-Second World War developments 29–32; pre-Second World War 23–9; Second World War 29–32
Holland 86, 131–2
Horner, General 138
hostage cases 131
Hotel Vitez (Bosnia) 68
humanitarian law 197, *see also* law of armed conflict

Human Rights Watch 157
Hussein, Saddam 1, 151, 212, *see also* Iraq
hydroelectric irrigation works 99

IACs *see* international armed conflicts
ICC *see* International Criminal Court
ICRC *see* International Committee of the Red Cross
ICTY *see* International Criminal Tribunal for the former Yugoslavia
IDF *see* Israel Defence Forces
IMFA *see* Israel Ministry of Foreign Affairs
industrial centres 18–19
Instant Thunder (operation) 219–20
Institute of International Law 32
Instructions Governing Aerial Warfare 25
Instructions Governing Naval and Air Bombardment 25
Instructions to Be Observed by the Royal Air Force 25
Intelligence Targeting Guide 101
intended future use *see* purpose criterion
international armed conflicts (IACs) 34–5
International Committee of the Red Cross (ICRC): API definition 32–3, 42; definite military advantage 116–17, 124; effective contribution 84–7, 91; military advantage, circumstances ruling at the time 139; nature criterion 47, 49–50, 53–4, 57; post-Second World War 30–1; purpose criterion 75–6; use criterion 72
international crimes 162–6
International Criminal Court (ICC) 121, 166
International Criminal Tribunal for the former Yugoslavia (ICTY) 158–61, 164–5
international law 173, 194–213; application 204–6; LOAC manuals 198–9; operational conduct 197–8; recognition 194–9; target concepts

290   *Index*

206–13; target process 200–4; target selection 199–206, *see also* Manual on International Law Applicable to Air and Missile Warfare
International Military Tribunal, Nuremberg 160–2
International Security Assistance Force operations 238
international war crimes, military advantage 131
Internet 71–2
Iran 99
Iraq 1, 99; doctrine 211–12; legal interoperability 239–44; military advantage 137–8, 140–1; nature criterion 55; problematic cases 151, 157, *see also* Gulf war
Iraqi Freedom (operation) 240
irrigation works 99
Israel: effective contribution 94; military advantage 133–4; problematic cases 150–1
Israel Defence Forces (IDF) 65, 94–5
Israeli government 56
Israel Ministry of Foreign Affairs (IMFA) 65
Italy 24–5

Jalalabad 234–6
Japan 22, 27, 28
jets 137
Joint Forces Command 205, 207–8
Joint Prioritised Target List (JPTL) 203, 204–5
Joint Targeting Cycle 202, 203
Joint Targeting Doctrine 101–4, 106, 114, 200
Joint Target List (JTL) 202–3
Joint Theatre Forces 72
JPTL *see* Joint Prioritised Target List
JTL *see* Joint Target List
Judge Advocate Corps 198

Kabul 234–6
Kalshoven, F. 54, 87, 93, 143
Kandahar 234–6
Kharg island 99
KLA *see* Kosovo Liberation Army
Korean War 99

Kosovo 1, 73; definite military advantage 116–17; doctrine 211; legal interoperability 217, 225–33, 244; problematic cases 150, 164–5
Kosovo Liberation Army (KLA) 116–17, 227–8
Kuwait 73, 99; definite military advantage 124; military advantage 138, *see also* Gulf war
Kuwaiti Theatre of Operations (KTO) 221, 223

landmines 64, 133
law 194–213; *Air Force Operations and the Law* 103–4, 199, 206, 207; AMW 49–54, 57, 77, 122–3; Colombia's Operational Law Manual 114; *Commander's Handbook on the Law of Naval Operations* 100, 104, 198; Convention on the Law of Treaties 3, 112, 170; Institute of International Law 32; international law 173, 194–213; *Law of Land Warfare* 102, 198; *Law of War Handbook* 102–3, 199; Manual of the Law of Armed Conflict 127; *The Military Commander and the Law* 103, 199; operational law 79, 102–3, 106, 114; pre-1923 treaty law 16–19; *The Law of Land Warfare* 198; *The Military Commander and the Law* 103, 199, *see also* legal interoperability
law of armed conflict (LOAC) 127; attack/attacker definitions 10; concept and definition 3; definite military advantage 113; doctrine 196, 197, 198–9, 204–6; effective contribution 102–3; issues beyond 7–8; practice 4
Law of Land Warfare 102, 198
Law of War Handbook 102–3, 199
lawyers 196, 232
Lebanon 56, 94–5, 133–4, 157–8
legal advisers 196, 232
legal interoperability 215–49; coalition operations 218–44; problems 244–7
Liban Lait Company 94–5
Libyan State Television (LST) 165–6

Lieber Code 97–8
Lieber Instructions 17–18
Limitations of the Dangers incurred by the Civilian Population in Time of War 30–2
Limitations of Disarmament 23–4
lines of communication (LOC) 52–3, 54–8, 238
LOAC *see* law of armed conflict
location criterion 36, 45, 61–5
London: Downing Street 151; Hague Rules of Air Warfare 28; nature criterion 58
lowest common denominator 217, 246–7
LST *see* Libyan State Television
lubricants (POL) 229
Luftwaffe 25

Maliban glass works 94
Manual on International Law Applicable to Air and Missile Warfare (AMW): definite military advantage 122–3; nature criterion 49–54, 57; purpose criterion 77
Manual of the Law of Armed Conflict 127
marines 124
master principles 188
Mazar-i-Sharif 237
metallurgical industries 74
MiG fighter jets 137
military advantage 129–46; capture 131–2; changing/evolving circumstances 142–3; circumstances ruling at the time 136–44; destruction 130–1; methods 129–35; neutralization 133–5; targets of opportunity 143–4, *see also* definite military advantage
The Military Commander and the Law 103, 199
military objective definitions 10
Milosevic, Slobodan 150, 159, 212, *see also* Kosovo
mines 64, 133
Ministry of Defence (MOD) 59–60, 149, 152, 222, 243
Ministry of Propaganda 160

missiles 46–7, *see also* Manual on International Law Applicable to Air and Missile Warfare
mission creep 189
Mitchell, Brigadier General 'Billy' 177
MOD *see* Ministry of Defence
morale, civilian 153–5
Mount Srd 65
municipalities 122
Muslims 56

NAC *see* North Atlantic Council
Nagasaki 22, 28, 119, 252–3
national security 187
NATO *see* North Atlantic Treaty Organization
nature criterion 36, 45–61; contemporary debates 51–8; object scope 49–51; political leadership infrastructure 58–61; state leadership infrastructure 58–61; type of object 49–51
Naval War College 230–1
naval warfare: convention 17–18; economic 92; effective contribution 100–1, 104; historical origins 17–18
NCB *see* nuclear, chemical and biological weapons
Netherlands 86, 131–2
neutralization: broadcasting facilities 161; military advantage 133–5, *see also* destruction, capture or neutralization
New Zealand 105
NGOs *see* non-governmental organizations
NIACs *see* non-international armed conflicts
non-democratic societies 61
non-direct coercion 187
non-governmental organizations (NGOs) 157
non-international armed conflicts (NIACs) 35
Non-Strike Lists 202–3
North Atlantic Alliance 229
North Atlantic Council (NAC) 202

292 Index

North Atlantic Treaty Organization (NATO): *Allied Joint Targeting* 101–4, 106, 114, 200; broadcasting facilities 158, 159–60; definite military advantage 114, 116–17; doctrine 183–4, 195–6, 200–1, 202–3, 204–5, 206–7, 211; international crimes 164–6; legal interoperability 215–17, 225–33, 238, 244–5; nature criterion 50; practice 5–7; problematic cases 150; use criterion 73
Northern Alliance 234, 238
North Korea 30
nuclear, chemical and biological (NCB) weapons 239
nuclear warfare, *see also* atomic bombs
Nuremberg Tribunal 160–2
nurseries 67–8

OEF *see* Operation Enduring Freedom
Oeter, S. 123
offer of definite military advantage 36, *see also* definite military advantage
OIF *see* Operation Iraqi Freedom
oil and lubricants (POL) 229
'oil plan' 93
oil refining and distribution facilities 73
operational conduct 197–8
operational doctrine 190–2
operational law 79, 102–3, 106, 114
Operational Law Handbooks 79, 106, 114
Operation Enduring Freedom (OEF) 233–4
Operation Iraqi Freedom (OIF) 240
Ossetian forces 67

Palestinian Legislative Council building 150–1
Pancevo petrochemical complex 73
Parks, Hays 38, 40; civilian moral 153; effective contribution 88; nature criterion 55; use criterion 74
parliamentary democracy 60–1
people as targets 147–8
petrochemical complexes 73
petroleum, oil and lubricants (POL) 73, 229

Poland: effective contribution 85; legal interoperability 239–40; World War II practice 28
political leadership infrastructure 58–61, 147–53
Portugal 239–40
post-Second World War developments 29–32
power supply sources 73–4, 89–91, 117–19, 134
pre-1923 treaty law 16–19
pre-Second World War influence 23
presidential systems 60–1
prime minister 151
Principles for the Conduct of War Against the Enemy's Economy 25
problematic cases 147–67; civilian morale 153–5; international crimes 162–6; political leadership infrastructure 147–53; radio broadcasting facilities 155–62; state leadership infrastructure 147–53; television broadcasting facilities 155–62
purpose criterion 36, 45, 75–81

radio broadcasting facilities 57–8; legal interoperability 228, 239; problematic cases 155–62
Radio Televisija Srbije (RTS) 158, 159–61, 164–5
RAF *see* Royal Air Force
rail networks: legal interoperability 235–6, 238, *see also* lines of communication and transportation
red card methods 217, 245
Rendulic rule 137–8
Republican Guard 211
Restricted Target Lists (RTL) 202–3
rivers 55, 211
roads *see* lines of communication and transportation
rocket-propelled grenades (RPGs) 46–7
ROE *see* Rules of Engagement
Rogers, A.V.P. 36, 77, 79
Rotterdam 27
Royal Air Force (RAF) 25
RPGs *see* rocket-propelled grenades
RTS *see* Radio Televisija Srbije

Rules of Engagement (ROE) 194–6, 222–3, 238, 242–4, 246
Russia 28

Sarajevo 56, 121
Saudi Arabia *see* Gulf war
Schmitt, M.N. 78–9
schools 67–8
Schwarzkopf, General Norman 219
scorched earth policies 96–7
Second World War 19; effective contribution 93, 98–9, 108; Hague Rules of Air Warfare 22, 23–9; nature criterion 58; post-developments 29–32; practice 23–9
semi-presidential democracy 60–1
Serbia 56, 64–5, 73; broadcasting facilities 158, 159–60; definite military advantage 116–17; doctrine 211, 212, *see also* Kosovo
Sherman, General William 96–7, 211
Short, General Michael 216, 230–1
sniper positions 67–8
Socialist Party 212, 228, 232–3
Spain 113–14, 120
Special Forces 234
Srd Mountain 65
state leadership infrastructure 58–61, 147–53
strategic bombing 18–19, 108
strategic military doctrine 185–9
strategic rings model 209–10, 211
Streicher, Julius 160
Stupni Do Hill 64–5
Sub-Committee for Limitations of Disarmament 23–4
subcontracting infrastructure 74
Sweden 105
Swiss Federal Department of Defence, Civil Protection and Sports (FDCPS) 59
Syria 57
'system essentials' 179–80

tactical warfare 192–3
Taliban/al Qaeda 1, 211, 233–9
Tanayel glass works 94

tanker war 99
Target Development 203
targets/targeting: *Allied Joint Targeting* 101–4, 106, 114, 200; centres of gravity 175, 178–9, 209, 212, 213; coalition operations 218–44; concept 206–13; defended targets 16–19; definitions 11; deliberate targeting 11, 201–2, 204; dynamic targeting 11, 201–2, 204–6, 239, 262; economic warfare 92–5; *Intelligence Targeting Guide* 101; international law 199–213; Joint Targeting Cycle 202, 203; Joint Targeting Doctrine 101–4, 106, 114, 200; *Joint Targeting Policy* 101–4, 106, 114, 200; JPTL 203, 204–5; JTL 202–3; legal considerations 199–206; legal interoperability 215–49; modern theories 175–80; of opportunity 1, 143–4; people as targets 147–8; RTL 202–3; sets/systems/lists 41–2; targets of opportunity 143–4; undefended targets 16–19
Télé Lumière 157–8
television broadcasting facilities 57–8; legal interoperability 228, 232–3, 239; problematic cases 155–62
temple of Ur 137
The Associated Press 156
The Law of Land Warfare 198
The Military Commander and the Law 103, 199
thought doctrine 180–1
Tokyo 22, 27, 28
transformers 134
transmission facilities *see* broadcasting facilities
transportation/lines of communication 52–3, 54–8, 238
Turkmenistan 236
type of object 49–51

UN *see* United Nations
undefended targets 16–19
United Front 234, 238
United Kingdom (UK): American–British Claims Commission 98; definite military advantage 120;

294 *Index*

doctrine 183–4; Downing Street, London 151; First World War 18; Hague Rules of Air Warfare 20–1, 23–4, 28; *Joint Targeting Policy* 200; legal interoperability 230–4, 239–41, 243, 245; location criterion 63; Manual of the Law of Armed Conflict 127; military advantage 139; nature criterion 58; prime minister 151

United Nations (UN) 3, 150–1

United States (US): Additional Protocol I 37; Air Force 101, 102, 196; American–British Claims Commission 98; broadcasting facilities 156; *Commander's Handbook on the Law of Naval Operations* 100, 104, 198; definite military advantage 124; doctrine 197–8, 206, 208–9, 213; effective contribution 91, 96–105, 109; Hague Rules of Air Warfare 20–1, 28; *Joint Targeting* 200; Judge Advocate Corps 198;

Law of War Handbook 199; legal interoperability 215–16, 218–21, 230–1, 233–45, 247; Naval War College 230–1; purpose criterion 79; Special Forces 234

Ur temple 137

use criterion 36, 45, 65–74, 148–9

Uzbekistan 236, 237

Vietnam 30–2, 85

Warden, Colonel John A. 178–80, 209–10, 211, 219–20

war-fighting/sustaining effort 19, 80–1, 83, 92, 95–109, 213, 253–4, 256

warheads 46–7

water reservoirs 70

weapons of mass destruction (WMD) 242

White House 150

Wilby, David 158–9

WMD *see* weapons of mass destruction

Wratten, Air Vice Marshal 224